London 1945

Also by Maureen Waller

1700: Scenes from London Life

Ungrateful Daughters: The Stuart Princesses
Who Stole their Father's Crown

Maureen Waller

London 1945

Life in the Debris of War

JOHN MURRAY

First published in Great Britain in 2004
by John Murray (Publishers)
A division of Hodder Headline

2 4 6 8 10 9 7 5 3

A CIP catalogue record for this title is available from the British Library

Hardcover ISBN 0 7195 6600 2

Typeset in Sabon by Palimpsest Book Production Limited,
Polmont, Stirlingshire
Printed and bound in Great Britain by
Clays Ltd, St Ives plc

John Murray (Publishers)
338 Euston Road
London NW1 3BH

For Roland Philipps

Contents

Illustrations

Acknowledgements

Enormous thanks, as ever, go to my husband, Brian MacArthur, whose idea it was for me to venture into the twentieth century, for his endless patience, wisdom, humour and support.

I should like to thank Jonathan Lloyd, wonderful agent and dear friend, and Roland Philipps, inspiring publisher, for their unfailing enthusiasm, dedication and kindness. I thank Lizzie Dipple at John Murray for her sympathetic assistance and attention to detail and Morag Lyall, who has done a splendid job copy editing all three of my books.

I wish to thank Mr Noel Mander for kindly giving permission to use the drawing on the endpapers, which was executed by his friend, the late Cecil Brown.

I am grateful to Professor Peter Hennessy and Mr Tom Pocock for generously giving their valuable time to reading sections of the script and offering helpful suggestions.

The historian of London is extremely fortunate in the wealth of material at her disposal and I wish to thank the staff of the following libraries and institutions for their helpful service: The Imperial War Museum, the National Archives, the Guildhall Library, the British Library and the Newspaper Library, the London Metropolitan Archives, the Trustees of the Mass-Observation Archive, University of Sussex, the London Library, the BBC Written Archives Centre, *The Times* Archives, the British Film Institute's National Film and Television Archive, Camden Local Studies and Archives Centre, Hackney Archives, Kensington and Chelsea Local Studies Library, Southwark Local Studies Library, Tower Hamlets Local History Library and Archives, and Westminster Archives Centre.

Every effort has been made to trace copyright holders and I should like to thank all those who have kindly granted permission to use quoted material.

Maureen Waller
London, October 2003

London 1945

Ministry of Home Security

Composition of Groups in Region No 5
London Region

GROUP 1
Chelsea
Fulham
Hammersmith
Kensington
Westminster

GROUP 2
Hampstead
Islington
Paddington
St Marylebone
St Pancras
Stoke Newington

GROUP 3
Bethnal Green
City
Finsbury
Hackney
Holborn
Poplar
Shoreditch
Stepney

GROUP 4
Bermondsey
Deptford
Greenwich
Lewisham
Woolwich

GROUP 5
Battersea
Camberwell
Lambeth
Southwark
Wandsworth

GROUP 6A
Cheshunt
East Barnet
Edmonton
Enfield
Hornsey
Southgate
Tottenham
Wood Green

GROUP 6B
Barnet RD
Barnet UD
Finchley
Friern Barnet
Hendon
Potters Bar

GROUP 6C
Acton
Bushey
Ealing
Harrow
Ruislip
Southall
Uxbridge
Wembley
Willesden

GROUP 6D
Brentford
Feltham
Hayes
Heston
Staines
Sunbury
Twickenham
Yiewsley

GROUP 7
Barking
Chigwell
Chingford
Dagenham
East Ham
Ilford
Leyton
Waltham Holy Cross
Walthamstow
Wanstead
West Ham

GROUP 8
Beckenham
Bexley
Bromley
Chislehurst
Crayford
Erith
Orpington
Penge

GROUP 9A
Barnes
Epsom & Ewell
Kingston
Malden & Coombe
Richmond
Surbiton
Wimbledon
Esher
Merton & Morden

GROUP 9B
Croydon
Beddington &
  Wallington
Mitcham
Sutton & Cheam
Banstead
Carlshalton
Coulsdon & Purley

(TNA/HO 198)

LONDON REGION

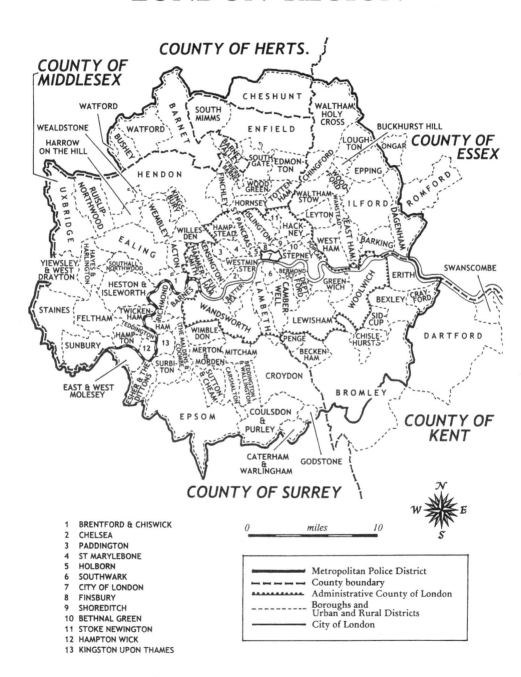

COUNTY OF HERTS.

COUNTY OF MIDDLESEX

COUNTY OF ESSEX

COUNTY OF KENT

COUNTY OF SURREY

WATFORD
SOUTH MIMMS
CHESHUNT
WALTHAM HOLY CROSS
BUCKHURST HILL
WEALDSTONE
WATFORD
ENFIELD
BARNET
LOUGH-TON
ONGAR
HARROW ON THE HILL
BUSHEY
SOUTH-GATE
EDMON-TON
CHINGFORD
EPPING
ROMFORD
HENDON
WOOD GREEN
TOTTEN-HAM
WALTHAM STOW
WANSTEAD
ILFORD
DAGENHAM
UXBRIDGE
RUISLIP NORTHWOOD
WEMBLEY
FINCHLEY
HORNSEY
ISLINGTON
LEYTON
EAST HAM
BARKING
YIEWSLEY & WEST DRAYTON
HAYES & HARLINGTON
SOUTHALL NORTHWOOD
EALING
ACTON
WILLES-DEN
HAMP-STEAD
ST PANCRAS
HACK-NEY
WEST HAM
STEPNEY
HESTON & ISLEWORTH
KENSINGTON
WESTMIN-STER
BERMOND-SEY
GREEN-WICH
ERITH
SWANSCOMBE
STAINES
FELTHAM
TWICKEN-HAM
RICHMOND
BARNES
HAMMERSMITH
FULHAM
BATTERSEA
CAMBER-WELL
DEPTFORD
WOOLWICH
BEXLEY
CRAY-FORD
TEDDINGTON
HAM
WANDSWORTH
LAMBETH
LEWISHAM
SID-CUP
DARTFORD
SUNBURY
HAMP-TON
THE MALDENS & COOMBE
WIMBLE-DON
PENGE
CHISLE-HURSTS
EAST & WEST MOLESEY
ESHER & THE DITTONS
SURBI-TON
MERTON & MORDEN
MITCHAM
BECKEN-HAM
EPSOM
SUTTON & CHEAM
CARSHALTON
BEDDINGTON & WALLINGTON
CROYDON
BROMLEY
COULSDON & PURLEY
CATERHAM & WARLINGHAM
GODSTONE

Legend

1   BRENTFORD & CHISWICK
2   CHELSEA
3   PADDINGTON
4   ST MARYLEBONE
5   HOLBORN
6   SOUTHWARK
7   CITY OF LONDON
8   FINSBURY
9   SHOREDITCH
10 BETHNAL GREEN
11 STOKE NEWINGTON
12 HAMPTON WICK
13 KINGSTON UPON THAMES

0   miles   10

N
W   E
S

——————— Metropolitan Police District
— — — — County boundary
▲▲▲▲▲▲▲ Administrative County of London
— — — — Boroughs and Urban and Rural Districts
——————— City of London

Prelude

'Through the long war, from beginning to end, London has
been the wedge that's kept the door of freedom open'
                                    – Macdonald Hastings

A visitor to London towards the end of 1944 would not be
seeing the city and its people at their best. The first impression was one of grimy, grey drabness. Buildings black with
soot cried out for a lick of paint. Boarded-up windows
presented a blank face to the world. Mean terraces, with now
and then a gap, fizzled out in piles of rubble. Acres of bomb
sites and bricks, bricks meticulously counted and piled up: so
many bricks in a devastated landscape. After five years of war,
the people looked tired and worn. There they were in their
shabby clothes, queuing for buses, or walking purposefully
along, not bothering to give the bomb sites a glance. Women
holding string bags stood patiently in long lines outside shops,
resignation on their faces. If he closed his eyes the visitor
became more conscious of the all-pervasive smell. It was of
coal smoke in the damp chill, but something else too. Dust!
Dust so acrid you could taste it in the mouth.

London was no longer filled with the buzz and excitement
of thousands of Allied and foreign servicemen, as it had been
in the build-up to D-Day, but there were still plenty of troops
on leave. The white helmets of the American military police,
known as the Snowdrops, could be spotted everywhere,
keeping an eye on any of their men propping up walls or
slouching along, the worse for drink. Wherever the GIs were,
the good-time girls were never far away. In Piccadilly Eros
was no longer the centre of attention: the god of love had

been evacuated with thousands of Londoners – mothers and children, the old and the sick. In his place stood a gigantic ugly box covering the empty plinth, a billboard urging people to buy Savings Certificates firmly plastered to its side. The crowd was drawn there all the same.

Just a few steps away on Shaftesbury Avenue stood Rainbow Corner, the most famous of the American Red Cross Clubs in town, where the American visitor would find his home from home. Groups of GIs would mass on the pavement outside, deciding how to spend their time: a dive straight into the flesh market in Piccadilly Circus, or a pub crawl, to get drunk on the warm, weak beer? Those in the know might nip round the corner to the back bar of the Café Royal, where whiskey from neutral Ireland was in plentiful supply. Otherwise, spirits were hard to come by. Or perhaps a trip to the famous Windmill Theatre, whose proud boast was that it never closed. Never clothed, more like. Here pretty girls in chorus lines were still indefatigably kicking their legs and nudes stood stock still, impassively ignoring the ear-splitting bangs and vibration of falling doodlebugs and rockets.

Step into the hall of Rainbow Corner and the visitor was instantly reminded why he was here at all, part of the friendly occupation force passing through London. An arrow, pointing vaguely east towards Leicester Square, bore the inscription: 'Berlin – 600 miles.' Another, pointing in the direction of Regent Street, said: 'New York – 3,271 miles.' There was everything here for his comfort. The voice of Bing Crosby blended with the clinking of Coca-Cola bottles, and over all there was a haze of smoke from copious supplies of American cigarettes. A thousand couples could jitterbug in the dance-hall. There were billiards, table tennis and pin-tables. There was a shoe-shine parlour, a letter-writing service and a juke box. One large comfortable lounge held a piano and plenty of armchairs, the other a big selection of classical records and a radiogram. There was a hobbies room, regular cabarets, weekly boxing shows and nightly free cinema. The GIs even had their own newspaper, the *Stars and Stripes*, packed with action from the battle zone, sports features and news from the States. Although it was printed on the presses of *The Times* at Blackfriars, there was little mention in the *Stars and Stripes* of the host city, London.

British visitors were admitted to Rainbow Corner by invitation only, but over 200 of the natives were paid employees, and nearly the same number of registered hostesses danced with the men twice a week. Through the hospitality section of the club, American servicemen were introduced into British homes, although they were advised to take their own rations to supplement the meagre fare of the hungry Brits. At the reception desk English women with cut-glass accents were on hand to give the visitors directions, should they wish to see the town. Taxis, like private motor cars, were scarce. Londoners had long given up and taken to walking. But London cabbies knew their market. The Americans were better paid than British boys and, never having got the hang of the currency, were notoriously careless with their change. At the club's behest, half a dozen tame taxi drivers who knew something of London's history would report to reception several times a day, taking American soldiers in groups of five at six shillings a head on a two-hour tour. Buckingham Palace, Westminster Abbey, Whitehall and St Paul's: all you had to do was sit in the cab and let the sights roll past you.

The more discriminating visitor might like to explore the town at greater leisure. Strolling along Piccadilly, past the burnt-out wreck of Wren's St James's Church, which had lost its spire, he might cut left, across Jermyn Street and down to the open green space of St James's Square. Like all London squares and terraces, it had lost its railings in the salvage drive of 1940. It certainly gave the town a more spacious feel, even if cabbages rather than flowers were hogging every inch of ground. Over on the right the façade of the famous London Library was intact, but there had been mayhem behind it. A few months ago, it had been a scene of twisted steel girders and yawning chasms with pulverised literature hidden under mounds of rubble. The whole area out to St James's Street and down to Pall Mall was badly scarred. Christie's auction house was a burnt skeleton. The clock on the front of St James's Palace was defaced and behind the red-brick walls of the Tudor building many of the rooms had been damaged by high-explosive and incendiary bombs and blast from a doodlebug.

Buckingham Palace looked as soot-grimed, gloomy and neglected as the rest of the town, its blackout still firmly in place. It had been damaged 14 times, yet the King and Queen were still in residence, relieved that after their own home had been hit they could, as she put it, look the East End in the face. Over in Birdcage Walk the Guards Chapel in Wellington Barracks had been destroyed by a flying bomb in the middle of a Sunday service in June, striking down the officer at the lectern reading the lesson and killing and maiming the rest of the congregation. Windows shattered all around and the blast tore the leaves off the trees. It was early summer and the curious thing was that the trees started to bud again at the end of the autumn just as others were losing their leaves.

If the visitor wandered along Constitution Hill towards the hidden police station at Wellington Arch, he might be lured by the music of the regimental band into Hyde Park. In the far north-east corner, by Marble Arch, Speaker's Corner was still the centre of free speech, no matter how many wartime restrictions there were. 'What are we fighting for?' a speaker shouted. 'Spam,' cried a wit in the crowd.

At lunchtime in Trafalgar Square a long queue outside the National Gallery might excite the visitor's curiosity. It was not to see the national collection, which had been removed for the duration of the war, leaving only the frames behind in the empty rooms. Visitors now were treated to the Picture of the Month, which the Gallery's inspired director, Sir Kenneth Clark, arranged to have brought up to London, one picture at a time, from the collection's wartime hiding place in a vast, specially prepared cave in a Welsh mountain: viewed in splendid isolation, the masterpiece would be all the more appreciated. Hundreds queued on weekdays for Myra Hess's concerts of chamber music, under the gallery's great glass dome or in the basement shelter, when for an hour the perennial favourites, Beethoven, Mozart and Bach, would transport them beyond their wartime cares. An added attraction for the lunchtime crowd of office workers was Lady Gater's canteen at the gallery, serving the best sandwiches in London.

Perhaps the visitor would be tempted to take a short walk along the Strand. To enter the Savoy Hotel, the hang-out of the American press in London, was to escape into a world of serene luxury. The Grill with its riverside view was one of the best dining rooms in London, although the recent crashing of a V-2 rocket into the Thames outside shattering the windows for the seventh time had been a bit close for comfort: some of its habitual customers had temporarily absconded to the Hungaria in the safer environs of Lower Regent Street.

At the southern tip of Trafalgar Square, the statue of Charles I on horseback had been replaced by a fake information bureau bearing the inscription, 'Closed on Sundays and not open all week'. Walking down Whitehall, there was no call to stop at the Banqueting House, as the Rubens ceiling had been removed to safety outside London. The whole row of sandbagged government departments in Whitehall had been hit by German bombs, some of them several times.

Outside the Houses of Parliament, the statue of Oliver Cromwell stood steady and resolute as Churchill, unharmed throughout the war, while round the corner the crusading Richard the Lionheart had had the tip of his uplifted sword bent and his horse's tail pierced by enemy action. Miraculously, Westminster Hall, completed by William Rufus in 1099, survived in spite of its roof catching fire. Big Ben had been hit, but the clock had not stopped. The House of Commons was *hors de combat*. In May 1941 the Commons' Chamber was entirely destroyed by a fire which spread to the Members' Lobby, causing the roof to collapse. Fortunately the Speaker's Chair, from which the Speaker of the day had told Charles I he had neither ears to hear nor eyes to see except as the House permitted, had been removed to safety outside London. In the

House of Lords a bomb passed through the floor of the Chamber without exploding. The Commons sat in Church House, Dean's Yard for the rest of the war and afterwards would sit in the Chamber of the House of Lords, while a new House of Commons was under construction. In July 1944 a doodlebug just failed to cross the river and plunked down on St Thomas's Hospital instead, breaking a large number of windows on the now deserted terrace of the Palace of Westminster opposite.

Westminster Abbey had been knocked about a bit, but nothing the workmen could not put right. The Coronation Chair, the stalls and bronze grille from Henry VII's Chapel and the statues from the royal tombs had been sent to the country for safety. The Stone of Scone was in a secret hiding place. It had been buried near the abbey and, in case of invasion, a plan revealing its exact whereabouts had been sent to Mr Mackenzie King, the Prime Minister of Canada. Over the river, Lambeth Palace, the residence of the Archbishop of Canterbury, had sustained damage from 10 high-explosive bombs as well as V-1s, or doodlebugs, crashing in the vicinity. Further east along the derelict wasteland of the South Bank, Southwark Cathedral had lost its stained glass windows when a high explosive bomb landed in nearby Borough Market. Guy's Hospital had sustained several hits.

Surprisingly, none of the bridges spanning the Thames was hit, although plenty of explosives had landed in the river. If the visitor were to cross Waterloo Bridge to the Aldwych – scene of one of the worst V-1 disasters – and turn right past a relatively intact Somerset House, he would soon come upon the burnt-out shell of St Clement Danes Church. Dr Johnson's pew had gone up in flames with the rest in 1940. The tower was still standing, but the bells – 'the bells of St Clements' in the old song – had fallen down and four of them had cracked. Nearby the Royal Courts of Justice had been damaged and the Inner Temple Library with 45,000 legal books had been destroyed. There was damage to Middle Temple Hall and the Temple Church, where only the effigy of Lord de Roos (died

1227) survived. Twinings Tea Shop had been hit, but part of the old counter at which Sir Christopher Wren had bought this little luxury had been salvaged.

Up in Chancery Lane the Public Record Office had removed all its documents, with those of some of the City livery companies and London parishes, to a number of destinations for safety. Two thousand tons of them in 88,000 large containers had left London.

Fleet Street, still the home of the newspaper industry, was relatively unscathed. Down a little alley on the north side, Dr Johnson's House in Gough Square had survived, while Sergeant's Inn and many eighteenth-century houses lay in ruins. On the south side Wren's St Bride's Church, completed in 1680, had been reduced to a shell. The exquisite wedding-cake spire, arguably Wren's finest, had survived, but the bells had fallen from the tower. The registers, including the one containing the baptismal entry of Samuel Pepys, had survived, but the font which had probably served on that occasion had been destroyed. Down in the crypt the bombing was to reveal a Roman mosaic on what was, after all, the approximate site of a Roman temple.

At Ludgate Circus the visitor would have to pass under the overhead railway running from Blackfriars up Farringdon Road. Climbing up the slope of Ludgate Hill to St Paul's was to enter a devastated land. There was nothing but wide open spaces, gaping cellars and rubble up here. That St Paul's survived at all was a miracle. On the night of 12 September 1940 a delayed action bomb buried itself 27 feet in the ground near the clock tower. Three days later it was successfully extracted and driven in a lorry at full pelt through the City to Hackney Marshes, where it was disposed of. It left a crater 100 feet wide. On 10 October 1940 a bomb went through the outer roof of the choir. A mass of debris fell and destroyed the high altar.

On the night of 29 December 1940, when the City was empty and its premises locked and unguarded, there was the greatest conflagration since the Great Fire of 1666. This was the moment when a photographer on the roof of the *Daily Mail* building in Fleet Street took the famous picture of the dome of St Paul's rising above the smoke as the City all around it was engulfed in the inferno. Flames from buildings to the north and north-west, eating up the stocks of the book trade in Paternoster Row, were practically licking the stonework. A telegraph was actually despatched to New York with the news that the great edifice was no more. The Thames was at low tide and firemen's hoses ran dry, but by foresight and good fortune the guardians of St Paul's had installed some of their own supplies and it was saved.

The danger was far from over. On 16 April 1941 a bomb fell on the north transept, pierced the saucer dome and exploded inside. The debris broke through the floor into the crypt. Almost all the stained glass was destroyed by the blast and the iron framework twisted and bent. Several monuments were damaged. That same night, a few feet from the eastern wall, a Civil Defence worker found himself staring at a land mine eight feet high. Slowly and painstakingly, it was removed. By the end of 1944 St Paul's was facing a new menace: the V-2s, indiscriminately hurled through the stratosphere and arriving without warning, penetrating the crash site at over 3,000 miles an hour and leaving a massive crater.

The destruction of so many buildings in the vicinity of the cathedral meant that its sheer immensity, dominating the City as it had been designed to do, could be appreciated for the first time. In Wren's day, St Paul's could only be glimpsed through narrow alleyways and from short distances. Now a person could stand near the damaged Old Bailey in Newgate Street or in the burnt-out shell of St Mary-le-Bow in Cheapside and enjoy an uninterrupted view of the cathedral, while the long length of Queen Victoria Street, whose buildings had been razed to the ground, afforded an unrivalled prospect.

The Monument, which recorded London's losses in the Great Fire of 1666, was untouched. The densely packed square mile of the City, with its jumble of tall, narrow-fronted offices and warehouses, proved almost as vulnerable to disaster during

8

the Blitz of 1940–41 as it had in the earlier conflagration. Out of a total of 460 acres of built-up land, buildings covering 164 acres were destroyed. The sirens sounded 715 times, a total of 417 high explosive bombs were dropped on the City alone, 13 parachute mines, 2,498 oil bombs and thousands of incendiaries. After the night of 29 December 1940 the fifteenth-century Guildhall was a smoking ruin, although the outer walls and tracery and the medieval porch and crypt survived. Nineteen churches, 16 of them by Wren, were reduced to the shell. Only 3 of 34 historic City livery halls – the Apothecaries' in Blackfriars Lane, the Ironmongers' in Aldersgate Street and Vintners' in Upper Thames Street – were undamaged.

In 1941 a high-explosive bomb had penetrated Bank Underground station, leaving a massive crater in the road which had to be spanned by a bridge. Surprisingly, the Bank of England, the Royal Exchange and the Mansion House, over-looking the crater, sustained only slight damage.

North of London Wall, the area between Aldersgate Street and Moorgate up as far as Cripplegate – the Barbican – was a wasteland. To the north of it, bombs had torn into the Non-conformists' burial ground at Bunhill Fields, leaving Civil Defence workers the distasteful task of gathering up the remains, although the graves of Bunyan and Defoe were undisturbed. To the west, in Smithfield, St Bartholomew's Hospital had suffered superficial damage, and London's most ancient church, St Bartholomew the Great, dating in part from 1130, was almost unscathed. The same could not be said of the fifteenth-century Charterhouse nearby.

Moving east to Tower Bridge, the visitor to the Tower of London would be amazed to find the moat turned into a vast allotment with row upon row of vegetables. So close to the cranes, wharves, warehouses and ships of the Port of London – now busier than ever, since it was the main source of supply to the Allied armies in Europe – the medieval fortress had received 15 direct hits from high explosive bombs, as well as countless incendiary bombs. Three V-1s were to fall within its walls. And yet it survived with only minor damage to some of the Tudor buildings and their glass. It was piquant to think that Hitler's deputy Rudolf Hess had been lodged for three days and nights in the King's House, where Anne Boleyn had spent her last days and Guy Fawkes had been examined. The axe and the block from the Tower and the armour had been removed to the country, but it was closed to visitors anyway.

Near the Tower, the Church of All Hallows Barking, from whose steeple Pepys had watched the progress of the Great Fire, was a burnt wreck. To the east, the Great Synagogue in Duke's Place – the oldest in London, dating from the seventeenth century – had been entirely destroyed and all its treasures lost. Further west towards Liverpool Street, Hawksmoor's Christ Church, Spitalfields had sustained considerable damage. It was one of the many London churches in whose crypt the living had sheltered from the bombing among the dead.

Returning from the City to the West End the visitor would pass the Church of St Sepulchre in Newgate Street, the church where the condemned had received a blessing before the long procession to Tyburn in the days when hangings were still public. The church was intact. Then he would cross Holborn Viaduct, where the bronze statues representing Commerce, Agriculture, Science and Fine Art looked out over the busy thoroughfare of Farringdon Road and Smithfield Market. A little further along, the City Temple and Wren's St Andrew's Church had been destroyed. Whichever route the visitor took then, either along High Holborn or down Gray's Inn Road and into Theobald's Road, he would find destruction. National Fire Service men were letting their pigs roam in the ruins of Lincoln's Inn Fields. The sixteenth-century Staple Inn and the hall of Gray's Inn were in ashes. Like Dr Johnson's house, Dickens' house in Doughty Street survived. The Royal Free Hospital had already been damaged several times, but the Germans were not finished with it yet.

Emerging into Bloomsbury he would find the British Museum closed. It had been hit by high explosive bombs several times, destroying the upper galleries and 150,000 books

– but all of them within the last century, so not irreplaceable. Some of its bigger exhibits from Egypt and Assyria had been too big to move and were left to take their chances, protected by blast walls and sandbags. The Elgin Marbles were spending the war in the London Underground in a disused part of the Aldwych-Piccadilly Line, along with the wax funeral effigies of kings and queens from Westminster Abbey, paintings from the Tate Gallery and exhibits from the Museum of London – both of which were closed for obvious reasons. Other exhibits from the British Museum joined those of the Victoria and Albert Museum in Corsham Quarries near Bath.

Bloomsbury was dominated by the thirties' high rise, the University of London's Senate House, where the Ministry of Information had set up its headquarters. It was both sinister and absurd, a bit of a public joke. Over the other side of Tottenham Court Road lay Fitzrovia, then part of Soho. The whole Soho area, squeezed between the Ministry of Information to the east and the BBC to the west, was the closest wartime London came to a literary haunt. Step into the smoke-filled atmosphere of the Wheatsheaf in Rathbone Place to find a sprinkling of poets in uniform spending their leave in the place they called home, or into the Highlander in Dean Street, south of Oxford Street, to see Dylan Thomas, drowning his boredom after a day working on film scripts for the Ministry of Information.

The really keen visitor with literary interests might travel out to Hampstead to see Keats House, damaged and still not open to visitors, or to bohemian Chelsea. Although the Germans had done their best to destroy Battersea Power Station, the borough had suffered far less damage than most others in London, although the number of casualties among civilians and Allied servicemen and women still ran into the hundreds. Chelsea Old Church, containing St Thomas More's chapel, was the main casualty. Ironically, the curious effigy of Sara Colville (died 1631) rising from a coffin remained intact, while that of Lady Jane Cheyne (died 1669) was found on a rubbish heap nearby. A pub crawl was the best way for the visitor to absorb the atmosphere of Chelsea. The visitor might even witness a police raid, when everyone would have to show his identity card and leave pass. In pubs and dance halls all over London this meant a hasty exodus to the ladies' toilets, where the deserters queued to push each other through the window. After licensing hours, drinkers could retire to illicit drinking clubs to while away the afternoon or drink until the small hours of the morning.

A galaxy of cheap and cheerful Soho restaurants, such as Bertorelli's, Schmidt's, and La Scala in Charlotte Street and Fava's in Greek Street, might appeal to the visitor. The White Tower in Percy Street was a cut above. For something grander and to impress a girl, there was the Berkeley Buttery on the corner of Piccadilly and Berkeley Street opposite the Ritz, but an American on good pay could easily afford the Dorchester, the Ritz or the Savoy, where to conform with the law a meal was only five shillings, although the cover charge and the wine drove up the price. The Dorchester charged extra to use the dance floor, but a good time could be had at the Royal Opera House, Covent Garden, where the stalls had been converted to a public dance floor, while the spectators sat at tables on the balconies and boxes.

So it was back to Piccadilly Circus. The new dim-out, which was supposed to replace the blackout proper in September, did not make much difference. Councils were slow to get street lights working again and people were too apathetic to take down the blackout. Prostitutes – the Piccadilly Commandos or 'dogs', as the Americans called them – continued to shine a torch on themselves as a means of soliciting. Londoners were still blundering about in the dark. It would be a while yet before the lights went on in London.

A Tribute to London

London has been in the front line in the final victorious phase of the greatest war that history has ever known. She was in the first battle and she is in the last one – so far.

It was London that, in the darkest days of the war when this country stood alone, gave hope and confidence to the free peoples of the world and set an example in courage, endurance, and unshakeable faith that has led the United Nations to the threshold of victory. It cannot be wondered at that Hitler has made a special target of London. No city in the world has done more to frustrate his ambition and ensure his downfall. In 1940 Hitler paid London this compliment, that if only he could knock her out he would win everything. He failed. In 1944 the compliment he has paid London is that if only he could have knocked her out he would stave off defeat. He has failed again.

History will be able to record the astonishing fact that when the German armies were being battered to pieces in the closing battles of this world war, Hitler and the German High Command left them with appreciably reduced air cover in order that men and material might be available for the high-minded military task of smashing people's homes in London. Immense resources which could have helped to protect Germany's fighting troops were deliberately reserved for use against the back streets and suburban roads of London. It might be thought this was just blind revenge. It was something more than that.

To Hitler London is and always has been a strong-point of immense significance in the fighting line against him. The enemy has stated time and again that the object of his flying bomb and other secret weapons is to break our will to win. That is what he has been trying to do – to break the spirit of London, to make London squeal to such a pitch that the Government would be forced to call off the war.

He calculated that after five years of war London could not possibly stand the strain of being shot at continuously 24 hours a day, day after day, week after week, month after month. He knows better now. London is invincible. There may conceivably still be trials in store for us before the allied armies have rooted out the last of the vipers' nests, but Hitler has already lost the Battle of London as surely as he has lost the main battle of France, of which the Battle of London was a part. It was a part, because our plan was to break the back of Germany's western forces, and to do it in Normandy.

Hitler's plan was to attack London with such ferocity as to make us divide our strength and abandon our strategy by attacking his flying bomb coast. His attack, which began a week after D-Day, was an essential part of his defensive plan. He was beaten partly because our guns and planes took toll of his weapons, but more still because what came through to London – and there was plenty of it at times – didn't make Londoners squeal. London stood fast. The Battle of Normandy was won – and the Battle of London helped to win it.

The Battle of London has been won by –

1. The people of London. They have suffered death and injury, loss of homes and worldly possessions, widespread damage to their houses, disruption of families by evacuation, miseries of shelter life, the trials and difficulties of travel and shopping – but through all anxieties maintaining an outward calm, confidence, good humour, and carrying on with the job.

2. The people of southern England living in Bomb Alley, on the coast and in the country places. They have been in the firing line almost without pause ever since the first Battle of France in 1940, and it is impossible for anyone who knows the facts to think of the Battle of London without thinking of the trials and sufferings of the townspeople, villagers, and country folk of battle-scarred southern England.

3. The Civil Defence services. The energy, speed, and enthusiasm with which they took up the challenge and adapted their methods

and organisation to meet the new form of bombing have brought fresh glory to their magnificent war record.

4. The airmen and the gunners. The fighters, gunners, and balloon crews of the Air Defences of Great Britain had to learn new tricks in dealing with the flying bomb, and were extraordinarily successful in the toll they took of those weapons which the enemy was able to launch. Great work was done by the bombers and fighter-bombers, both British and American, in the offensive counter-measures that were taken against the firing sites, supply organisations, communications and production centre of the new weapon.

The day has come when London can openly rejoice in the great part she has played in the overthrow of Nazism by the sturdiness of her resistance, first in 1940 and now in the last battles of the war.

— Statement issued by Herbert Morrison, Home Secretary and Minister of Home Security, and published in *The Times* on 7 September 1944.

The next day the first supersonic weapon, the V-2 rocket, landed in London. The Battle of London continued.

I

Rockets Fell like Autumn Leaves

'There is no siren warning now. No time to take shelter. For this is the most indiscriminate weapon of this or any other war. It is a sinister, eerie form of war'

– Daily Herald

New Year's Eve 1944 was the sort of clear moonlit night that had once been a gift for German bombers following the shining Thames towards the heart of the capital. Symbolic of London's long struggle and survival, St Paul's Cathedral stood majestically among the ruins, a miracle after five and a quarter years of war. In the wasteland surrounding it, the jagged outlines of bombed buildings, their foundations exposed to the elements, and the occasional surviving spire of some City church, rising naked above the ruins of its blackened structure, looked ghost-like in the moonlight.

In daytime wide-open vistas and ruined buildings afforded better views of the cathedral than had ever existed. Purple-pink rosebay willow herb softened the edges of the torn land-scape. In empty cellars and vacant plots National Fire Service and Civil Defence men and women ran their poultry, pig and rabbit clubs, or cultivated vegetables where once businesses had flourished. Stray cats, refugees from thousands of bombed homes, behaved as if they owned the place. Nestling beside the cathedral, large emergency tanks promised 1 million gallons of water should incendiary bombs ever again bounce off the dome or rain down on the roof as they had done during the Blitz, and incidentally provided a home for waterfowl. It was surprising how quickly nature had reclaimed its own in the financial capital of the world.

Even after the conflagration of 29 December 1940, when nearly one-third of the City was destroyed and the smoke from its still burning buildings choked the air, St Paul's had opened its doors to worshippers next morning, so that the service tonight was part of a proud tradition. Deep inside the crypt a congregation composed mainly of the Watch – those brave, selfless men who had given up their nights to protect St Paul's – and of servicemen and -women waited expectantly for the BBC's red light, signalling they were on air. Just as it flicked on, the hush was shattered by an explosion and the prolonged rumbling, like an express train coming through a tunnel, that in the last few months had become all too familiar to Londoners: a V-2 rocket had landed, not necessarily in the vicinity, but sounding so loud after it penetrated the earth at over 3,000 mph, travelling faster than sound, that anyone could be excused for thinking it was. By some acoustic quirk, those in its direct path barely heard a V-2. If you did hear it, it had missed you. But that knowledge did nothing to quell the primeval fear each time one exploded.

Not for the first or last time in this war, Wren's masterpiece rocked and vibrated, but owing to the solidity and elasticity of its structure settled again. There was a splintering of glass and the last window in the cathedral cascaded in shards over the marble floor in the empty darkness. Damage to add to the earlier wreck of the high altar and of Wren's own monument with its words, 'If you seek a monument, look around you', which lay in rubble. Still, the monument the inscription referred to had so far survived the worst the enemy could throw at it.

For one tense moment, the Dean worried there would be panic and a rush to the exit. Instead, the congregation laughed and prepared themselves for the first hymn. There had already been a short rehearsal, since the St Paul's choirboys were not there to lead but still in their wartime billets in Truro and singing in that cathedral, but now the singing began in earnest and it was wonderful. Listeners at home in cold, draughty, damaged houses sat back to enjoy the service ushering in the

New Year, fervently hoping that this year of 1945 would bring peace at last.

Londoners entered the New Year in low spirits, the lowest since the war began. After the D-Day landings of June 1944, they had hoped that the war would be over by Christmas, only to be disappointed. It was worse than disappointing. Just before Christmas the Allies had suffered a serious reverse, meeting a fierce German counter-offensive in the Ardennes. For civilians – particularly those in London Region, the front line – five years of war had taken their toll. In the coldest winter for over half a century they were living in primitive conditions with tarpaulins for roofs, blown-out boarded-up windows, missing doors, smashed or frozen water pipes and desperate fuel shortages. Many were homeless, living in tube shelters and rest centres. They were tired of rationing, queuing and making do. 'We are suffering, here at home, the worst period of the war,' George Beardmore noted in his diary. 'We are all – all of us, at the office, in the shops, and at home – weary of war and its effects.' Most of all, their nerves were stretched to breaking point by the unremitting onslaught from the skies.

The V-2, which so many listeners heard during the Watch Night Service at St Paul's, was a timely reminder that the Battle of London was far from over. 'Just as all these wonderful sounds were coming over the air,' wrote Vere Hodgson of Notting Hill, 'behold I heard a rocket bomb drop in the distance. It was a long way away but it was there to remind us that there are still some very unpleasant things about and that THE WAR IS NOT OVER.'

This cautious note was one that Duncan Sandys, the junior Minister in charge of the V-weapon problem, might ruefully have wished he had adopted at the press conference held on 7 September 1944, in which, taking his cue from Herbert Morrison's speech of the previous day and printed in *The Times* that very morning, he told journalists: 'Except possibly for a few last shots the Battle of London is over.' It was the most extraordinary misjudgement. As early as 1943 the Government had been well aware that the Germans were working on two new secret weapons, the first a pilotless missile, or flying bomb, the second a supersonic rocket. The Prime Minister Winston Churchill had admitted as much in Parliament on 22 February 1944. Intelligence as to the nature of the new weapons had been gathered from Poland, Sweden, France and the production site on the island of Peenemünde off the Baltic coast. Peenemünde and the launch sites in the Pas de Calais had been the subject of heavy aerial Allied bombardment – taking a huge toll of aircraft and airmen. The bombardment, Hitler's initial lack of faith in the rocket, and inter-service rivalry on the German side, had delayed the unleashing of the two weapons, while in London the Civil Defence Committee of the War Cabinet had debated how they were going to cope with the likely scale of attack.

By the time Duncan Sandys made his regrettable statement, London had taken the brunt of Hitler's first 'Vengeance' weapon, the V-1, launched indiscriminately at civilians all through the summer of 1944. At sunrise on 13 June 1944 a curious chug-chug sound, like a motorbike scraping across the sky, had suddenly stopped, followed by an almighty crash. It had landed at Grove Road, Bethnal Green, cutting the railway bridge and rendering 266 people homeless. Looking at the remains of the weapon in the enormous crater, onlookers assumed that a piloted plane had crashed, but it was puzzling that there was no evidence of a pilot. As these curious missiles arrived in salvos over the following days, the public were still unaware that they were pilotless. At St Olave's Hospital, Bermondsey, for instance, a group of young nurses – my mother among them – marvelled at the pilot's bravery in flying so low. The bombardment was so intense that on 16 June Herbert Morrison, who as Home Secretary and Minister of Home Security was responsible for Civil Defence, agreed to make a statement, announcing that London was under attack by pilot-less planes, but refusing to disclose the extent of the destruc-tive power of the weapon.

Life had become uncertain again. This was far worse than the earlier conventional bombardments. In the Blitz, there had been sufficient warning of impending attack to take shelter. Sirens at local police stations had given clear warning of an 'Alert' and of the 'All Clear', when it was safe to emerge again. The V-1s were arriving so thick and fast – on average 73 every 24 hours, although in overcast weather as many as 200 might evade the fighters sent out to deflect them – that alerts would go on all day with only brief periods of respite or even continue for days at a time. It was easy to lose track as to whether there was an alert on or not. Alerts were a huge interruption to the working day, so much so that many offices and factories employed roof spotters, to inform them if a V-1 was getting sufficiently close to warrant the staff taking shelter. Such precautions were impractical for the ordinary household, although some might have followed the practice of Joyce Barrett, living in Sutton Dwellings, Shoreditch, who acted as lookout while her mother and the other women in the block defied the warnings in order to cook the Sunday lunch.

Frightening and exhausting as the constant alerts were, Londoners had not lost their sense of humour. A member of the Women's Voluntary Service for Civil Defence (WVS), who was helping a family in Clapham, recalls that the father 'grabbed each of his small children almost as if they were puppies and popped them into the Anderson shelter. He then turned round to look for his wife. Things were hot. But she was upstairs. He called out to her to hurry up. She yelled: "Wait a moment, I've got to find my dentures." "Listen, you," came the reply, "they're dropping doodlebugs, not sandwiches."'

Londoners took to staring at the sky, now bereft of the silver barrage balloons that had protected them throughout the war. Briefly missed and soon forgotten, the balloons had been moved south, part of three lines of defence against the new weapon: first the fighter pilots over the Channel and patrolling the Dutch and Belgian coasts – some became adept at using the wing to tip over the flying bomb, so that it would crash outside urban areas; then a gun belt stretching along the south coast, where they had a clear line of vision to blast the missiles as they were catapulted from their camouflaged launch sites at 350–400 mph, flying as low as 1,000–2,300 feet; then the barrage balloons on London Region's outer rim.

Above all, Londoners' ears were constantly attuned to the possibility of attack, listening for the distant hum which would ascend to a raucous rattle as it drew closer. They flinched at sudden noises, such as a slamming door or a car backfiring. It was the peculiar mechanised sound and the unpredictability of the weapon that suggested the terms 'buzz bombs' and 'doodlebugs'; perhaps it was also the Londoners' natural urge to poke fun at something Hitler had so portentously called his Vergeltungswaffe, literally, Vengeance Weapon – his retaliation for the bombing of German cities.

They found themselves praying that it would keep moving and land somewhere else.

The V-1 played tricks. Sometimes as it drew close it would suddenly veer away again, or make a circle and return, just when you thought the danger was past. A sudden cutting out of the engine when the fuel ran out and the missile began its descent signalled the moment to dive for cover. In the street people launched themselves on to the pavement or in the gutter. Inside, they crouched under tables and desks, or the Morrison shelter if they had one. The tenseness of those few seconds, waiting for the explosion, was unbearable.

The never-ending vigilance and frequency of explosions were wearing on the nerves. As George Britton of Walthamstow told his daughter in California, it 'makes you feel that you are just waiting your turn'. A chunk of his letter had been removed by the censor, but he continues, 'I can't make myself go far from home, in fact I can't stand any noise in the house, for fear of not hearing one of the robot planes coming over ... everyone seems to feel the same, we are all on edge.' Irene Byers worried about her elderly parents, especially her father: 'He dreads the doodlebugs so much that he is in danger of a nervous breakdown. They have even stopped using the Hoover because the noise blots out the cutting of the bug's engine. Just the effect Hitler wishes for us all. Total dread.' Even the bells of St Paul's had been silenced since June, when it was decided they 'might drown out the sound of an approaching robot'.

The impersonal nature of the new weapon, the fact that death was being doled out by a robot rather than a human being risking his own life in the process, had a strange psychological effect. 'You accepted a plane with a man in it,' Odette Lesley said, 'you couldn't accept something that was automatic. It was this that struck psychologically at us in such a way that it destroyed our nerves.'

Death could fall out of the sky at any moment and was completely random, as Stanley Rothwell, a Civil Defence worker from Lambeth, recalled:

The doodlebugs kept us busy both day and night. Our services were extended almost to the limit. No sooner had we attended one incident than we were met with another even before we had time to get back to our depots to report the casualties. We had been detailed to West Norwood, there was a heavy casualty list there which we cleared. On our way back we could hear the oncoming doodlebug behind us chugging like a motorbike. In front of us on a rise to the left we saw two semi-detached houses. A man was digging in a garden alongside, a little boy was running up the garden path towards the house, his schoolbag slung across his shoulder. At the doorway was a woman beckoning him to hurry indoors. The engine of the flying bomb shut off, we crouched waiting for the crunch. It glided over and past us and settled on the two houses all in the space of seconds. There was a loud explosion, a mushroom cloud of dust. Everything went up; no houses, no man, no mother and no boy. We picked up three dustbins full of pieces out of the rubble. The only way to identify where they were was the dampening dust and the cloud of flies.

If death was random, so too was survival. When Mary Beazley, an admiral's daughter working in a parachute factory in Heal's in Tottenham Court Road, was kept awake all night by the noise of ack-ack guns, she decided to give her usual service at the Guards Chapel a miss that Sunday morning, so avoiding the V-1 which totally destroyed it, killing half the congregation and injuring the rest. Later, during the V-2 period, someone cursed missing a bus; catching the next one, he found that the one he had missed had been completely destroyed by a rocket a mile up the road.

The effect of a V-1 with its one ton of explosive power (equivalent to a 1,000 kg bomb) crashing on a dense urban area was devastating. Within a half mile radius of the point of impact, roofs would be ripped off, doors blown out, window frames wrenched from their casements and glass shattered – the crunch of glass underfoot was a constant sound. In the West End the modern steel-reinforced buildings stood up reasonably well to blast, but the flimsy Victorian back-to-backs of the working-class districts were extremely vulnerable. Whole streets would collapse like packs of cards. The force of the explosion would hurl victims against obstacles, crash them into walls, knock them down and in some cases rip them apart. Anyone in the vicinity might be lacerated, even blinded, by flying glass and injured by flying debris. Blast played funny tricks, good as well as bad. Its tendency to rip off clothing left two elderly spinsters in Belgravia emerging from the ruins stark naked but clutching their Pekinese. On another occasion the blast from a V-2 rolled a sheet of linoleum into a tube, which allowed the baby boy wrapped inside to breathe until the rescue men found him buried in the debris of his home.

As it was being catapulted at London day and night, the V-1 caught people in the rush hour, or out at the shops. They might die in the office or in the lunch hour, as many did at the Aldwych when a V-1 exploded outside Bush House. Five young WAAFS leaning out of the window at Adastral House, the Air Ministry, 'to see the beastly thing', were drawn out by the blast, their bodies flying through the air to crash on the pavement below. Walking back to Fleet Street from

Simpson's after lunch that day, Ronald Hyde, the news editor of the *Evening Standard*, noticed that the trees had lost their leaves and were adorned instead with human flesh. Someone had stepped from the shelter of a doorway after the explosion and been sliced vertically in two by a falling sheet of glass. Victims generally would be covered with dust or with soot, sucked out of chimneys by the blast. A three-year-old boy covered in soot was found in a ruined house. While being washed he kept repeating, 'Nasty, dirty, noisy chimney-man.'

Londoners had long ago adopted an air of insouciance under aerial attack and there was evidence of the same now. Life went on, although the sound of an approaching V-1 might have a dampening effect on conversation. Lunching in a private room at the Savoy, John Lehmann was in earnest discussion with Sir Kenneth Clark about the war artists when

the familiar splutter began to be audible in the distance; as it grew louder, we all became a little more thoughtful; conversation faltered, dried up here and there for some seconds though the thread was never entirely lost; gestures were inhibited, not a fork was lifted to a mouth for the brief span of time that seemed an eternity. When the machine had evidently veered away again, it was satisfactory to observe that no member of the party had actually disappeared under the table.

On his way to a meeting at Euston Square, Harold Nicolson noted: 'a doodlebug comes over our bus and we all crouch down to avoid the shattering of the window-glass. People are very calm, and when it passes, they just go on reading their newspapers.'

Through all the vicissitudes of war, Londoners had shown spirit and resilience. As Nancie Norman, a young civil servant, recalls, 'You didn't complain, you didn't need to be counselled, you just got on with it.' Nevertheless, the old camaraderie that had been such a feature of the Blitz of 1940–41 was on the wane. The frequency and unpredictability of the new weapon, combined with a desperate wish not to die now the war was so close to its end, seem to have produced an element of panic. 'I can still remember my horror and disgust at seeing grown men avidly pushing women and children aside to get down into Warren Street tube station when the doodlebugs were coming over,' Odette Lesley recalls. 'I was actually shoved out of the way myself once or twice. People's nerves had gone – their nerves were shot to pieces.'

Certainly everyone was very tired and this must have accounted for a great deal of the irritability. Living at Sissinghurst in Kent, Harold Nicolson and his wife Vita Sackville-West were in 'Bomb Alley', literally on the flight path of the V-1s as they headed towards their principal target, Tower Bridge and its environs – though more often than not falling several miles short of it on Croydon, Wandsworth, Lewisham, Woolwich and Camberwell, which had the distinction of being the most bombed boroughs. 'Viti has been kept up and rendered sleepless by the robot 'planes,' Nicolson complained on 16 June. And 10 days later: 'The doodle-bug attack became so serious last night that Viti and I waited up in my room for the midnight news. There was nothing new. We are kept awake during the night by the rocket-bombs [*sic*] howling overhead, and we hear as many as twelve explosions. It gets better after 2 am and we get a little sleep.'

How much worse for the citizens of south London, who were either the recipients of the bombs themselves or had the unnerving experience of hearing them constantly flying low overhead to explode nearby. Irene Byers in Dulwich was one of them: 'On June 15th we go to bed and have an all night warning with the long rumoured secret weapon in action for the first time. It is an unmanned rocket shaped like a small aeroplane whose putt-putting engine cuts out, glides to its target and then explodes. Being a warden, Cyril [her husband, who worked in the Bank of England by day but did duty as a part-time, unpaid ARP warden at nights] has long since known about it and said nothing to me, but the shock and the silent attack petrifies me.'

Not surprisingly she found the tension, the broken nights

and lack of sleep so unbearable that she was among the first to leave London, taking her children to the safety of Somerset. Over a million Londoners left town, a third of them children under the Government evacuation scheme, others privately. In August 15,734 hospital patients and staff were evacuated to Scotland, Wales and the north, while another 8,179 were discharged to their homes. Many hospitals were to be hit by the V-1, including St Thomas's just across the river from the Houses of Parliament, the Royal Free in Gray's Inn Road, the Middlesex in Mortimer Street, St Mary Abbott's in Kensington, St Olave's in Bermondsey and the Lewisham, but the purpose of the evacuation was to free up the beds for the expected V-1 casualties. Plans were drawn up to evacuate 85,000 civil servants, only a proportion of the 130,000 on headquarters' staffs of government departments based in London – testimony to the bulging bureaucracy of wartime.

Londoners took to sleeping in the Underground again. At the height of the V-1 terror, 73,600 of London's night-time population of 6,750,000 were sleeping in the tubes – as opposed to 150,000 during the Blitz of 1940 – 41 and during the Little Blitz in the first four months of 1944 – although by early August the figure was halved. There was shelter capacity in London for 7,250,000, but only 40 per cent of Londoners ever took any shelter at all and of these only 4 per cent resorted to the Underground shelters. Once again travellers alighting from the tube would be greeted by the smell of hundreds of bodies in close confinement and have to step past their recumbent forms. People drew comfort from being in the company of others when they were under attack, but they might also pass the evenings enjoying some of the entertainment laid on for them, borrowing books from the 52 lending libraries serving the tube shelters, listening to programmes of gramophone music or taking night classes. Trains would draw in, bringing refreshments for sale and endless cups of tea.

On the platforms London Transport had painted white lines: the first eight feet from the edge, the second four feet from the edge. Until seven thirty at night shelterers had to keep behind the eight-foot line; after that they could move up to the four-foot line. At ten thirty the trains stopped for the night and the current was switched off, allowing shelterers to move forward to the edge of the platform, to the escalators or even on to the lines themselves to snatch a few hours' sleep. Now the lights would be dimmed on the platforms, although not in the corridors.

Before the war steps had been taken to safeguard the Underground system from flooding in the event of a direct hit to the Victoria Embankment or the under-river tunnels: the two Bakerloo Line tunnels running between Charing Cross and Waterloo, the two Northern Line tunnels between these same stations and between Bank and London Bridge, the two East London Line tunnels between Wapping and Rotherhithe; two disused tunnels between Monument and London Bridge; and one partly under the river at Charing Cross. A single bomb dropped in the proximity of the Charing Cross–Waterloo tunnel could have flooded half London's Underground system, from Shepherd's Bush to Liverpool Street, Hammersmith to King's Cross, Clapham Common to Euston, Elephant and Castle to Marylebone. Therefore, flood-gates and diaphragms to act as a second line of defence had been installed at every vulnerable point. Fortunately, the old Strand–Charing Cross loop tunnel, which had been out of use for years, had been sealed at either end. In 1940 it received a direct hit – the only one suffered by any of the Underground's Thames tunnels – and a section over 200 yards long was flooded by the river and would have swamped the Underground in all directions.

Large sums of money had also been spent on constructing various protective devices in the neighbourhood of important water mains and sewers. Hydrophones had been installed on the Thames river-bed so that the impact of a delayed-action bomb or mine falling near any of the under-river tunnels could be promptly detected. The sound was recorded in the control room at the South Kensington Regional Office's headquarters of the Chief Engineer. The flood-gates were manned round the clock, controlled collectively from a small room in the passage between the Piccadilly and Northern Lines at Leicester Square station. The time required to close them was 30 seconds. Miraculously, none of these vulnerable areas was to be pierced by flying bombs or rockets, since the latter came without warning and allowed no time to act.

These precautionary measures did not mean that the Underground was exempt from accidents, however. In January 1941 a high-explosive bomb had caused the road to collapse into the subway tunnel at Bank station, leaving a 1,800-foot crater. Blast shot down the escalator, which collapsed, killing many of the people on it. Others were blown off the platform into the path of an approaching train. Worst of all, at Bethnal Green station in 1943 people were filing into the tube shelter after an alert when there was a sudden deafening noise, possibly an ack-ack battery trying out a new kind of gun in nearby Victoria Park. Whether this made the crowd press forward too quickly or not, a woman carrying a baby tripped down the final steps. People tumbled down on top of her, leaving 173 dead, dead mainly from suffocation. The results of the Home Office inquiry into the disaster were published on 19 January 1945, when the cause of their deaths was given as loss of self-control. There were indignant protests against this verdict and a *Daily Mail* article revealed that the noted London architect Mr O. Howard Leicester, who had designed Arsenal football stadium, claimed that the entrance to the station contravened LCC public safety rules, since there were 20 steps without a landing when the maximum number of steps permitted was 14 per flight. The dead left 400 dependents seeking compensation and the damages amounted to £100,000.

Eighty tube stations, including disused stations at British Museum, South Kentish Town and City Road, and non-traffic tube tunnels at Aldwych, Bethnal Green and Liverpool Street were used as shelters. Southwark's 70-foot-deep shelter in the old City and South London railway tunnel was the largest with space for 10,000 people, although the disused tunnel to the east of Liverpool Street had similar capacity. Bethnal Green's tunnel was so capacious that 7,000 were habitually using it during the summer of 1944, and there was room to spare for a canteen, a sick bay with a visiting doctor and a trained nurse in attendance, a concert hall where at least 200 were entertained three times a week and a branch public library with 4,000 volumes. In addition there were the Southwark and West Ham tunnels with about 4,000 bunks between them. Two of the tube traffic stations which were interchange points – Piccadilly Circus and Leicester Square – were not being used for dormitory purposes, while the other interchange stations – Bank, Paddington, Euston, Leicester Square, Tottenham Court Road, King's Cross, Oxford Circus and Strand – had limited dormitory space.

In the early days of the war organised gangs had exploited the situation by bagging spaces on the tube platforms and selling them to the public at 2s 6d each, while many people clutching pathetic bundles had queued all day – or sent one of their children to queue for them – to be sure of a place that night. By 1944, however, a system had long been in operation whereby a standard reservation ticket corresponding to a specific bunk or platform position was issued by the local authority to each shelterer, assuring the holder of a place. In addition 10 per cent of the total accommodation at each station was kept free for casual shelterers. No charge was made to shelterers to enter the station. Notting Hill Gate had pioneered the idea of six people occupying six feet of platform length – allowing three to sleep in a three-tier bunk and three stretched out on the platform in front of it.

Frequent routine visits were made by local authority public health inspectors to tube shelters to eliminate rodents, bed bugs, fleas and mosquitoes. There had always been a danger that bugs would be introduced to the shelters on people's clothes and bedding. The Central Council for Health Education had issued abundant publicity material to educate the public about the dangers of infestation and local councils established stores where shelterers could keep their bedding during the day in a clean, disinfected environment. Laundries were opened at or in the vicinity of certain Underground stations so that bedding could be washed and aired the same day, ready for the evening. Any family with a recognised tuberculosis sufferer was forbidden to use a public shelter: private shelter arrangements were made for them. In the Underground and other public shelters, the medical officer in attendance was to keep an eye out for anyone showing signs of the still common disease of tuberculosis and isolate the case. Anyone breaking shelter rules would be summarily arrested by the police, who might also be called on by the paid shelter warden or voluntary marshal to eject those exhibiting drunken, disorderly or quarrelsome behaviour. Noisy children – such as the particularly rowdy and undisciplined offspring of Gibraltarian refugees who were living in hotels in the Kensington area and liked to colonise Notting Hill Gate station – were an irritation.

On 9 July 1944 the first of London's new deep bomb-proof shelters, 130 feet below ground, was opened at Stockwell Underground station: Clapham North, Camden Town, Clapham South and Belsize Park deep shelters opened over the following two weeks. These bunkers, capable of being closed off from the world for months at a time, had been constructed because the Government feared that the new V-weapons would be used as a delivery system for chemical or biological warfare. 'When the first V-1 attack was launched in June '44,' the Canadian Major Brock-Chisholm later revealed, 'and the first flying bomb went off with a big bang, showing that it only contained normal high explosives, the General Staffs all heaved an immense sigh of relief.' The new bunkers had been intended for Government personnel, not the public, but now that the fear of chemical and biological attack had receded the metropolitan boroughs – with the exception of Bethnal Green and Southwark, who already had plenty of capacity in their own deep tunnels – were each given an allocation of tickets to distribute. Civilians who habitually sheltered at the nearby Underground stations and a certain number of homeless women and children under local authority direction were admitted by ticket into four of the deep shelters.

Bunkers in the South Group lay beneath Clapham Road, under the existing Underground stations of Clapham South, Clapham Common, Clapham North, Stockwell and Oval. Those in the North Group lay under Camden Town, Belsize Park, Goodge Street, Chancery Lane and St Paul's. They were each about 1,400 feet in length and held 8,000 bunks. The main access shafts to the streets above were enclosed in steel-reinforced concrete pillboxes, to minimise risk of flooding from shattered pipes, as had happened at the Balham tube station disaster in October 1940, when many sheltering there had drowned in water and sewage. As for the bunkers to which there was no public access, the Railway Executive Committee had set up quarters in Down Street, between Hyde Park Corner and Green Park or Dover Street, as it was then called: from here they organised Britain's rail system, which as the main carrier could not afford to be interrupted by war.

The Government was using other deep shelters to house British and American troops in transit and on leave, as storage for historical and official documents and as armaments factory and telecommunications sites. Brompton Road station was being used by Anti-Aircraft Control and Earl's Court station for the manufacture of torpedo sights and other equipment. Goodge Street deep shelter, of all places, took on historic significance on 6 June 1944 when General Eisenhower made his famous broadcast from there announcing that the invasion of Europe was under way. There was also a warren of tunnels and deep citadels under government buildings in Whitehall for its personnel, and a new citadel had been constructed under Curzon Street House for the royal family, replacing the one beneath the North Terrace at Buckingham Palace.

By the end of August 1944 the V-1 onslaught was petering out, as the Allies overtook the launch sites in northern France. They would not cease altogether, however, because the Germans next reverted to launching them from Heinkels off the east coast and from Delft in Holland; by the end of the war they had almost succeeded in improving the technology to launch them from as far away as Germany. Altogether, 9,251 V-1s were unleashed, 5,890 crossed the coast, of which 2,563 reached the London Civil Defence Region, where, excluding those that blew up in the air or landed harmlessly on open ground, they caused 2,220 incidents. The death toll was 5,375, while 15,258 were seriously injured and retained in hospital and over 28,000 received minor injuries. In August Churchill told Parliament that 18,000 houses had been totally destroyed and 800,000 damaged by the V-1 – by no means the final tally – causing homelessness and housing problems on a vast scale. Indeed, across London as a whole there were 50,000 removals during this period. The extent of the damage was hushed up to maintain morale and confound the Germans, but anyone venturing out from central London to the southern suburbs, as James Lees-Milne did one day on a visit to Peckham, was shocked at the devastation. He reckoned that at least two-thirds of the housing in the area had been destroyed or damaged.

After a few quiet days in early September, Londoners had begun to relax. This was no time to be complacent, however. If the Government thought the danger of Hitler's second new weapon, the V-2 rocket, had passed now that the Allies were sweeping across France, it was in for a rude surprise. Bombing the experiment and production site at Peenemünde had not been enough; the rocket was being manufactured by slave labour at a secret location in the Harz Mountains. Unlike the V-1, the rocket could be fired from mobile launch pads, or indeed, from any flat surface such as a road. On 7 September, the very day Duncan Sandys was making his optimistic statement to the press, the SS descended on a quiet residential district of The Hague in occupied Holland, roused the residents and summarily evicted them from their homes. A convoy of trucks arrived next morning, bringing the first of the rockets, 45 feet long and 6 feet wide, which were set up and ready to fire by late afternoon. Concealed among the houses of the innocent-looking suburb, they pointed due west, in the direction of London.

* * *

Just before 6.45 on the evening of Friday, 8 September 1944 an enormous explosion with a sort of prolonged rumbling was heard all over London. In Staveley Road, Chiswick, one of those spacious suburban tree-lined streets of solid, red-brick detached and semi-detached houses, a crater about 40 feet wide by 10 feet deep suddenly appeared in the roadway outside Number 5, puncturing the utility services. Seven houses were demolished immediately and five others damaged beyond repair. There was major blast damage to nearly 600 other houses within a radius of 600 yards of the crater – a noticeably narrower area of damage than that usually associated with the V-1, but then the penetration of a weapon with a warhead of approximately the same weight and explosive power but travelling almost 10 times faster at 3,000 mph created a much deeper crater, one that contained more of the blast. Obviously the denser the housing the higher the damage and the casualties, but Staveley Road had only eight houses per acre. Many of the residents had not yet returned from work, so that casualties were relatively light: 3 dead, 10 seriously injured and 10 slightly injured.

The curious double bang of the explosion – because the rocket travelled faster than sound, the explosion on impact was followed a split second later by the sonic boom as the missile re-entered the earth's atmosphere – was clearly heard seven miles away at Westminster. Those in the know realised that what they had planned for and dreaded but then tentatively shelved had arrived. At his office at Shell-Mex House on the Embankment Duncan Sandys telephoned the Home Security War Room – secure in its bunker 30 feet under a strange round concrete rotunda near Millbank – to find out where the incident had taken place and then called for his car.

At the summit of a hierarchy of control rooms, the Home Security War Room would have been informed by the people at London Region's Headquarters – housed in and under the Geological Museum in Exhibition Road, South Kensington – who in turn would have got their information from Group Control. For the purpose of Civil Defence the country had been divided into 11 regions. The London Civil Defence Region – Region 5 – had such a massive circumference that it was subdivided into nine groups: Group 1, for instance, embraced the City of Westminster, the boroughs of Fulham, Hammersmith, and the then separate boroughs of Chelsea and Kensington. Group 2 swept from St Marylebone up to Hampstead and round via St Pancras to Islington and up to Stoke Newington. The City of London fell into Group 3, along with the eastern boroughs of Bethnal Green, Finsbury, Hackney, Holborn, Poplar, Shoreditch and Stepney.

Groups 1 to 5 incorporated the 28 metropolitan boroughs that came under the umbrella of the London County Council (LCC), as well as the City of London, while the rest embraced those in Greater London, the area roughly matching that of the Metropolitan Police District. For instance, Group 6 included all the local authorities in the Middlesex County Council and some in Hertfordshire County Council, Group 7 some in Essex County Council as well as East and West Ham, Group 8 some in Kent County Council and Group 9 some in Surrey County Council. Some of these groups in turn – 6 and 9 – had been subdivided, reflecting the size of their population.

Down in Staveley Road the local Air Raid Precautions (ARP) warden in his distinctive dark blue beret and battledress with the yellow badge would have arrived speedily to assess the situation: type of bomb, existence of fire, damage to housing, an estimate of the number and type of casualties, whether or not broken gas or water mains were presenting hazards. Either running or cycling to his post – each borough was divided into districts which were then subdivided into wardens' posts, each covering a number of sectors – he would have telephoned the full details through to the borough Control Centre – usually situated in a bomb-proof shelter under or near the Town Hall – who in turn would have passed on the information to Group Control and so on up the hierarchy. Each one would mark the site of the incident on their wall map, always up to date with the resources currently available to be deployed at any incident. The whole exercise took minutes.

Communication was the key. Connected to Group Control on one hand, on the other the borough Control Centre was linked by banks of telephones and messengers to the wardens' posts, fire and ambulance stations, rescue depots, first-aid posts and the cable and utility services. The latter – the Gas Light and Coke Company, the County of London Electric Supply Company and the Metropolitan Water Board – all had their own control centres, working closely with the local authorities' control centres. The Borough Surveyor had plans showing the exact location of pipes, wires and cables under every road, so that he was able to gauge the extent of subterranean damage not always apparent to the warden on the spot. This was especially useful in the V-2 period, because the depth of penetration caused considerable damage to the utilities: for this reason, wardens henceforth would be asked to report the size and position of craters. Once the call came through from the ARP warden at Staveley Road, the officer in charge at the borough Control Centre – supported by specialists such as the City Engineer, the Medical Officer of Health, the Director of Public Cleansing, the Chief Warden and the District Rescue Officer, or their representatives – would immediately have organised his response to the incident.

Within an hour of the Chiswick explosion VIPs were converging on the site. They included the Home Secretary and Minister of Home Security, Herbert Morrison – who had been Leader of the LCC and chairman of its General Purposes and Civil Defence Committee during the 'phoney' war – and his Parliamentary Secretary, Ellen Wilkinson. London Region was represented by the junior of its two Regional Commissioners, Admiral Sir Edward Evans, as ever resplendent in his naval uniform. There were people there from Group Control and the local Control Centre, as well as NFS and Civil Defence personnel already at work, all of them realising they were witness to a new and terrible phase in the Battle of London.

The Government's first instinct was to keep the arrival of the V-2 secret. If they were not mentioned in the news, the

Germans would be left wondering whether the rockets were landing at all, and not knowing where they were landing, they would have no chance to correct their aim. 'Actually the V-2 began nearly a fortnight ago,' William Hall, a part-time Civil Defence worker in Hackney noted in his diary a few days later, 'but the papers have not said a thing. In fact it is one colossal bluff; the Jerries must think their V-2s are getting lost in the stratosphere.' A rumour that the Chiswick explosion was caused by a flying gas main soon gained currency, although the absurdity of such an explanation quickly became an in-joke among Londoners. Even children began to see how ridiculous it was. The silence of the authorities, the fear of the unknown, perhaps made the new weapon seem all the more frightening and sinister. In her diary, Mrs Bell of Mortlake noted her first reaction:

One Friday evening the children were playing on the balcony. I was sitting on the settee. There was an unholy crash, I think I bounced three feet into the air. The kids came in looking like ghosts. 'Oh Mummy, what's that?' Looking out of the window we saw a pall of smoke, rising like a ghoulish old monk, even the cowl was well over the face. It had a weird air about it, it gave me an odd feeling. We were puzzled, we had heard no warning, no sirens, nothing. WHAT THE HELL WAS HITLER UP TO NOW?

Well-meaning members of the public were soon writing to the Home Office to describe strange phenomena in the sky:

At 7.20 am on Saturday morning, the 17th of September last [wrote a resident of Robin Hood Way, SW15], my wife, on pulling the bedroom curtains, called my attention to a most startling phenomenon in the sky to the east. Owing to the fact that this house is situated on the edge of Wimbledon Common, it has a clear view of the horizon to the east. There are no houses to obstruct the view in this direction. The phenomenon was due east and took the form of a long streak of brilliant light, running up from the horizon vertically. 'Frozen lightning' exactly describes it. It must have been several miles high. It was so bright it was difficult to look at.

Nevertheless, it was a long way away. I should put it from ten to twenty miles, due east of this house, although of course I have nothing to go on in estimating the distance of such a strange thing. The streak persisted in its straightness and brilliance for a minute or two. Then, very gradually, it began to turn into a spiral. The coils of spiral became bigger and fainter until the whole thing dissolved. A minute or two later came the noise of the distant explosion from that quarter.

Those who realised what was causing the latest series of explosions discussed it in hushed tones, complicit with the Government's policy of silence. But there was growing frustration at the lack of any official statement. The majority felt that such a statement was necessary to deter evacuees from returning to London, although a few appreciated that such an admission would only help the Germans. Ironically, the Government had announced the end of official evacuation on 7 September. Thinking it was safe to do so – and possibly seeing the relaxation of the blackout and the introduction of the dim-out in September as another optimistic sign – thousands who had left during the summer to escape the V-1s poured into the capital again. 'The silence of the authorities observing a hush-hush attitude gave them the impression it was safe to come home,' Stanley Rothwell complained. 'This was misleading to the people in the provinces; they were unaware of this new diabolical terror weapon which was beginning to rain upon us, so back my family came.'

Irene Byers, returning with her children from Somerset, was shocked by what she found: 'We catch a much earlier train than planned, arriving at Paddington Station at five o'clock to an ear-splitting explosion. My heart gave a sudden lurch and for a moment I stood stock still. It could not be, yet I had heard rumours of a deadly and more lethal weapon – the dreaded and scarcely believable V-2. It was. What a nerve-wracking welcome home.' Her husband was soon reproaching himself for allowing the family to return and before long the lodger – one of thousands of builders up from the provinces to repair damaged houses – had suffered a nervous breakdown and had to go home.

Not until 10 November – significantly, after the failure of the Arnhem campaign, which if successful would have released Holland from the German grip so much sooner – did Churchill admit in the House that London was under attack from the V-2 rocket. The admission meant that the pros and cons of the two V-weapons were soon being debated openly, as Mollie Panter-Downes, the *New Yorker*'s witty reporter in London, records:

Since the Government's admission that the rockets had landed in this country made it unnecessary to go on talking about them in whispers, the question whether they are harder on the nerves than the robots has been much discussed and usually answered in the affirmative. People dislike the newcomers' nasty and unpredictable habit of plunking out of the blue with a truly appalling explosion which leaves the air thrumming and twanging like a plucked guitar string. Still, as someone remarked the other day, they arrive so abruptly you don't have time to get scared – you're either dead or simply startled.

George Orwell was exasperated by the debate, as he revealed in *Tribune*:

People are complaining of the sudden unexpected wallop with which these things go off. 'It wouldn't be so bad if you got a bit of warning,' is the usual formula. There is even a tendency to talk nostalgically of the days of the V-1. 'The good old doodlebug did at least give you time to get under the table,' etc. Whereas, in fact, when the doodlebugs were actually dropping, the usual subject of complaint was the uncomfortable waiting period before they went off. Some people are never satisfied.

The new space-age missile left the British defence system of fighter aircraft, anti-aircraft guns and barrage balloons completely redundant. The lack of any signs of defence gave the rockets an air of invincibility – 'cosmic terrors', as one Londoner described them. All the RAF could do was bomb the railway lines bringing the missiles to The Hague: an attempt to bomb the suburb where they were being launched from proved disastrous. The rocket took all of four minutes to reach its target in London. As it shot up four or five miles into the stratosphere and was visible for perhaps only four seconds in its final 20,000 feet of descent, no defence was possible, nor any sort of warning.

Gwladys Cox was quick to realise this: 'The rockets, if less frequent, are a worse affliction than the flying bombs, as their entirely silent approach cannot be heralded by sirens and clear weather does not deter them. Travelling faster than sound, they are well-nigh impossible to stop.'

Whereas the V-1 could be seen and heard, so that measures could be taken to dodge them, the V-2 arrived like 'a bolt from the blue, completely unheralded'.

'We don't stand a chance against these bloody things,' moaned Mrs Bell, 'they'll blow us all to hell.'

Mass-Observation – an independent sociological organisa-tion set up by the anthropologist Tom Harrisson and others in 1937 to study British society by canvassing public opinion on the streets, as opposed to what the press and politicians assumed to be the public's opinion – noted that the fact that the V-2 was completely indiscriminate and that you could do virtually nothing to protect yourself provoked a fatalistic attitude. 'What I says is if your name's on it you'll get it,' was the typical Cockney response. 'No good worrying 'cos you can't do nothing about it.' Some were still mercifully obliv-ious, or understandably confused, as one old lady revealed when she told Mass-Observation, 'The rockets, dearie? I can't say I've ever noticed them.'

George Britton was philosophical. 'It is no good worrying about them,' he told his daughter. 'If you *hear* the bang, you are out of danger.' Nevertheless, he and his wife had taken to sleeping outside in the Anderson shelter again and she at least would not be lured from it until the official announcement that the war was over. Like the Morrison tables indoors – which had the advantage of offering shelter within seconds –

the Andersons stood up well, except in the case of a direct hit, and protected the occupants from flying glass and debris. The main problem with the Anderson was that it was often water-logged and there was not sufficient room for more than two to lie down. Shelterers would emerge in the morning cold and stiff from a long uncomfortable night. Reg Neal in Hoxton loathed the whole idea of Andersons: 'It was like putting you in your coffin before you was dead.' Street shelters, the low concrete blocks which offered accommodation to passers-by or those who lacked private shelters, were vulnerable to blast, which stripped the bunks off the walls. Many London houses and blocks of flats had had their cellars converted into shelters.

A Walthamstow woman called the V-2s 'bombs with slippers on', because of the silence of their approach. A confidential Government report, 'Lessons from Recent Raids – Long Range Rockets', confirmed that the first sound was that of the explosion, 'though some have reported a short "swish" before the explosion'. There had been several reports of a 'feeling of pressure or a premonitory instinct of impending disaster immediately before the explosion, but it is possible this may be due to confusion of time in the memory afterwards'. Some people do seem to have been blessed with extraordinarily sharp hearing or a sixth sense and animals certainly were, for they always leapt for cover moments before an explosion. The explosion was followed by 'a drawn-out rumbling sound, caused by the passage of the missile through the air faster than sound'. For this reason, the explosion had been described as 'more echoing and more prolonged than a flying-bomb – like a peculiar peal of thunder'.

The document noted that 'sound seems to be no indication of either the distance or the direction of the explosion. Explosions have been heard distinctly twenty or thirty miles away. At ten miles they have been loud enough to give the impression the incident is very close, yet to people within half a mile of the incident it has sounded too far away to be of their immediate concern.' The people of Croydon had the unnerving experience of being aware of an instantaneous lightning-like flash of white light as a V-2 passed over the town, although it was too high and too swift to be seen, then the sound of the explosion as if it were there. In fact the explosion was usually many miles away but the sound was thrown from hill to hill, giving an enveloping and stunning effect. To the north and perched on its high ground with the whole vista of London before it, Hampstead had a similar experience.

The suspected target for the V-2 was Waterloo Bridge and its environs, but as the rocket was still at an early stage of development, targeting was poor and most were falling short – this time, as they were being launched from Holland over Essex, on to the 11 boroughs of Group 7 on the eastern side of the region, which were to receive 199 V-2s in all. Ilford with 35 was to be worst hit, although West Ham's 27 rockets were to cause more fatalities. Barking was to have 21, Dagenham 19 and Walthamstow 18. The inner eastern boroughs such as Stepney, Bethnal Green, Hackney, Finsbury and Islington would have some of the highest number of incidents with fatalities commensurate with the density of their housing and population.

Anyone venturing over the river from Westminster and Chelsea could be forgiven for thinking he had entered another world – the real battle zone – for this was the area that had already suffered so badly from the V-1s. The boroughs of Battersea, Camberwell, Lambeth, Southwark and Wandsworth were to receive 23 rockets, but the density and poor quality of the housing in these working-class districts accounted for the above average number of deaths – 245 – and nearly 500 seriously injured. The south-eastern suburbs sweeping in an arc from Croydon up to the Thames were to receive 76 rockets. Bermondsey, Deptford, Greenwich, Lewisham and Woolwich would suffer badly, the first of these boroughs being just a couple of miles east along the river from the target.

Most boroughs were to receive a steady drizzle of V-2s, with casualties and damage of note only to those in the immediate locality. However, it was an 'outstanding incident' in the borough of Deptford – the 251st V-2 to arrive – that was to be the worst of the entire offensive. It would leave no doubt as to the full, horrific reality of Hitler's second new weapon.

It was Saturday, 25 November 1944, and Woolworth's in New Cross Road, Deptford was full of housewives doing some early Christmas shopping and children buying their sweets ration. The rumour that a rare consignment of saucepans had come in (how women must have regretted yielding up so much of their aluminium kitchenware in the salvage drive of 1940) had drawn many extra shoppers on this cold day. The blow fell at lunchtime. Everyone from four-week-old babies to adults in their seventies was hurled in the air along with the debris. On the road outside, part of the main A2 to Dover, the bodies of passers-by were flung great distances like bundles of rags. A bus that had been passing stood still in the road, its passengers staring ahead, killed by the force of the blast. In shock, a woman pushing a pram, her clothes torn and askew, continued towards the store, intent on buying that saucepan, until a kindly Civil Defence worker told her to go home. A baby's arm still in its woolly sleeve lay in the enveloping dust. It took 3 days and nights for 21 rescue squads and others to extract the dead and injured from under the debris. A constant procession of mortuary vans could not keep pace with the stream of bodies and fragments of bodies recovered. The final toll was 168 dead, 123 seriously injured and countless others with lesser injuries. Some were completely obliterated, one man's presence being confirmed only by his wedding ring.

By some strange fluke, the more prosperous boroughs received the lowest number of V-2s. The City of London itself would have none, although its immediate working-class neighbours in Group 3 were to suffer so badly. There were to be only five incidents in Group 1, which incorporated the City of Westminster and the wealthy 'Royal Borough of Kensington', as well as the more westerly Chelsea, Hammersmith and Fulham – although the more proletarian Fulham proved the exception by having none at all.

The West End was by no means exempt, however, and an

incident there always received full public attention. At eleven o'clock on the night of 6 December a rocket fell on the Red Lion public house in Duke Street, off Oxford Street at the side of Selfridges, causing widespread damage. A taxi carrying three American sailors and a woman was blown by the blast into a large display window of the store. It took some time to locate the woman's torso. The body of a woman who had been holding her husband's arm as they walked nearby was later discovered at the other side of the building. A canteen used by US Government employees was located in an annexe of Selfridges, accounting for 8 American dead and 32 injured; 10 British civilians also died and 7 were injured.

Next morning, as the shop girls with their brushes and pans swept the glass off the pavements and cleaned up the debris in their departments, Oxford Street was as crowded as ever, as frantic shoppers hunted down something, anything from the uninspiring range of goods on display for Christmas gifts. Walking through streets strewn with glass, the wife of Harley Street consultant and broadcaster Anthony Weymouth went to help the WVS manning the Incident Inquiry Point, an essential fixture at the site of any bomb disaster. The WVS offered housewives like Audrey Weymouth the opportunity to do some war work on a voluntary basis, often working part-time so as to be able to combine it with their other commitments.

The WVS always worked in close co-operation with the local authority. They manned Incident Inquiry Points under the direction of the Incident Officer, who was in charge of the whole rescue operation. Here the WVS, in their uniform of green tweed suits with red piping and matching hats, would check the census cards against the names of casualties recovered and they would answer queries from anxious relatives: confirming whether someone had been sent to hospital or escaped unhurt, or taking the relatives aside to break the news of a death. They would take charge of valuables, which were to be handed in to the care of the local authority, until their owners claimed them. They might even look after pets, which would be handed over to Nargac – the organisation that looked after animal victims of raids, tending their injuries, tracing their owners or finding them new homes.

At Duke Street a nearby school had been commandeered for the purpose, the children's hand-made Christmas decorations hanging forlornly on the walls; one room was utilised by the WVS and another converted into a mortuary. 'Audrey told me afterwards that one of the most pathetic instances concerned a woman's shopping-bag which was found and brought in. The owner had evidently been shopping, for it contained odds and ends obviously intended for Christmas presents,' Weymouth confided in his diary. 'There were also three little Union Jacks bought, I suppose, in readiness for the peace.'

There was to be no let-up for Christmas. In the week of 20–27 December there were six V-2 incidents in London Region. On Christmas Eve in Wanstead 18 houses were demolished and 177 seriously damaged, leaving 7 dead and 7 seriously injured and a great many homeless or living in discomfort in what should have been the most peaceful night of any year. On Boxing Day Islington residents were enjoying a pint at their local, the Prince of Wales, on the corner of Mackenzie Road and Holloway Road, when disaster struck.

At 9.26 that evening a rocket burst in the eight-inch concrete roadway outside, leaving two large craters in the stiff clay: the deepest craters were always those where the surface was hardest, like this one. This was just the sort of housing that was most vulnerable to the V-weapons' one ton of explosive power. As the Incident Report states: 'Blast caused demolition of about 20 mainly 3-storey houses and shop premises, including the Prince of Wales pub, of poor construction with 9" walls, wood floors and slated roofs, erected 80 to 90 years ago, damage beyond repair to about 20 other houses and shops, and damage to properties calling for first-aid repairs within a radius of about 200 yards from the crater [comparatively narrow as the craters were so deep]. Gas and water mains were broken.'

It was a cold, frosty night with heavy fog: visibility was

down to six feet and London buses were crawling in convoy, guided by conductors carrying hurricane lamps and torches. Visibility was bad enough anyway after a V-2 incident, when the air would be thick with smoke and dust and the acrid smell left in its wake. Artificial lighting in the form of Army (AA) mobile searchlights – part of Ack-Ack Command – was brought in. The use of lighting to aid rescue workers in the hours of darkness had been possible since the relaxation of the blackout. The blackout was still compulsory in the event of an alert – in fact, most people had not bothered to take their blackout down and street lighting, if it existed at all, was so low that the dim-out offered very little improvement on the former blackness – but alerts had become rare. In conventional aerial attack lighting a rescue operation would have acted as a guide to succeeding bombers, but now that bombing was almost totally robotic it made no difference whether the lights were on or not. This was a bonus, as the V-2, coming without warning or allowing time to take shelter, caused comparatively large numbers of trapped casualties, requiring many hours of patient work on the part of the rescue workers.

Each heavy and light rescue squad had a lorry containing cutting and lifting tackle and baulks of heavy timber for shoring up buildings. The men tended to come from the building or engineering industries, because they had to have the knowledge and experience to be able to foresee how brickwork, floors, steel-framed structures and reinforced concrete might behave when subjected to the eccentric strains and stresses that followed bomb damage. Combing through the debris in search of casualties was a delicate art, as J.H. Forshaw, the deputy to the LCC's chief architect, describes in his unpublished history of his department in wartime:

He knows that the steel joist above him would hold the collapsed roof of timber and the weight of the tiles piled upon it, but he also knew that the fractured pier upon which the joist itself was resting might at any moment give way, crushing him and the casualty he was trying to reach. He knew how to cut through the cast-iron of the bath which lay across the route he was tunnelling and how to use the mahogany frame of a wrecked piano to shore up the walls and roof of his cave-like working space so that he could bring the casualty safely away. He learned to sense the value of every brick and piece of wood that lined the dark dust-filled channel. In the hours of patient working, handing out piece by piece and handful by handful the crumbled plaster and rubbish, he did not stop to think of the many places which needed only a touch to set the whole mass moving, but he knew them as he knew his own hand. He did not let bombs, flaming debris, rising water or escaping gas deter him whilst he was physically able to carry on. Not until he had guided, carried or dragged his casualty inch by inch to safety did he open his mind to the risks he had himself undergone, and then it was only to dismiss them as a joke.

Twenty thousand Londoners, he concluded, owed their lives to this dogged, persistent work in the worst conditions imaginable. The rescue workers were also responsible for many personal acts of kindness, often risking their lives to burrow into the debris to recover some object which would mean so much to the person who had just lost her home. The Reverend George Markham, working many hours a week as an unpaid Civil Defence worker on top of his parish duties at St Peter's Walworth, recalls one such occasion: 'We cut a hole through a pile carpet, so that one of my wardens could squeeze under the old lady's bed below, and find the tin box which contained her few treasures. It was hot, dusty work, after a long noisy night, but I always felt that these little salvage efforts were worthwhile. It is hard to realise that it was these small things that made such a difference to the morale of so many people.'

Inevitably, there were times when the rescue men discovered that it was their own family buried in the ruins: one such fireman in Bermondsey was led away sobbing by the parish priest. But they had their rewards as well, not least in being witness to the stoicism and good humour of many of those they saved. Typical was the old woman in the East End brought out from under the debris of her ruined house, where for many hours she had been protected by the solidity of the dining table. Spotting her son among the rescue workers she yelled triumphantly, 'I told you that was a good table!'

The use of trained dogs to locate the dead and injured – preferably two working simultaneously so that they could scent a casualty from different directions – was a relatively recent novelty and seen here at the Mackenzie Road incident.

The licensee, his wife and the barmaid were on the ground floor and escaped with minor injuries, but the cellar was full of people drinking and smoking and proved a death trap. A fire started immediately and although as ever the grey-helmeted NFS had been quickly on the scene – from their lookout posts they were often first to pinpoint the location of an explosion and from training and practice were used to exiting their stations and arriving at an incident at maximum speed – many of the dead were charred beyond recognition; others suffered from fractures of the skull and limbs from falling beams. When casualties were lying injured in the debris, almost smothered in the all-pervading dust that filled their noses and mouths, rescue workers would try to thread in a rubber tube of drinking water or soda-bicarbonate to ease their discomfort.

It was the task of the duty doctor at the borough Control Centre, working on the information supplied by the ARP warden, to allocate and plan the medical response. Mobile first aid units – otherwise known as the Heavy Mobile Unit (HMU) – operating in parties of four with a driver would be sent out to help the rescue workers and organise the despatch of casualties by ambulance either to hospital or to a nearby fixed first-aid post. The incident doctor provided on-the-spot diagnosis and treatment. Doctors and nurses might have to crawl through tunnels of debris after the rescue men to help the injured or amputate on the spot in the dust and grime, sometimes even with water rising or leaking gas from fractured mains threatening their own lives while they worked.

Unlike the female ARP wardens and those in the Auxiliary Ambulance service, who wore trousers, the unfortunate nurses had to do all this still wearing their uniform dress. Too bad then if they found themselves – as doctors and nurses some-times did – being lowered head first into a void in the debris to administer aid to a trapped casualty: at Mackenzie Road a doctor managed to squeeze into the cellar to give a morphine injection, diminishing the pain of a woman who was later brought out dead. The decision as to whether a casualty was dead or alive rested entirely with the medical personnel, never with the rescue workers. Certification of a death would be given by the duty doctor at the incident, or later by the doctor in attendance at the mortuary.

By the time the Regional Commissioner Admiral Sir Edward Evans visited the borough of Islington on 1 January 1945 the casualty figures of the Mackenzie Road incident were given as 71 dead, 56 seriously injured and 202 slightly injured. But Islington was not to see in the New Year without another tragedy. At 11.40 on the evening of 31 December a rocket exploded at the northern end of the borough, at the corner of Hanley Road and Regina Road in Holloway.

This was the one that distinguished itself by being heard by everyone tuned in to the St Paul's Watch Night Service. Late-night revellers remembered it for obvious reasons. In Mayfair Mrs Robert Henrey was admiring the beauty of London by moonlight; she was thinking it would never be seen in such a flattering light once the lights were turned on again, revealing its wartime drabness. She heard the explosion and noticed that it was followed by the frantic barking of dogs in the neigh-bourhood. James Lees-Milne was on his way home to Chelsea with a friend. They were at Hyde Park when the crash came, followed by the roar of the rocket. Like the congregation in St Paul's, Lees-Milne and his friend laughed – a release of tension, another score for survival. It must have been midnight by the time they reached Sloane Square, where a crowd was singing and sounds of merriment poured from lighted windows. The merriment sounded false, he noted, and there were no church bells.

Up in Holloway the rocket penetrated dwelling houses and formed a large crater, while blast caused the demolition of

12 houses of the same poor calibre as those in the previous incident. Twenty-five houses were demolished and damage requiring first-aid repairs was inflicted on properties within a radius of 300 yards of the crater. By 2 January it was confirmed that there were 13 dead, 29 seriously injured and another 102 slightly injured. Seven were still missing. A Sound Locating Unit as well as dogs had to be employed in the search, since the Incident Officer directing the operation – often now from a mobile van – had been able to give very little clue as to the number and position of likely casualties.

It was the duty of the ARP warden – originally there was one for approximately every 1,000 people – to keep a census of residents in his area, so that the Incident Officer would be able to tell the rescuc workers the number and probable location of people in any building. It was up to householders as well as wardens to ensure that the register was kept up to date. The author of the Government report 'Lessons from Recent Raids – Long Range Rockets' deplored the fact that this practice had grown slack. Many who had left London in the great exodus of the summer of 1944 had failed to inform their warden of their return. In November 1944 the Government had started to cut down the Civil Defence force – 'almost as if it had never heard of the V-2' – by just over 10,000, leaving a total force of 24,000 paid Civil Defence workers, with the result that a number of wardens' posts had closed. People simply would not go to the trouble to walk to a more distant post to give information as to their movements. Wardens might even have to resort to checking with local traders, since they would be aware of the return or any prolonged absence of customers through the ration book system.

It was much more difficult to know how many casualties to look for in a street incident, where there were lots of random passers-by. Civil Defence workers and police would have to pay special attention to snatches of conversation by people who had witnessed the occurrence and might be able to indicate the presence and location of casualties. Sometimes relatives could give vital clues as to the movements of their loved ones. At an incident in Shoreditch a girl's insistence that her parents would have reached a certain point on their return from Petticoat Lane Market one Sunday morning led to them being found alive under a collapsed building after rescue workers had decided there were no further casualties. In a residential neighbourhood friends and relatives would be admitted to the incident site if they could indicate the probable whereabouts of casualties. A young girl insisted that her grandfather was in the lavatory at the back of the house at the time of the explosion: he was brought out unscathed but bemused. 'I pulled the chain and the whole house fell down,' he told his rescuers.

On the morning of 3 January Tom Pocock, a young journalist, left his lodgings in Oakley Street, Chelsea, glancing nervously at the sky, as was now an ingrained habit. The previous week 12 V-2s had landed in London, and this week there were to be both V-1s and V-2s, with an average of 9 V-2s every 24 hours. He walked to the bus stop and caught a number 11 to Fleet Street. Two minutes later at 8.50, as the bus swung from Pimlico Road into Buckingham Palace Road and Pocock was peering through the diamond-shaped mesh designed to protect passengers from the splintering of glass, an explosion split the air. 'On the pavement,' he noticed, 'people ducked, pitched forward and ran (the image was of wind-blown leaves) and the bus slewed to a stop.' Behind him, the Royal Hospital, Chelsea, built by Wren and home to the red-coated old soldiers, the Chelsea Pensioners, had been hit. The north-east wing and the medical officer's house had sustained damage, killing him, his daughter and a friend. Two pensioners standing just inside the chapel were killed and 20 seriously injured. By a stroke of fate, one of the pensioners who died had been standing roughly in the same spot and survived when the Hospital had been hit at the end of the First World War. Many of the old soldiers insisted on helping the rescue workers.

Typically, there was widespread damage to buildings in the

vicinity. James Lees-Milne, working for the National Trust as an expert on historic houses, knew what damage to expect since his own house near the river had been badly affected a few weeks previously when a V-1 had landed only 100 yards away. A few days later he visited a friend:

I walked down to St Leonard's Terrace and asked after L. He was in bed, but he and his servants were unhurt. All his windows on both sides of the house were smashed, doors wrenched off, both outer and inner. And partitions and ceilings down. Much of his furniture was destroyed. Yesterday rockets fell like autumn leaves and between dinner and midnight there were six near our house. Miss P. and I were terrified. I put every china ornament away in cupboards.

Later, Tom Pocock castigated himself for staying on the bus when it resumed its journey, instead of running back to see what had been hit and offering his help in the rescue work. As he rightly surmised, he would only have been in the way. One of the disadvantages of there being no alerts during the V-2 offensive, as opposed to earlier conventional air attack when civilians would be in the shelters, was that there were far too many would-be helpers and onlookers at daytime incidents. Some of them even endangered the rescue operation by climbing on to the debris – 'live debris' as the experts called it. It had always been the job of the Metropolitan Police to throw a cordon round an incident and redirect traffic, but with the standing down of the Home Guard at the end of 1944 a valuable source of help in crowd control at incidents had also been removed and now it fell to the police alone.

By this stage in the war, Tom's 'blasé and pragmatic' attitude was not unique. As John Lehmann admitted: 'One grew hard about other people's misfortunes; one had to. One did not try to picture the scene . . . One registered a moment's relief at not having been present, shut it out of one's mind, and carried on. Life went on, in a way that would have seemed incredible if one had imagined the situation before the war.'

Nowhere was this phlegmatic response to the bombing more apparent than in the cinema. The cinema provided the people's great escape from the horrors outside, let them relax and forget their own troubles for a short time. So determined was the audience to maintain its weekly or bi-weekly visit to the Granada, Walthamstow, that when its roof was lost and covered in tarpaulin in freezing weather they brought their blankets and hot water bottles. During a period of 3 days and 2 nights when 31 rockets fell in the vicinity of the Empire, Edmonton, the sound of a revolver on screen followed by the question from one of the actors, 'What was that?' prompted the response, 'Only a bloody rocket!' from a voice in the stalls. When a V-2 fell near the Granada in Tooting, interrupting the lunchtime show and shaking the building, the exit doors were blown in and the windows shattered. Two to three hundred people made a concerted rush for the open exits, but seeing the smoke outside and realising the danger was over, they all trooped back in to see the rest of the show.

This attitude was evident at an 'outstanding incident' in Hackney, one of 10 V-2s to hit the borough. Even though the force of the explosion rocked the building and dust fogged the screen, the audience of a crowded cinema elected to stay on to finish the film, ignoring the carnage nearby. In Woodland Street, school was out for the day. Some of the children were just leaving the building when they were caught by the blast; others were trapped under toppling masonry. The keener ones had just reached the Forest Road Public Library, to change their books and select new ones. 'Some, especially the clever ones, call at the library every day,' the head teacher proudly told a reporter, while waiting anxiously to find out how many of her pupils were among the dead and injured. Two of them, 13-year-old Janet Bircham and 11-year-old Louis Crane, were already leaving the library with their books when they were killed instantly. Reg Neal, who as a 14-year-old school leaver had joined Hackney Civil Defence as a messenger, recalled that blast had pulled down the front of neighbouring houses, leaving families who had been having their tea at the moment of the explosion still sitting there – covered in white mortar dust and 'dead as doornails'.

William Hall, working part-time for Hackney Civil Defence, was soon on the scene of the disaster:

Arrived home from office at approx 17.20 hours found more windows smashed, evidence that a V-2 had dropped near. Had a spot of tea and went off to the incident. Arrived and found that the bomb had dropped on side of library. There were quite a few children inside, the main reserve operations were in the library. But there was digging going on at various nearby houses . . . There were a good few 200 watt floods placed at various points. We also had two cranes . . . The IIP [the Incident Inquiry Point] was a main job for a good while. At approximately 23.15 hours the IIP closed. We reported to the IO [Incident Officer]. By now, most of the houses had been cleared, and we were working on the library. There were some more people still in there. At 00.25 two bodies were recovered one of a youth and the other of an old man. Apparently they were in the reading room.

It was a very cold night and starting to snow. Standing for hours while the rescue teams patiently worked their way through the debris, distraught mothers ran forward in fear every time a body was recovered. After waiting all night, the father of five-year-old Barry Hughes was still standing there next day, hoping for news of his only child. 'I know he was in the library,' he said, 'because his grandmother who went with him said so before she died.'

That same day a block of flats in Lambeth was hit leaving 41 dead and 26 seriously injured, but the Hackney incident with 15 dead and 102 seriously injured seemed especially poignant since 10 children had died. 'It was *sick*!' recalls Reg Neal. It was by no means the only school incident, however. On 6 March the children of Nutwell School in Battersea were having their lunch when a V-2 crashed into a previously blitzed site, demolishing flats and some of the newly erected prefabs in Nutwell Street and Selincourt Road. Children lying about badly cut and bleeding presented a pitiful sight. A week later at Tottenham Grammar School two 14-year-old boys who had finished lunch early and gone out to the playing field were killed when a V-2 landed on waste ground nearby: 10 minutes later, half the boys still at lunch would have been on the playground and lost their lives.

The week after the Hackney incident there were 9 serious V-2 and 2 V-1 attacks, one causing 10 fatalities in Southwark. At six on the morning of 13 January a V-2 demolished another 12 houses in Islington, leaving 29 dead and 36 seriously injured. A week later a V-2 at Woodville Road, South Woodford, gave the eastern borough of Wanstead and Woodford one of the highest numbers of casualties in a single incident for the whole war. The borough history gives a perfect description of the incident, its characteristics shared by hundreds of others. It started off with a pretty typical wartime evening: 'The day, Saturday, 20 January 1945, was cold and bleak. Snow lay on the ground, iron hard from a spell of severe frost. Evening brought a biting rawness in the air which kept people by the fireside and suggested early retirement to bed. Many, however, sat up to listen to a play on the wireless. This, they are persuaded, saved many lives.'

Then the rocket struck.

In the immediate neighbourhood the people heard nothing – for that was the way of the rocket – but saw their homes begin to disintegrate before their eyes. Further away, a violent explosion was both heard and felt. Wardens at Post 28 in Chigwell Road had no doubt that the rocket had fallen in their area. Within a few seconds a report had been sent in. Two wardens went to investigate, a third stood by to man the telephone. Post 27 (Elmhurst Gardens), Post 29 (Daisy Road) acted with similar speed. Thus, within a few moments of the fall, the incident was being investigated from three directions. All three Post areas were, in fact, involved.

The wardens found the all too familiar scene – heaped wreckage, people, some in night attire, standing bewildered in the street; casualties, bleeding from flying glass wounds, calling for aid. Some men and women were already philosophically clearing up the mess of fallen ceilings and broken glass.

The NFS was quickly on the scene, finding some houses on fire (unlike high-explosive and incendiary bombs, the V-2 did not cause fire, but obviously if domestic fires were alight the force of the blast would cause the flames to be thrown out of the grate). The Incident Officer, distinguished from the rest of the Civil Defence workers by his light blue helmet, took up his post outside Cowslip Road School gates. A blue light indicated the spot from where the entire rescue operation was being managed. Wardens and the police directed service vehicles to park in such a way that no one was blocked in, especially the ambulances which needed to execute a quick turn-around. An Incident Inquiry Point with its blue flag was set up in a house thrown open for the purpose and members of the WVS took up their places, ready to give anxious relatives news of casualties. Census cards and the information provided by neighbours enabled the rescue party leaders to estimate the number of people trapped and their probable position in the demolished and damaged buildings. There had to be silence while the rescue workers tapped and listened, waiting for any response from under the debris that would enable them to locate and uncover a casualty as quickly as the fallen structure allowed.

A mobile first-aid unit dealt with 47 minor casualties, consisting mainly of cuts by glass. Forty-three others were seriously injured and sent to hospital. 'Stretcher bearers [from the Light Rescue squad] move cautiously, with a minimum of jarring, they bear a casualty to an ambulance. The extreme cold makes necessary increased precautions to ensure the injured, always affected by shock, are kept warm.' An urgent call for extra blankets may have been answered locally by neighbours – if, after five years of war they had any to spare – or more probably by the WVS, the recipient of so much bedding and clothing from generous charities in the United States and Canada. Vans ferried the 18 dead to the mortuary.

The last body, of a small girl crushed by a falling chimney stack, was recovered on the Monday afternoon. An incident would not be closed until the Incident Officer was satisfied that all casualties were recovered and everyone accounted for: if necessary, he might have to open an incident again, if someone was subsequently reported missing. As the operation was wound up, wardens and NFS personnel made a systematic house-to-house search for minor casualties or cases of shock. 'Every house visited was labelled on the outside CDS – to prevent duplication of effort.'

Two days later, on 23 January, Hither Green cemetery was hit by a V-2, strewing human remains about the gardens and roadway of Verdant Lane, presenting Civil Defence workers with a difficult and unpleasant task. It was not the first time a cemetery had been hit. The next day a V-2 landed in the centre of Greenwich. The Town Hall was badly shaken and the Mayor, who was just entering the public hall, was lifted off his feet 'as if some giant, invisible hand had taken me up by the back of the neck' – whereupon he was deposited without ceremony on the dance floor, suffering only from injury to his civic dignity.

In February the V-2 offensive reached a new intensity with 31 incidents a week in London Region – just at the time when the part-time Fire Service was being disbanded. From Walthamstow George Britton complained to his daughter in California: 'Our life here is a constant strain. All during the day and night we are hearing loud bangs. One minute there is a street of houses. The next, without any warning, two, or three, or four or more are not here. Just a big hole in the ground surrounded by half an acre of devastation. Glass windows *sucked* out of the house by the explosion.'

In the borough of St Pancras the Central London Eye Hospital and the Royal Free Medical School were hit, leaving 31 dead and 54 seriously injured. On St Valentine's Day a V-2 killed 29 in Hammersmith and left 41 seriously injured. On the 20th the photographic works at Ilford were hit. The following week the Royal Victoria, the Royal Albert and the

King George V docks were hit again and extensive damage inflicted on warehouses in Silvertown: it was the seventh time the area was hit by a rocket and the fifth this year.

In the first week of March there were 36 incidents. Woolwich, site of the Royal Arsenal, had seven, the largest number in any borough in any one week. On the very day a mother and her three young children had moved there, they were all killed. To add to the misery, the V-1s resumed for the first time since mid January, being launched either from piloted aircraft or from launch sites in Holland; the most serious of seven incidents was at Wood Green in north London, when seven people were killed and seven seriously injured. Recalling Duncan Sandys' words from the previous September, Mrs Uttin of Wembley was thoroughly exasperated: 'He talks through his hat!'

In West Hampstead, Gwladys Cox, who like many British civilians had obviously been listening to German propaganda on the wireless, was equally harassed: 'Goebbels kept his word. During the past week the bombing has got much worse again, not only rockets and flying-bombs, but piloted raiders as well. We have had several alerts, both day and night, and heard many explosions . . . although we realise it is Hitler's last fling, it is nevertheless very unpleasant, for we are all utterly weary, and feel we do not deserve this flare-up, even if it is the finale.'

The Western Allies crossed the Rhine on 5 March, but Holland was not yet taken and the Germans were to make the most of their last month there to fire a frenzy of V-2 rockets against their favourite target. Living in King's Cross, Anthony Heap complained: 'Several V-2s over during the night after a short weekend lull. I suppose that one of these days our armies will make some attempt to advance northwards into the Netherlands as well as eastwards into Germany. Then we might get some peace from the damned things.'

On 7 March they killed 52 people in their beds when in the early hours of the morning a V-2 fell in the courtyard of blocks of flats known as Folkestone Gardens in Trundleys

Road, in the borough of Deptford. Two of the blocks were destroyed, together with a row of terraced houses in Trundleys Road. In the dawn light a huge pile of debris could be seen, with 3 cranes aiding the work of 20 rescue squads and firemen as they struggled to release the dead and injured.

We heard a child whimpering underneath a collapsed house, [one of the rescue workers recalled]. The supervisor gave orders that no one was to pull out any long timbers, no one was to get on top of the debris, and digging was only to be done with bare hands . . . The baby kept quiet for a while, and supervisor said, 'Cry, you little bugger, so we can find you'. A voice said, 'Mind my face.' It was the child's father, completely wedged, couldn't move at all. The supervisor told us to edge through and scrape a passage, 'And be bloody quick about it', seeing as both casualties were right under the collapsed home . . . He wormed his way to the baby's cot, working in an awkward position, with an obstruction pressing on his abdomen, while also trying to direct the rescue of the father. He reached out to get the baby, which was quiet but moving, when he was suddenly overcome by nausea. He edged aside to allow another to take the baby.

Twelve were rescued that night by that particular rescue squad, but residents of more than 20 flats, including whole families, died. Sixty-four were seriously injured and 70 sustained lesser injuries.

Shortly after eleven o'clock next morning, a V-2 struck Smithfield Market at the junction of Farringdon Road and Charterhouse Street, in the borough of Finsbury but right on the border with the City. By unlucky chance, word had spread that a consignment of rabbits would be in, so that the market was unusually crowded with queues of housewives and children. Along the Farringdon Road a man conveying over £1 million in banknotes from the Bank of England to his own bank escaped when his van burst into flames.

A quarter of a mile away two men working on the roof of the Deanery of St Paul's were almost blown off by the blast. Inside the cathedral, a member of the Watch was thrown against the table of the high altar and feared for a moment that the inner dome was splitting, so violently did the whole structure quake. Fourteen-year-old Joyce Barrett was working as a cutter on the fourth floor of an old factory in Aldersgate Street. She had always worried about working in the proximity of such large windows – her employer being too mean to stick tape on them to stop the glass blowing out in lethal shards in the event of an explosion – but now found she had 'a second sense' and ducked just before the terrific blast of the explosion. As it happened the windows bulged in and out – someone who witnessed such a phenomenon at another incident noticed that the glass caught the reflection of the blue sky and clouds as it moved – but did not break.

This was the worst sort of incident, when hundreds of people not from the neighbourhood were buried under huge heavy mounds of debris. It would be hard to find them, to retrieve them and to identify them. The destruction was worse than usual. The rocket had penetrated several shops and the fish market and detonated well below the roadway, bringing the whole structure of heavy iron girders, bricks, stone and timber down into the goods yards of the London and North-Eastern Railway running below. The depth of the rocket's penetration at least meant that the extent of damage in the surrounding area was narrower than usual. When Admiral Sir Edward Evans pitched up within the hour, he was told that it was impossible to estimate the number of casualties.

An Incident Officer from the City Police (the City had its own Police Force, distinct from the Metropolitan Police) took up his post in Farringdon Street, directing nine heavy and seven light rescue parties and NFS personnel. Several cranes were beginning to remove the debris, while down below railway trucks were able to convey some of it away, but it would be days rather than hours before the casualties could be counted and identified. The Incident Report noted that the City Police had the area well under control. Roadways were being cleared of debris and repairs were being put in hand to overhead cables so as to allow the trolley buses in Farringdon

Road to operate a one-way service from dawn the following day.

A much overworked Incident Inquiry Point had been set up by the WVS in a local public house, before moving to Pearce's Restaurant in Charterhouse Street, where they were still working at full pressure on the 10th. The WVS was also operating a number of canteens for the rescue workers.

Anticipating heavy casualties, 15 ambulances were standing by, while several doctors were administering to the injured and dying. Casualties were being sent to St Bartholomew's Hospital at the far side of Smithfield Market, where by prior arrangement with the head porter 14 volunteers from *The Times* who were conversant with first aid were helping to unload ambulances, carry stretchers and escort the wounded into the hospital. By one o'clock St Bart's had to close its doors. It had received 256 cases. Four surgical teams operated with short breaks until noon next day. The worst injuries were penetrating wounds to the abdomen and compound fractures of the arms and legs. Others had suffered eye injuries. Succeeding casualties were sent to the Royal Free, Great Ormond Street, the Homeopathic Hospital and University College Hospital. Those who had been buried for any length of time were being watched for signs of crush syndrome. Many were treated as outpatients suffering from shock, cuts from glass and abrasions: these might be labelled 'minor injuries', but having glass splinters removed from one's face, back or limbs was hideously painful and disfiguring and often necessitated time off from work to recuperate.

At six o'clock the Regional Commissioners Sir Ernest Gowers and Admiral Sir Edward Evans, together with the Lord Mayor of London, Sir Frank Alexander, came to view progress, just as the mobile searchlights were being put into place to aid the night-long rescue operation. The next day, the smell of decomposing fish – and probably human bodies – was so bad that the Ministry of Health at Holborn had to arrange for the debris to be sprayed, so that the rescue workers could continue. They did heroic work in the worst conditions, but understandably some never became inured to the horrors they witnessed. Bagging 'pieces of flesh' was among the worst of it. At least one person remembers his father coming home and being physically sick after a rescue job.

It had always been a cardinal rule that the dead must not be left exposed to the gaze of onlookers – apart from the obvious reason such a sight was considered bad for morale. In the earlier, conventional air raids, Civil Defence workers would have had time to remove the dead and bag parts of bodies before civilians emerged from the shelters. Now, under sudden rocket attack, that was more difficult, especially as onlookers would quickly converge on an incident. On no account must the dead be taken to hospital. Temporary mortuaries would be set up on an incident site, or at the very least an area would be put aside in which to store the bodies until the stretcher parties could take them away to the local authority mortuaries. The Reverend Markham recalled that he would always ask a couple of wardens to guard the dead. 'Otherwise their clothing would be rifled, there in the midst of the darkness and dust, and falling bombs.'

Temporary mortuaries had no post-mortem facilities; they were simply storage areas. Bodies had to be numbered consecutively in the order in which they were brought in to the mortuary (the numbers being quoted on all subsequent documents and lists). At Smithfield a temporary mortuary was established in a market building on the south-east corner of the Farringdon Street and Charterhouse Street crossing: so many bodies were being brought out of the debris that it was still in use two days later. There were special procedures to observe. A body must be labelled ideally with details of name, address, sex, age, place of death, time and date of finding the body – these labels to be attached to the body by the rescue workers, stretcher bearers or mortuary vehicle attendants.

Amazingly, very few bodies were unidentified or unclaimed in London in wartime. In heavily bombed Bethnal Green, for instance, there were only 23 unidentified victims in the whole course of the war. When a body was first brought out of the debris it would usually be so covered in mortar dust (giving an aged appearance), filth and blood that it was unrecognisable even to close relatives; after being cleaned up the task might prove just as difficult. Parents in particular would find it hard to make that extra leap of the imagination to identify their child in the broken, mangled remains they saw before them.

It was a gruesome task for the mortuary workers to reassemble bodies, or to get them into a sufficiently recognisable state for identification by a relative. As an art student at the Slade, the young Frances Faviell had studied anatomy and found herself engaged in this grim task:

We had somehow to form a body for burial so that the relatives (without seeing it) could imagine that their loved one was more or less intact for that purpose. But it was a very difficult task – there were so many pieces missing and, as one of the mortuary attendants said, 'Proper jig-saw puzzle, ain't it, Miss?' The stench was the worst thing about it – that and having to realise that these frightful pieces of flesh had once been living, breathing people. After the first violent revulsion, I set my mind on it as a detached systematic task. It became a grim and ghastly satisfaction when a body was fairly constructed – but if one was too lavish in making one body almost whole then another one would have some sad gaps.

A considerable amount of detective work might be required before identification could be certain. Naturally relatives could not be asked to view badly mutilated or dismembered remains, so that mortuary workers might have to resort to some ingenious methods to get identification confirmed. Setting up the remains in such a way that something – the long hair, the set of the head – was familiar sometimes worked. Or they might describe some distinctive feature to relatives without showing them anything. Personal effects or a strip of clothing might prove sufficient. Of course it was particularly helpful if the dead person had worn an identity disc – as some people had taken to doing during the war – but the Minister of Home Security was not inclined to press civilians to wear discs, for reasons of morale. Some carried a slip of paper inside their National Registration card giving the name and official particulars of a serviceman they wanted notified in case of injury or death in an air raid; local authorities kept stocks of postcards to send to armed forces personnel informing them of the death of a relative, upon receipt of which they were usually granted compassionate leave. Women tended to be more difficult to identify than men, since they carry everything in their handbags, which invariably became separated from the body during the incident.

The Metropolitan Police would visit all hospitals and mortuaries to take particulars of casualties. Lists of casualties occurring in any Metropolitan Police district would be distributed to all police stations, so that relatives who had not had the opportunity to inquire at the Incident Inquiry Point might approach their local police station for information. The information was collated at Scotland Yard, whose Casualty Bureau kept an alphabetical list of all casualties. Official reports were compiled at regular intervals and sent on to the Regional Headquarters.

If a casualty died in hospital, his relatives would be informed by the hospital authorities. Otherwise, it was the duty of the police to inform the next of kin of the death as soon as possible; the local authority also had an obligation to notify next of kin and to send a message of sympathy reading, 'The Minister of Health asks me to express the deep sympathy of His Majesty's Government with you in your loss.' A certificate of death due to war operations would be issued. Relatives had to attend the registrar's office to register the death and to obtain permission for the disposal of the body.

As the author of the official paper, 'Emergency Mortuary and Burial Arrangements', stated, 'two essentials must be safeguarded – public health and public morale'. It was the duty of the local authority to bury victims of air attack, where they were not satisfied that proper arrangements had been made for disposal of the body. At the mortuary Form CWD had to be completed, establishing identity and indicating whether the relatives proposed to bury the victim privately or to leave the burial to the local authority. In fact, three-quarters of all burials were done privately. Local authorities made every effort to distinguish between burial of air raid victims and the 'pauper' burials they were otherwise responsible for, but the stigma attached to the latter persisted and was never sufficiently dissociated from the former. The fact that local authorities were at pains to assure relatives that they would use wooden coffins *if* they were obtainable at the time of burial probably had the opposite effect. Bethnal Green offered an extreme case in that the local authority did not use coffins at all for its burials, only shrouds.

Local authorities were reminded that the burial of a civilian who had died as a result of enemy action 'should be regarded as no less honourable than burial of a soldier by his comrades'. Members or a member of the council should attend burials, especially those of Civil Defence workers. 'The use of the Union Jack as a pall at such funerals is also encouraged and is adopted by the majority of local authorities in the region.' Funerals must be carried out 'in a seemly fashion and while avoiding any unnecessary display or expense should be of the most dignified kind that circumstances permit'. Local undertakers were employed to carry out the burial 'at the lowest contract figure', providing a coffin (not necessarily wooden), hearse, bearers 'and sometimes a coach of mourners'. Mass graves were laid out to look as if the graves were individual.

The Government grant to the local authority of £7 10s per burial might *not* be 'topped up' by relatives to provide a more lavish funeral. The Ministry of Health's view was 'either burial by a local authority or burial privately, but not both at once.' The father of a girl killed when a V-2 hit Borough High Street, Southwark, in late January 1945 complained that his 'daughter could be buried by the Government alias the parish with a cheap box and put in the communal dump and this they would have graciously paid for', but they would not grant him an allowance to provide something better for her. 'We could afford £15,000,000 a day for the war,' he concluded bitterly, 'but for people who could take it – parish relief.' He signed himself off in a letter to the *South London Press* as 'A Disgusted Londoner'.

Wartime, with its complex bureaucracy, demanded extra paperwork at death. The dead person's National Registration Identity card had to be marked 'Dead: War Operation' and forwarded by the mortuary superintendent with Form CWD to the Clerk of the Council for transmission by him to the local registrar, who would forward it to the Register General. Ration books were to be forwarded by the mortuary super-intendent to the Clerk of the Council for transmission to the Food Executive officer. Lists of bodies in mortuaries were also to be made available to the Food Executive officer in order that he might be able to trace and recover any ration books not found on the bodies of identified persons – before they fell into the hands of the unscrupulous black marketeers.

In the week that the V-2 at Smithfield Market killed 110 and seriously injured 123 people, there were 33 other incidents in the London Civil Defence Region.

When a V-2 on Sunday, 18 March had been described in the usual anodyne news bulletin which came a few days later as having landed 'on waste ground in Southern England' Vere Hodgson pounced triumphantly. Living at the other end of the Bayswater Road, she knew this one had landed a few yards from Speaker's Corner, damaging the Regal Cinema, the Cumberland Hotel and Mount Royal, a block of flats. Fortunately it landed about three hours before the crowds habitually converged on Speaker's Corner – ironically, to exercise the free speech that the Ministry of Information had done so much to curb in the wireless and press reports of enemy air attacks.

An American officer, Colonel Bigelow, was fortunate in that his room was at the back of the Cumberland, where windows were shattered, doors warped and plaster parted company with ceilings. He gave up on breakfast, but reckoned without London *sangfroid*. 'In less than ten minutes after the explosion a maid appeared with my breakfast tray. She was a bit white and shaky, but all she said was, "Here's your breakfast, Sir. I'm afraid it's a bit dusty. The ceiling's down in the kitchen." He chuckled as he described the scene: 'These British!'

On 21 March a V-2 fell on Wanstead Golf Course and killed a rabbit. Another landed as far off course as the Great West Road, the major highway leading out to Oxford, lined with factories and modern semis – cheaply constructed and not too well able to withstand the blast: nearly 700 of them were damaged in this incident. Of the 33,000 factories in London Region engaged in essential war work – half a million munitions workers alone were using London Transport every day – over 900 were damaged by the V-weapons. At 9.39 on this particular morning the rocket scored a direct hit on Packards, where marine engines were being assembled, but 13 other factories in the vicinity were also affected. Thirty-three people were killed, 98 seriously injured and several hundred received minor injuries.

On 25 March the West End was struck again when the Methodists' Whitefield Tabernacle in Tottenham Court Road was completely demolished, killing seven people sheltering in the basement. 'Naturally the traffic was diverted away from the scene, so the silence, broken only by the mobile generators feeding the lights and the sharp sounds of picks and shovels striking the rubble, added to the eeriness,' noted John Sweetland, a young man living in Marylebone, who found the power of the V-2 rocket 'awesome'. 'The scene, lit against the backdrop of a dark sky, had the unreality of a film set.'

The V-2s were to stop at the peak of their ferocity, but not before one final, terrible 'outstanding incident'. It occurred in the hard-hit borough of Stepney, which together with its neighbours in Group 3 was to suffer a disproportionate number of 'outstanding incidents' with its 45 rockets. On a visit to the area, James Lees-Milne felt that the extent of the bomb damage was matched only by the squalor and deprivation. At 7.21 on the morning of 27 March the residents of Hughes Mansions in Vallance Road, Stepney, were just getting up and having breakfast. The 5-storey flats, built as local authority housing about 30 years previously, consisted of 3 parallel blocks and were home to 89 families, many of them working in the local trades of tailoring and cabinet making. The missile scored a direct hit on the middle block, completely demolishing it, and practically destroyed that to the east, while causing serious blast damage to the west block, to St Peter's Hospital on an adjoining site and to a local school.

Mrs Annie Friedmann, a tailor's wife, had just gone out for some hot rolls for breakfast: she never returned. A few weeks later, two children were able to tell a newspaper of their experiences. Fifteen-year-old Ben Glaizner recalled: 'I saw a blue flash, but never heard a sound. Next thing I was buried. Father had just called us. If he hadn't he might be alive today. He went to the window and caught the full blast. Glass knocked out both his eyes and as he turned away a wall fell on him.' The day after his father's funeral, the paper noted, Ben carried on at his father's hairdressing shop where he had been apprenticed for a few months.

The Starkman family were extremely lucky to escape with their lives. Nikki, 11, remembered:

Mummy was in hospital and she was supposed to come home the day before, but her temperature had gone up again. I was in the kitchen helping with breakfast when bricks began to fall out of the wall. I was so surprised. Then the kitchen things started flying about and my mouth was full of dust, and everybody was crying and shouting. I ran to my parents' bedroom, but it was gone, bed and all. Father was in the passage and wasn't hurt, but my brother Marcus was on his hands and knees in bed holding the wall off him with his back and there was a piece of glass in his eye.

A Whitechapel fireman described the scene when he first arrived: 'As we stopped near what had been a large block of flats we were met by many people, some trying to find relatives or friends, others demented and just running around wildly. I remember one chap covered in blood running down the road carrying what had once been a whole, live baby, calling his wife, and some people grabbing him and leading him away.'

As in all collapsed buildings, some people had managed to survive in empty pockets in the debris, so that they were still being recovered alive all that first day. The last living person was brought out at 10 p.m. From then on floodlighting enabled rescue workers to carry on their search for the dead throughout the night. By six next morning, it was reported that 99 were dead, 43 seriously injured and 48 slightly injured, but that the 'search was still proceeding for an unknown number of missing persons'. The final toll was to be 134 dead and 49 injured.

The Hughes Mansions disaster seemed particularly futile and poignant, since it was the penultimate V-2 incident of the war. Shortly after half past four in the afternoon of the 27th the last of over 1,300 rockets to be unleashed and the 517th to fall within the boundaries of the London Civil Defence Region fell at Orpington, killing one person. Hitler's rockets had killed 2,500 and seriously injured 5,869 in London Region – of these over 1,700 had died, nearly 4,000 had been seriously injured and another 7,500 had received minor injuries in the first 3 months of 1945 alone. Two days later at 9 a.m. on 29 March the last V-1 to land in England crashed down near Hatfield in Hertfordshire, appropriately burying itself in a sewage farm. Three hours later another was shot down into the sea off the Suffolk coast.

By the end of the first week in April Londoners had enjoyed several days' respite. The only noise disturbing their nights now came from the heavy drone of planes passing over the capital on the way to bomb Germany: 'London is now on the air-bombing bus-route,' Anthony Heap complained.

'No bombs!' Vere Hodgson noted gleefully on 11 April. 'Ain't it lovely!' Warm spring sunshine added to the pleasure of Londoners rejoicing in the novelty of being able to walk about without fear of death from the skies. Flower sellers were doing a brisk trade selling Cornish daffodils, violets and forsythia and window boxes in woefully down-at-heel residential streets began to look more cheerful.

Could it all be over? Not wishing to repeat the fiasco of

the previous September the Government made no announcement until 26 April, when the Member for Ilford raised the question in the House and Churchill replied: 'Yes, sir. They have ceased.' On 2 May the remaining 23,000 Civil Defence workers enrolled with local authorities in London Region were disbanded 'quietly and smoothly'.

For thousands of Londoners whose homes had been destroyed or damaged, however, their troubles were far from over.

2

The Word from the Ministry

'If one treats the British people as intelligent, they behave surprisingly intelligently'
 – report on 'Home Front Propaganda'
for the Ministry of Information

In the New Year of 1945 the Home Security Weekly Appreciation report stated that the Germans were claiming the destruction of three bridges in London and huge devastation and disruption in the capital:

The Houses of Parliament have been damaged extensively. There is not a building standing within 500 metres of Leicester Square. Piccadilly Circus has been devastated. The Tower has suffered considerable damage from blast. The number of V2 bombs exploding right in the centre of London is considerable. Since thousands of buildings have been destroyed, the evacuation of the population to the north of England continues at high speed.

The following month the Germans seized on a quote from an American prisoner of war, who had apparently been heard to say, 'In another month there will be nothing left of London.' He must have been listening to German radio, perhaps Radio Hamburg, the notorious Lord Haw-Haw's broadcast base.

Of course, this was all nonsense. Deprived of feedback from London as to if and where the rockets were landing and the havoc they were creating – mainly in the outer boroughs – the Germans were reduced to making it up, if only to boost the flagging spirits of the German people. They were depicting Hitler's dream scenario, not reality. In a totalitarian state, a

Goebbels-like Ministry of Propaganda spewing out all sorts of lies was possible. In a democracy like Britain it was not. It was inappropriate for Britain to adopt the same unsavoury weapon as the regime it was fighting. There had to be a certain amount of negotiation between the Government, the BBC and the press as to what news was permissible and how and when it was to be presented, but there could be no question of deceiving the public. On the whole, the Government could rely on the patriotism of newspaper editors – and the people when it came to it – to co-operate.

The Government also had to recognise that the British public was not stupid. It was too discerning to accept a diet of lies. Nor could the British sense of humour be discounted. Far from being in awe of the state's propaganda machine, as the Germans were, the British regarded it as a national joke. After a disastrous start, the Ministry of Information – based in the University of London's Senate House, the skyscraper in Malet Street – quickly earned the titles Ministry of Muddle, Ministry of Malformation and the Mystery of Information. Its early absurdities were captured in Graham Greene's *Ministry of Fear* and Evelyn Waugh's *Put Out More Flags*. Later, in *Nineteen Eighty-Four*, George Orwell's Ministry of Truth, with its looming architecture and endless corridors, was a parody of the Ministry of Information and the BBC.

It remained the graveyard of ministerial reputations until the arrival of Churchill's confidant, the assertive Brendan Bracken, as Minister in July 1941, when the whole ethos of the Ministry changed for the better. The Government gradually came to understand that it could rely on the common sense of the British people, who responded best to plain speaking and sound information, while understanding the need for a certain amount of official silence and disinformation if it meant not helping the enemy.

Britain could not fight for freedom, yet subject its press and wireless to excessive censorship. London, after all, had been the birthplace of the free press. As a press proprietor himself and on good terms with Lord Beaverbrook and other proprietors,

Bracken was determined to allow the press as much scope as possible. Far from being an instrument of government suppression, the Ministry of Information was to protect the freedom of the BBC and the newspapers, albeit within certain constraints imposed by the exigencies of war. Both BBC News and the press were to have complete freedom to keep the public – and, indeed, the rest of the world – informed as to the progress of the war, as long as what they broadcast or wrote did not assist the enemy. Broadcasting to occupied Europe, the BBC's European Service in Bush House, Aldwych, was an instrument of war, acting as a beacon of freedom with its bulletins starting, 'This Is – London . . .' Even its audience in Germany was huge, as a bulging postbag of letters of thanks revealed when the postal service with Europe was restored at the end of the war.

At home the BBC Home Service and Forces Programme – the only two that were on air, until the advent of the independent, popular American Forces Network – in Broadcasting House, Langham Place, pervaded nearly every home, factory and many air raid shelters and had an equally vital role in disseminating information and in keeping up morale through entertainment. The Forces Programme, providing light music, was particularly good for morale in maintaining the link between servicemen and their families. Mass-Observation noted that the Forces Programme was so popular that it might as well be called the 'Housewives Programme' and, indeed, in July 1945 it evolved into the Light Programme: linking with the new British Forces Network in Germany, in August 1945 it introduced the much-loved music request programme, *Family Favourites*.

Good relations between Government and press suffered a setback in 1942 when the *Daily Mirror* (circulation 1,900,000) published Zec's cartoon depicting a merchant seaman adrift on a raft in the Atlantic, with the words '"The price of petrol has been increased by one penny" – Official.' The Government had authorised an increase in the price of petrol of one penny, but the idea behind the cartoon was not to criticise government policy so much as to shock the public into awareness of what their profligacy cost the ordinary seaman. The Government took exception and decided to prosecute the *Mirror*, which had become a thorn in its side. As Herbert Morrison told the House: 'The cartoon is only one example, but a particularly evil example of the policy and methods of a newspaper which, intent on exploiting an appetite for sensation, and with reckless indifference to the national interest and to the prejudicial effect on the war effort, has repeatedly published scurrilous misrepresentations, distorted and exaggerated statements and irresponsible generalisations.'

The best way to deal with a newspaper 'which persistently disregards its public responsibility and the national interest', Morrison believed, was to make use of the powers contained in Defence Regulation 2D. 'This authorises the suppression of a newspaper that systematically publishes matter calculated to foment opposition to the successful prosecution of the war.'

The Home Office had already closed down the communist newspaper, the *Daily Worker*, believing that it might tap in to the social unrest the Government feared would be the outcome of wartime disruption. Its pursuit of the *Daily Mirror* provoked a sense of unease about infringements on the freedom of the press, however. There was a debate in the House. The National Council for Civil Liberties expressed their grave anxiety and organised a protest meeting in London. Labour backbenchers were critical and Lord Camrose of the *Daily Telegraph* intervened to say that surely a warning to the *Mirror* would be enough. The Government retreated.

Nevertheless, there had to be some restrictions on press freedom. Newspaper editors, like all British citizens, were prohibited under the Defence Regulation No. 3 from 'obtaining, recording or communicating to any other person or publishing information which might be useful to the enemy'. The press had been issued with Defence Notices, a set of guidelines which were updated from time to time on what was safe or unsafe to publish without running the copy past the censors, but since they could not be prosecuted for material that had been stamped 'Passed for Publication', this was an obvious course for many editors to take if there was any doubt. For the British press, submitting material for censorship was voluntary rather than compulsory; whereas for the foreign press, including Americans, based in London it was compulsory to submit their copy for censorship – an unpopular policy which was relaxed after D-Day in June 1944. In the same way as the newspapers, the BBC News Department came under Ministry of Information control, but the onus was on the Home News Editor to censor and edit bulletins, referring to the Ministry only when he was in doubt. By the end of the war, the BBC was operating almost totally independently, thanks to its integrity, reliability and good sense. Television, of course, was off the air for the duration, dying in the middle of a Mickey Mouse cartoon at 3.35 p.m. on 1 September 1939 and returning, at first only to the London region, in 1946.

A free press was best for civilian morale. The British public preferred to get its news straight, no matter how bad. To offer them inadequate or false news would only have fostered anxiety and rumour. There were some omissions from the press in the interests of national security, however. For instance, it was never revealed that after the bombing of the House of Commons in 1940 and 1941 the Members had earmarked Church House as an alternative to the House of Lords for their sittings. Nor did the press ever announce the date of the opening of a new session of Parliament, when the King attended. It was forbidden to reveal the whereabouts of the royal family in wartime.

The press co-operated with the Ministry in instances where disclosure might not have helped the enemy, but would have had a detrimental effect in the war on the home front. For instance, if the press got wind of some new rationing scheme, the onus was on them not to publish the news until it was officially announced, as otherwise there would be a run on stocks before the ration could be honoured.

BBC News, broadcast at 7 a.m., 8 a.m., 1 p.m., 6 p.m., 9 p.m. – drawing an audience of 16 million – and midnight, won a reputation for reliable, impartial reporting. Throughout the war, news readers introduced themselves by name, apparently to foil fifth column attempts to spread disinformation over the airwaves: this practice ceased on 4 May 1945. Weather reports were suspended, since they were considered helpful to the enemy – even the publication of photographs of sunbathers in Hyde Park was banned as they revealed the state of the weather – but resumed in April 1945.

Every newspaper with an office in London and the large news agencies maintained their representatives at the Ministry of Information on the ground floor of Senate House. Two of the main functions of the Ministry were to handle news and censorship. The press representatives attended daily press briefings, submitted material for censorship, telephoned the contents of briefings and deletions made by the censor to their offices, and liaised with other government departments, all of whom kept representatives at the Ministry of Information.

At a higher level, the Minister of Information would send 'Private and confidential' letters to newspaper editors, for their eyes and those of their top editorial staff only. In this way, a privileged few would be furnished with information on a need-to-know basis, but it was also a subtle means by which the Ministry could influence the press. As news of Hitler's secret weapons began to emerge – indeed, Hitler frequently alluded to them in his speeches – Herbert Morrison, who as Minister of Home Security was responsible for Civil Defence, called newspaper editors to the Ministry of Information for a secret briefing about what to expect and urged them not to give undue prominence to the subject in the press, so as not to spread public alarm, and to submit any material to censorship.

In February 1945 a *Daily Express* headline ran, 'Where do my V-2s Go? Hitler is Asking' – as he might well do, since the press was giving very little away about them. When the V-2s arrived in September 1944 the Government had wanted to impose a news blackout, so that the Germans would not know if the weapons had succeeded, even though ignorance meant that thousands of evacuees were returning to the capital, oblivious of the new menace descending from the skies. It was essential that the Germans did not know exactly where the weapons were landing, because that knowledge would allow them to correct their aim, meaning that far more would land on the desired target of central London.

Duncan Sandys, who was in charge of co-ordinating the response to the V-weapons, raised the possibility of actively feeding disinformation to the Germans, to ensure that the weapons would land in the outer boroughs rather than the centre of London. In a report on German Long Range Rocket Development for the War Cabinet Chiefs of Staff Committee dated 12 May 1943 Sandys suggested: 'The enemy would naturally be most anxious to determine accurately where the projectiles fell, in order that he might, if necessary, correct his fire . . . It might be possible to evolve a deception plan which would mislead the enemy and might make him divert his fire away from the real target.'

Rather more sensitive than Sandys to the political and social consequences if such a ruse ever became public knowledge, Herbert Morrison firmly quashed this idea. As a Londoner, formerly Mayor of Hackney and Leader of the LCC, he was only too aware of the dangers of dissatisfaction in the East End when they felt they were getting a rougher deal than their more privileged and prosperous neighbours in the West End. After all, it was to mollify the East End that the Ministry seized the opportunity to send a pack of journalists to report the bombing of Buckingham Palace in 1940. Morrison had asked newspaper editors to publish absolutely nothing about the rockets and they were happy to comply. There was tacit understanding on the part of the public that if details of the new secret weapon, the V-2, were not being published it was for a good reason. Even 16-year-old Kenneth Holmes in Islington was able to write phlegmatically in his diary in September 1944: 'I have been looking in every paper to see if there was any mention of these "explosions" but there is nothing at all. Why are we not being told about these? Obviously security measures – which convinces me that they must be rockets.'

Frustrated by the silence emanating from London, on 8 November 1944 the German Government issued a communiqué stating that V-2s had been used against London 'for some weeks past. The British Government is concealing the truth from its people.' Consequently, two days later the Prime Minister made a statement in the House confirming that V-2s had been landing for some weeks, although no specific details were released. This policy of vagueness, economy of information, would continue.

Very strict guidelines, right outside the scope of the Defence Notices, were given to the press on how to report V-weapon incidents. On 14 November 1944 a meeting was held between the Newspaper and Periodical Emergency Council – a body of influential journalists representing and speaking on behalf of the various newspaper and periodical societies – and representatives of the Ministry of Information, the Air Ministry and the Ministry of Home Security. At that and a further meeting held on 4 January 1945 the importance of concealing from the enemy information about the localities where the V-weapons were falling was unanimously recognised. It was agreed that nothing should be published to reveal date, time or place of an incident. It was not permissible to specify London, let alone any area of London. A line was drawn from the Wash to the Bristol Channel and every locality within that area was to appear in news reports under the general term 'Southern England'.

The Air Ministry and the Ministry of Home Security initially drew up the wording of the typical bulletin, which gave virtually nothing away: 'There was intermittent enemy air activity yesterday and last night directed against Southern England. Damage and casualties were caused.' 'Yesterday and last night' soon evolved into 'recently', although even that was felt to give too much away. The 30-day rule which had hitherto applied, permitting newspapers to identify damaged buildings and places after that interval, was suspended. Press reports concentrated only on major incidents, were sparing of the facts, and appeared some days or weeks after the event.

Reading them, it is very hard indeed to gauge which incident they refer to, the exact location, the extent of damage or number of casualties.

All reports of V-weapon incidents were to be submitted for censorship. This proved to be less than fail-safe. On 12 January 1945 the *Daily Mail* (circulation 1,507,913) reported: 'Cinema takings in London have fallen off to such an extent that the Cinematograph Exhibitors' Association are to convene a meeting to consider the question of an appeal for a cut in "Entertainment Tax".' Naturally the Germans might deduce from this careless slip that West End audiences had declined owing to V-weapon activity. But the *Mail* was only picking up on an article entitled 'Audience Audit' that had appeared the previous day in the *Daily Express* (circulation 2,738,500), referring to a crisis in entertainment sales in central London. The article indicated that the audience figures for West End theatres had fallen and that there was a drastic reduction in audiences in suburban cinemas. The Ministry was quick to intervene, claiming that the article was entirely against the spirit of the V-bomb censorship regulations as laid down in the 'Private and confidential' letter of 16 November 1944, following the meeting that had taken place between the press and the various ministries on the 14th.

'No one, after considering the facts and the figures published in your article, could feel any doubt that V bombs have recently been falling in the London area and that the enemy's aim is now such that it is likely that bombs may fall in Central London,' a letter from the Ministry of Information 'Scrutiny Section' lambasted the editor of the *Daily Express*, Arthur Christiansen. 'Moreover, the reference which you make to the absence of a warning makes it clear that the falling of rocket projectiles is feared; in view of this, and in view of the very few occasions on which flying bomb attacks have been launched against Southern England during the last three weeks, the enemy is likely to draw from your article the correct inference that rocket projectiles have been falling on London.'

Apparently, the Duty Assistant Director at the Ministry of

Information had spotted the article in an early edition of the paper and advised the night editor at the *Express* by telephone that the article should be removed. He 'declined to accept the advice' and the article was published in subsequent editions.

'Your publication of this article is regarded as a contravention of Defence Regulation 3, and the Chief Press Censor would be glad to hear whether you would care to put forward any explanation,' Christiansen was informed.

Not to be cowed, on 15 January he replied: 'It seemed to the Editor-in-Charge only natural that the threat of V-bombs would keep people at home – quite apart from the question as to whether any had actually landed or exploded. There was, in fact, nothing in the article to indicate whether any V bombs were landing in London or not.'

The argument rumbled on and there was much consternation behind the scenes that if the Ministry referred the matter to the Director of Public Prosecutions, the *Express* would engage the best defence lawyers if charges were pressed. The lawyers would argue that it could not be *proved* that the article was useful to the enemy. It only *might* be useful.

Undoubtedly it would be harmful if a particular incident could be related to a particular time for the enemy to correct the range, but the *Express* article had not done this. Hitler's avowed aim in using the V-weapons was to break British morale, in particular the morale of the Londoners, the people of the capital which had dared to defy him for five long years. 'The enemy has stated time and again that the object of his flying bomb and other secret weapons is to break the spirit of London, to make London squeal to such a pitch that the Government will be forced to call off the war,' Herbert Morrison had stated in his tribute to London speech on 7 September 1944. As Sir William Brown of the Ministry of Home Security pointed out to Rear-Admiral Thomson, the Chief Press Censor known as the 'Blue Pencil Admiral', the *Express* article was a gift for Hitler: 'Quite apart from all question of fall of shot, the article shows that rockets are having a considerable effect on morale in the London area and thereby assists the enemy in deciding whether his expenditure is worth while.'

There was no question, Thomson believed, that the article should have been submitted for censorship. But the *Daily Express* had a good record of co-operation with the censorship department and 'certainly better than some of its contemporaries' – probably referring to the less pliable *Daily Mirror*, although even the *Daily Telegraph* had fallen foul of the censors. The matter would be allowed to drop, but the *Express* would not be able to rely on an unblemished record if there were any further infringements. After all, as the cool-headed former barrister Sir Cyril Radcliffe, the Ministry's Director-General, reasoned, to expect the press to be completely silent about the situation was 'to misconceive the intensely competitive nature of the business that is involved in news reporting'.

As late as 7 March 1945 the press were being issued with fresh, tighter instructions on the reporting of V-weapons. The enemy must not know how many V-2s were landing and where, but advantage could be taken of the fact that he was sending over both V-1s and V-2s. No distinction was to be made in the press between V-1s and V-2s and at the daily morning briefings at Senate House news of V-bomb incidents would not be released by the censorship department until there were a sufficient number of both types to 'marry' them, again to minimise the usefulness of any information going to Germany. If there were four V-1 incidents but six V-2 incidents, the total number of 'bomb' stories released would be four and the enemy would not be able to tell which of his weapons was responsible. Reports of incidents were to be staggered, so that the enemy could not gauge what had happened to any particular rocket fired on a particular day.

Only a month after the arrival of the V-1 in the summer of 1944 the Ministry turned its attention to obituaries in the press. From obituary columns in *The Times* and the *Daily Telegraph* (circulation 165,000 and 648,317 respectively) it had apparently proved possible to deduce where the V-1s were landing. In the case of 70 obituaries in *The Times* and 80 in the *Telegraph*, the mean points of impact worked out in the case of the former at Streatham Hill and in the case of the latter at Clapham Junction. As Churchill's friend and influential private adviser, the ex-scientist Lord Cherwell told Sir Findlater Stewart at the Ministry of Information, 'the results are dangerously near the truth'. Rear-Admiral Thomson sensed the absurdity of this, maintaining that the Germans must realise that of the number of people killed in the whole of the London area, there were comparatively few 'whose relatives can afford or desire to insert obituary notices in *The Times* or *Daily Telegraph*'.

Various formulae were examined to make the obituaries 'safe' for publication. At first it was stipulated that there might not be more than three obituary notices of people killed in air raids from the same postal district in any one edition. Then the private or business address of a person killed was to be deleted if it was within 15 miles of Charing Cross – in which case there was to be no limit in any one edition of the paper as to the number of obituaries of persons killed as a result of enemy action in southern England. Death might be admitted to have been caused by enemy action, but the date of death must be no more precise than within a month.

The Times indicated that it was willing to comply with any reasonable amendment, but that it would not accept an absolute prohibition: it insisted on maintaining the right of relatives to announce a death in the family. The Ministry's new instructions of 7 March 1945 included further reference to obituaries: it stated categorically that if a death were to occur in a period when only V-1s or V-2s were landing, the notice should take the form of an ordinary obituary notice, with the date and address given but with no reference made to 'enemy action'.

In April 1945, when V-weapon activity had ceased, Herbert Morrison sent a memo to Churchill suggesting that press restrictions on publishing reports of rocket attacks should be lifted as soon as possible to allow the full story to be told, especially in the United States, of what the people of London and other parts of England had had to endure. The same request was made by the press and rejected, on the basis that the Germans might still use the weapons on the Allied troops in Europe and that the reports might be studied by the Japanese for use in the Far East. There was to be some relaxation of the rules, but in a fresh batch of instructions issued by Rear-Admiral Thomson on 26 April the press were forbidden to give specific dates of incidents, maps, diagrams or statistics; there was to be no complete list of V-bomb incidents in any one place, which would give information as to the intensity or pattern of attack; there was to be no tally of casualties in any one incident, or value put on damage caused; nor were there to be any details revealed of defences.

Even after the Chief Press Censor wrote to all newspaper editors to tell them that the machinery of press censorship was to be dismantled as from 9 a.m. on 2 September 1945, following the signing of the Japanese surrender terms in Tokyo Bay, it was still not permissible to publish all the details of the V-weapon attacks. In October the *Ilford Recorder* found itself in trouble for publishing a complete list of the number of rockets that had fallen on the borough with details of casualties and damage inflicted. Although this was in contravention of existing security rulings, the Air Ministry decided not to take proceedings against the paper. Among a rush of local histories describing London's war, *Ordeal in Romford* was denied approval for publication, as it revealed specific information about V-bomb attacks and incidents which, although the war was over, might still be useful 'abroad'. The copy was to be rendered 'innocuous'.

The main goal of 'propaganda' in a democracy had to be to promote action to win the war on all fronts, but at the outset the Ministry of Information was badly out of touch with the popular mind. Posters such as '*YOUR* COURAGE, *YOUR* CHEERFULNESS, *YOUR* RESOLUTION WILL BRING US VICTORY' generated cynicism. With the First World War still fresh in some memories, the public read into this poster the implication that once again sacrifices would be made by the many for the few. The problem was that the senior personnel at the Ministry was drawn mainly from the old boys' network, the privileged few from the public schools and Oxbridge who approached their task wearing the social blinkers of their class. In due course they were amazed that all their preconceptions about the ordinary British people were confounded. Far from panicking and running away and begging for peace when the Blitz started, the people – best exemplified by the East Enders who took the brunt of it – stood firm. In various long-winded and obtuse slogans the men – and it was men – at the Ministry tended to employ a literary way of thinking to which most people were unaccustomed. Eventually they discovered that a short, clear message such as 'Be like Dad, Keep Mum' worked wonders.

Gradually it dawned on the Ministry that exhortation did not work. Nor was there any need for it. The public could not be patronised, but it did respond to reason and explanation. In spite of his aristocratic background, Winston Churchill never talked down to the people, but it was clear that his speeches came from the heart, which was why the people responded so well to his leadership. Lord Woolton at the Ministry of Food had the popular touch and understood better than any other minister that the best results were obtained when the Government took the people into its confidence. Other ministers did more harm than good when they spoke on the wireless, and the Ministry of Information and the BBC eventually won the point that they should be kept in the background. At the BBC early on in the war J.B. Priestley provided the sort of plain-speaking, simply expressed ideas that endeared him to the nation – if not to the Ministry, the BBC and the establishment – and, incidentally, prompted the quest for more speakers with a regional accent, which was considered more 'trustworthy' and 'reassuring' than the traditional BBC 'educated Southern English', more accurately termed Received Pronunciation. The Yorkshire character actor Wilfrid Pickles was brought in alongside such BBC stalwarts as Alvar Lidell, Stuart Hibberd and John Snagge to read the news.

The Ministry came to have a better understanding of the mind of the people from the feedback it was receiving from a number of organisations. First of all, there were the regular reports from its own Home Intelligence Division on the state of morale, the effectiveness of propaganda and all aspects of wartime life. These reports were circulated throughout Whitehall. The division received its information from its regional intelligence officers, while bodies such as the Citizens' Advice Bureaux, W.H. Smith and Sons, managers in the major cinema chains and officials of the London Passenger Transport Board reported directly to Senate House, often filling in questionnaires provided by the Home Intelligence Division. The BBC's Listener Research unit was a valuable source of information. The Home Office passed on the Police Duty Room reports. Postal and Telegraph Censorship, whose staff exceeded 10,000, gleaned vast amounts of information about the state of public morale and opinions from its scrutiny of mail leaving Britain. The Ministry also placed heavy reliance on the work carried out by Tom Harrisson's independent organisation, Mass-Observation, which supplied regular reports on a wide range of subjects by observing, interviewing or eavesdropping on the public. This material was bolstered by the statistical reports of the Wartime Social Survey under the aegis of the London School of Economics. The Ministry of Information acted as a filter, passing on information to the various ministries as well as carrying out specific surveys on behalf of those ministries, so that they might adapt their policies accordingly.

Under Brendan Bracken the Ministry stopped bombarding the public with myriad exhortations and demanded that after doing their homework all ministries submit their proposals for publicity campaigns to the Ministry, who would decide the type and reach of the publicity. The Ministry's output would become more professional and more focused. Its aim would be to use one voice which was in tune with the people. Public morale would be safeguarded by more considered campaigns which married up with reality and with the correct administrative response: for instance, it was no good the Ministry of Labour exhorting people to work harder when they were already working at full capacity and would resent any implication by the boffins at Whitehall to the contrary. It was demoralising for people to give up their iron railings or saucepans, only to see them rusting in a great heap locally, rather than being taken away to be transformed into Spitfires. Similarly, public anger was roused by a campaign persuading them to spend their holidays at home, when it turned out that the railways were running special holiday excursion trains. The whole emphasis was to be on explanation and education. If the public understood why the Government wanted to adopt a particular policy and could see a good reason for it, it was much more likely to co-operate.

The Ministry's posters covered every billboard. It advertised extensively in the press and women's magazines and ran flashes in the cinemas. It ran successful campaigns for the Ministry of Health to combat VD, the incidence of which had risen alarmingly since the outbreak of war, and also to immunise children against diphtheria. 'Coughs and sneezes spread diseases', encouraging the public to use a handkerchief and cover their mouth when coughing, was a bid to minimise infection and keep up productivity for the war effort. The 'Dig for Victory' poster and advertising campaign was successful and there was the added benefit that gardening was already a popular topic on the wireless, so that the BBC could lend its weight to this campaign.

The BBC, penetrating nearly every home or workplace in the land, proved the most effective medium for getting most of the Ministry's messages across – one of the few exceptions being the VD campaign, which was considered too risqué for the wireless. The challenge was to achieve the right balance between advice and entertainment. The successful *Kitchen Front* programme was a prime example of this, attracting 5 million listeners, four times the audience of any other daytime talk. Unlike so many other Government ministers, Lord

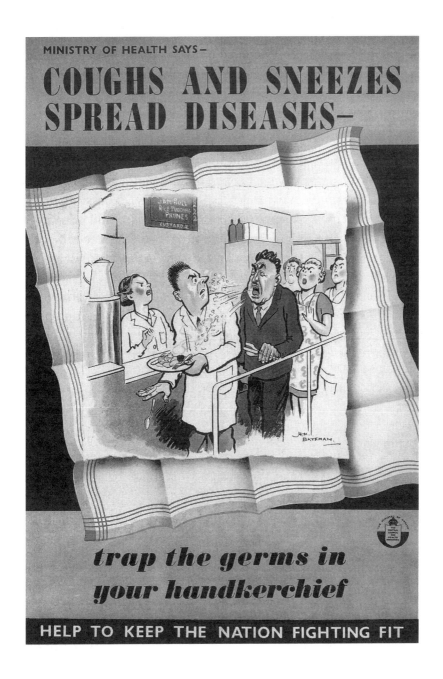

Woolton knew exactly how to pitch it. He did not cajole; he informed in a light-hearted manner. The slot just after the eight o'clock morning news proved to be the best time to catch the housewife, just before she did her shopping. Whereas in the past food programmes had largely been made to appeal to the middle classes, now a five-minute sketch, *Feed the Brute*, attracted a high proportion of working-class women. The comedy duo 'Gert and Daisy' (Elsie and Doris Waters) and the actress Mabel Constanduros playing the cantankerous Grandma Buggins made the lessons more palatable.

No matter how hard the Ministry tried, a campaign could only work if the British public was in sympathy with it. In contrast to the Kitchen Front campaign, which reconciled the public to the inevitable – rationing – the Ministry of Fuel and Power's Fuel Economy campaign fell on deaf ears. The Ministry of Information and the BBC were sceptical about this campaign from the start and their doubts were proved right: in due course, the BBC was able to exert its authority to scrap it, since propaganda that no one listened to was a waste of airtime.

There was to be no rationing of fuel, partly as a result of the opposition of Tory MPs with big country houses to heat and a well-founded Tory fear that Labour was manoeuvring to nationalise the mines. Instead, it was hoped that the public could be persuaded to ration themselves voluntarily. Rationing worked because people understood that it meant fair shares for all, but people were suspicious that voluntary sacrifice would not be made by all. There was always a suspicion that 'it's the poor that pays', while the rich were able to slide out of their obligations. Coal production was a persistent problem, yet no proper explanation was ever forthcoming as to why people should conserve fuel in an island literally sitting on it. At any rate, they remained unconvinced.

The poor, for whom higher wages and rationing, subsidies and price controls on food meant improvements on their pre-war lot, were unlikely to respond to a campaign that showed itself so ignorant of the facts of their existence. They could hardly cut fuel consumption when they were already down to the barest minimum. They did not have the ready money to buy coal in the summer when it was cheaper and more available, nor in many cases did they have anywhere to store it. It was irrelevant for them to save bath water, as they had no bath; they could not opt to eat in the kitchen instead of the dining room as they lived in one room; they could not collect 'kindling from the garden' when they were living in an urban slum.

Overt propaganda and too much exhortation were counter-productive. Some of the most successful morale boosters came from the BBC's entertainment programmes. *ITMA – It's That Man Again* – was by far the most successful radio comedy show of the war. Starring the immensely popular Tommy Handley, it picked up on the topical news of the day, parodying the war. It was a case of bringing archetypal British humour to the rescue. Comedy brought a sense of relief and restored a sense of proportion. One of the BBC's wartime functions was to unite the nation in the war effort and *ITMA*'s 'in jokes' provided some of that cement. Forty per cent of the population tuned in to *ITMA* at 8.30 on Thursday evenings and it was also picked up by the forces in the Middle East and West Africa, so that phrases such as 'Can I do you now, sir', 'I'm going down now, sir', 'It's being so cheerful that keeps me going' and 'I don't mind if I do' became common currency. The sting was taken out of wartime conditions by poking fun at ministries, bureaucracy, rationing and all the other restrictions and, for good measure, a German spy, 'Funf', was thrown into the equation.

It didn't always require humour to entertain the wartime audience. The success of *The Brains Trust*, a serious programme in which Cyril Joad, Julian Huxley, Donald McCullough, Commander Campbell and guests discussed science, politics, philosophy and the arts, probably took the BBC by surprise, but it was perfect for those long, dark evenings when the blackout discouraged excursions outdoors and families sat round the wireless together.

If *ITMA* was widely acknowledged to have been the show that helped Britain to win the war, the BBC's *Music While You Work* and *Workers Playtime*, blasting out of loudspeakers in the factories, had a far more stimulating effect on wartime production than any amount of 'Factory Front' propaganda. Again, it was popular with the forces and another link between the fighting front and the home front was fostered.

The cinema's contribution to public morale through its ability to provide a few hours of escape from the reality of total war cannot be underestimated. Long queues would stretch outside cinemas, the most famous being that at the Empire, Leicester Square, for the epic, *Gone with the Wind,* which played in the West End continuously from the Blitz to Easter 1944. Starring the British beauty Vivien Leigh and Clark Gable, it provided nearly four hours of sheer escapism in glorious technicolour. The air raid sirens might be sounding outside, but no one was going to leave the cinema, so transfixed were they by the passion and the fires of Atlanta up on the screen. Margaret Mitchell's novel, on which the film was based, was one of those wonderful big absorbing reads which proved so popular during long nights spent in the shelters.

The popularity of the cinema made it an ideal forum for Ministry propaganda. In addition to the main feature film, the B film and newsreel, at least one official short film on anything from salvage to mending old clothes was included. *Food Flashes* urging the virtues of potatoes, say, were as common on the cinema screen as they were in the press. The public wanted news, as the long queues outside the News Cinema in Oxford Street attested. In the cinema, newsreels showing the battle front, when relatives strained for a glimpse of their men, were enormously popular. Shots of enemy defeats with the RAF shooting down German planes or German and Italian soldiers being taken prisoner provoked loud applause: they were definitely morale-boosters.

If the public went to the pictures for a few hours of escapism, they also welcomed realism. Propaganda documentaries produced by the Crown Film Unit, such as *Western Approaches* which told the story of the ordeal of the merchant seamen on the Atlantic convoys, were well received. There was a spate of factual films, such as *In Which We Serve*, starring Noël Coward as Lord Louis Mountbatten on the ship HMS *Kelly*. *Millions Like Us* depicted factory life and *This Happy Breed* a working-class family in wartime. The first really successful fictional film about army life, *The Way Ahead* starring David Niven, came in 1944. It showed how a group of men from different backgrounds united as an effective fighting unit. In June the following year, *The Way to the Stars* depicted life in wartime England near an RAF station and the impact made by the Americans.

Sentiment was popular. In January 1945 audiences were much taken with *Waterloo Road*, starring John Mills and Stewart Granger. It was such a convincing cameo of London life in wartime: the lonely wife of an absent soldier being seduced by a small-time racketeer in a flashy suit and armed with a phoney medical certificate. Love and loyalty triumph in the end. Noël Coward's play *Blithe Spirit*, which ran for over 2,000 performances and captured the spirit of London at the time with the song, 'London pride has been handed down to us, London pride is a flower that's free', was released as a film at the end of the war, but it was less well received than the stage version.

Escapism meant returning to a past heroic age, when England won all its battles. Films such as *Lady Hamilton*, with Vivien Leigh and Laurence Olivier as the hero Lord Nelson saving his country from invasion at Trafalgar, were popular. Olivier's *Henry V*, which appeared in the run-up to the invasion of France in 1944, was appropriately inspiring and patriotic.

Comedy films, especially those starring George Formby whose *She Snoops to Conquer* was drawing the crowds early in 1945, with lots of songs, suggestive *double entendres* and slapstick comedy, were morale boosters. Sunshine, cheerfulness, good nature and lots of song and dance routines were the popular ingredients of Hollywood musicals, which with the likes of Bing Crosby, Bob Hope and Dorothy Lamour provided perfect escapism. When Ginger Rogers did not dance in one of her films, the manager of a Granada cinema in his monthly report could not be sure if a slight decline in takings was down to that or the number of V-2 incidents in the vicinity. But the public could also be moved by more serious Hollywood fare, such as *A Tree Grows in Brooklyn*, about a family living in a New York tenement, which was showing in London in the week of VE Day.

Apart from the prevalence of the cinema, the war was a stimulus to the appreciation of books, paintings and music. There was a great revival of the arts, actively encouraged by the Government and CEMA (the Council for the Encourage-ment of the Arts), who took concerts, ballet, drama and art exhibitions to the people to sustain morale. The Government learned that its involvement in the arts could be a force for good and in 1945 the Coalition Government decided that CEMA should be made permanent and granted a royal charter as the Arts Council of Great Britain. In the spring of 1945 Mollie Panter-Downes noted:

During the war years, more and more Londoners have taken to reading poetry, listening to music, and going to art exhibitions, although there is less and less of all three to be had in this shabby, weary capital. Most of the poets are too personally involved in the war to have attained that state of impersonal tranquillity which generates good poetry. Louis MacNeice, whose most recent collec-tion, *Springboard*, was quickly sold out, is working at the BBC, C. Day Lewis has a job at the Ministry of Information, Stephen Spender is a full-time fireman, and most of the younger poets are in uniform. Several have been killed, among them Alun Lewis, who was considered one of the most promising. The output of good poetry is small, but the public hunger for it is pathetically great. The demand for music is probably not much greater now than it was in peacetime, but it looks greater because the supply of concert halls and orchestras is sadly limited.

The Queen's Hall near Langham Place had been bombed early in the war and the Royal Opera House, Covent Garden had been transformed into a public dance hall. The V-weapon threat in the summer and autumn of 1944 meant the cancellation of the Proms at the Albert Hall: instead, the BBC arranged to broadcast them by wireless only. In March 1945 Mr Gerald Cooper resumed his concerts at the Wigmore Hall on Tuesday evenings at 6.45 p.m. They lasted an hour, 'which is really as much as a busy public can comfortably assimilate on an empty stomach after a day's work'.

Art flourished in wartime, in spite of the removal of the National Gallery's collection to Wales and the closure of the Tate, which was bombed several times. Both galleries continued to add new works to their collections through the war. The empty rooms of the National Gallery were filled with paintings bought by the War Artists Advisory Committee on behalf of the Ministry of Information. During the war, official permission had to be obtained to paint outside, but artists such as Graham Sutherland, Stanley Spencer and Paul Nash were commissioned by the Ministry to paint the destructiveness of the bombing, coal mines, factories, the construction of aircraft, and other aspects of the war. Henry Moore painted his figures sheltering in the Underground quite spontaneously, before he was taken on officially. All work had to be submitted for censorship. Some artists were on salary, but Leonard Rosoman's *House Collapsing on Two Firemen, Shoe Lane* was bought by the committee for £30.

The purpose of the Artists' International Association, whose members included Augustus John, Vanessa Bell, David Grant, Frank Dobson, David Low, Henry Moore, Paul Nash, Ethel Walker and Lucien Pissarro, was to close the gap between the artist and society by 'democratising' art. Art was not only to record what was happening, but to give pleasure and recreation, to stimulate and encourage by vividly showing what Britain was fighting for. An exhibition held at Charing Cross Underground station was seen by 150,000, while the *News Chronicle* sponsored the 'For Liberty' exhibition in the basement air-raid shelter of John Lewis's bombed-out department store in Oxford Street in March 1943. Exhibitions were taken on tours of British Restaurants, the communal eating places that had been set up in wartime to provide cheap, nourishing meals for those too busy to shop or cook and the bombed-out, and to save on fuel.

Many of London's artistic community dispersed to the countryside for the duration of the war. Cut off from continental influence in their island fortress, artists such as John Piper once more explored the English landscape. By the spring of 1945 Bond Street's galleries, including some new private galleries, were tentatively opening their doors again. The Lefevre Gallery was showing superb drawings by the Scottish artist Robert Colquhoun and 'works by John Minton, Lucian Freud, Keith Vaughan and other young men who have yet to make their names'. In April newcomer Francis Bacon was appearing at the Lefevre Gallery, while the *Spectator*'s critic was bemoaning the fact that Henry Moore showing at the Berkeley and the Lefevre 'is a gifted sculptor, for the moment highly overrated. He produces an endless series of sculptors' drawings, window-dressed with washes of colour, which seem to supply an inexhaustible market.'

The end of hostilities meant the end of isolation for English art. Not surprisingly perhaps, the public was unprepared for the Picasso exhibition held at the Victoria and Albert Museum in November, not knowing what to think of it and disliking it intensely. 'Disgusting,' said one. 'A child of ten could do better,' said another.

Many writers were employed by the Ministry of Information. Unlike art, there was no great flowering of literature. This war lacked the brilliance of the First World War poets and many of the novels produced have not stood the test of time. Ironically, the war created the conditions for a reading boom. There was a definite increase in reading as an activity, just as publishers were drastically limited in their output by the paper shortage. The Publishers Association voluntarily negotiated among its members a Book Production

Economy Agreement, laying out minimum production standards: thinner books, narrower margins, more words per page, chapters running on without a break were all devices employed to eke out the paper supply. After a rocky start, in which publishers were reduced to 25 per cent of their pre-war paper quota, the quota settled at about 42 per cent. New publishers did better, not having a pre-war paper level to measure against, and there was a rash of new publishing houses in consequence.

Print runs were severely reduced, as was the number of new titles published. In 1937, 17,137 new books were published, in 1939, 14,094 and in 1945 only 6,747. At the same time, expenditure on books rose from £9 million in 1939 to £23 million in 1945. These figures represent sales alone: it is impossible to gauge how many people read each copy, sharing the book as they shared equally limited print runs of newspapers and magazines. There was the Boots Lending Library, and local authorities arranged for large quantities of books to be available in Underground shelters: Bethnal Green station had a thriving lending library, while at West Ham they secured a supply of Penguin paperbacks and slightly damaged books for the occupants.

It was unfortunate that many London publishers had lost their backlists in the great conflagration of 29 December 1940, when 27 publishers in the vicinity of St Paul's – the home of the publishing business for more than three centuries – lost their offices and warehouses in a single night. Five million books were destroyed. Those publishers who managed to retain some backlist found that they were unable to replace it once it had sold out. To improve the poor standard of wartime book paper – which George Orwell likened to lavatory paper, while lavatory paper, he said, was now like sheet tin – the Ministry of Supply in its wisdom had ordered a massive salvage of old books, which were to be pulped in order to improve the paper quality of new publications. Fifty-six million volumes were collected, of which 5 million were sent to the Forces; the rest, including who knows how many rare books and first editions, were pulped.

The classics enjoyed a boom. Jane Austen transported readers back to a world of discreet English gentility and Anthony Trollope to the solid security of the Victorian age. There was plenty of time on long dark evenings when people were kept indoors by the blackout or spending hours in the shelters or on some endless wartime train journey to work through the whole of Dickens or Proust and other great authors. Series such as Hugh Walpole's *Rogue Herries* books and John Galsworthy's *Forsyte Saga* were perfect for the same reason. Tolstoy's *War and Peace* was *the* big read of the war. A mention on *The Brains Trust* and then a BBC serialisation triggered off the demand. It coincided with the British passion for all things Russian after their entry into the war.

Even when there was so much violence in the world, readers were hungry for thrillers. Dorothy L. Sayers was popular. Escapism came in the form of historical novels, such as those by Georgette Heyer, and in September 1945 with the publication of the mildly salacious Restoration romp, *Forever Amber*, by the American Kathleen Winsor. There was enormous excitement about this novel, which according to the *Daily Mail* had 'already burst on the American market with the effect of an atomic bomb'. How would the British public receive Amber St Clare? it wondered. It was considered risqué, so much so that some librarians had banned it and Anthony Heap, rather than endure a long wait at his local library, splurged on his own copy. The novel's detractors did not feel it warranted the 800 pages it was printed on. The Public Morality Council was keeping its eye on the forthcoming film, which it suspected would be sufficiently immoral to warrant censure.

More serious contemporary writing was represented in *Horizon*, launched by Cyril Connolly in 1940 with editorial help from Stephen Spender, and in John Lehmann's *Penguin New Writing*. Thanks to a generous allocation of paper this 6d Penguin paperback became a highly successful venture. Elizabeth Bowen maintained that it was difficult in wartime to obtain the focus necessary for art and this may explain the preponderance of the short story, Julian MacLaren-Ross's *Better than a Kick in the Pants* in 1945 being one example.

Like so much writing of the time, Evelyn Waugh's novel *Brideshead Revisited* was touched with regret for the splendours of the recent past. '*Brideshead* has been a success,' the author wrote in his diary soon after it was published in the spring of 1945; 'sold out in the first week and still in continual demand. Most of the reviews have been adulatory except where they were embittered by class resentment.' His only concern was that if he did not take steps to prevent it most of the money he earned would be going to the state in tax.

Mirroring the cinema, there was an appetite for history, particularly of the kind where Britain's enemies were soundly defeated. Arthur Bryant's *The Years of Victory* came out in 1944, as did G.M. Trevelyan's *English Social History*. Anthony Heap only managed to obtain a copy in October 1945 'after a wait of many months', indicating the frustrations of the book business, which had an eager audience but never enough copies.

The theatre was obviously restricted in its appeal to those who could manage to get to the West End and be there in time for the 6.30 p.m. start demanded in wartime (or as early as 5 p.m. during the worst of the V-weapon period), since transport closed down so early. The hints in the *Daily Mail* and the *Daily Express* in January 1945 that the theatre and cinema were suffering a decline in audiences might have been as much due to the quality of what was on offer as to the bombs. The V-weapons certainly do not seem to have deterred the young from going out to enjoy themselves, as Mollie Panter-Downes remarked:

The theatres and cinemas are losing the business of customers who feel that it's better to take precautions than be sorry, but the V-bombs have not affected such established sell-outs as the Lunts, who have opened at the Lyric with their usual much-admired performance in a not much-admired play called 'Love in Idleness'. The big funny-man shows starring the English comedians Tommy

Trinder and Sid Fields are also booked for weeks ahead. Even the audiences at the musicals appear to have come out dressed to meet any emergency, from bombs to a long tramp home. The women in the London theatre audience usually look as if they have come straight from their jobs. The young things who go out and dance at night get themselves up rather more festively and every dance place in London is jammed with boys and girls on leave. Dancing is having a healthy boom right now despite the menace in the stratosphere.

The wartime theatre enjoyed more success in provincial runs and, of course, CEMA brought drama to new audiences in the forces and the factories. The propaganda, morale-boosting element which worked so well in the more pliable medium of film was less apparent at the theatre. In January Daphne du Maurier's *The Years Between* at Wyndhams explored the topical problem of long separated husbands and wives. The recently formed Old Vic Repertory Company formed by Ralph Richardson, Laurence Olivier, Tyrone Guthrie and Sybil Thorndike was staging *Uncle Vanya* and John Gielgud was appearing in *A Midsummer Night's Dream* at the Haymarket Theatre. By October the keen theatre-goer Anthony Heap was reporting that 'the biggest entertainments boom ever known is in full swing' with every theatre in the West End packed out every night. But, of course, by then the war was over and the entertainments industry had fulfilled its role of boosting wartime morale.

Nothing the Ministry did actually decided the state of morale and once it recognised this, around the time Brendan Bracken became Minister, it stopped hectoring the public. Morale was really only affected by how the war was progressing. From September 1939 to May 1940 the long period of the phoney war – or 'Bore War', as it was known at the time – when there was little activity was a low point. There was a definite boost when France capitulated and everyone from the King downwards sighed with relief that now there were no allies to please. Britain would go it alone. The defeat at Dunkirk in May 1940 had been turned into a triumph, partly as a result of J.B. Priestley's *Postscripts to the News* which followed the nine o'clock News, when he paid tribute to the little boats that had courageously set out from England to rescue the remnants of the British Expeditionary Force from the beach: 'so characteristically English, so typical of us, so absurd and yet so grand and gallant, that you hardly know whether to laugh or cry when you read about them.' The following year was a low point, when there was no news of victory on any front to cheer people up and when food stocks were seriously endangered by the success of the U-boat campaign in the Atlantic.

The entry of the United States into the war in December 1941 at least meant that eventual victory was assured, although the news continued depressing, especially in the Atlantic. Montgomery's victory over Rommel at El Alamein in October 1942, when the church bells all over England rang out after three years of silence, was a high point. The defeat of the Germans at Stalingrad in February 1943 was also a boost to British spirits. After that, there was a lull and a dip in morale – output in the war factories and turnaround time in the docks slowed – until the successful invasion of Italy, when it picked up again. Ironically, just as the end of the war was in sight in the grim winter of 1944 and first three months of 1945, morale reached its lowest ebb.

On 29 December 1944 the final Home Intelligence weekly report stated that 'spirits have continued to fall in some cases considerably.' This was 'mainly due to von Rundstedt's offensive and the situation in Greece'. There had been 'shock and surprise at the success of the German counter-offensive . . . People cannot understand how we could have been taken so much by surprise – misjudging German resources of men and material.' The euphoria felt after the success of D-Day in June 1944 and the rapid advance of the Allies across France, followed avidly by listeners to the BBC's pioneering *War Report*, had led many to hope that the war might be over by

Christmas 1944. Instead, the Allies had failed to penetrate the German frontier by the end of the year and, worse, were encountering serious German resistance in the Ardennes. The war would definitely not be over by Christmas; indeed, it might drag on for another year. There was 'considerable anxiety and depression that the war will last longer than expected', the report continued, and that 'the war may not be over for a long time – even by next Christmas'. After the American breakthrough in the Ardennes and the Allied crossing of the Rhine, spirits picked up. The last months and weeks saw daily newspaper headlines along the lines of 'only 200 miles to Berlin' and 'Russians in the suburbs of Berlin', while private diaries also record the increasing excitement of this countdown to the end.

With the exception of the fall of Singapore in February 1942, arguably the biggest, most shaming capitulation in British history, morale was never seriously affected by what was going on in the war with Japan. In the middle of 1943 General Wavell complained that his troops in the Far East were depressed by the apparent lack of interest shown by the British public in their operations. After VE Day in May 1945, the Ministry of Information tried in vain to arouse any interest in the continuing war in the Far East. The apathy was hardly surprising, since it was happening in a distant part of the world, whereas for so many years the Germans had been just 20 miles across the Channel and frequently directly overhead.

The home front was the front line and what was happening there affected morale, too, although the British people never lost sight of the fact that the prime goal was to win the war, and that sacrifices made on the home front to that end were only to be expected. Hitler was badly mistaken in thinking he could break the spirit of Londoners by attacking them from the skies. Unlike smaller cities, such as Coventry or even Hamburg and Dresden, London was too large to be subjugated by bombing: if one area was knocked out, it was business as usual in the rest of the metropolis. The effect of the Blitz in 1940–41 was only to stiffen resolve. American reporters in

London, such as Ed Murrow, did much to foster the image of a brave and stoical London. Indeed, in the end it might be said that Londoners themselves began to believe the 'myth' of the Blitz and act accordingly. They were apt to complain if they felt the rest of the country was not sufficiently aware of what they were enduring and this was particularly the case during the V-weapon period, when there was official silence on the subject.

With the onslaught of the V-1s, Herbert Morrison worried that morale might falter. People were suffering badly from lack of sleep and under the constant bombardment there was no relaxation from the strain. More to the point, he told the War Cabinet: 'After five years of war the civil population were not as capable of standing the strain of attack as they had been during the winter of 1940–1. If the flying bomb attacks were supplemented by rocket attacks . . . there might be serious deterioration in the morale of the civil population.'

When the V-2s came, morale held, probably because the end of the war was in sight. A resident of Chigwell, hearing at least 20 rockets a day, might have been right, however, when he said: 'You know, if the Germans had had those things in 1940, I think we might have cracked.'

At the height of the V-2 bombardment in January and February 1945 the Government was forced to consider the possibility of reopening facilities for evacuation from London. The Senior Regional Commissioner for London maintained there was little real demand to evacuate, believing that a few requests on the part of some councillors and MPs had been magnified. Nevertheless, local authorities in the heavily bombed Romford, Leyton, Barking, Chigwell, West Ham, Dagenham and Walthamstow were pressing for the provision of free travel vouchers and billeting allowances for people of the priority classes – pregnant women, mothers of small children, children, the old and the disabled – so that they might leave. The Minister of Health agreed, but stipulated that 'no publicity is to be accorded the scheme', so as not to trigger public panic: 'Such facilities would undoubtedly provide a useful safety valve by removing from the affected areas some of the less stable elements of the population . . . The chief dangers from press publicity are the giving of encouragement to the enemy to reinforce his attacks and the depressing effect on public morale.'

In the civil histories series drawn from official papers, Richard Titmuss in his *Problems of Social Policy* maintains that aerial bombardment did not cause an increase in mental disorders or neurotic illness. Nevertheless, there came a point in the V-weapon campaign when some could stand it no longer, as a report of a suicide in the *Croydon Advertiser* illustrates:

'This war lasted too long for me; I can't go on', was the pathetic yet fateful message awaiting Mr Edward Gordon Noyce when he came home from work. Lying dead from carbon-monoxide poisoning on the sitting room floor, her mouth connected to a gas point by a rubber tube, Mr Noyce found his wife, Stella, 57. She had written little notices, 'Danger, gas on', and pinned them up in the hall. At the inquest her daughter told the Coroner her mother had been depressed by the war, and particularly by the V bombs. She was worried about her son in the RAF and suffered from headaches, giddiness, insomnia, but would not see a doctor.

The daily discomforts and inconveniences of wartime continued to affect morale, or at least to wear down a tired population, irritated that the war was dragging on so long. On the brink of the New Year, 1945, the Home Intelligence report noted that although Christmas 'has given some pleasure, rest and relief' there had also been 'widespread and bitter complaints about the price, poor quality and scarcity of toys and gifts and much grumbling over unequal food distribution'. There was comment about 'the bad distribution of turkeys, nuts and oranges', with turkeys going for ridiculously high prices on the black market and a revival 'of complaints generally about under-the-counter sales'. In a winter of freezing temperatures, people were 'anxious about the shortage, uncertain deliveries and high cost of coal and shortage of coke'. There were 'complaints about the inadequacy of the clothing coupon allowance and the poor quality, shortage and high price of footwear, especially children's'.

The last few weeks of the war saw a breakdown of the communal spirit that had been such a marked feature of the Blitz. 'The danger has gone and we are becoming individuals again,' a Kensington woman noted in March 1945, 'losing completely that communal feeling we had in the fight common to all.' With the end of the fighting, people did not see why they should make sacrifices any more and they were making their disenchantment felt. As Mrs Bell of Mortlake recalled: 'The mood of the people was changing, they were no longer polite, snappy, irritable, some downright rude.'

Far more critical for morale were the larger questions of post-war housing and employment. There were bitter complaints about the current shortage and high price of accommodation in the capital and widespread fears about the future. 'Workers continue anxious about redundancy in the war factories.' Redundancy was recognised as a new name for unemployment and they dreaded it, as wartime industry was dismantled and peacetime industry was slow to follow. Men feared that women, who had invaded the workplace during the wartime emergency, were there to stay. Workers were apparently saying, 'We well remember the savage reductions we suffered after the last war and we are getting ready for the fight; we won't readily surrender any progress we have made during this war.'

It is interesting that there was evidently so much cynicism about the post-war world, when for some time the Government had been holding out the prospect of an improvement in social conditions as a morale-boosting incentive. One of the reasons that morale was so low during the first months of the war was that Chamberlain's Government steadfastly refused to state what Britain's war aims were supposed to be. His successor Winston Churchill was always more interested in the grand strategy of the war than he was in the home front, despite the pleas of the first three Ministers of Information – Lord Macmillan, Sir John Reith and Duff Cooper – to set some agenda of Britain's war aims. Churchill's declared aim that Britain was fighting for 'Victory, victory at all costs' was apparently not enough. They felt that unless the Government made a firm pledge of post-war social reform the people would not be persuaded to give all their energies to the war effort. It was only with the launch of the German offensive against Russia and the receding of the invasion threat that Churchill's Government was free to pay some attention to the question, 'What are we fighting for?' although Churchill himself seems to have been reluctant to offer any hostages to fortune.

The concepts of freedom and individuality were constantly stressed, as was the fact that under the Nazi regime, the state encouraged children to betray their parents. But perhaps something more tangible was required than these theoretical reasons for war and sacrifice. The working class had to be disabused of the notion that they would be no worse off under the Germans. They had to be assured of a better world if only they employed all their efforts to defeating the enemy. In September 1942 the Army Bureau of Current Affairs launched a new propaganda campaign: 'Your Britain – Fight for it Now'. The war had shown that conditions could be improved if the state was willing: it seemed there was an enormous amount that the state could do when it was in its interests to do it. The war had done much to break down class barriers and to arouse the middle-class conscience to the plight of the poor. Only when confronted by the dire state of child evacuees from the slums of the East End did the rest of society appreciate the appalling conditions in which so many of their fellow countrymen were living.

As George Orwell expressed it in *The Lion and the Unicorn*, 'We cannot win the war without introducing Socialism, nor establish Socialism without winning the war.' The Beveridge Report in 1942 recommended comprehensive social insurance and the elimination of the five giant evils of want, squalor, greed, poverty and disease. It became a bestseller and Home Intelligence noted that it was 'the most discussed topic in recent times'. Yet the Ministry declined to give the report any further publicity. R.A. Butler's report culminating in the Education Act of 1944 raised the school leaving age to 15 and promised secondary education for all, although a Wartime Social Survey indicated a certain amount of indifference to these changes, probably because the public was already disillusioned about the silence surrounding the Beveridge report.

From October 1944 the BBC, on its own initiative, attempted to dispel the gloom in *The Friday Discussions*, to help listeners decide what they wanted from the post-war world. The official silence on post-war reform continued, which probably accounts for the fact that Home Intelligence reports revealed widespread scepticism about the likelihood of the Government actually delivering on its promises. Taking its cue from the current Government's equivocal attitude, the people no doubt reasoned that wartime plans for social reform were probably more to do with bribery than idealism. But they would not be cheated this time: the massive landslide victory of Labour in the General Election in July 1945 ensured they would have their reward.

Throughout the war, the Ministry of Information had to manage propaganda regarding Britain's allies as well as its enemies. Ironically, it had more trouble maintaining good relations between the British and their English-speaking, democratic American cousins than it did between the British and communist Russia.

In contrast to their scorn for America, so slow to join the fighting, the British people were enormously impressed by Russian fortitude and the advances the Soviet army was making against the Germans. Churchill loathed communism, but reasoned after the German invasion of Russia in June 1941 that 'if Hitler invaded Hell I would make at least a favourable reference to the Devil in the House of Commons'. However, there was a brief hiccup when the Government could not bring itself to allow the 'Internationale' to be played on the BBC, along with all the other national anthems of the Allies on Sunday nights prior to the nine o'clock News. The Russian ambassador in London, Ivan Maisky, was impervious to Duff Cooper's argument that to call the 'Internationale' a national anthem was a contradiction in terms and refused to substitute it with some other Russian music. After six months the Government had to climb down. The challenge for the Ministry was to praise the new Russian ally while giving no lip service to communism and denying British communists any reflected glory from the Soviet war effort.

The Ministry established an Anglo-Soviet liaison section and was responsible for arranging exhibitions on all aspects of Russian life, except the political, to extol Britain's new ally and to feed the British appetite for all things Russian. Publishers were encouraged to bring out translations of Russian literature and the BBC broadcast programmes with a Russian content and Russian music. Russian films described their war effort and in a final compliment a poster with the sort of heroic socialist realism so typical of Soviet propaganda encouraged British women to emulate their Russian sisters and come into the war factories, while another plainly told them to cover their hair for safety as 'Your Russian Sister Does!'. The Ministry's efforts were motivated less by altruism than a determination to prevent the British Communist Party seizing the initiative and seducing the British people into joining it. It would be counter-productive to organise direct anti-communist propaganda, however: all the Ministry could do was continually stress the benefits of indi-vidual liberty and freedom of choice. At the same time, any criticism of Stalin and his regime was suppressed and the Ministry went so far as to advise George Orwell's publishers not to publish *Animal Farm*. Victor Gollancz did not want it anyway, but it was eventually published by Secker & Warburg in August 1945, by which time Anglo-Soviet relations had turned distinctly frosty.

The Ministry was to be responsible through its American Forces Liaison Division for smoothing relations between British hosts and American servicemen, who started to arrive in Britain in 1942. There was already a history of resentment and sore feeling because the Americans had been so slow to enter the war, although President Roosevelt himself was seen as a true friend of Britain. Everyone appreciated that his Lend-Lease programme had provided a life-line when Britain was at its most desperate. The entry of America into the war was greeted with joy and relief, although Home Intelligence also reported 'a malicious delight' that at long last the mighty isolationist would now have a taste of war.

In contrast to the Russian ally, who was far away and out of sight and therefore more likely to be mythologised, America was all too familiar, at least from the perspective of Hollywood movies and the common language, and soon from the presence of 1,500,000 American servicemen in Britain – many of whom spent their leave in London, even if they were not actually based in the capital. Consequently, Home Intelligence reported that 'America is not really regarded as a foreign country, to be wooed with praise, but as a close relative to be chided freely for her shortcomings.' Concerted efforts were made by the Ministry to depict the new ally in a sympathetic light, and the American ambassador in London, John Winant, introduced a series of talks on the BBC, *Let's Get Acquainted*, to prepare the way for arrival of the US troops.

There would inevitably be friction that this late-comer was to be the senior partner. There would be cultural clashes, not least over the thousands of coloured troops unleashed on a Britain where – with the exception of parts of London, where black people had been part of the scene for 400 years – black faces were unfamiliar. The British Government was fearful of the public response and in particular worried about fraternisation between British women and black troops, but Brendan Bracken refused to initiate a campaign to deal with the problem of coloured troops. As it turned out, the black GIs won much sympathy from the British people, and problems usually arose only because the British objected to the segregation imposed by the white GIs on their coloured colleagues. The British people took the view that since the black GIs had come 3,000 miles to help them win the war, they saw no reason to distinguish between them and white Americans. No discrimination was exercised by the British authorities and the Ministry's regional officers often had to liaise with the American commanding officers to dispel tension or explain Britain's non-discriminatory policy.

The Ministry arranged for a film, *Welcome to Britain*, to be made by the Strand Film Company and shown to American servicemen. Booklets provided by the United States War Department, such as *Over There: Instructions for American Servicemen in Britain, 1942*, helped a great deal. We may gauge from its suggestions some of the pitfalls before the visiting Americans and no doubt some of the *faux pas* some of them were making. 'It is always impolite to criticize your host; it is militarily stupid to criticize your allies,' they were told. They must avoid falling into the trap of boasting 'that America won the last war or make wise-cracks about the war debts or about British defeats in this war', since 'Nazi propaganda now is pounding away day and night asking the British people why they should fight "to save Uncle Shylock and his silver dollar". Don't play into Hitler's hands by mentioning war debts.' They were warned not to brag, show off, or throw their weight about. A potential source of friction was that 'You are higher paid than the British Tommy. Don't rub it in. Play fair with him. He can be a pal in need.' Of course, the well-built, ebullient Americans with their superior uniforms and free spending inevitably attracted British girls. There was a particular danger that the morale of British troops serving overseas would be affected by the knowledge that back home their women were cavorting with Americans.

Working closely with their British counterparts in the Ministry, the American censors produced a number of directives affecting American troops serving in Britain. British editors were often asked to suppress news – such as the details of a disturbance between GIs and locals in a pub – that had no security significance, but which might have a detrimental effect on relations between the two main Allies.

The Americans were greeted with excitement and curiosity; they were fun and enormously generous to British children.

Generally, they were liked and appreciated, especially after D-Day, when their troops actually went into action. At the beginning of 1945 a Home Intelligence report touched on the current state of opinion about US troops in Britain and the sort of niggling little differences that affected relations between the Allies: 'People praise the Americans' fighting qualities, their good and polite behaviour (there's a realisation that bad behaviour is confined to a conspicuous few), and the entertainments they have planned for children. However, they are boisterous, drive too fast and waste petrol, and have better pay and living conditions than our boys. A lorry takes them back from a dance, whereas our boys have to leave early and queue for a bus.'

Some Londoners – men, anyway – could not wait to see the back of the Americans, as Anthony Heap sourly noted in his diary at the beginning of April: 'One of the things I most look forward to after the war is the prospect of seeing fewer and fewer – and eventually I hope no more – seedy, sex-crazed American soldiers sloppily slouching along the streets, clutching, as often as not, the crimson-nailed paws of the common little sluts, for whom "Yankin" has become a full-time occupation.'

Whatever people might think of the American servicemen in their midst, there was enormous shock and grief at the death of President Roosevelt. An American in London, Mollie Panter-Downes, noted the reaction to his death:

Because the British have been prepared for the last few weeks to receive the good news which obviously nothing could spoil, the bad news knocked them sideways. President Roosevelt's death came as a stupefying shock, even to those Britons whose ideas of the peace do not run much beyond the purely personal ones of getting their children home again, a roof back over their heads, a little car back on the road, and plenty of consumer goods in the shops. To the more internationally minded, the news seemed a crushing disaster. People stood in the streets staring blankly at the first incredible newspaper headlines which appeared to have suddenly remodelled the architecture of the world. They queued up patiently for succeeding editions as if they hoped that something would be added to the first bald facts to make them more bearable. The flags hung limply at half-mast along Whitehall, where knots of lugubrious people gathered at the entrance of Downing Street, hoping for a glimpse of Mr Churchill as he came back from adjourning the House of Commons' business of the day.

A woman who worked at the Central Telegraph Office near St Paul's was one of thousands who expressed her feelings in her diary on 14 April: 'Terribly shocked to hear this morning of the death of President Roosevelt. Can hardly believe this to be true . . . Everyone is very grieved – he was one of the best ever – Winston will feel this – they were such buddies. All the papers speak so highly of him and what he did for Britain.'

A typical Cockney comment was picked up by Mass-Observation: 'I went all cold, as if I'd lost a friend I'd known for years and years . . . shame, isn't it? He was a fine man, a proper gentleman if ever there was one. I don't know where we'd be if it wasn't for Roosevelt sending us food and munitions on that Lend-Lease plan.'

There was heartfelt regret that Roosevelt, who had done so much to achieve the Allied victory, had not lived to see the peace. Anthony Weymouth noted in his diary: 'People are saying that it is pathetic he shouldn't have lived to see Germany completely defeated, but I look at it another way. He lived long enough to see the plans (for which he was so largely responsible) to liberate the world from German aggression bear fruit. He must have known it was only a matter of months or even weeks before the war in Europe at any rate came to a victorious end.'

The first shocked response was that, at this juncture, Mr Churchill could have been better spared than Roosevelt. The Prime Minister's supreme task had been to steer Britain through the war, and this he had done. But it was felt that Roosevelt was crucial for the forging of the post-war world. Many people elected to cancel whatever plans they had to go out that Friday night and stayed at home quietly, perhaps remembering those dark days of the war when the only note of cheer was Mr Roosevelt's voice on the radio.

Only a week after the memorial service of Britain's former Prime Minister in the previous war, Earl Lloyd-George, at Westminster Abbey, there was a memorial service for the American President on 17 April at St Paul's. A London evening newspaper's headline disclosed, 'Churchill in Tears in Roosevelt Service' – perhaps an early example of press intrusion.

Just as it was essential for the Ministry to paint Britain's allies in a good light, it had to decide how to vilify the enemy. A campaign of atrocity stories, such as that in the First World War, was clearly not going to work. The public was more sophisticated than that and the jingoism that had been so pervasive in the earlier war was lacking in this one. In the early days of the Second World War, when the Chamberlain Government was still in power, a distinction was made between the Nazi regime and the German people, but this had long since faded. The broadcasts of Lord Vansittart, the former diplomat and fierce denouncer of Nazism since 1936, and the publication of his *Black Record*, claiming that the Germans had from the earliest times always been violent and aggressive and must be squashed once and for all, were widely discussed, if not accepted. The V-weapons revived anti-German feelings: they were so patently just a vicious attack on defenceless civilians, with no military benefit, even though at the time Bomber Command, in the Dresden raid and others, was wreaking even worse atrocities on German civilians.

By the spring of 1945 popular opinion had hardened against the Germans, who seemed to be needlessly prolonging the war instead of accepting their inevitable defeat. The BBC took a positive stance, producing a series of discussion programmes about the future of Germany. A *Listener* leader in February 1945 appealed to the British to show some pity and to concentrate on laying the foundations of a lasting peace. Newspapers such as London's *Evening Standard* were inviting readers' suggestions as to how the Germans should be treated. A vicar from Enfield, who had obviously imbibed Vansittart's philosophy, was uncompromising in his hostility:

How shall we treat the Hun? The first step is to recognise the German character is essentially brutal and understands only force. For fifteen hundred years the Hun, to give him his proper title, has been a menace to his neighbours . . . and one is driven to the conclusion that God will Himself intervene and by some natural calamity obliterate such parts of Germany as may render her for ever afterwards impotent to be a menace to the world.

The British Government had long been aware of the concentration camps and there had been mentions of them in the press. In the course of the war, survivors who had witnessed and escaped the Nazi regime were given airtime on the BBC. It had been decided not to use the knowledge of the camps as a weapon in the propaganda war against Germany, however, because anti-Semitism was so common, particularly in London's East End, where Home Intelligence reports frequently noted there were accusations that the Jews were always bagging the best places in the tube shelters or avoiding conscription or were heavily involved in the black market. Needless to say, popular rumour was blaming the Jews, quite erroneously, for the Bethnal Green tube shelter disaster of 1943. It was felt that to draw the public's attention to the plight of the Jews in occupied Europe would only serve to incite further anti-Semitism at home. But the publication of the photographs and press reports on the liberation of the camps by the Allied armies showed the full horror for the first time and generated feelings of revulsion and disgust directed against the German perpetrators. As Mollie Panter-Downes noted in her journal:

It has taken the camera to bring home to the slow, good-natured, sceptical British what, as various liberal journals have tartly pointed out, the pens of their correspondents have been unsuccessfully trying to bring home to them since as far back as 1933. Millions of comfortable families, too kind and lazy in those days to make the effort to believe what they conveniently looked upon as a news-

The great edifice of St Paul's stands surrounded by the devastation of the City of London. The cathedral owed its survival to sheer good fortune, to its surveyor with his unrivalled knowledge of the building and to the selfless courage of its volunteer fire watch. It could not have withstood a direct hit from a V-2, but none fell close enough to do more than shake the structure and shatter the remaining windows.

Under the v-weapon onslaught dense Victorian back-to-back housing of flimsy construction, such as this example in working-class Islington, collapsed like packs of cards. Street surface shelters stood up surprisingly well.

Casualties would be covered in mortar dust and grime, which had an ageing effect. It meant that the dead were often unrecognisable to their next of kin.

ogs, preferably two working together the better to sniff a casualty from different
rections, were useful in indicating the exact location of bodies beneath the debris.

ver on hand to dole out tea and sympathy, the Women's Voluntary Service was present in
ome capacity at every 'incident'. Here rescue workers stop for a quick 'cuppa'.

Above From the roof of St Paul's, a trail of devastation can be seen all the way to Tower Bridge and beyond.

Left The facilities in the London Underground shelters had improved enormously since the Blitz. After the onset of the v-weapon attacks in the summer of 1944 a series of deep, bomb-proof shelters beneath some of the tube stations were opened to the public. Admission was by ticket only.

Above After an 'incident', households might be without water, gas or electricity for days. Here the Church Army is doing an invaluable service providing women and children with hot drinks and snacks. The little boys perched on the rubble are all too familiar with it – it has become their playground.

Below One of the worst v-2 attacks came on the morning of 8 March 1945 at Smithfield Market. Word had spread that a consignment of rabbits had come in, so that the market was unusually crowded. Hundreds of casualties had to be located and retrieved from mountains of rubble after the ground had collapsed into the underground railway below. The process of identification took several days.

At 7.21 on the morning of 27 March 1945 the residents of Hughes Mansions, a trio of local authority flats in heavily bombed Stepney, were just getting out of bed or having breakfast when a V-2 scored a direct hit on the middle block, completely demolishing it and severely damaging the other two. As in many such 'incidents' bodies were hurled through the air and found on the rooftops of nearby buildings. A distraught widower was said to return to the scene calling out for his wife, who had just popped out for some bread rolls and was caught in the impact as she returned.

Rescue workers usually came from the building industry, as they had to have an understanding of how a structure was likely to react under the eccentric stresses and strains following bomb damage. It took these heroic men hours of patient, painstaking work to pick their way carefully through the debris, sometimes with escaping gas or rising water threatening to engulf them, to retrieve casualties.

paper propaganda stunt, now believe the horrifying, irrefutable evidence that even blurred printing on poor wartime paper has made all too clear. The shock to the public has been enormous, and lots of hitherto moderate people are wondering uncomfortably whether they will agree, after all, with Lord Vansittart's ruthless views on a hard peace.

Vere Hodgson was one of those who felt the German people as a whole must take the blame: 'It is no use the German people saying they did not do it. They are all guilty, because they allowed such people to come to power and cheered them when they were winning. Now they disown their acts. Naturally. They are losing. That is the German all over.'

The *Daily Express* staged an exhibition of photographs of the camps at Trafalgar Square on 1 May 1945, under the sign 'Seeing Is Believing'. Londoners filed past in horrified silence. A more comprehensive exhibition was being held at the *Daily Express* reading room in Regent Street. Visitors were interviewed on the way out and left no doubt that the evidence of their own eyes had removed the last vestiges of sympathy for the Germans: 'After seeing the exhibition I feel we ought to shoot every German. There's not a good one amongst them.'

'Dreadful. They should show it to the whole world so that such cruelty will never be forgotten; every man, woman and child should see it, it would give them some idea of the rottenness of the German race.'

On the BBC Edward Murrow described Buchenwald and Richard Dimbleby Belsen in a 14-minute despatch for *War Report*, graphically but in measured tones. The cinemas and news cinemas, such as Studio Two at Oxford Circus which always drew huge queues, were also showing newsreels of the camps. In some cases, women were crying or leaving rather than look at them. An anonymous diarist in Kensington felt it was her duty to see the scenes of the concentration camps, but warned her mother not to go. 'What I thought was, if we had not won, these things would have happened here and anywhere in the Nazi world.'

The State Cinema at Kilburn High Road proclaimed: 'Scenes of unbelievable Nazi atrocities at Buchenwald and Belsen. See Them – Lest You Forget.' One customer emerged saying, 'I feel we could have prevented a lot of it. I feel our Government must have known all about it. I don't think we could ever be hard enough on the Germans; their behaviour is more like animals. Why, savages wouldn't behave that way, yet the Germans are supposed to be a highly cultured race.'

Someone else expressed a more thoughtful view:

It made me feel pretty sick, but somehow I feel too much is being made of it. So much commentary – I mean, it makes you wonder what they're up to . . . I'm afraid it doesn't make me feel anti-German, it makes me feel anti-humanity; that man could do such a thing to man. Would the same have happened here, I wonder, if we'd had the same government? I've heard some violent anti-Semitic talk which makes me think it would. I feel it's the fault of humanity at large, not the Germans in particular.

The British people – even Londoners, who had suffered so much – were not vengeful. They only wanted a guarantee that the peace terms would render Germany harmless in the future. They did not want to 'do the job' a third time. However, the revulsion felt at the evidence of the camps, coming as it did on top of a period of intense V-2 activity, hardened hearts. Mollie Panter-Downes continues: 'If, as some people think, the sudden piling on of the horrors is an attempt to prepare the British and American publics for the stiff terms Moscow seems determined to impose on Germany, it has certainly succeeded here. Whatever the Russians ask, it will not be enough to wipe Buchenwald and the rest from shocked British minds.'

Contrary to popular suspicion, there does not seem to have been a Ministry brief to harden opinion against the Germans. The BBC ended the war pleading for restraint towards the German people, as exemplified in a broadcast by Patrick Gordon Walker, formerly of the BBC's German Service and, in 1945, elected to Parliament as the Member for Smethwick.

In *Belsen: Facts and Thoughts* he described in graphic detail the scenes he witnessed after the liberation of the camp and argued:

The world can and must, in a tremendous act of justice, stamp out this horror, and punish the guilty. But may I add this? I have seen these things myself and perhaps because I have I am convinced that vengeance must not be indiscriminate. We must not punish the innocent and the guilty alike . . . I mean that if we do not discriminate in our vengeance we shall be doing what the SS would have wanted us to do, namely as they did, to destroy the respect for human life. We want to restore it.

The anonymous Kensington diarist who was horrified by the newsreels of the concentration camps was also shocked when she viewed the newsreel of devastation of German cities wrought by the British and American air attacks. ' "It's awful," I whispered in the dark to my friend. "Yes", she murmured back, "but if we had not done it, it would have happened here." '

The British public had been well aware that Bomber Command's campaign was directed at civilians as much as it was against military and industrial targets and, if anything, morale was sustained by the knowledge that the Allies were dealing out to the Germans rather more than the Germans were to Britain. On 11 April Mollie Panter-Downes noted:

The first photographs that really show the results of Allied strategic bombing in Germany have just been released here, and they have further convinced Britons that the Reich's days are numbered. Londoners, who have had plenty of experience in calculating piles of rubble in terms of human misery, are apt to whistle incredulously at the shots of Cologne street scenes. The evidence of what the enemy is trying to withstand makes it easier for people here to accept the latest crop of V-bombs and the sudden return of piloted bombers in a series of small and apparently merely vindictive attacks. The bomber raids were the first of the kind on England since last June, and many people had got so accustomed to being bombed by robots that the idea of being bombed in the old-fashioned way seemed almost as strange as a Jules Verne fantasy.

It was Churchill himself who expressed some concern after the destruction of Dresden in February 1945, namely that the Allies would be taking possession of a ruined land.

The debate on how to treat the vanquished continued throughout the year, with the former Tory MP Harold Nicolson pleading in the *Spectator* in September for Britain to exercise clemency in occupied Germany:

How can we hope to re-educate Germany if we behave to the Germans exactly as the Nazis have behaved in the territories which they occupied? If, on the other hand, we are prepared ourselves to make further sacrifices in order to diminish, if only by a small proportion, the coming death-rate in Germany, then we can in all sincerity claim that we practise Christian principles as well as preach them . . . I am suggesting only that, within the measure of the possible, German displaced persons should not be allowed to starve. There are those who sincerely believe that all Germans are evil and deserve terrible punishment . . . I know that the vast majority of Germans, although prone to inhumanity and devoid of political intelligence, are capable under wise government of great domestic and civic virtues. The re-education of Germany can never be effected by precept; only by example, and if the example we give them is one of indifference to human misery, then indeed we shall have failed in our opportunity.

Never before had the Government involved itself so much in the lives of the people or gained such a thorough knowledge of the conditions in which they lived. During the war the Government had been forced to care for their condition, since their well-being and productivity were essential for victory. Through the work of the Ministry and coinciding with the wartime social revolution, the Government had learned to replace patronage and fear with trust and respect for the people. The knowledge the Ministry gained through its various intelligence-gathering bodies to maintain morale during the war had provided insights on subjects that transcended the wartime emergency – housing, the national diet, transport, education, social welfare, working conditions – which would be useful for the enormous task of post-war reconstruction. The downside was greater interference by the state in people's lives, although after nearly six years of war the British people had become inured to increased bureaucracy. With the coming of peace, it was appropriate that the Ministry, shorn of its censorship powers and executive authority, evolved into the Central Office of Information, working for succeeding governments as a research and information service. Its wartime achievement, liaising with Whitehall, Westminster and the people, had perhaps been to show that a frank and open relationship between Government and people was not only possible, but also the most productive.

3
Shelter

'If your house is damaged tell your Air Raid Warden. Get
Form C1 from the local council or from the regional officer
of the War Damage Commission and send it to that officer
within 30 days of the damage occurring'
                    – ARP at Home: Hints for Housewives

On the afternoon of 9 January Gwladys Cox and her husband
decided to brave the freezing temperatures to take a walk
round the neighbourhood. After all, with the fuel shortages
and several of their windows broken, it was not as if it was
so warm and comfortable indoors as would make much difference. She was probably curious to trace the source of
yesterday's explosion: Hampstead's first V-2 had exploded at
4.16 in the afternoon on the railway embankment between
West End Lane and Kilburn High Road. Before long they stumbled on a pitiful but all too common sight:

After lunch, it stopped snowing, and as the air was invigorating,
we walked, or slithered in the slush, down to Iverson Road. Here,
rows and rows of small houses had been blasted from back to
front; doors, windows, ceilings all gone. Whole families were out
in the street standing beside the remains of their possessions, piled
on the pavements waiting for the removal vans; heaps of rubble
everywhere, pathetically showing bits of holly and Christmas
decorations.

The reason they were standing about in the cold – probably unwashed, their bodies and clothes covered in white
mortar dust and filth, tired, shocked and upset – was not just
that they were waiting for the removal vans. The bombed out

did not dare leave the site of their ruined homes, in case the looters moved in. By rights, the police should have been guarding against this, but of course they could not be everywhere at once, and the Home Guard was no longer available to deter looters. After an incident it was comforting for the victims of air attack to pick through the rubble to rescue any memento of their former lives, no matter how small or insignificant. But these people, or rather the rescue squads working at the incident, had obviously managed to salvage quite a few possessions from the wreckage. The owners could not afford to let them out of their sight until the council removal men came to take them into the local storage depot. It might be a while before they showed up, because the manpower and vehicles to do the job were desperately overstretched – so much so that the NFS, Civil Defence, the RAF, the army and even the US army were being asked to lend a hand.

At an incident scrupulous care was taken to safeguard valuables, so that they could eventually be returned to their rightful owners. Money, silver, jewellery and any other valuables recovered by wardens, rescue workers or demolition men were to be handed to the Incident Officer or the leader of the working party and from him to the police, in exchange for a receipt. They were then passed to the borough treasurer at the Town Hall, where they were listed and checked by two members of staff, before being placed in a store or strong room. The owners could claim them upon showing proof of identity and ownership. If the owners had been killed, the next of kin might claim them, but only on production of a will proven to be valid.

The Reverend Markham, working in Walworth, knew how essential it was to secure valuables from the debris before the looters arrived. In wartime, people tended to keep all their most important possessions – cash, documents such as marriage and insurance certificates, ration books and clothing coupons, as well as jewellery – in their handbags or in a bag ready to pick up in a hurry. 'As soon as it was daylight,' he recalled, 'I used to take two of my wardens, and tunnel through mountains of rubble to find these handbags. We dare not leave them even for a few hours, or they would be gone.' The borough treasurer's men also needed to be on the scene quickly to empty gas and electric meters, or else they too would be rifled within hours.

If a house was badly damaged but still just about habitable, the occupants preferred to stay there, rather than leave it to the mercy of looters. Stephen Woodcock, a civil engineer living in Kensington who did some ARP work, remembers such a family in Finchley: 'The house was badly blasted – roof damaged and all internal walls gone, and glass splinters sticking into the walls and woodwork, and all doors and windows gone. They themselves were not hurt. Her mother refused to leave the house, for fear of looting, and they slept in the only secure room. It was bitterly cold weather, followed by heavy rain, which made the house a muddy wreck.'

James Lees-Milne encountered a similar case:

Mrs P. went at luncheon time to see our bombed charwoman in Battersea. She was shocked by the condition of her house. No ceilings, or rather no plaster left to them, no glass, no light, and dirt and dust indescribable. No doors fitting and woodwork torn off. Mrs Beckwith dares not leave the house for fear of looters. Mrs P. said she did not understand how humans could live in such conditions. And the borough says it can do nothing for Mrs P. because she is lucky to have a roof over her head.

To add to the misery, people living in damaged houses in the immediate aftermath of an incident would often be without water, gas or electricity. At the incident itself, the Queen's Messenger Convoys – purchased with funds from the United States and dominion and colonial organisations – the WVS and various charities would be on hand to provide tea, sandwiches and cakes from mobile canteens: during the V-2 period the Salvation Army alone provided over 292,500 refreshments and their canteens went out on 360 occasions. These refreshments were free for the first 48 hours after an incident, but voluntary contributions were invited. They could only be a temporary stop-gap; what these people needed were regular hot meals and here the LCC's emergency Londoners' Meals Service stepped in, delivering hot meals on payment at the doorstep to the occupants of damaged homes. Those who felt able to leave home briefly might repair to their local self-service British Restaurant, where a good three-course meal was available for 11d. Similarly, mobile bath units and laundries parked outside in the street enabled the inhabitants to wash and do the washing – more than ever essential, since the blast caused so much dust and dirt, leaving every item of clothing in need of a wash. The soap company Lever Brothers led the way in introducing mobile laundries with their own generators, which operated two domestic washing machines, rinsing apparatus and an electric drier on a lorry.

For the bombed out the local rest centre was often the first step on the road to rehabilitation. Not everyone resorted to a rest centre, of course, but during the worst of the V-1 offensive in the summer months of 1944 as many as 64,121 were admitted to London's rest centres, the highest number on any given night being 10,129 on 3 July. Altogether, there was accommodation for 35,000 at a time across 153 centres, often located in school buildings. During the period from December 1944 to March 1945, 8,307 bombed-out people were admitted, the centres in the eastern boroughs of Bethnal Green, Islington and St Pancras being the busiest. There were a handful of Jewish rest centres in Stoke Newington and Stepney, where Yiddish was spoken and kosher food provided. Almost every rest centre was damaged by blast from flying bombs and rockets, but only four were destroyed, two of them by rockets on 17 and 28 March 1945, killing five members of staff.

At an incident, the homeless were counted and the information passed on to the local authority report centre for transmission to the billeting officer, whose job it was to arrange for their transfer to the rest centre: the Incident Officer could not send people on to the rest centre until authorised to do so. London's rest centres, under the aegis of either the LCC or the MCC but ultimately funded by the Government, were open only to people made homeless as a result of enemy action and who were unable to make any alternative arrangements for their accommodation. Board and lodging were free of charge. A great deal of progress had been made since the early days of the war, when rest centres were overcrowded and lacking adequate facilities and the bombed out were treated like 'public assistance' cases: pre-war planning had assumed that aerial attack would leave thousands dead, it had not envisaged thousands homeless.

Now every effort was made by the rest centre staff (often schoolteachers who were unemployed while their pupils were evacuated to the country, receiving pay in line with Civil Defence rates), voluntary helpers, nurses and social workers to ensure that they were welcomed with kindness; after their trauma, they needed to be given sympathy, comfort and a sense of security. Rest centres were encouraged to be in competitive mode, vying with each other to provide the best facilities and most attractive surroundings, while the LCC arranged for ENSA (Entertainment National Service Association) to entertain the occupants.

The war brought social workers into the Government orbit for the first time, initially helping children under the evacuation scheme, but then the homeless in the rest centres. Working for the Ministry of Health, who had responsibility for the welfare of the homeless through the local authorities, social workers – or welfare inspectors, as they came to be called – were to manage the difficult rehousing cases arising in the rest centres, shelters and elsewhere. People abusing the system by refusing offers of suitable accommodation could be evicted, but only after consultation among various officials. Liaison between the welfare officer and the borough's billeting officer responsible for rehousing was essential: this was the best way to focus on individual needs and to ensure that the rest centres did not become 'dammed up': that there was a smooth flow of homeless in and out of their doors.

It was quite likely that all personal documents, cash, clothing, furniture and household goods had been lost in the incident; although the early wartime leaflet, *ARP at Home: Hints for Housewives*, advised people to pack a suitcase of spare clothing and leave it at a friend's house in another part of town, probably this advice had been largely ignored. At the rest centre the WVS was on hand to provide some essential clothing, very often from generous donations made by Canada and the United States in their 'Bundles to Britain' drive, but also financed by the Lord Mayor's Air Raid Distress Fund; a full wardrobe would not be forthcoming, but at least enough to enable the person to go to work next day. Grants were obtainable to replace clothes, spectacles, false teeth (they were very common in an age when so many had their teeth removed in their twenties, either because they were already rotten or to save on anticipated dental bills), furniture and tools essential to the person's work. A sum in cash was offered for immediate needs. When Frances Faviell received hers, she looked at in disbelief, never before having obtained money without actually earning it. 'It's all right,' she was told, 'it'll come off your War Damage claim, it's not charity.'

If they had lost them in the incident, the bombed out would have to apply for replacement National Registration identity cards, ration books and clothing coupons. The National Registration card, containing the holder's name, address and National Registration number, was supposed to be carried at all times and produced for police inspection on demand. Replacement documents could be organised through visits of the relevant officials to the rest centre, unlike in the early days of the war when the dispossessed would have to trudge from office to office and queue to apply for new ration books, cash advances and war damage compensation, to arrange the removal and storage of furniture, the reconnection of water, gas and electricity supplies and to inquire about evacuation. Now, the facilities for all this were available at the rest centre.

The thousands of Londoners who did not resort to a rest centre after they were bombed out still had the same problems to confront. Help was at hand. There was a choice of two main bodies to approach. The Citizens' Advice Bureaux were voluntary organisations, run in central London by the Charity Organisation Society (later known as the Family Welfare Association) and in other London areas by the London Council of Social Service: such was the burden they carried through the stresses of five long years of war and the many questions they had to answer arising from complex and unfamiliar wartime bureaucracy that they received up to half their funding from the Government.

Alternatively, there were the local bureaux of information established since the Blitz by every borough or district council. The foremost of these was at 71 Park Lane. These information services offered advice on such questions as how to claim compensation for damage and removals, what to do about hire purchase on furniture that had been destroyed, how to obtain grants for lost clothing and other goods, how to apply at the local branch of the Ministry of Pensions for an injury allowance or for a pension for the dependents of men who had been killed. They speeded up the process of resettlement by directing people to sources of assistance and by helping them to help themselves. The sooner they were settled, the sooner they could return to essential work.

The leaflet *After the Raid*, which was frequently updated, advised tenants that they should serve a 'Notice of Disclaimer' under the Landlord and Tenant (War Damage) Act, 1939, on their landlord, if they did not wish to continue to pay rent for a house that had been destroyed or damaged. Householders who had suffered damage to their property were advised to make a claim immediately, or at least within 30 days, on Form C1, obtainable from the District Valuer's Office, which was generally in the Town Hall or council offices, for compensation for damage to houses. For furniture and other belongings they should complete either form PCS3 or PCS4: the former was for those who had an insurance policy under the War Damage Act and was obtainable from an agent of the insurance company; the latter was for those who were uninsured and could be obtained from the Town Hall or Customs and Excise.

Home ownership among the middle classes and skilled manual workers had increased with the building boom of relatively cheap, suburban housing between the wars, although private renting was still the most common form of tenure. For owners whose houses were destroyed or damaged there was compensation and for those who had a mortgage the loss of that home was not quite as complicated as it might be. Before the war Lloyds had made its position clear that it would not accept insurance against war risks to property, thereby following the position taken for many years by the insurance companies. The Government would have to foot the bill. In 1940 the War Damage Commission was established, charged with the duty of making payments in respect of damage to land and buildings by enemy action, and for the collection by the Inland Revenue of war damage contributions from owners of property. This was not an insurance scheme, as compensation and contributions could not be related as they were in ordinary insurance. Owners were rather surprised to find that their contributions did not cease automatically with the end of the war.

The Commission's headquarters were at Devonshire House, Piccadilly, but there were four London offices at Acton, Kingston, Clifton House in Euston Road and Leadenhall Street in the City. During the summer of 1944 the V-1 generated 69,000 claims and by the end of May 1945 this figure had climbed to 1 million claims. The precious files of these four London offices, along with sufficient staff to create a working unit, were moved to a place of greater safety on the outskirts of Leeds.

The War Damage Commission would pay either the cost incurred in the repair of war damage, or if it was uneconomic to repair the property, a value payment on the basis of its value on 31 March 1939. An owner might opt for a hybrid payment: costs to cover a proportion of the repairs, as well as a value payment on damage he did not wish to repair immediately – for instance, it would be madness to reconstruct a conservatory before the cessation of hostilities. Value payments were to be made at some future date to be specified by the Treasury, except where the claimant needed alternative accommodation for either his home or place of business, in which case an advance up to a maximum of £800 would be immediately forthcoming. For those who had a mortgage outstanding on a ruined property, this advance had in the first instance to be used to repay the original mortgage. It was done on the understanding that the mortgagee was willing to renew the mortgage for the property to be acquired in substitution for the former property – a general arrangement to which the Building Societies Association had readily acquiesced. For those in line for value payments, there would be a long wait. Not until November 1947 was the Treasury to pay out the first £88,684,000 in respect of 101,600 properties – a very small proportion of the number destroyed or damaged in London.

The amount of value payment or payment of cost of works would be reduced accordingly if the owner failed to take reasonable steps to preserve his property from deterioration following war damage. Properties left unoccupied or unprotected after bombing sometimes became the hunting ground of looters who removed lead, floors, doors, mantelpieces. This sort of damage was not categorised as war damage.

It was up to the claimant, not the Commission, to see that the builder engaged in the repair work was doing the job properly. The Commission with its panel of experts – architects, building and quantity surveyors – had to be satisfied that the payment of the cost of works represented the 'proper cost' of war damage repairs. The applicant had to make his claim on a form signed by him, accompanied by itemised accounts, paid or unpaid, and a certificate signed by the builder. Inevitably, there were some who were tempted to cheat, putting in claims for damage which was the result of years of neglect rather than enemy action. A deposit of 30 shillings was charged if a roof had to be inspected. This would be forfeited if the surveyor's report showed that the roof had not sustained damage as a result of bombing and the owner was simply 'trying it on'. There is no doubt that a considerable amount of so-called air-raid damage, rectified at Government expense, was the result of past neglect; the number of prosecutions for fraud probably represented only a proportion of fraudulent claims.

Some people were innocent but unfortunate, like Verily Anderson's husband's landlady, whose back wall collapsed on VE Day. 'Today of all days!' she exclaimed at the injustice of life. 'They'll never accept it as war damage now. Why couldn't it have fallen down yesterday?'

It was the business of the War Damage Commission to pay for war damage, to repair the property to the state it had been in originally; it was not its job to make improvements, rectifying what should have been done properly, say, two centuries ago. Many disputes as to what was attributable to war damage and what was owing to the original shoddy workmanship were to reach the courts after the war. Agents set themselves up in business, offering to handle damage claims in return for a percentage of the money they obtained in compensation from the War Damage Commission. The Poor Man's Valuers' Association gave technical help to those who could not afford the services of a valuer. For everyone the cost of professional fees was covered in the sum of damages received.

When his house was damaged, it was the responsibility of the owner to ensure that his furniture was protected from the elements. If the owner could not be found, it was incumbent on the local council to remove or protect furniture in danger of deterioration. No compensation would be forthcoming for furniture and possessions that had sustained damage after the actual incident by being left in a house taking in rain. Furniture would be removed and taken to store by the borough only from homes that were uninhabitable. If the house was damaged but habitable, furniture was not to be removed, but stored in parts of the premises where it would be reasonably safe from weather and thieves. Removal into the local authority storage depots was carried out by the borough's workmen. Alternatively, the owners could arrange for private removals and storage to any address in the London region, the local Council paying up to £10, but only in case of need, for removal expenses on production of a receipt from the removal firm; any claim over £10 would have to be referred to the Ministry of Home Security, which had responsibility for salvage of furniture, working through the local authorities. Costs of return of furniture from store to a new home would be similarly re-imbursed. The owners did not have to pay the costs of furniture being stored as a result of enemy action; that would be covered by the Government.

By 1945 London's storage depots were overflowing. The situation was so desperate that local authorities had resorted to requisitioning large empty houses in such prestigious addresses as Chester Square, Eaton Terrace, the Boltons and Kensington Park Gardens. Once inside, there was no guarantee that the furniture would be free from theft or damage. Storage depots were not exempt from enemy action. The Regional Commissioner Sir Ernest Gowers' report to the Minister of Home Security in the New Year of 1945 revealed that inspections by Regional Officers to the stores discovered a high degree of infestation by moth: the Ministry of Health was to be asked to supply insecticide and advice on how to deal with the problem. The number of claims for loss of furniture and damage to it in store had increased. There was 'evidence of systematic thefts of carpets and wireless sets, but in view of the enormous amount of movement of furniture in the London region the losses have not been disproportionate.' He warned that the Government must expect a rash of claims once the wholesale removal of furniture back to owners' homes got under way. Some of the furniture would undoubtedly remain in store for a considerable time after the war, until the owners were housed or servicemen returned from abroad.

After the V-1 offensive during the summer of 1944, it was a race against time to make houses weatherproof for the coming winter. They had not caught up with the V-1 damage – of the 1,104,000 homes damaged by the V-1, only 700,000 had received first-aid repairs – when the V-2 offensive began, exacerbating the problem. Thousands of building workers were drafted in from the provinces to speed up the repair work, but it was impossible to keep pace with demand, first as the V-2 continued to create further devastation, and later when a flood of civilians and demobbed servicemen and women started returning to the capital after the cessation of hostilities. No one with experience of the building trade was now called up into the armed forces: labour exchanges throughout the country were instructed to send all suitable men to London, where they would work under contract to the local authorities, while living in emergency camps, rest centres and private billets. As they had done for centuries, many building workers came over from Ireland and skilled tradesmen were released from the services to help out. Nevertheless, the housing shortage was to remain the most vexed question central Government and the local authorities had to contend with during 1945.

The sight that would greet a newcomer to London's inner and outer suburbs in 1945 would be mile upon mile of flapping tarpaulin, used as an immediate stop-gap remedy – 'first aid repairs' – where the roofs of domestic dwellings had been destroyed by blast. The demand was so great that there was a shortage of tarpaulin. The prevalent sound was the tap of hammer on tiles, as roof after roof received 'second stage' repairs. Clear glass was also in short supply, so that it had to be eked out sparingly, according to the number of occupants in a house, and applied only to the living rooms; the rest would be covered first with two-ply roofing felt, later with windows made of 'R' glass – coarse, unpolished and almost opaque. The result was that London's damaged homes were dark as well as draughty. In south-west London, where 127,200 houses still awaited repair at the end of January, it was estimated that the amount of glass required to replace windows in Battersea, Wandsworth and Lambeth alone amounted to 9 million square feet, enough to cover Clapham Common. Hackney flatly refused to replace any glass windows during the era of the V-1s and V-2s, but by October 1945 glass representing one and a half million feet had been used in the borough.

Hackney's policy was pragmatic, because many houses would be repaired only to be damaged again. In neighbouring Stepney, for instance, over 45,000 houses had been repaired in the course of the war, some as many as three, four or five times. Down in Camberwell some houses had been damaged six or seven times; in the New Year it was particularly frustrating that repairs there were being held up by the failure of about 600 building workers to return to work after the Christmas holiday. By mid February 132,000 men were engaged on repairs in London and, according to Sir Malcolm Trustram Eve – the man appointed by Lord Woolton, the Minister of Reconstruction, to co-ordinate the various agencies (the Ministries of Health, Works, Supply, War Transport and Labour, among them) engaged in dealing with the housing problem in London Region – the rate of repair rose from 27,300 in January to 33,700 houses a week in February.

Local papers would keep an anxious tally of houses repaired in the course of the week, the numbers outstanding often seeming to stretch into infinity. In the third week of January, for instance, the *Hampstead and Highgate Express* noted that of 470,900 bomb-damaged houses in north-west London, 240,008 had been made 'tolerably comfortable'. In Hendon, Hornsey and Finchley 56,788 out of a total of 94,100 damaged houses had received attention. In Islington half of 65,900 bomb-damaged houses awaited attention: there would be many more to add to the tally before aerial bombardment ceased. Inevitably there were hiccups, on at least one occasion literally, when six men working on bomb-damage repairs filled demi-johns with wine from the cellar of a blitzed public house in South Lambeth and were afterwards found by the police lying in the street in a drunken condition. Small wonder, as they had stumbled on 27 gallons.

Each local authority had to prepare a programme of work, deciding what to do with their available labour force, either making houses fit for occupation or adapting houses for multiple-family occupation. The idea was to do essential, first-aid repair work – making the property 'wind and weather tight' – as quickly as possible, so that people could return to their homes, as they preferred to do, no matter how rudimentary the repairs. House damage was divided into four categories. Class A signalled that it was totally destroyed; Class B that it was to be demolished; Class C that it was uninhabitable, but capable of repair; Class D that it was habitable and capable of repair. The Ministry of Health, which was responsible for first aid repairs to houses, also saw to it that the local authorities gave broken drains immediate attention, to prevent drinking water being contaminated by sewage and to keep the rat population – which was threatening to run out of control, not least since so many domestic cats had been put down in 1939 – in check. 'In wartime every live rat is a potential enemy agent,' warned the Ministry of Food. During the last year of the war a sustained campaign destroyed 4 million rats, 1 million of them in the London sewers alone.

The bombed out were rehoused only if their home was destroyed or if repairs would take longer than six weeks. In 1943 the Government had given local authorities the power to requisition empty houses, so that they would have a pool of accommodation for the homeless. They could stay rent free for the first two weeks, then for a rent within their means. Otherwise, they might be billeted with private families, or rehoused in flats owned by the council. If accommodation could not be found within the borough, the bombed out might find themselves housed in another part of town. This was not an ideal solution, since Londoners had proved resistant to being moved away from their 'village'. To encourage his 'good neighbours' scheme' Sir Malcolm Trustram Eve had loaned his 12-room town house in Chelsea as accommodation for the homeless. East Enders were being housed in big houses in Mayfair and Chelsea under the 'house pooling' scheme, operated by those London boroughs – Westminster, Chelsea, Kensington, Paddington and St Marylebone – that had suffered comparatively lightly from the bombing. Big houses in Gloucester Terrace, Hyde Park Gardens and Westbourne Terrace were being converted by Paddington Council into flats for 1,000 homeless people. In October 1945 householders who had spare rooms were advised to let them. Otherwise, Aneurin Bevan, the new Labour Minister of Health warned, the Government would requisition them. He hoped to be able to rely on voluntary effort.

Requisitioning of empty houses was obviously controversial. Local authorities were required to give 'reasonable notice' – usually a month – to the owners of such properties. Some owners were holding their properties for 'speculative' purposes, as the housing shortage became more acute. These 'unpatriotic persons' were installing stooge tenants to prevent the local authorities requisitioning their property until the most advantageous moment. In July 1945 the Government told the local authorities they could requisition empty houses for distressed families if the owners were not living there themselves – without asking permission of anybody.

In spite of the LCC's powers of requisitioning, not all empty property in London was suitable for the homeless. Dry rot was a common problem and families could not be housed in such properties – the floors would not stand it. Timber was in very short supply and only a small percentage of it was available for house repairs. It did not help that in July there was a go-slow at London's docks: Canadian, American and Swedish timber ships were held up in the Thames waiting to unload while dockers sat inside playing cards. Naturally frustration mounted at the sight of these empty homes, while there was little appreciation of the problems.

By the summer of 1945 some members of the public had taken matters into their own hands. A latter-day Robin Hood, Harry Cowley, was to be heard addressing the crowd at Hyde Park Corner: he and his Vigilantes — mainly ex-servicemen – would use strong-arm tactics to seize empty properties and place the homeless in them. In mid July the leader of the Paddington group, John Preen, moved a mother of seven who had been bombed out in 1941 from two rooms in a basement into a seven-room house. The Paddington Vigilantes moved 23 families in 9 days into unoccupied houses in the borough. They cannot really be compared with modern squatters, because the Vigilantes were mindful of the law. Each of the families housed by Preen signed an agreement to do no damage and to pay rent when demanded by the owner or agent at the controlled rate. They also agreed to accept suitable alternative accommodation if offered by Paddington Council. Preen himself was taking a list of desperate cases to the council. If he had no joy, he warned, he would continue seizing houses on behalf of the homeless.

Even *Woman* magazine praised their achievement: 'The Vigilantes deserve all our thanks for showing that the people of Britain are not unendingly patient. We have given authority big power over our lives, but not the right to be complacently inefficient. Now that authority has been jerked awake the work of the Vigilantes is over.'

However, those illegally occupying a property could be dispossessed by the local authority, as Mrs Joyce Yardley, a pregnant mother of one, found to her cost at a flat in Paddington, while she was waiting for the return of her husband on leave from the RAF. The council had padlocked the kitchen and bedroom doors, so that she was unable to wash or cook and was sleeping on bare boards. 'I was desperate,' she told the *Daily Mirror*, 'if they chuck me out, I'll sit on the Town Hall steps with my baby until they do something.' She was unable to leave the flat, because if she did so the police would lock her out. An official of Paddington Council said that the flat had been requisitioned and promised to another woman 'with an even stronger case than Mrs Yardley. We sympathize with her, but she had no right to take the law into her own hands, and she will have to go.'

For those who were successfully rehoused, there was the problem of setting up home again, at a time when household goods were extremely hard to come by. In 1941 the Utility Furniture Scheme was introduced, with the emphasis on good design and economical use of timber. The furniture was available only to newly weds or people who had been bombed out of their houses and lost all their belongings. Prospective buyers had to get an application form from their local fuel office for a permit. Each permit carried 60 units and was valid for 3 months. Alternatively, some of the East End's traditional furniture makers were redirected to repair work or reconstructing old furniture and wood to make new pieces.

For those not entitled to Utility furniture or unable to afford to replace their furniture, there was a scheme by which they could acquire it second-hand. Some of the provincial counties, cities and towns adopted their own London boroughs, the most generous being those, like Plymouth, Bristol and Bath, that had been badly bombed themselves. Oxford adopted Bermondsey, where 4,242 homes had been obliterated and practically every one of its 19,020 dwellings had been damaged in the course of the war. A grateful Hackney sent an exhibition of its bomb damage to the people of Shropshire, who had contributed so generously to their adopted borough: they had sent 45 loads each of about five and a half tons of household goods to Hackney. Furniture, pots and pans, lamps, china, cutlery and carpets were taken to WVS depots to be transferred to the boroughs, for the WVS to distribute to the needy on a points basis.

The local authority would supply the WVS with a classified list of people who had lost their homes. Upon showing their identity cards they would be admitted to browse the store. Each household would be entitled to goods up to a value of 50 points and each person in that household up to 30 points. The allowance did not buy much. A double bed cost 50 points, a large carpet, an armchair, a dining table or a sideboard could be had for 40, an ironing board for 30, a kettle or a saucepan for 10, a lamp for 5, a scrubbing brush, a knife or a fork for 3. The bombed out were given priority in acquiring precious new sheets, but there was a six-month waiting list even for priority cases. When a consignment of sheets came into Pontings in Kensington High Street one day in February, 10,000 women queued from five in the morning for a chance to buy. The WVS had three central stores where blankets were kept for desperate cases. The American and Canadian Red Cross had generously given 25,000 blankets and 30,000 quilts for distribution to the needy.

It was depressing to set up home again with second-hand goods. Rosie White, whose family lost everything when they were bombed out, was eventually resettled in a council house:

So we came back on the Sunday to this house and stuff that Dad's sister had bought us from the gratuity money, the bombed-out money, about £68 I think it was. His sister got us what she could find and that's what Mum came home to. It was very basic. Mum sat down and cried when she looked round the house. Secondhand everything, cups and saucers with cracks and chips. Even though we were poor we had our pride and principles, and to drink out of cracked cups was bad. But during the war you were lucky to have cups. You were sometimes drinking out of small jam jars.

After the shock and trauma of being bombed out, some elected to leave London, at least for a time. The *After the Raid* leaflet advised the homeless that they would be given a free travel voucher if they did not otherwise have the means to get to relatives and friends. They must also ask for a certificate to enable the person they were planning to stay with to obtain a billeting allowance for them. This was hardly generous and many were left out of pocket, as Irene Byers discovered during her stay in Somerset:

I met a lovely young wife from Streatham. She had a six-month-old baby and was staying at Croydon when her own house was bombed. She lost everything, furniture, wedding presents – the lot – and is now staying with friends at Bridgewater, who charge her 30s a week for one small room. Some friends! The Government only contributes 5s and the rest she has to find out of army pay. Her husband is fighting in France and she is very bitter about money-making opportunities in Somerset. It certainly gets under my skin the way some people are profiteering from other people's misery.

Country people were sometimes less than welcoming to bombed-out Londoners, as a 33-year-old RAF widow discovered:

We had a flat in London and my husband joined the RAF in 1939. My home was completely destroyed last June. I went to live with my mother-in-law, and my father-in-law was killed and his house, the only remaining resemblance of a home I had, was wiped out one week later. Two days later my husband was killed in action. I have, of course, a pension, a few sticks of furniture, and I can still see the funny side of things though you may wonder at this. I have come down here to the country and I live in one room. I have tried everything I know to get a little cottage. Other people get them round here, but they are all locals. Londoners like me are not wanted, and all I seek is to make up to my little boy for the home he has lost while his father was fighting for these people.

On the other hand, some Cockneys were difficult guests in the country, as Irene Byers noticed when she overheard a London evacuee in the local pub: '"Anyone 'ud think we was foreigners the way they treat us." She fixed a baleful eye on an innocent local and added, "If I'd known I was to be sent down 'ere, I'd 'ave drowned meself first!"'

Those who found their own accommodation were advised to send their new address to the Secretary, London Council of Social Services, 7 Bayley Street, Bedford Square, London WC1. In this way, anyone who had had to relocate might be found through the Town Hall, the local council offices and the Citizens' Advice Bureaux, all of whom kept the information on record. Anyone in the forces would be able to trace relatives through their commanding officers.

The Ministry of Health was responsible for evacuation and through local authorities arranged for old people to be evacuated, where they were willing. Many of them were unwilling to leave the place and people they knew, but on the other hand many of them were not sufficiently mobile to take shelter when necessary. The National Council of Social Service was asked to find private billets for the elderly, who would receive the billeting allowance of five shillings a week for their accommodation alone. Alternatively, they might be sent to old people's homes out of London. It did not always work out for the best. The Reverend Markham remembers a couple in their eighties who had been married for 60 years: they were evacuated to different old people's homes in different towns in the north, so that they did not see each other. 'They quickly pined and deteriorated,' he says. 'They both died.' At the end of the war, decisions had to be taken about those who had been evacuated. In view of the housing situation in London, those who were billeted privately were advised to stay put for the time being, although the billeting allowance no longer applied. Alternative arrangements had to be made for those who had become institutionalised, or lost the habit of living independently, in the course of the war.

As a last resort, the homeless took to living in the Underground stations and deep tube shelters. Christmas 1944 had been miserable for them. Strikes were illegal during the war on pain of fines or imprisonment, but they were occurring with increasing frequency, as managers and workers flexed their muscles in anticipation of the post-war world. Underground workers went on strike when the London Passenger Transport Board refused to grant them Christmas leave. This meant that most of the stations were closed over the Christmas period. Alternative accommodation for the homeless still sheltering in the Underground had been provided by most local authorities, but some shelterers, namely those at Knightsbridge and Hyde Park, fell out of the loop. Mr Mackenzie, the head shelter warden at Knightsbridge, told the *West London Press*: 'The Christmas Day muddle revealed a wanton disregard for the safety and comfort of many homeless souls. There were hundreds wandering the streets all night with their pathetic bundles and their sad-eyed little children. It was disgraceful and quite unnecessary.' The newspaper called it 'bungling inefficiency wedded to bureaucracy with a vengeance'.

Living in the Underground cannot have been comfortable at the best of times, but some seemed to thrive on it, so much so that they sought refuge there even if they were not actually homeless. Mrs Squibb of Stepney, the wife of a serviceman overseas and the mother of four children aged two to fifteen, had taken to the Underground because her house was so badly damaged that only one room was habitable. Others enjoyed the company and the camaraderie that life in the tube offered. A 90-year-old woman, who had spent five years in Hampstead Underground station, told the *Hampstead and Highgate Express* that her 'greatest delight is to watch the people getting in and out of the trains'. During the Blitz 3,000 had sheltered in Hampstead, London's deepest Underground station. By the late spring of 1945 a few hundred were doggedly hanging on for the final All Clear. 'Most of us have been here for five years,' one woman told a reporter, 'so we might as well see it through to the end.'

Undoubtedly many would be sorry to leave when they were finally winkled out. Mrs Johnson of Mansfield Road, Gospel Oak, was a regular at Belsize Park and told the local paper: 'I am very happy here and I shall certainly miss all the friends I have made when we leave. It is ridiculous of people to say that the Tubes are unhealthy. Why, I have had only one cold in the five years I have been here.' During the first quarter of 1945 the number of shelterers remained fairly constant at 12,500 in the Underground and about 5,000 in the new deep tube shelters. By mid April, with the cessation of the V-weapons, these numbers had dropped to 6,000 in the Underground and about 2,500 in the deep tube shelters. Seventy-eight-year-old Mrs Helen Bolan was still living in Elephant and Castle Underground station at the end of April, even though she was not homeless. 'I stay here because I like it,' she said, 'I like the company and the noise of the trains. I shall be sorry to go home.' Her sister-in-law had lost her home in Dulwich six months previously, so that she had come to join her. In Holborn there were still 180 regulars at the end of April, including Jock, whose house had been damaged in October 1944. He and his wife had been given a new home, but preferred the shelter. 'I like the early morning cup of tea we get here,' he told a reporter. 'At home I have to make it myself.'

In addition, many had taken shelter in Chislehurst Caves, which had been a popular refuge for thousands of Londoners during the Blitz. Not all of them were homeless; some had homes which were at least in part habitable. They were simply too nervous to emerge during the period of the V-1s and V-2s. To discourage them from staying in the caves all the time, hot meals were not served, only tea and sandwiches night and morning. Nevertheless, some stuck obstinately to the caves. The fact that they were relatives of servicemen had a detrimental effect on morale in the forces.

Evacuees with no habitable London home were forbidden to return to the capital, but inevitably many ignored the advice and had to be given shelter. 'It would be repugnant to public opinion,' a London Region circular stated, 'to leave the evacuees with no option but to resort to ordinary poor law relief. The Government has decided, therefore, that they should be accommodated in the first instance in the rest centres.' About 10,000 places were kept open for returning evacuees in rest centres, while others found temporary accommodation in the Underground and deep tube shelters. The idea was that they would be given accommodation for a week, in which time they would be put in touch with the local housing officer. Adults and children over 14 were to be charged 2s 6d a day for their board and lodging, children from 5 to 14 1s 3d a day and children from 1 to 5 8d a day. Those without the means to support themselves were to be referred to the Assistance Board.

On 4 May it was announced that although canteen facilities were to be discontinued, some of the Underground shelters were to remain available to the homeless for a little while, a decision welcomed by those boroughs where the housing problem was particularly acute. On VE night, 8 May, at least 1,200 people were still sleeping in the Underground stations. On 31 May the last of the bunks were removed. By July 1945 the Regional Commissioner reported that all public shelters had been closed, the Ministry of Health having found alternative accommodation for homeless persons and returning evacuees. Three of the new deep shelters had been taken over by the War Office, although they were soon found to be redundant in the new atomic age. They were no longer open to members of the public. Local authorities were being pressed to demolish street shelters, since children and other 'irresponsible persons' were breaking into them and causing damage and general unpleasantness. In a final piece of housekeeping, those who had been issued with Anderson shelters by the Government (in 1939 they had been provided free of charge to any householder in the danger zone earning less than £250 a year) were told to dismantle them and have them ready for collection by their local council. Alternatively, they might purchase their Anderson for £1 or their Morrison, which many had found useful as a table, for £1 10s.

The sight of bomb damage was considered bad for morale, so that as soon as the valuer had done his work, the demolition crews moved in to demolish dangerous buildings and the debris men started clearing and levelling the site. The Ministry of Home Security was responsible for the clearance of debris and salvage work, but the LCC undertook the tasks in all the metropolitan boroughs. It had set up the War Debris and Disposal Service with J.H. Forshaw of the LCC architect's department as director: his department was responsible for 'demolition, shoring and rescue work', the three tasks being closely linked. The Borough Engineer and the District Surveyor were responsible for carrying out the work in each borough under the direction of their Group Engineer and Group Surveyor respectively. The Group Centre would be responsible for sending reserves of men and materials to whichever areas needed them and for diverting local resources from one borough to another.

Not everything went smoothly. In May 450 lorry and crane drivers employed by the LCC on bomb damage repairs went on strike in protest against the Ministry of Works' decision to suspend Sunday overtime. Unrest continued and in October bomb repair men downed tools again in protest against the reduction of their working hours and pay from 54 to 44 hours a week. Four thousand of them joined a demonstration in Hyde Park demanding an increase of three shillings an hour for craftsmen and an 80 per cent increase for labourers for a 44-hour week.

On the other hand, German prisoners of war were brought in as extra labour to clear bomb sites, London acting on the principle that they could now clear up the mess they had made. At the end of May men from Rommel's Afrika Korps, camped at Lewisham, were earning 6d a day preparing sites for prefabs. German POWs were kept separate from British workmen, but working a 54-hour week they were paid at British trade union rates by their employers. The money went to the War Office and from it the cost of billeting and feeding the prisoners would be deducted before they received 1s for an 8-hour day for skilled work and 6d a day for unskilled labour, according to the rates laid down by the Geneva Convention. In the first instance, they were volunteers. They were reported to be good workers and 'quite docile'.

The salvage of building materials was of equal importance to the clearance of sites when so much of the country's industry was given over to war production and there was both a demand for and a scarcity of building materials. Large quantities of salvaged timber were stored away from danger outside London, although there were dumps of firewood from bombed houses – such as the one in Lillie Road Recreation Ground, Fulham – where the public were invited to help themselves. Iron and steel were sorted and removed to foundries, bricks were cleaned, slates and tiles reserved for first aid repairs. Rubble had been diverted to build new airfields for the US air force in East Anglia, as well as roads. London debris had been transformed at London's docks to make floating harbours to be towed over to France after D-Day. Cast iron baths, sinks, fireplaces, radiators, counters and safes were either sold to the public or stored in salvage dumps like the one in Hyde Park.

By May 1945 the War Debris and Disposal Service had managed the salvage and removal of 331,865 tons of steel, 298,810 tons of timber and firewood, 132,659,000 bricks, 2,578,000 slates and tiles, 6,726,246 tons of hardcore and 3,897,000 tons of debris.

The LCC architect's department was also responsible for the preservation of parts of scheduled buildings of historical or architectural interest. A plan had been prepared by the Ministry of Works and Buildings with the assistance of the Royal Institute of British Architects and the Society for the Protection of Ancient Buildings, whereby expert advice was available to those engaged upon the treatment of such buildings when they were damaged by enemy air activity. Decorative plaster ceilings were carefully removed in sections, and fanlights, doors, balustrades, panelling and fireplaces were all carefully stored to prevent further damage by exposure. Anything that could be salvaged from a historic building or church was preserved for its future reconstruction. At the same time, the destruction of buildings in the City had revealed a harvest of antiquities beneath: these were to be studied and preserved.

As soon as the site was levelled, it was ready to be built upon. The question was should the building be permanent or temporary? Given the desperate housing shortage, the temptation was to erect quick temporary housing. As early as March 1944 Churchill had mentioned that his friend Lord Portal at the Ministry of Works was 'working wonders' with a new type of temporary home, a prefab, and aircraft factories were being given over to constructing them. Unfortunately, the early Portal was made of steel and the projected number would eat up the nation's entire steel supply. Even with a change of material by 1945 the cost of a prefab had risen from £600 to £1,000. At the same time, about 30,000 asbestos huts were being imported from America.

It was the responsibility of the Minister of Works to supply prefabs to local authorities. They would then arrange with the contractors for the preparation of the sites and the speedy erection of the 'huts' or 'hutments'. The local authority would manage the properties and draw rent from them; all expenditure would be reimbursed by the Ministry of Health, offset by the rents received. There were mixed feelings about temporary housing. After all, it was expensive for the amount of space it provided – only 655 square feet – and unsightly. In a debate in the Lords in February, Lord Rennell asserted that the desire for perfection was the enemy of all progress. 'Better to live in a Nissen hut than to have no home of your own at all.'

Not every council was as radical as Shoreditch, which was the first to erect temporary hutments on a disused burial ground. Here, the wife of a young soldier and their children who had lost their home to a V-I were to have a distinctive address: I The Graveyard, Shoreditch. Her hutment home would be built over old graves and her view would be of tombstones. Sixteen temporary hutments were to be built on this, London's first graveyard estate, at the side of St Mary's Parish Church, Haggerston. Permission to build on the consecrated ground had been given by Dr Fisher, the new Archbishop of Canterbury, when he was still Bishop of London.

In more conventional surroundings, Hornsey Housing Committee was one of several who had misgivings about building 200 temporary hutments; they felt the labour, time and money would be better spent on repairing permanent homes. Indeed, some temporary home sites proved more expensive to prepare than originally estimated. The Ministry of War Transport – which diverted the labour engaged in road reconstruction to lay down the concrete bases for the huts – admitted to the Ministry of Health on 9 July 1945 that the work of preparing 50 hutment sites for Croydon Borough Council cost £7,600, when the original estimate had been £4,137, the two chief reasons being the sloping ground and the remoteness of the mains. If temporary housing was erected on a cleared bomb site, it would delay the building of permanent housing for up to 10 years. It was obviously more convenient, if more expensive, to place it in the public parks or open spaces, as St Pancras Borough Council was trying to do in the Gospel Oak area of Parliament Hill Fields, Regent's Park and Primrose Hill. In Parliament Hill Fields alone 50 acres could accommodate 1,000 families.

In February the editor's letter in *Woman* magazine pleaded:

We are still waiting, but with dwindling patience for action on the housing front. The temporary homes about which we have heard so much are still missing from our bombed towns – in many cases it has not even been decided where they will stand. If they are put on the sites of demolished houses where are the permanent houses to go? If, on the other hand, they are put up in the parks, vacant lots and undeveloped areas, think of the increases in time, labour and costs of bringing roads, water, light and heat to the new estates. Looked at in this way does not the cost of each temporary home soar sky-high out of the realms of practical achievement? Many building experts insist that permanent homes in brick are quicker and easier to build than the pre-fabricated houses – and brick houses do not raise this desperately knotty problem of sites, since they would be permanent structures.

It was time, she concluded regally, for the Ministry of Works to make up its mind. It had had long enough to decide: if it now believed that the temporary housing scheme was a poor idea then it should get down to the urgent job of building proper houses.

In fact prefabs proved rather popular with those who obtained them. They were compact but well designed and far more modern and convenient than many of the occupants had been used to. Of course, these people were desperate, so that they were disposed to like them, but the fact that some continued to live in them for years and would not be parted from them is a tribute to their qualities. Joe Linsell, who was living with his wife Mary and two children in a single room at the home of his mother-in-law, applied to the LCC and was invited to view a prefab:

After we looked round Mary was worried, and me – would it be our luck to get one? When we came on the Friday, there was the council people outside with a table, there was nine families lining up. 'Course, Mary's got my hand and says, 'Oh, there's only eight prefabs.' Well, someone was going to be unlucky and as number two went, then number three, number four, so the tension was getting worse, but when it came to number eight he called my name to the table, I said, 'Yes, I'll have it'. And of course we took it and we moved in a week after but I did feel sorry for the person who was left out and she even cried. But it's the happiest day that ever happened.

Even when a local authority was planning to build permanent housing there could be a problem, such as when the residents of Hampstead protested against its council's plans to erect working-class flats on a partially cleared bomb site at New End Square and Well Walk.

There was concern that speculators had their eye on bomb sites and at least one clever entrepreneur – Donald Gosling – had post-war car parks in mind.

The Government had given the LCC the power to acquire bomb sites for temporary housing and other purposes, allowing only a fortnight's notice for the owner of the land – the freeholder – to appeal against its requisition. The local authority had merely to post a notice on the site announcing its intention of applying to the Ministry of Health to enter and take possession. The chances of owners actually seeing the notice, since so many bombed-out families had moved to other districts, with heads of families very often in the services, in time to take action were remote. In Wandsworth, where 2,500 sites were urgently needed for temporary dwellings, the situation was acute. Nevertheless, the council was honest enough to condemn requisitioning as 'sharp practice'. More pragmatically, it stated that portal-type homes would hold back the building of permanent housing on the site for 10 years. In July home owners in Streatham were organising a protest against the procedure. A man whose house was destroyed in 1940 appealed against the notice served on his property, only to be told his letter arrived nine days too late. 'I don't want to sell my freehold,' he wrote. 'I want to rebuild my house. My three sons are abroad. What are they fighting for? The sooner they come home to liberate this country from bumptious bureaucracy the better.'

The requisitioning of bombed sites was a highly contentious issue: it was usually absolute and permanent, unlike the requisitioning of an empty house to 'borrow' accommodation for the homeless for a time. Some local authorities seemed to be exploiting their powers to grab as much land as they could to the detriment of the private owner, as an editorial in the *Croydon Advertiser* illustrates:

The person whose house has been totally destroyed gets a raw deal. First he has to wait until the end of the war before he can rebuild. It rests with the War Damage Commission whether he will be allowed to rebuild at all or whether he will have to accept some arbitrary sum – payable at some future date and probably bearing no relation to the cost of reinstatement – as full compensation. Of course some old houses had outlasted their usefulness and should have been modernised or replaced – the bombing only anticipated what was inevitable anyway. Granted there is a shortage of housing and the local authorities have to provide for the bombed out who cannot pay an economic rent and must therefore be placed in houses subsidised by the community at large. Still, it seems like kicking a man when he is down to tell him that simply because his property has been completely destroyed his site – his sole remaining asset – is to be requisitioned or acquired compulsorily for a Council house, whether permanent or temporary. The panic legislation is being used by some authorities to secure possession of as many as possible of the available sites irrespective of the rights or wishes of the owners.

To add insult to injury, the Croydon Housing Committee stated in June 1945 that 'where an owner-occupier's site has been acquired by compulsory purchase he shall be offered the first refusal of a tenancy of any permanent Council house subsequently built on the site.' The article concluded vehemently: 'The man wants justice, not charity!'

Londoners whose houses were intact but which had been requisitioned while they had been absent during the war often returned to find them still occupied. Sometimes it was years before they could take possession of them again.

At the same time there was much dissatisfaction at the way some local authorities were treating the homeless. In Croydon the pregnant wife of a serviceman was apparently told 'beggars can't be choosers' when she complained about the standard of accommodation offered her. The first was an attic flat up 40 stairs: she would have to carry coal up from the basement and go out and round the back to hang up the washing; the second was a damp basement without cooking facilities and so dark the light had to be kept on all day; the third was a ground floor flat with broken windows, doors that would not close, a broken fireplace and only a small gas stove. She was currently living with her parents and when her husband came home on leave they had to sleep on the kitchen floor (normally she shared a room with her two sisters). Clearly none of this would be suitable once the baby arrived.

Some tried to exploit the situation, such as a couple of Shoreditch families keen to relocate to Southend. The responsibility for rehousing the homeless lay with the borough in which the bombing incident occurred. The homeless had to take the housing they were offered; it was not up to them to pick and choose. In January 1945 an article in the *Daily Mirror* drew readers' attention to the plight of Mr and Mrs Pollington and Mr and Mrs Fisher and their daughter, who were ostentatiously living in a surface shelter in the street and doing their cooking on a brazier made from an old dustbin used as a stove. Mrs Pollington had a sideline rounding up homeless cats and sending them to be 'painlessly destroyed'. Apparently the families had been offered accommodation by Shoreditch, but had turned it down, holding out for Southend, whose scheme of allocating houses to homeless Londoners (but only respectable types who could afford to pay the rent and fares to their workplace) had been receiving good publicity. Both councils were apoplectic at the misleading nature of the article,

Southend because it had never received an application from either family, since Shoreditch had rightly decided they were unsuitable for the scheme.

Throughout the war rents had fluctuated, according to demand. During the Blitz, for instance, it had been very easy to find accommodation, especially a top-floor flat. By the end of 1943 a joke was going the rounds about a man found drowning in the Thames: a passer-by had stopped, not to rescue him but to ask his address. Arriving breathlessly at the house, he found it already occupied. He accused the man who opened the door of having no right to be there, since he had just seen the owner in the Thames. 'I know,' he replied, 'I pushed him in'. The housing shortage was at its most severe after the V-weapons' offensive. It was a bonus for private landlords, rent racketeers were much in evidence and rents were spiralling out of control. In Chelsea it had been possible before the war to rent a furnished room for 15s or £1 a week; now the rent would be 35s or £2 2s a week. 'How are people earning £3.10s or £5 a week to pay such a rent?' moaned one resident. 'And where are we to live?'

Even if prepared to pay inflated rents, the accommodation was not easy to find. Typically, when two flats were advertised to be let at 22s and 21s a week respectively in Brixton in June the advertisement drew 300 people from all over London. The queue formed at 6.30 in the morning. The first 12 were admitted at 10 a.m. and left their names. An expectant mother collapsed during the long wait. 'Four families are living in three rooms at my home and another woman besides myself is expecting a baby,' she told the *Daily Mirror*. 'It is terribly disappointing to come here so early and find so many people in front of me.'

When Labour came to power a Rent Act was rushed through, strengthening the control over furnished tenancies and establishing rent tribunals in many areas. For those wishing to buy their own home, however, a property boom was clearly under way. In July a Hampstead resident wrote to the *Daily Mirror*: 'I enclose the agent's quotation for a house built for £1,200 about twenty-three years ago. It was sold some time back for £2,500. Now the owner wants £4,750.'

The returning middle classes found that they could no longer afford houses in Kensington or Chelsea. Mollie Panter-Downes noted:

Londoners whose war jobs took them out of the city or who could afford to move their children out of bombing range are now beginning to return to town, and, as a result, the prices of London property are starting to show the same alarming upward curve they developed after the First World War. Depressed couples in search of a small family house in which to settle down as Londoners once more are finding that the good things are prohibitive in price and that the moderately priced houses appear to have received a little too much attention from the bombers. The new government limit on house repairs is ten pounds [no repairs costing more than £10 could be done without a licence from the local authority, to prevent the labour force seeping away from the main job to deal with inessentials], so the problem of getting a dirty, leaking house into habitable shape is a difficult one. However, some amateur house-decorating help is available. For example, the charwoman's husband, on leave from the Navy, may oblige with a little distem-pering, or a friendly air warden may come around in off-duty hours and do a bit of carpentering.

It was a good time to scoop up a house if one had the cash, however. When Verily Anderson found a bomb-damaged house in Holland Park (not then the fashionable area it is today) she slapped down an offer without bothering with a survey. The house was bomb-damaged, but the War Commission would cover the cost of repairs.

Exhibitions to promote the goodies that would be available in the post-war world were popular. Some of them were to advertise the new post-war kitchens with all the latest labour-saving gadgets. 'These kitchens are the gas industry's post-war present to them,' waxed the promoters of one such exhibi-tion, referring to the women of Britain. In London, women flocked to the exhibitions, but most of them could only dream.

A middle-class woman who emerged from the *Daily Herald* Post-War Homes Exhibition in July spoke for thousands when she said: 'They could just give me *any* of it, and I should think it wonderful. Honestly, I liked it all. I'm so desperate for a house I'd like anything. I can't criticize or judge it at all – four walls and a roof is the height of my ambition.'

Housing was to be the first problem of the peace and, in many people's eyes, the key issue at the general election in July. The Coalition Government had produced no white paper on housing as it had for education and health. The war had destroyed 50,000 houses in the County of London and 66,000 in the rest of Greater London. Another 1,300,000 were in need of major or minor repairs. In addition, there was a huge backlog. The pre-war boom in house building largely fed the private sector. There was still a huge deficiency in the public sector, where many outworn and unsanitary slums remained and needed to be replaced, if the people were to have the rewards they had been promised. All houses had been neglected for five years at least and were overdue for maintenance repair work. Very little building had been done during the war and now builders were short of materials and labour – in 1939 there had been 1,008,000 building workers in Britain, in mid 1944 there were only 345,000 – and subject to tight government controls.

At a conference of London's local authorities held in January 1945 Henry Willink, the Minister of Health, estimated the immediate need at 1 million additional houses and the long-term need as between 3 and 4 million in 10 years' time. 'I tell him he is wrong,' declared Councillor J. Cochrane, a JP of Uxbridge, Middlesex. 'During the war two million couples have got married and will want homes soon after the war. We want three or four million houses as quickly as we can have them. Not in ten years' time.' He was one of those who had the heart-rending task of sending applicants away empty-handed. 'I have seen a young mother leaving our Council meeting with a child in her arms and tears in her eyes, and a young couple saying, "We can't afford to have a family because we have no place to lay our heads." It is a disgrace to England,' he concluded.

At the annual general meeting of the Family Planning Association in June, Mrs Godfrey Pyke said that many more married women were seeking advice on birth control simply because of the housing shortage. There had been many wartime marriages where the couple had been content for the wife to live with the in-laws while the husband was in the forces, but now those couples wanted a place of their own. There would also be a rise in the marriage and birth rates after the war, adding to the pressure for housing. In truth, the authorities had no real idea of the number of houses required: they did not have the data, but it was far, far beyond the 750,000 houses 'to afford a separate dwelling for every family desiring to have one' that the incoming Labour Minister of Housing, Aneurin Bevan, believed was the correct estimate. The Government was also reckoning without the people's increased expectations. They had been promised the houses, not to speak of the extra space, and now they demanded them as their right.

There was a widespread feeling that the Coalition Government was not being aggressive enough to remedy the housing problem. When Lord Woolton, the Minister of Reconstruction, had told the Lords in February that the Government aimed at half a million houses (300,000 permanent and 200,000 temporary) built or building at the end of two years after the defeat of Germany, the Archbishop of York said he 'could not imagine anything more disappointing or more likely to cause bitterness among the men in the Services than to find when they came back that there was no possibility of the home to which they had looked forward so keenly'. In April the Labour peer, Lord Latham, leader of the LCC, complained in the Lords at the Coalition Government's 'indecisive footling' of the housing problems, protesting that 'there were plans by the bucketful but no production.'

Looking at the number of ministries involved in the

housing programme, it is a wonder any progress was made. The Ministry of Health was in overall charge of housing, controlling the plans and the loans of the local authorities; the Ministry of Works was responsible for the production of prefabs – emergency, temporary housing; the Ministry of Town and Country Planning controlled the use of the land; the Ministry of Labour directed the building operatives and the workers in the factories who were producing the prefabs; the Ministry of Supply was concerned with materials. In addition, the Board of Trade was concerned with the issue of import licences for house-building materials such as timber and steel. 'It is as though in an orchestra each instrumentalist were playing a different tune, or at best, the same tune but in a different time,' *Picture Post* suggested. Many were asking if it would not be more sensible in the present crisis to create a Ministry of Housing with full powers over the whole business.

In the run-up to the general election Labour's Ernest Bevin had glibly promised 5 million houses in quick time, which certainly sounded more attractive to the voters than Churchill's more realistic pledge, repeating the promises already outlined by Woolton. The arrival of the dynamic Aneurin Bevan as Labour's Minister of Health put paid to any more attempts to create a separate Ministry of Housing. He was more than able to fight his corner, pressing for the labour – the brick makers as well as the brick layers – to be released from the forces: he succeeded in bringing the labour force back up to over 1 million by May 1946. He secured for housing as opposed to other ministries' needs the lion's share of the limited materials. Where the Tories' natural inclination had been to let private enterprise take care of itself, Bevan's policy was in sharp contrast. Speculative builders had almost always been responsible for London's housing and look at the mess they had made of it, Bevan argued. Left to their own devices these builders would satisfy only the private sector.

Labour's new 'democratic' policy would allow only one private dwelling for every five in the public sector. Bevan thought it reprehensible that housing in the public sector should only be for the working class, and substandard at that. He took seriously the provisions of the 1944 Dudley Report, whereby a 3-bedroom dwelling should be no less than 900 square feet. It was little enough to expect. Bevan resisted all pressure to speed up the housing programme by cutting corners. His houses must be built to a decent standard. Most radical of all, housing was to become the responsibility of the local authorities. They, rather than private builders after profit, would now be the driving force in the housing market. And they had every incentive. If councillors wanted the votes, they would have to supply the housing. With private builders squeezed out of almost all but public enterprise and frustrated, black market activities thrived.

Owing to the new powers they had been granted to requisition bombed and derelict sites for building, local authorities already had in their possession enough land to provide 600,000 new houses. Much to the consternation of the Tories, the procedure whereby the local authorities could acquire land was now speeded up by lifting the requirement for public inquiries and hearings, thus removing the impediment of protracted negotiations by landlords. Permits had to be obtained from the local authority for all building work, putting a definite dampener on any initiative or progress. It was up to the local authorities to draw up their own programmes, prepare the sites, make the contracts with private builders or establish direct labour departments, fix the rents, allocate the tenants and supervise the estates.

Meanwhile, as 1945 drew to a close the housing queues seemed to be getting longer and the clamour louder and more insistent. Over on the Opposition benches the Tories were in the novel position of attacking the Government for their dilatoriness. Bevan was quick to retaliate that 'only a very grave concern for the public weal could have inspired them [the Tories] to put down a motion on a subject so embarrassing to themselves.' He could hardly have achieved more in so short a time, but Churchill was not going to let his old foe off the hook. 'The Minister of Health has already allowed four months of excellent building weather to slip away,' he said witheringly at the censure debate on 6 December.

Quite so, but it would take years to build that elusive land fit for heroes.

4
Don't Waste It

'To throw your bus ticket away is to destroy material which is still vitally needed to make more munitions. So don't drop your ticket in the street – please! Your waste paper is urgently needed for salvage'

– Ministry of Supply

It was the coldest January for 50 years. There were sheets of ice in the Straits of Dover and in London Big Ben froze. Children, wrapped up in mufflers and mittens, returned to school to find the ink in the pots frozen. On Hampstead Heath tobogganing was in full swing. The National Fire Service detailed its men to visit every emergency water tank in the capital to break holes in the ice to prevent the tanks from bursting. On the doorsteps, milk froze in the bottles, which did burst. Thousands were suffering from burst water pipes, including a group of Southwark housewives, who besieged their Town Hall demanding help. The Arctic weather seriously hindered progress on the repair of bomb-damaged houses: it was virtually impossible to do roofing and external brickwork in such conditions. Trains, which were unheated, were to be avoided at all costs, as James Lees-Milne found when a journey from Darlington finally got him into King's Cross at three in the morning, 'frozen to the very marrow'.

Lack of coal supplies resulting from the steady run-down of the mines during the war – when 20,000 men had left the coal industry annually and there had been no new intake – together with restricted manpower and transport, meant that the capital was facing a fuel crisis. All over London women queued at emergency coal dumps, carrying away in prams and pushcarts the little they were allowed. In Southwark Lil Patrick recalls:

You had to get fuel where you could. There was a place down by Rotherhithe Tunnel – a gasworks – where you could get the coke. Then of course you had to have something – push chairs or whatever you could get – to wheel it home, because it was about a mile away. Then there was a little shop where coal used to be delivered from time to time. And the message would go round – 'Maggie's got coal! Take the push chair round!' And so we'd get in the queue and we'd get a bag of coal. And it was thick snow, and of course the stuff we had on the push chair far outweighed what the push chair could take, and pushing it across the snow didn't help! So there we were with the wheels gradually going out like this! And we ended up by dispensing with the push chair, and pulling the coal along in the sack on our way home, sliding it along the ground. And if there was bomb damage anywhere and there were beams, wood, or whatever, you'd get the push chair round there, and load the beams on there, and then bring it home and saw it all up.

Emergency coal dumps were set up in each borough. The maximum load in the Hampstead area, bought on a cash and carry basis, was 56 pounds. In Stepney a 6d ticket entitled its inhabitants to 14 pounds of coal. Six thousand tickets were sold in the first few days. In Lambeth women who had queued only to be told that no more tickets would be given out rushed the dump and began to help themselves. The police had to be called. Living near King's Cross, Anthony Heap was able to obtain reasonable supplies of coal, yet he noted in his diary at the end of January: 'The fuel situation continues to go from bad to worse. Still unable to get deliveries, distracted housewives daily besiege the newly opened coal dump in their thousands to buy 14 lbs for 6d. Gas and electricity supplies are liable to be suddenly cut off without notice.'

It was hard luck on old people who could not physically manage to haul coal back from the dump or who were living in top-floor flats, to which the few coal men about were refusing to deliver. Two elderly women in Sutton Buildings, Chelsea admitted: 'We're managing, but only just. It's been a very hard time. We've had half a hundred weight a week – so we have to count the lumps! You have to go out and walk all day – look at the shops or go into the library or something and then you can have a little fire in the evenings, but it won't run to one a day.' The old and the sick were dying for lack of warmth.

Edna Bucknill was a war widow, living with her mother:

We were frozen, like everyone else. No coal had come for weeks and in a tiny room with a scrooge-like fire in a tiny grate, we had burned all we could think of to keep a modicum of warmth to heat the little kettle on a trivet and ourselves – when [my mother] remembered the clothes line prop. We could not saw it up, so it was placed across the landing into the room and into the grate. It was slowly fed through the bars as it burned. The kettle boiled and a joyous evening resulted, the prop keeping us warm for about two and a half hours. My younger brother, aged about twelve, was the official threader. The laughter warmed us, too, for there had been little of that for a very long time.

Not surprisingly in the depth of winter, Londoners were apparently using too much gas and electricity. There were fears that there would be a complete collapse of the electric grid system unless greater economy was exercised by domestic and industrial consumers. The Ministry of Fuel and Power urged people through the BBC and the press not to turn on the electric fire in the morning, but to pile on extra clothes instead. The Ministry also suggested they 'go without toast for breakfast'. Housewives were asked to leave inessential cooking until after ten o'clock: 'The needs of munitions factories are heaviest between 8am and 1pm. Housewives can make a very real contribution to the war by cutting the use of electricity and gas to a minimum between these times and, if possible, by dispensing with them during the peak period.'

Of course, saving fuel was nothing new. At the beginning of the war it had come as a surprise to a nation used to copious

supplies of coal. 'Five lbs of coal saved in one day by each household will provide enough coal to make thirteen bombers,' they were told. Every household had to guard against wasting fuel: sometimes a small boy, who was deemed the man of the house if his father was away serving in the forces, was put in charge of monitoring the family's use of scarce supplies and making sure they did not exceed targets. Those London families who possessed baths – about one in three – had long been used to restricting their bath water to a maximum of five inches, something which astonished the American President's wife Eleanor Roosevelt when she stayed with the King and Queen at Buckingham Palace in 1942 and was confronted with the painted line around the bath indicating the maximum permitted depth of water. And this was for one bath a week, which was the norm in ordinary households, not one a day.

Housewives had been urged to save fuel when cooking by using only one ring or by taking the opportunity to heat water in the oven while cooking. As an extreme fuel-saving measure, the Ministry of Food's pamphlet *Food without Fuel* was anxious to demonstrate how a meal could be cooked in a hay box. A hay box was made of a strong packing case with a lid, or an old trunk. It had to be well lined with clean newspaper, which in turn had to be covered with a blanket. The remaining space was filled with hay, which could be made from old grass cuttings. Food had to be heated up in a saucepan to boiling point on the stove and then placed with the lid on the saucepan in its nest in the hay. A meat stew that would take 30 minutes to cook on the stove would take three and a half hours in the hay box. Not surprisingly, the hay box method did not really take off.

During the fuel crisis of early 1945 the readers of *Woman*, always a faithful purveyor of Government messages, were reminded that 'your fire may come out of a tap instead of a scuttle, but it's a coal fire just the same. Gas comes from coal, and coal reserves must be used economically if the country is to have enough for all its needs . . . Cut your gas and electricity. They both come from *coal*!'

Even in the gloom of a British winter, there was no need to turn on all the lights. Here, too, housewives could save fuel, if only they would take the trouble. *Woman* explained how:

No dim-out indoors! How to get the maximum brightness from your electric fittings: keep your bulbs clean by monthly dipping them in warm suds and polishing with a soft duster. Did you know that one 100-watt bulb is brighter than four 25-watt bulbs? Glass shades, especially inverted reflectors, are always grime collectors. A regular tickle with a feather duster or ceiling brush and a periodic wash in sudsy water is recommended. Parchment shades can be dusted and wiped with a cloth dipped in lukewarm soapy water. Fabric and silk shades need as much care as your best, flimsy undies.

Even someone like James Lees-Milne, who led a comparatively rich and privileged existence, was affected by the fuel crisis. 'The cold persists. It is appalling, and I have run out of anthracite,' he moaned on 11 January. 'I only have two bucketfuls of coal left. I ordered ten hundred weight of anthracite, my first order since March last year, in November. It has not been delivered yet.' At least he did not have to stay at home. He dined out and on 20 January resorted to his club: 'It is so appallingly cold – snowing again and freezing – that I cannot, without anthracite, face my room in Cheyne Walk. Went to Brooks's and there worked before the fire.' He was reduced to going to bed in his clothes, but on 26 January had the consolation of having 'a late tea with Emerald [Cunard] at the Dorchester, which was beautifully heated'. Indeed, everyone followed the same pattern of going out to public places as often as possible. There were record cinema audiences, as people sought the warmth they were denied in their own homes.

There was anger too at the quality of the coal on offer: 'And rotten bad stuff it is – more like steam-coal – it's so hard to break up, and it's all slaty. Paying 3/10 for bad coal, it's hard, it's very hard on the poor people,' Mass-Observation heard. 'I suppose it's the coal owners, selling off just what they like while the war's on – they know they can get the price for it, whatever it's like.'

The crisis inevitably brought its tragedies. Mrs Doris Segal of Shepherd's Bush, the wife of a soldier, had been unable to obtain any coal. She left the gas oven alight and the door open to provide warmth for her three children, a baby of three months and twins of fourteen months. They were left in the care of a neighbour while their mother went out in search of coal. He was chopping wood in the yard when the room caught fire and all three children died from fumes.

Londoners were invited to help themselves to the firewood from bomb-damaged houses. Bill Goble recalls: 'There was a large empty site on the White City Estate, next to Bloemfontein Road, where now the General Smuts pub is; and this site was used as a dump for air raid debris. Behind this was another site, used for damaged furniture. We used to go there to collect wood for our fire as it was difficult to get enough coal to keep the fire going.'

The irony of the situation was not lost on Gwladys Cox: 'At the moment we are burning a piece of Buckingham Mansions, which gives me a sinking feeling, for, at this very moment, Buckingham Mansions might quite as easily have been burning a bit of *us*!' Down in Mortlake Mrs Bell looked to the river for driftwood: 'Old Father Thames is good to the people who live alongside her,' she wrote. 'The tide brings in wood by the ton. When dried it lit many a fire when coal was short, and so was money.'

An inordinate amount of time and energy had to be spent in trying to secure what supplies were available, as Clive Beardmore noted:

Gas and electricity are cut off at times but so far not in Harrow. Potatoes are scarce. Coal and boiler-fuel also. By this I mean that we do a vast amount of scheming and worrying to obtain these things. I should not like to add up the number of fruitless expeditions I have made in the search for paraffin. On my rounds, when I see a queue of people with cans outside an ironmonger's, I make it my business to hurry home and fetch our cans and join 'em. Owing to these endeavours we have not so far run short of our creature comforts. But Mrs Amos next door looks pinched and half-starved.

Anyone who arrived in London, say from the United States, in these first few months of 1945 would have noticed how tired, pinched and grey the people looked, particularly the women. There were queues for everything and it was mainly the women who were queuing. 'Your Best Friends Today Are Your Feet', a *Daily Mail* headline informed its women readers, as if they did not know. When Lola Duncan returned from Canada in the New Year of 1945 she was soon introduced to the British habit of queuing, a wartime invention: 'The bus queue was another innovation. And I was nearly mobbed for fighting to get on first as of old. I tried to explain my ignorance. But it was no use. I crawled to the end of the line – a cheat and an outcast.'

Of course, with the bulk of Britain's petrol supplies being diverted to the RAF and the United States air force for their bombing raids on Germany and to other military needs, buses were few and far between, except in the rush hour when they maintained an almost full service. The service from central London closed at ten thirty at night; apart from the fuel shortage, it was a tremendous strain to drive in the blackout. To save fuel, dozens of buses parked overnight at Hyde Park, rather than go all the way back to their depots. Even after the service was increased when extra petrol was made available after VE Day, it was hampered by the tyre problem, owing to a continuing shortage of rubber from the Far East. Once on the bus, passengers were condemned to sit on uncomfortable wooden slatted seats, which had been introduced to save the labour and material needed to produce upholstered seats, or they had to stand tight up against each other in the extra space provided by the removal of some of the seating. The paper shortage meant that bus tickets were smaller and leaner, and passengers were urged to place their used tickets in the boxes provided. The lighting was so dim – as an economy as much as in accordance with blackout regulations – that the women bus conductors, the clippies, had problems seeing the coins.

Queuing had become a way of life. 'If you saw a queue you got on it' was the general principle. It was not always rewarding, as Mrs Bell remembers:

It became a habit to get alongside anyone who stood just waiting – it had to be near a shop. A queue formed one day outside the butcher's. When I asked the woman at the head of the queue what it was for she was quite haughty, 'I don't know what you are waiting for, I'm waiting for my husband.' My friend and I fell about laughing all the way home, we could not tell anyone why. Many times we waited over an hour, for just one pound of potatoes, half a pound of liver.

Women would go to extraordinary lengths to track down food, as a resident of Shepherd's Bush remembers:

As Dad and I were at work during the war my mother did the shopping and cooking. A neighbour would call and say, 'They have opened a box of fish at Mac Fisheries' so Mother would race up – usually it was all gone. One day she went to Hammersmith because she heard there were some apples. After queuing for ages, they ran out so she got on a bus and went to Acton, queued for an hour and returned triumphantly with two cooking apples.

There were many complaints about the attitude of shop-keepers, to whom customers were tied through the ration book system. Housewives could register the whole family's ration books with one retailer, in a bid to ensure preferential treatment if a scarce item became available, or spread them across a number of retailers. Whichever, they had to work very hard at keeping in with the shopkeepers with whom they were registered, although as new ration books were issued annually there was a chance to move to another if the previous one had proved unsatisfactory. Women, who had to queue almost on a daily basis when few owned a refrigerator, felt bullied and slighted by shopkeepers, who sometimes seemed to take a malign pleasure in not opening until a sufficiently long queue had formed, or else in pronouncing, 'Sorry ladies, that's your lot', before slamming the door in their faces.

Anthony Weymouth agreed that shopkeepers were often offhand or downright rude. 'We shan't know ourselves after the war when once again the various tradesmen solicit our custom,' he speculated, 'at present we're busy soliciting theirs, or rather trying to persuade them to enroll us among their favoured customers.' A great deal of grovelling over a sustained period of time meant that the retailer might keep something 'under the counter' for the fortunate few. Some went to the most extraordinary lengths to ingratiate themselves, as an article in the *Spectator* about how to keep in with your butcher explained: 'The crude way is to tip him heavily. Of course, that is not paying more for your meat, which would be illegal. I have known others who invite the butcher to their parties; others again, who teach their children to call the butcher "uncle".'

Weymouth acknowledged that it was not the shopkeeper's fault if supplies were low and was much taken with a witty notice he saw displayed outside a shop: 'We regret that only customers over ninety can be served and then only if accompanied by both parents' – a more tactful way than the manner usually employed in indicating that the proprietor had nothing to sell.

In spite of understandable complaints about queuing and shortages, feeding a population of just over 45 million on a beleaguered island in wartime was a triumph of Government planning and organisation. Under the inspired leadership of Lord Woolton, Minister of Food from April 1940 to November 1943, the Government did a brilliant job both in taking the public into its confidence, explaining the problems so as to win its co-operation, and educating it about the values of nutrition. 'Food is a munition of war. Don't waste it' urged one of the Ministry's advertisements in its Kitchen Front campaign, which received wide publicity through press and wireless. An evocative poster showing a sailor adrift in the Atlantic, losing his life to bring supplies to Britain, had a powerful influence on the public. 'Remember the little economies are multiplied by every home in the land,' the Ministry urged. 'In this way British housewives can lighten the heavy load of our Merchant Navy.' Indeed, every house-wife soon understood that sacrifices had to be made to save

Our Sailors don't mind risking their lives to feed you—and your family—but they do mind if you help the U-boats by wasting food.

valuable shipping space and to conserve the lives of seamen and most of them became adept at stretching the rations and juggling the points to provide as nutritious and interesting fare as possible for their families.

At the outbreak of war Britain was importing two-thirds of its food. Clearly, this was a situation that had to be addressed, and quickly. 'The outstanding problem in feeding the nation became that of finding the necessary shipping space,' Lord Woolton recalled. 'The country never realized how nearly we were brought to disaster by the submarine peril.' Shipping space was required for the import of materials for making munitions, as much as for the import of food, drugs and other commodities. Having run the gamut of the Atlantic, supplies were again vulnerable to air raids on the docks and warehouses:

the sight and smell of burning sugar spilling out of Silvertown's warehouses is one of the enduring images of the Blitz. Woolton devised a system whereby ships were unloaded hastily and established new cold stores and warehouses away from the ports. Every locality had its emergency food stores, so that the population could be fed for a few days in the event of invasion or an interruption to transport links.

It was the task of the Ministry of Agriculture to stimulate British farmers to produce some of the food that had hitherto been imported. Pre-war, 22 million tons of food and animal feeding stuffs were being imported annually, the key suppliers in order of importance being Argentina, Canada, Australia, New Zealand, India, Burma, the United States and the remaining small proportion, enemy or occupied countries in Europe. Imported food provided more than two-thirds of the calories and over half of the total protein supply. Early in 1941, when British dollar resources were nearly exhausted, the passage of the Lend-Lease Act in the United States enabled Britain to obtain from them supplies of valuable foods that could no longer be had elsewhere. This created a sorely needed improvement in the national diet.

With the entry of Japan into the war in December 1941, however, Britain lost most of its sources of tea, and all its sources of sago, tapioca, pepper, copra and coconut oil. The fall of Thailand, Burma and Indo-China meant that 80 per cent of Britain's supplies of rice were lost, while the Dutch East Indies could no longer supply sugar, tea and vegetable oils. The supply of palm oil to make soap was suddenly stopped by the Japanese occupation of Malaysia. Nigeria became an alternative source of palm oil, but soap still had to be rationed. The presence of the Japanese in the Indian Ocean jeopardised food supplies from Australia, New Zealand and India – source of wheat as well as tea. Much of the food from Australia and New Zealand – consisting largely of meat, wheat, butter and cheese – was redirected to American troops in the Pacific, while to compensate larger Lend-Lease supplies were directed from the United States to Britain across the Atlantic, with notable economies in shipping. Among tins of unfamiliar meat came Spam – Supply Pressed American Meat – and corned beef.

British farmers had to increase the output of food for human consumption: by 1945 only one-third of the pre-war tonnage of food was being imported. There had been a 90 per cent increase in the domestic production of wheat, an 87 per cent increase in the production of potatoes, a 45 per cent increase in the production of vegetables and a 19 per cent increase in sugar beet production. Onions, which had been imported from Brittany and the Channel Islands prior to the German occupation, were such a rarity that they were offered as coveted prizes in raffles. A Shepherd's Bush woman remembers: 'One day a relative gave my aunt in Fulham three small onions. She was always generous and brought us one. We kept it for a long time for a special occasion.'

The ordinary householder was urged to 'dig for victory' and in every domestic garden – even the gardens of Buckingham and Kensington Palaces – flowers gave way to vegetables. Anderson shelters, whose tin roofs had to be covered with five inches of soil, were a good spot to grow marrows. London's window boxes were given over to herbs,

its balconies to tomatoes and soft fruit, and tubs outside exclusive shops and men's clubs sported vegetables instead of flowers. The LCC allocated land for allotments and in the public parks 16,000 allotment holders were encouraged to grow vegetables. School playgrounds, bomb sites, railway sidings, dumps, even cemeteries were pressed into service. In

West Ham alone, in spite of dense housing, shortage of open spaces and poor soil, there were over 2,000 allotments, comprising an area of 124 acres. When the Tooting Bec Allotment Association petitioned the LCC for a continuation of the grant of allotments in 1945, it claimed that each allotment holder was producing an average of half a ton of food a year.

The LCC co-operated with the Royal Horticultural Society to give help and advice to London's allotment holders: there were exhibitions and gardening classes and every newspaper carried its gardening column, specifically devoted to the growing of vegetables. Gardening hints were swapped at the bus stop. Publishers produced a spate of books on the subject. Amateur Gardening's *War-Time Gardening for Home Needs* came with the label 'A National Food Handbook' and the dictum, 'By Helping Yourself You Help the Nation'. On the jacket flap there was a message from the Minister of Agriculture: 'To smallholders, allotment holders and those who have a reasonably sized garden – to those also who may be termed backyarders – you can help, help perhaps more than you realize, to feed yourselves and others. I ask for the fullest possible co-operation. The results of your work are of vital importance.'

Allotments were scrutinised for signs of neglect. At the Croydon and District Federation of Allotment Societies' annual meeting in March 1945, for instance, complaints were heard about untidy and badly kept allotment sites. In January 1945, 9,000 allotment holders in London's parks and open spaces had not yet paid the rent for the renewal of their tenancies for the year, despite reminder notices being posted on the sites since November. The LCC warned that there was a 2,000-long waiting list for its allotments and unless rents were received by 15 January the council would have no alternative but to re-let the plots to those on the waiting list.

In January 1945 Mary Rose's gardening column in *Home Chat* carried a sketch of a housewife tending the family allotment. In contrast to the harsh winter, February and March

1945 saw some of the warmest days in London for over 40 years. By April the temperature was in the eighties and on the 16th it reached 82 degrees in Regent's Street, before turning cold again. With the good weather and the end of the war in sight, Irene Byers was longing to grow flowers rather than vegetables in her garden, but the *Evening Standard*'s 'In a London Garden' column warned readers not to get rid of vegetables straight away, but to introduce flowers gradually. It would be some considerable time before Londoners could afford to forsake their vegetable growing and the LCC closed its allotments.

Before the war, large quantities of animal feeding stuffs had been imported with which to maintain the domestic output of meat, bacon, poultry, eggs, milk and dairy products: several tons of animal feed were required to produce one ton of meat or eggs. British farming managed to adapt to the loss of imported animal feed, to the extent that almost none was imported by the end of the war. It was particularly important that it should be able to provide feed for cows to keep up and increase the supply of milk for liquid consumption, while some meat continued to be imported. Shipping losses meant that the maximum quantity of nutrients had to fill the minimum space, so that bones were removed from the meat and the carcasses compressed and folded. The redirection of crops from beast to man meant that the pig and poultry population had to be reduced, the first by half and the second by one quarter. The reduction was partly compensated for by the import of substitute proteins from the United States and Canada: dried egg, which occupied one-quarter of the shipping space of shell eggs and did not need refrigeration; canned meats and fish, condensed milk, cheese and bacon.

Wasting food was a crime punishable by substantial fines, as a woman in Barnet found when she was caught putting out crumbs for the birds, and the Ministry of Food's inspectors made regular checks of restaurant and domestic dustbins; they also had the right to inspect domestic store cupboards, as a guard against black market activities. 'It was no use relying

on the enunciation of patriotic and moral persuasion,' Lord Woolton wrote. 'One had to have the stick also so that sinners were brought to speedy and heavy repentance.' But there was no need to throw food away. Westminster City Council initiated a system for the collection of kitchen waste – it had the highest yield per 1,000 of the population – to be passed through its concentrator to provide food for pigs: 35,000 tons of waste fed 31,000 pigs from birth to maturity. Pig bins for kitchen waste were set up in restaurants and the streets of every borough. Even bomb-damaged food carrying dirt, debris and broken glass was not to be discarded. The borough's chief sanitary inspector would examine it and decide whether it should be treated and made fit for human consumption or passed on for animal feed, or else destroyed.

Small groups of people banded together to run their own clubs keeping poultry, rabbits, pigs and bees under licence from the Ministry of Food. Living in the metropolis was no bar to such activities. While sheep grazed in Green Park and pig clubs thrived in Hyde Park, hens clucked on the roofs of Harley Street or wandered in smart streets. Each member of the pig club would contribute his kitchen waste to the animal's feed for the year and the pig, having reached the statutory 100 pounds in weight, would probably be slaughtered at Christmas under the supervision of a Ministry inspector and divided among them. In January 1945 there were reports of foot-and-mouth disease in pigs, especially in the Paddington area. Lawn clippings, dandelions and pot scrapings fed domestic rabbits, until such time as housewives could screw up their courage to kill one for the pot.

Strict limits were placed on the number of animals that could be kept: more than 20 hens meant that some eggs had to be handed over to the Ministry. Domestic poultry keepers had to surrender their entitlement to shell eggs in order to obtain feeding stuffs for their hens. By April 1945 there were 1,310,000 domestic poultry keepers in Britain providing eggs for 6,690,000 people. Local newspapers ran informative columns for such clubs and lectures were given: 'The Upper Norwood Domestic Poultry and Rabbit Club enjoyed a talk given by Mr A. Eisen, area organizer, Ministry of Agriculture, illustrated by coloured lantern slides' on the 'various breeds of rabbits most suitable for the production of flesh and fur'.

The Government was keen to avoid the problems of the First World War, where food shortages and panic buying led to galloping inflation and social unrest, as food prices soared beyond the reach of the ordinary and poorer sections of society. At the outbreak of the Second World War strict price controls were imposed, at the expense of the Exchequer. Prices were fixed through all stages of distribution to the point of sale to the public. Traders were to get a fair return, but no more. Those who infringed the controls incurred heavy fines or imprisonment. In the course of the war the cost of food rose by only 20 to 30 per cent above 1939 levels, as opposed to 130 per cent during the previous war, while the average wage doubled. The Ministry of Food became a bulk buyer of food with agencies established all over the world to procure supplies at the best prices. Eventually the Ministry increased its purchasing power still further by procuring, say, supplies of tea for all Allied and neutral countries, buying the total exportable surpluses in all producing countries. In Britain the Tea Brokers' Association of London, acting as the Ministry's selling agent, allocated the tea to the primary wholesalers. The state became the owner or virtual owner of all food imported into the country.

The Government also became the owner of all home-produced food – except that produced in private allotments or clubs under licence – in that the Ministry of Food was the sole buyer, with responsibility for its distribution into legitimate rather than black market channels. All animals had to be sold through specified collecting centres, graded and bought by the Ministry at fixed prices, and slaughtered on the Ministry's behalf at a selected slaughterhouse. Milk was bought at fixed prices by the Milk Marketing Board, who sold it to the Ministry, who determined how much should be used for dairy products, how much for liquid consumption. It was then re-sold by the Ministry to distributors and manufacturers. Eggs were sent to packing stations under the Ministry's control. Fish was not taken into Ministry ownership, but it had to be evenly distributed, so that the Ministry paid the carriage charges, reimbursing itself by a levy on primary buyers. In this way, it destroyed any incentive to sell all the fish to traders in areas nearest the ports of landing to the exclusion of inland towns.

The food industry itself and the way it operated had to be drastically overhauled. The munitions industry needed buildings for plant, so that factory space previously allocated to food had to be reduced. The idea was to concentrate an agreed volume of production into a smaller number of factories economical of manpower. Output per employee was strictly measured: if it fell below a certain level those employees might find themselves transferred by the all-powerful Ministry of Labour into munitions. As food manufacturing became concentrated, the variety of manufactured foods was reduced. In soft drinks, for instance, the wartime manufacturers' association agreed to eliminate all their brand names for the duration and sell standardised products under such designations as 'Orange Squash S.W.153', the code letters and number being the sole indication of the manufacturer's identity. In biscuits, the number of varieties produced by any one manufacturer was reduced from 350 to only 20. But manufacturers were keen to ensure that customers would not forget their brand names or specific products and advertised the fact that they would be available again after the war. Peek Frean, manufacturers of biscuits in Bermondsey, was very anxious not to be forgotten: 'A Peek into the Past,' the advertisement began. 'Ah, those Bourbons – a royal line of Peek Frean biscuits! They were crisply crunchy, with a sandwich layer of rich chocolate cream. To-day, Peek Frean Biscuits are zoned, and supplies are limited. Mr Peek's and Mr Frean's peek into the past is also a pre-view of the future when their biscuits will again be plentiful and varied. Peek Frean's Britain's crispiest biscuits.'

All non-essential transportation had to be eliminated in wartime. Londoners were urged to spend their holidays at home and the onus was on the local authorities to arrange sufficiently attractive entertainment – concerts, sports fixtures, competitions and open-air dances – to keep them there. Every railway booking office sported a sign asking, 'Is your journey really necessary?' Trains, whose main task had to be to carry troops and freight, were overcrowded, cold, dimly lit, slow and frequently late. Travellers had to arrive at the station long before the train was due to leave just to be sure of getting on it. Private motoring had virtually been extinguished with the demise of the petrol ration, except in cases where it could be proved that no other transport was available, which was hardly the case in London. Even a Harley Street doctor like Anthony Weymouth, who because of his profession was among the privileged few still entitled to a petrol allowance, had laid up his car on blocks and taken to taxis and bicycles. Most people walked whenever they could, took the tube even if it meant climbing over the recumbent bodies of shelterers, or joined the long queues waiting for scarce buses.

With the shortage of petrol and rubber tyres, as well as labour, the transport of food had to be rationalised and restricted, too. The Ministry of Food transformed the way milk was collected from the farms and taken to the primary buyers, with a resultant saving of 75,000 vehicle miles daily and 2,225 billion gallons of petrol a year. Milk had been distributed by a large number of companies, including the Co-op, to an immense number of small retailers. One street might be served by six or more milk delivery carts. Under the Ministry's direction, everyone who had their

milk delivered had to register for it, so that supplies could be regulated, and delivery in each area was divided among the dairymen so that each served a compact block of streets. Glass milk bottles, of course, were precious and scarce and had to be returned promptly; alternatively, milk was served straight into the householder's jug.

Britain's main sources of timber and paper lay in the United States and Scandinavia – in occupied Norway and neutral Sweden. The paper shortage meant that London's book publishers – who had lost millions of books when their City warehouses went up in flames during the Blitz – were given a paper quota, as were newspapers. The quality press, *The Times*, the *Daily Telegraph* and the *Manchester Guardian*, ran to six or eight pages, while the popular press, including the *Daily Mirror*, the *Daily Mail* and the *Daily Express*, shrank to as little as four pages. Even carrying plenty of advertisements for the Ministry of Information, the shortened newspapers managed to convey all they needed to. All newspapers restricted their circulation and quickly sold out. It was bad form not to use both sides of the paper when writing a letter, as wartime Government correspondence in the National Archives shows. Among its many salvage drives, Westminster City Council collected 13,113 tons of paper in the course of the war and sold it for £72,303. Housewives got into the habit of sorting through their rubbish, putting aside kitchen waste, rubber, tins, bones, rags and paper for salvage. 'Waste paper isn't rubbish,' a Ministry of Supply advertisement reminded them. Paper was needed to make munitions. 'Enemy Ships Torpedoed with the Help of Old Rags' ran another Ministry headline, telling women that their old rags had been transformed into charts for submarine commanders, as well as other military purposes.

In the food industry, timber packing cases had to be reused. The use of packaging was strictly controlled. Paper and board could be used to package food only as far as bare necessity required, to convey the goods to the public in a proper condition. Paper bags were not provided in shops and customers

had to carry goods away unwrapped, using their own carefully preserved paper or baskets or the ubiquitous string bag.
The tin mines of Malaya had been lost to the Japanese and
the scarcity of tin was aggravated by the ever-growing demand
for tinned goods by the armed forces serving overseas.

Not the least of inconveniences for civilians was a shortage
of lavatory paper, as an anonymous diarist in Kensington
records one grim day in January 1945: 'I had a free day to
go from shop to shop to find toilet paper, now scarce, and
hear a distant explosion like an exploding rocket shell. If only
there were no war, no shelling, no shortage of paper, no lack
of pressure from the gas supply.'

In wartime the lives of the people were controlled to an unprecedented degree. They were subject to the sort of restrictions that,
had it not been for the war, would have been possible only
under a totalitarian regime. Taking its cue from the Germans,
in January 1940 the British Government adopted a policy of
rationing, but it improved on their system. In Germany everything was rationed, customers in a restaurant could not eat
without surrendering coupons, and certain workers had privileged status. Lord Woolton believed that this was too onerous
and impracticable. 'I was determined that we would not ration
unless we could ration successfully: on this issue I was not
prepared to risk public confidence in the coupons for essential
foods. Also I was chary about burdening a somewhat exhausted
department with further claims on their administrative efficiency.' Woolton, formerly a social worker in the Liverpool slums
turned successful businessman running a string of northern
department stores, referred to the Ministry of Food – which
from its Colwyn Bay wartime headquarters employed 50,000
civil servants nationwide – as 'the greatest shop the world has
ever known'. Ironically, Britain had to keep larger reserves of
food in store than it had done before the war, not only because
succeeding supplies might be lost at sea, but also to ensure that
the ration would always be honoured.

Lord Woolton believed that for rationing to work, it had

to remain essentially simple and have the appearance of justice and impartiality. The British people accepted the principle of rationing, and most of them were happy to co-operate, because they recognised that it meant fair shares for all. Everyone had to be registered at a food office to obtain a ration book. Even the King and Queen were issued with ration books, although the Minister concerned was advised to present them to the royal couple personally. Ration books came in different colours according to category. Adults had buff-coloured books, while the green ration books of pregnant women, nursing mothers and children under five earned them a place at the front of the queue. Children between the ages of 5 and 16 were given blue ration books, allowing them priority on fruit and an extra allowance of milk. If a precious ration book was lost, it could be replaced on payment of one shilling and on signature of a declaration witnessed by a responsible person.

Initially, the rations consisted of 4 ounces of bacon or ham per person per week, 12 ounces of sugar, 4 ounces of butter – later reduced to 2 ounces – and 4 ounces of margarine, 2 ounces of cooking fat (at this time, the British used vast quantities of animal fat rather than olive oil), 2 ounces of tea per person per week, 1s 10d worth of meat – later reduced at various times to 1s 1d and 1s 2d (equivalent to two small lamb chops) – for a person over six and 11d worth for a child below the age of six per week, cheese varying between 1 and 2 ounces per week – except for miners, agricultural workers and other heavy workers, who were allowed an extra 8 to 16 ounces, since they lacked canteens and had to carry their midday meal to work. Vegetarians were also given extra cheese instead of the meat ration. The dietary requirements of religious minorities were taken into account, although at the outbreak of war the Chief Rabbi had excused Britain's Jews from observing the Jewish dietary laws for the duration.

Adults could have two pints of milk each a week in winter and up to three or four in summer, for both liquid consumption and to be used in cooking. Expectant mothers and mothers with children under one year were entitled to seven pints a week. Children up to 5 could have seven pints a week, 5- to 18-year-olds three and a half pints a week. For poor children, many of whom had suffered from poor teeth, bone deformation and rickets, the increased intake of milk showed definite benefits by the end of the war. Certain classes of invalids were allowed up to 14 pints a week. Control of scarce milk supplies meant that its use for the manufacture of cream, ice cream and chocolate had to be stopped. However, in November 1944 limited amounts of ice cream went on sale again. In addition to liquid milk, every family was allowed one tin of dried skimmed milk – equivalent to four pints – a month. Children under one, later two, were allowed a full-cream product nearer the real thing.

Jam, marmalade and syrup were rationed, as well as mincemeat, lemon curd and honey. During the jam- or marmalade-making seasons, when the WI, WVS and housewives everywhere laboured to produce vast quantities, there was an extra sugar allowance, there being a Ministry rule that every pound of home-made jam must contain 60 per cent sugar to preserve it longer and enable it to travel. A north London woman remembers: 'We made jam from hedgerow fruits and the small amount of extra sugar we were allowed for the purpose. Crouch End Playing Fields in particular were a rich source of blackberries, elderberries and rowan berries.' Although it was all right to give the odd pot of jam to a friend, it was a finable offence to sell jam made with both real fruit and rationed sugar outside the rationing system – hence the phrase 'money for jam'.

Later, in December 1941, points rationing was introduced. Those who found that their neighbours had occasionally been able to get tinned salmon or sardines, various tinned meats, tinned fruits or beans, cereals, pulses or dried fruit, demanded that the Ministry of Food should ration all these items. As Lord Woolton said, they did not realise the impossibility of the task. 'It is only possible to ration if there are sufficient supplies for everybody to have some, and this multitude of different articles that indeed made life tolerable for people, were all in such short supply that it would have been impossible for everybody to get even the smallest quantity.' In practice, small consignments of these foods were often squeezed into the odd cabin or small space when a ship was being loaded. There was never a sufficiently large or consistent quantity to honour a blanket ration for the whole population. So the Ministry devised a new, ingenious scheme.

Every holder of a ration book received 16 points a month, later raised to 20 and then to 24 before dropping to 20 again, to spend them as he or she wished, at any shop that had the items. The articles that were in the shortest supply cost the largest number of points and vice versa. 'It was a "Stock Exchange" in points and it varied frequently,' Lord Woolton wrote. 'The number of points that were called for was subject to change: if we found, for example, that we had a considerable quantity of sardines, then we advised the shopkeepers that they were in good supply and presently we reduced the number of points for which they called.'

For months before the introduction of the points system the Ministry had stockpiled the food, so that there would be enough in the shops to launch the system with confidence. It offered an incentive to break the routine of the dreary wartime diet. Housewives scanned the 'Changes in Points Value' that appeared in the newspapers. 'For women it became "shopping" instead of "collecting the ration",' Woolton continued, 'and this gave them a little pleasure in their harassed lives and an exercise in their natural skill.' It offered the Ministry the means of controlling the market. 'If the demand for any one article became excessive the points' value of it was put up until consumption had been checked.' In addition there was 'personal points' rationing for chocolate and sugar confectionery.

Wholesalers were given up-to-date population statistics, based on ration book returns, so that they might adjust their distribution where necessary. This was particularly important in London Region, as a considerable section of the population was evacuating the capital or returning in the

course of 1944 and 1945. Each local authority had a food
supply committee, consisting of food traders and employees
as well as consumers, to organise the distribution of food to
the shops. Before the war, local authorities had been asked
to select Food Executive Officers and key personnel from
their staff to run local Food Offices. By 1944 there were
1,250 Food Offices, each catering for 30,000–40,000 people.
The Food Executive Officer, often Clerk to the Council, was
secretary of the Food Control Committee and in charge of
the Food Office. The Food Office was concerned with the
administration of rationing. It issued identity cards on behalf
of the Registrar General, clothing ration books on behalf of
the Board of Trade, and food ration books on behalf of the
Ministry of Food. It dealt with changes of address, answered
queries on food matters and acted as a local focus of food
propaganda. It licensed retail traders and caterers and operated the Ministry's new welfare schemes for milk, orange
juice (concentrated, from the United States) and cod liver oil
to children and expectant mothers.

When a member of the public bought rationed food, he
would have to hand his ration book to the retailer, who would
cut out the coupons. The retailer would put all the coupons
in a large envelope, certify how many were in it, and send it
back to the Food Office. It was impractical for the Food Office
to count all the coupons, so that they carried out spot checks
only. On the basis of the number of coupons returned, the
Food Office would issue the retailer with a buying permit so
that he could replenish his stocks. Fred Barnes, who had
worked as a legal clerk in the town clerk's office in Romford
before the war, became Food Officer in that district. He recalls
an amusing incident with the coupons, which were stored
above the office:

And they were stacked and kept for so long in these attics, and
one of the girls said to me one day, 'You know we've got mice up
there and they're playing havoc with the coupons.' She said, 'The
strange thing is, they're not touching the tea or the sugar, they're

going for the cheese and bacon.' I said, 'Don't be silly, they can't read.' But when I checked it was a fact. No tea, no sugar coupons touched, but cheese and bacon had been ravished. Of course the answer was perfectly simple, the shop assistants when they handled the ration books had grease on their fingers which came off on the coupons and the mice could smell and enjoy them.

Lord Woolton later attributed the fact that the British were adequately nourished in wartime to the application of science to nutrition. Before the war half the population of Britain was not getting enough nutrients. The diet was generally deficient in calcium, vitamin A, vitamin B1 and vitamin C; it was also short of animal protein and iron. The war focused official minds wonderfully on how to provide the best nutrition for the people to keep them fit and productive for the war effort, making the best use of shipping space and what could be grown at home. At the beginning of 1945 the total calorie value of the diet was 3,008 per head per day, the same as pre-war. There were less fats and sugar in the diet, although there was a lot of starch; as one woman quipped, she was surprised when she stood up after a meal that she wasn't stiff.

The consumption of protein, though not of animal protein, was higher than it had been before the war. The intake of calcium and iron increased substantially during the war, as did that of vitamin B1 and riboflavin, vitamin C and nicotinic acid, although there had been a reduction in the intake of vitamin A. The wartime diet might have seemed tedious and restricted, but it was a sensible one and no one went hungry, even though a Wartime Social Survey carried out for the Ministry of Food revealed that men in particular thought they were not getting enough to eat. It was a question of changing habits and attitudes. It was not necessary to overeat to be well fed; quite the contrary. To do so was wasteful and unpatriotic: 'If you eat more than you need, you are wasting food as surely as if you had thrown it away. So eat what you need, no more. Buy wisely and cater strictly. For your health's sake, as well as your country's, remember that "Enough is as good as a feast." Save food! Save money! Save cargo space for munitions!' the Ministry tirelessly impressed on the public.

Nor was anything to be left on the plate, as the wartime poster proclaimed: 'A clear plate means a clear conscience. Don't take more than you can eat.' Like it or not, the British emerged from five years of war leaner, fitter and healthier and women could take pride in their slim figures.

The Ministry of Food embarked on a food education programme for the nation. A small staff of dieticians and cookery specialists provided expert advice, which was passed on to the public in a barrage of advertisements, broadcasts and film flashes at the cinema. Every morning after the BBC eight o'clock News Freddie Grisewood would introduce the *Kitchen Front* programme. Dr Charles Hill would broadcast hints and tips on food. It was stirring, positive and upbeat – especially when he got on to the subject of bowels. Ambrose Heath and Mabel Constanduros gave recipes. Anyone who had something interesting to contribute was invited on to the programme. Lord Woolton would appear with the popular characters 'Gert and Daisy'– Elsie and Doris Waters – the content of their comic dialogue being easily absorbed by listeners. Food slogans would be interspersed with encouragement, such as 'Carry on Fighters on the Kitchen Front! You are doing a great job.'

Magazines invited readers to send in helpful hints for other women, paying half a crown for each one published. Recipes devised as part of the Kitchen Front campaign peppered the press in the form of weekly 'Food Facts'. A survey carried out for the Ministry of Food showed that only 40 per cent of housewives kept 'Food Facts' cuttings, however, and poorer women were least likely to read them or keep them.

Women could arm themselves with a copy of *Food Facts for the Kitchen Front: A Book of Wartime Recipes and Hints* with a foreword by Lord Woolton. The book was very didactic, explaining at length the values of various foods. 'In these days, when we are all beginning to concern ourselves with essentials and to discard the things that do not matter,' it preached, 'it is necessary to remember these two facts: 1. What we *can* get is good for us; 2. A great deal of what we *cannot* get is quite unimportant.'

Practical demonstrations were arranged by food advice centres in the larger towns. Marguerite Patten worked for the Ministry as a food adviser and demonstrator at Harrods in Knightsbridge. Many of the Harrods customers had never cooked in their lives before and, now that their cooks and maids had left for more vital and lucrative employment doing war work, these women had to absorb cooking and rationing all at once. If asked advice on a dinner party, Marguerite Patten's first question would be, 'What have you got?' There was no point in dreaming up the ideal meal, because the chances of acquiring all the ingredients were remote. Women had to learn to make the best of what was available, to be imaginative. Like Dr Hill, Marguerite Patten would emphasise the positive, stressing that a recipe needed 'only one egg!'. She soon exhausted the official repertoire of recipes and had to invent new ones, improvising as she went. Her eggless fruit cake, in which tea was the magic ingredient, was pronounced a triumph.

Thanks to the Ministry's educational drive and their own ingenuity, British women became adept at juggling rations and points to provide nutritious meals. The wife of an American journalist arriving in 1945 was flummoxed: 'For a month now I have been trying to co-ordinate my culinary talents with British rations. The cookery book I brought with me is about as much use as an atomic bomb formula in a school laboratory.'

The contents of *The Stork Margarine Cook Book* convey something of the grimness of preparing food and keeping a family fed in wartime: 'Cooking in times of emergency', explaining, for instance, what to do if you have a cake in the oven when you suddenly have to run for shelter; 'Stretching and shrinking your family meals, and money-saving meat dishes'; 'Scrap-saving and new ways to do up meat and fish'; 'Making the most of tinned food'; 'Sauces to make wartime food more interesting' and 'Making the most of vegetables, rice and macaroni'. Touchingly, there is a small section for 'grass widowers', whose wives were either evacuated or engaged in war work. The fact that it contains such basic instructions as to how to put the kettle on indicates how far there was to go to achieve equality of the sexes.

Most wartime cookery books, especially *Food Facts for the Kitchen Front*, laid heavy emphasis on a vegetable-based diet, which would provide vitamins A and C, compensating for the loss of citrus fruit, as well as a certain amount of protein. 'Even if you like a meat and vegetable meal best,' it advised, 'you can feed well on a course of vegetables alone. Or if you are near the end of your meat ration, an extra vegetable will transform it into a substantial meal.' Anthony Weymouth, a Harley Street doctor who was taking a considerable interest in the new science of nutrition and its application to health, worried about the inadequacy of a totally vegetarian diet. To gain sufficient daily protein from vegetables alone, he argued, 'you would require the stomach of a cow comfortably to digest an adequate amount of green leaves.' Readers of *Food Facts for the Kitchen Front* were reminded to 'preserve the vegetable water for soup or stock'. The British had always had a tendency to over-boil vegetables until there was no goodness left in them, but now they were advised to eat them raw or steam them. The fact that many of the vegetables they ate were home-grown and therefore fresh accounted for a nutritional benefit rarely present in shop-bought vegetables today.

'Potato Pete' became a popular cartoon character in the Ministry's campaign to encourage the public to eat more

P's for Protection Potatoes afford;
O's for the Ounces of Energy stored;
T's for Tasty, and Vitamins rich in;
A's for the Art to be learnt in the Kitchen.
T's for Transport we need not demand;
O's for old England's Own Food from the Land;
E's for the Energy eaten by you;
S's for the Spuds which will carry us through!

potatoes. Potatoes, although scarce in the early months of
1945 because of bad weather, were not rationed and were 'a
rich store of all-round nourishment.' 'It is an energy food and
a protective food,' the public was informed. 'It contains
Vitamin C – the vitamin we miss when fruit is scarce.' Potatoes
were not to be peeled, which was wasteful, but cooked in their
skins and then peeled. One of many memorable Ministry of
Food ditties reminded the public that:

> Those who have a will to win
> Cook potatoes in their skin
> Knowing that the sight of peelings
> Deeply hurts Lord Woolton's feelings.

There were dozens of recipes involving potatoes, including a
potato omelette which only involved 'one egg (if you have it)'.
Women were even advised that 'well-seasoned mashed potato
and chopped spring onion and parsley make an excellent sandwich filling!' Any left-over potato could be used to thicken
soups or stews, as could oatmeal.

Similarly, the Ministry's 'Doctor Carrot' cartoon character,
carrying a doctor's bag marked 'Vitamin A', advised people to
'Call me often and you'll keep well.' The idea was to promote
'carrots, bright treasures dug from good British earth'. 'Carrots
help you see in the dark' the Ministry advertisement told a
nation constantly bumping into each other and immovable
objects in the blackout. An apocryphal story is that Goering
picked up on this propaganda and, ignorant of the invention
of radar, believed that a heavy consumption of carrots must be

the reason British pilots seemed to have such excellent eyesight. Consequently, the Luftwaffe was condemned to eating vast extra helpings of carrots. Potatoes and carrots, as well as the much-promoted vegetable swede, were the main ingredients in the famous wartime dish, Woolton Pie, which was essentially a vegetable pie thickened with the ubiquitous oatmeal and topped with either potato or pastry made from national wholemeal flour. It was considered far too dreary a dish to warrant the name of such an imaginative and avuncular minister. Carrots, like beetroot, were used as sweeteners in cakes and to make marmalade. Children munched on carrots rather than sweets.

Like potatoes, bread was promoted by the Ministry as an energy-giving filler. Bread was not rationed during the war, although it was in 1946. The public was reminded that bread was made from wheat, some of which had to be imported, so that it must not be wasted. Lord Woolton admitted he hated to see a waiter throwing away an unused roll. The menus in the popular Lyons Corner House carried the notice: 'We are co-operating with the Ministry of Food by serving bread or rolls only on request. Won't you co-operate by not asking?' Throughout the war the Ministry's scientists were constantly tampering with the 'National Loaf', employing nearly all the wheat including the husk, while trying to increase the content of vitamin B1, iron and nicotinic acid, adding pure calcium carbonate, bran and oats to boost its nutritional value.

It was not popular, being darker and rougher than people were used to, although by January 1945 improved milling techniques and a decrease in the bran content meant a whiter loaf was being produced, as Anthony Heap noted gratefully: 'Duly delighted to learn that bread is to regain some of its former whiteness. What with this and the reappearance of ice cream [in November 1944], we seem to be getting right back to – well, 1941, anyway.' He confessed he would will- ingly exchange white bread and ice cream for a bottle of Heinz tomato ketchup, which he had missed most during the war. Flour was not rationed, which was just as well, as the British diet relied so heavily on sweet and savoury pies and pastries. Meals were not considered complete without a pudding: stale bread could be used in bread and butter pudding and in trifle, while a fruit crumble was a wartime improvisation when there were insufficient ingredients to make a proper pastry case.

With butter in short supply, margarine made from whale oil and nuts was promoted as an alternative, but it was not popular. 'So long as you have plenty of Stork in the house, you and your children are safe from one wartime hardship: shortage of good, economical fat,' *The Stork Margarine Cook Book* proclaimed. Margarine was doctored by the Ministry, which added vitamins A and D. If butter or margarine ran out, a substitute could be made with marrow fat from marrow bones, eked out with a teaspoon of vinegar. Mock cream could be made by mixing margarine with sugar, dried milk powder and a tablespoon of milk.

There were wry chuckles from the audience in performances of Shakespeare's *Henry* V at the words, 'Aye, but these English they are shrewdly out of beef.' Indeed, a nation of heavy meat eaters was reduced to bolstering its meat ration with oddities like horsemeat, rabbit, sheep's hearts and sheep's heads, which, like offal and sausages of rather dubious content, were off the ration. Vere Hodgson found she was rather reliant on sausages:

The meat ration lasts for three evening meals. I don't think anyone can make it go further, whatever you have. This covers Saturday, Sunday and Monday. Tuesday and Wednesday I have a handful of rice or macaroni doffed up in some way with curry or cheese. But the cheese ration is so small now that there is rarely any left. Thursday I have an order with the dairy for a pound of sausages. These do for Thursday, Friday and Saturday lunch. They do not however taste much of sausage. I understand they are nearly all soya bean flour and the flavour is nothing much. However they look like sausages and we pretend they are. Of course a little fish would help a lot but there are always long queues for it and my dinner hour is only one hour and I never have time to wait. But you see, we manage and we are not hungry.

Wartime cook books described what could be done with the cheaper cuts of meat to make the meat ration go further, while there were ideas as to what to do with offal, such as 'sweetbreads and brussels sprouts' and 'brains au gratin'. A new regulation in August 1941 permitted the sale with a licence of horsemeat for human consumption. Unlike some of their continental neighbours, the British had never eaten horsemeat and found it abhorrent. Irene Byers tried it once only: 'We dine off a piece of horsemeat – an experiment never to be repeated. The meat was stringy, tough and with a strange sweet taste. We throw it all away and enjoy our home-grown vegetables instead.' Some recall being served horsemeat for school lunch, while many adults surreptitiously bought it for their pets, as an anonymous diarist in Kensington records: 'By rushing backward and forward between one horse butcher and another I got a good steak for the cat. Of course I did not say it was for the cat, the butcher would have been insulted, of course I asked politely and was surprised to be served politely and have it wrapped in the paper I brought, in an almost deferential manner.'

In bohemian Chelsea where she was frequently entertaining her literary and artistic friends, including the poet Dylan Thomas and his wife Caitlin, Theodora Fitzgibbon was less scrupulous about horsemeat:

The search for food took more and more time, for with the many callers, some who stayed for hours, even days, meals had to be provided. I would make huge pots of onion soup, and when the horseflesh shop opened in Chelsea Manor Street not only the dogs profited, but also ourselves, for I had no scruples about making enormous horse-liver pates and jellied tongues. Would everyone's enjoyment have been so great had they known, I wonder? I even made a rook pie one day, which was eagerly devoured.

Rabbit was a bit more popular. 'I never thought the day would come when I would look upon rabbit as a treat,' Mrs Uttin of Wembley ruminated. Perhaps she enjoyed the Ministry's Kitchen Front recipe for rabbit stew with prune dumplings. As a child in wartime, Ruth Tanner remembers her mother queuing from dawn for a wild rabbit, and afterwards making Ruth slippers of rabbit fur.

A short story in *Woman*, featuring an English girl who had been evacuated to the United States and had just returned home, brilliantly captures the desperate business of obtaining something, no matter how obnoxious, to put on the family's dinner plates:

'What do you think I have found?' cried Mrs Chester, delighted.

Lisa raised her pencilled eyebrows slightly, and looked at her parent. 'I don't know,' she said listlessly. 'A gold mine?'

'No, dear. A sheep's heart!' said Mrs Chester. 'That darling man at the butcher's shop had kept it under the counter for me! What do you think of that?'

Lisa's lip curled slightly. It was pretty dreadful to return grown-up from America to find your parents become not only trivial, but greedy. Really, thought Lisa, in this house we talk of nothing but food. In the Delaneys' house in Washington they never talked of food at all! There it just was!

In 1945 there was less meat available than in the previous year, but this was balanced by larger supplies of fish. Fish had never been rationed, but the few men and boats available for fishing had to work in enemy-infested waters or under threat of enemy fire from the air. Long queues would form at the fishmongers. 'At the fishmonger's this morning, a very long wait, fish being late owing to fog,' Gwladys Cox noted one morning in February. 'As the queue stood patiently waiting, there was a loud explosion in the distance. The whole queue gasped, looked at each other knowingly, said nothing and made no move.' Women in a queue were long past ducking or running for cover in the event of an explosion. Even the British favourite dish was in jeopardy, as Anthony Heap complained in May: 'The majority of fish and chip shops, like many pubs, are now only open about two nights a week. If it isn't a shortage of fish, it's a scarcity of potatoes. And if it isn't potatoes, it's frying fat.'

Again, oddities such as salt cod, whale meat and snoek were used to bolster supplies, but found little favour. Marguerite Patten points out that snoek from South Africa was very similar to tuna, but even tinned tuna was unknown to the British then. They had no idea how to cook it. They lacked the peppers, olives and other ingredients that make tuna at least such an appetising dish in the Mediterranean. One desperate advertisement in *Home Chat* ran: 'Sardines are worth their cost in points; with them you can concoct some really delicious dishes: dressed sardines, grilled sardines, devilled sardines, sardine rolls, savoury sardines, sardine spread.'

Lola Duncan had several shocks when she returned to wartime London from Canada, not least in trying to buy eggs: 'The first was asking for half a dozen eggs! The elderly man behind the counter looked at me more in sorrow than in anger. He took off his glasses, wiped them, and put them on again – as if to visualize better what had drifted into his shop. Then he scribbled something upon my [ration] book, handed me one egg, minus a paper bag, and retired.'

Before the war eggs had been imported from as far away as China and Poland, both now under enemy occupation. Eggs could not be rationed, because the number laid could never be relied on. On average townspeople were receiving about 36 eggs a year by the end of 1944, although in 1945 Mrs Bell noted that she was getting about 1 egg a month if she was lucky. No wonder she attempted the art of stretching an egg to feed four: 'Each woman would pass on to others any tips in saving. The best one caused a wry kind of merriment. It was found by using a razor blade an egg could be cut thin enough to make four sandwiches. I only tried it once, nearly took the top of my fingers off.'

Shell eggs were supplemented with dried eggs. Early in 1945 the dried eggs' ration was reduced to two packets every four weeks, while in September it was reduced again to one packet every eight weeks. Dried eggs were new to the British housewife, so not surprisingly she resorted to the Ministry's 'Food Facts' recipes for this more than any other food. They could be used to make scrambled eggs, omelettes, or in cakes and puddings. One packet of dried egg powder was equivalent to 12 eggs. It was necessary to mix one level tablespoonful of dried egg powder to two tablespoonfuls of water. If too much powder were used the dish would taste of sulphur.

Given that tea was the great panacea – handed out after every incident – it is amazing to think of Londoners managing through the war on such a tiny ration. The Ministry recommended 'One teaspoonful per person and none for the pot.' Women were reduced to scrabbling at the bottom of the packet for loose leaves. Some resorted to the black market, as Lil Patrick recalls:

We can't survive without a cup of tea, you know. I suppose it's like the French with wine. The first thing we do when we've got a problem is to get the kettle on, so the amount of tea that was allocated to us was obviously insufficient. And this is how it was done: people you knew, friends, would say, 'I can get my hands on some tea if you want!' I can't remember the prices now, but it was always twice as much. And that was obviously stolen from somewhere, wasn't it? I mean it had to be, didn't it, when you stopped to think about it. But you know, the moral side of it, when you're gasping for a cup of tea, you kind of put that in the grey area don't you, and think, No, that wasn't me – I didn't do that!, but we did. We all did it.

In January 1945 the tea ration was increased by one ounce a week for the over seventies. In Walthamstow Mrs Britton went straight down to the Food Office for the extra coupons. 'So we shall now be able to offer any visitor a cup of tea with a light heart,' George Britton told his daughter in America. In fact, it had long been the habit of anyone visiting friends for tea to bring their own supplies of tea, sugar and milk.

After five years of war, many British children either could not remember what a banana looked like or had never seen one in their life and had no idea how to eat it. They might have eaten the substitute, consisting of mashed parsnip with banana essence. There was a tantalising advertisement showing a banana. The caption read: 'Bananas? No, not yet – but the next best thing – Lingford's Banana Flavoured Barley Pudding Mixture'. 'Oranges, lemons, bananas were almost antiques,' Mrs Bell writes.

Home-produced fruit was scarce, too, as the Ministry frowned on market gardeners using valuable land to grow fruit rather than vegetables, so that even in the summer and autumn months when apples, pears, rhubarb, plums and soft fruits, such as strawberries, raspberries, red and black currants, blackberries and gooseberries, came into the shops they were in short supply and therefore expensive. 'Native strawberries in their short season are gold-plated,' noted an American living in London. The Ministry's Food Facts reminded women that when using acid fruits in a pie they could reduce the sugar required by as much as one-third by the use of bicarbonate of soda, while if stewing fruit a piece of bread in the pan reduced acidity and saved sugar.

On 9 January 1945 the *Evening Standard* reported the great excitement as a boatload of oranges – 22,500,000 to be precise, or '1lb per head for everybody in the London Metropolitan Police area' – arrived from Palestine. Needless to say, they came with a fresh batch of instructions from the Ministry for tired housewives to absorb:

These new imports include 20,000 cases of bitter marmalade oranges for which ration books will not have to be marked. Thanks to the improved supplies of citrus fruits a small addition is to be made to the preserves ration from 1 April. The result will be that starting on 1 April the ration will be modified to allow consumers to obtain 2 lb, instead of 1 lb, of marmalade in each four-weekly period. The preserves coupon will then be worth 2 lbs of marmalade or 1lb of sugar. The present option to take preserves in place of the sugar ration will be withdrawn.

Tracking down and securing one's quota of oranges proved another challenge, as Vere Hodgson discovered:

Oranges today in Notting Hill. I went on a reconnoitring expedition yesterday to my little back-street shop and they were to be in today. So I went again this morning and they were not unpacked – and I must come later in the day. I humbly asked if I might have two ration books – the Fat Husband responded cheerfully – 'Yes, as many as you like'. This was very good news, as in some places they were only letting one book have them. Meanwhile Barishnikov went on baiting Mr White, who is a particularly bad-tempered green-grocer round here. B. is determined to get the oranges from this Gruff and Grum, if he can. He just goes in every two hours to annoy him. The man keeps saying he has sold out – when B. can see cases of oranges in the shop. To continue, I sent Mrs Harry Johnson with full directions to get hers at my shop. I thought they would let her have them if she said she had been bombed out. They did, and she was very pleased. So at 1.30, my dinner hour, I hastened up the Hill. The Fat Husband again appeared and served me with THREE RATION BOOKS. This is very good. I got for Mr H., Miss M and myself at one fell swoop. They were immense jaffas and he gave me five. I looked rather doubtfully at these, and then sorrowfully asked if he could spare me one more orange, as it was difficult to divide five oranges among three people. The Fat Man considered and caved in. He weighed another jaffa and we had two each. I was much elated.

There were 457,000 marriages in Britain in 1945, but none of these couples could have an iced wedding cake – any more than they could have a proper gold ring where part of the gold content was not substituted with alloy. There had been a ban on using sugar icing since July 1940. The common practice was to borrow from the baker a cardboard cover to make a wedding cake look like the traditional iced cake. Marzipan, too, had to be improvised, using sieved haricot beans with almond flavouring. By this time, housewives had perfected the knack of making an eggless fruit cake, as was often the case with the family Christmas cake. If the cake was sponge, liquid paraffin might be used instead of scarce cooking fat. For a wedding the whole family, and friends too, pooled precious rations to provide a feast of sorts.

In their guidebook *Over There: Instructions for American*

Servicemen in Britain, produced by the United States War Department in 1942, American servicemen in Britain were warned: 'One thing to be careful about – if you are invited into a British home and the host exhorts you to "eat up there's plenty on the table", go easy. It may be the family's rations for a whole week spread out to show their hospitality.' Indeed, the American visitors soon caught on and would come to British homes loaded with food as gifts.

Inevitably, women quite often went without so as to give their husbands or children an extra portion of food. 'We always had something to eat, perhaps not always the best things but something. My mum would go without quite often,' recalls Marina Welch. 'Everyone would come home and we would sit down to eat and she would always say, "Oh, I've had mine." You knew she hadn't, it was just to make it go round.' Ruth Tanner from Walthamstow says, 'You was never really hungry – our mums were very economical.' Sometimes, she recalls, the women all got together to do something collectively, pooling their supplies to make, say, a cake, which individual rations would not run to.

One of the Government's new welfare schemes provided children with a hot meal at school five days a week, which helped working mothers and eased the pressure of eking out the rations. The meal contained 2d worth of meat, to ensure that children had an adequate intake of protein, while the Milk in Schools scheme was extended to ensure all schoolchildren received extra calcium. The Vitamin Welfare scheme provided small children, as well as expectant mothers, with vitamins A, C and D. Nevertheless, food remained sparse at home: 'It was hard not to fall into the habit of watching the kids to see they did not put too much of anything on their bread,' Mrs Bell confessed. 'If they had butter no jam. Jam no butter. What a luxury to have both.'

The tendency of women to go without themselves to feed their families led some of them to take up smoking, to the detriment of their health. Mrs Bell remembered: 'Mums often went short. Cigarettes were only eleven halfpence for twenty.

Often a smoke would ward off hunger. That's how many of us turned to smoking. When we first went to live in the flats in 1940 it was no bother to climb six flights of stairs with two buckets of coal. Now it was a struggle to climb them with only one.'

Rationing meant fair shares for all but, as ever, the rich were different. Those who had money could avoid much of the stringency by dining out. After the outbreak of war, Chips Channon and his friends had spent rather a lot of time eating in the Ritz, which 'has become fantastically fashionable; all the great, the gay, the Government [Chamberlain's]; we knew ninety-five per cent of everyone there. But Ritzes always thrive in wartime, as we are all cookless.' Losing their domestic staff to war work might have provided the impetus for more frequent dining out, but it was already a habit and a way of life for the rich and privileged, taken for granted and preferably not to be interrupted by war.

The hedonistic atmosphere, which was one aspect of wartime London, continued. For the diplomatic corps, according to the memoir of Count Edward Raczynski, the Polish Government-in-exile's representative in London, social life consisted of 'a round of Embassy lunches, dinners and cocktail parties'. James Lees-Milne, a bachelor who moved in the highest social circles, ate at London's best restaurants and clubs on a regular basis. Reading his diary, it is sometimes as if the war were happening somewhere else, to other people. His friend the *grande dame* Emerald Cunard seemed impervious to the food problem, as he found one day at the Ritz: 'Emerald began in true form by grumbling to the waiters about the food. She ought to know that in the fifth year of the war choice of food for luncheon after two o'clock on a Sunday is limited.' Dining in a private suite at Claridges a couple of months later, however, he reports, 'We had a delicious dinner, and a white wine like nectar. There were pats of butter like cricket balls, and peaches.'

There was nothing to stop people procuring as many meals as they could afford in a day. At least one old boy would arrive at his club for a quick lunch at 12.30 and then move on for another meal somewhere else. No coupons were surrendered for restaurant meals, although anyone staying in a hotel for more than three days had to hand in his ration book, or the emergency ration card obtainable for journeys away from home. Churchill's Government realised that some restrictions must be applied to eating out, not only to guard scarce supplies but also to obviate social tension. The supply of rationed food to the catering industry was strictly controlled. For hotels, boarding houses, hospitals, boarding schools and prisons, food was allocated on the basis of the number of ration books held by the residents. For restaurants, inns, canteens and tea shops providing occasional meals, food was allocated on the basis of the number of meals or hot beverages served. London hotels and restaurants had to be on good terms with food suppliers, but were not above indulging in a certain amount of black market trading.

Further controls were deemed necessary, however. In July 1940 it became illegal to serve more than one main course per person in a restaurant, the restricted dishes being marked on the menu by one or two stars. This rule might not always have been strictly observed, as James Lees-Milne revealed: 'Dined excellently at the White Tower – soup, coquille St Jacques, and veal. I was sure these two courses were illegal, and felt guilty.' In less august surroundings, a supper menu served from 6 p.m. to 7.30 p.m. in Lyons Corner House offered the following two-starred dishes: spam salad, pilchard salad, cheese and pickled cucumber salad, chopped meat and white bean salad, ham omelette, creamed fish with mashed potatoes, stewed lamb with mixed vegetables and potatoes, all served with a baked jacket potato. At the foot of the menu was a large boxed notice: 'The Meals in Establishments Order, 1942. This order restricts meals consumed in this room to three courses of which only ONE may be a "TWO STARRED" DISH. For convenience of patrons all "TWO STARRED" DISHES are served on LARGE PLATES.' Patrons could have either one two-starred main dish and one subsidiary dish marked with one star, or two subsidiary dishes marked with one star.

In June 1942 a maximum charge of five shillings was imposed on all restaurant meals, although grand establishments like the Savoy could demand an extra cover charge, for the flowers on the table and so on, and luxury foods such as oysters and caviar fell outside the restrictions. The five shillings maximum charge meant that previously exclusive restaurants became more accessible: it was a democratising process, just as much as rationing was. The relatively impecunious Theodora Fitzgibbon and her friends would occasionally eat at the Ritz and the Berkeley and she noted that 'many impoverished or elderly people took to lunching at the Ritz or similar hotels, as much as a return to prewar graciousness as for the meal itself, which was often disguised Spam or a similar product.' A young man could treat his girlfriend to dinner at the Savoy Grill knowing that the meal would cost five shillings, the cover charge another three shillings and sixpence and, the real extravagance, a carafe of wine thirty shillings. At the Dorchester, where the cover charge was as high as seven shillings and sixpence, there was also a charge of two shillings and sixpence to use the dance floor.

Top restaurants certainly seem to have found ways to circumvent the five shillings' rule, perhaps by overcharging for the drink. When Lees-Milne dined with Daisy Fellowes at the Basque Restaurant in Dover Street, he complained that 'there was no wine, so we had to be contented with two glasses of sherry each, nothing more. The bill came to £4 10s 0d, which was monstrous.' Establishments like the Café Royal would not accept bookings after 9.30 p.m., but that was probably as much to do with the blackout and the fact that public transport shut down so early as with food shortages.

A less affluent, middle-class professional like Anthony Weymouth seldom ate out in London's restaurants:

An unexpected treat. Dinner at a certain fashionable restaurant with Edward Boyle. I haven't been in this place since war broke out and I therefore looked about me with inquiring eyes. I had heard that the smart London restaurants were no longer so smart, but I had no first-hand knowledge, as I no longer feed in such places. Truth to tell, I've given up lunching and dining out, except when I'm invited for the food is usually so indifferent that it's simply not worth spending money in this way.

When he did eat out, he was usually disappointed: 'Lunch in a West-End hotel. Watery soup, omelette a la dried egg, and cold apple-tart. Waiting very offhand and, on our part, a good deal of waiting,' he complained. It is tempting to think that wartime stringency was the origin of the indifferent cooking and 'we're doing you a favour' attitude that were such marked characteristics of hotels and restaurants for decades after the war. The food was often doctored to disguise its poor quality.

'Lunch at the East India Club. Curry,' Weymouth continues. 'Like most other things, it has suffered from the war. So far as I could judge the meat was spam. But it was certainly tastier than most of the concoctions of vegetables and sausage-meat which to-day masquerade, under various French names, as cutlets and steak. The food is getting much worse in London, which I suppose is not surprising considering that we are now well into the sixth year of war.'

As early as 1943 Weymouth lamented that 'Wine, of course, has now disappeared from clubs and restaurants, although I heard of someone the other day who ordered a bottle of claret with his lunch, for which he paid £3.' But James Lees-Milne and his friends did not seem to be too badly affected by shortage of distilled spirits and lack of wine imports from continental Europe, perhaps because some establishments boasted substantial cellars at the outset, as well as clients who were able to pay the high prices. 'Hamish dined alone with me at Brooks's. A boozy evening. I had three whiskies and soda before dinner. We had a bottle of burgundy at dinner, and two glasses of port each after dinner,' he records. After 1943 supplies were bolstered by imports of rough red wine from North Africa.

Spirits were in very short supply because only so much precious grain could be diverted to making it. When Anthony Weymouth's daughter got engaged he ordered gin for a party of 30 from his usual supplier, but the case despatched to him was stolen on the railway – a common occurrence. The family then had to grovel to a number of other wine merchants: 'Ave [the bride-to-be] has been to a shop that has occasionally let her have a bottle of gin before. A local wine merchant, whose stony heart was moved when he heard why we wanted the gin, has promised us another for this afternoon, and a kind friend who has been given a bottle of gin for a Christmas present has promised to lend it, and we on our part have undertaken to pay her back as soon as we can.'

Unfortunately, when Mrs Weymouth went to collect the precious bottle of gin from the wine merchant, she slipped in the blackout. 'As we were counting on the case of gin, so rudely snatched from our grasp by some unknown railway man, we felt the loss of that one bottle to be a minor tragedy. But all was well. Audrey persuaded another wine merchant to disgorge, however unwillingly, a bottle of gin.'

A certain amount of bartering went on, especially if alcohol was involved. Marina Welch, who lived over her parents' off-licence in Deptford, recalls: 'Because of having the off-licence, if the whisky came in the butcher was informed and then my mum knew she would get a joint of meat that weekend. John and Dennis [her brothers] used to tell their schoolteacher, "The whisky's in", and he would swap his tea rations for it.'

In the April 1945 budget whisky went up to 25s 9d a bottle, even supposing a bottle could be obtained. Pubs, which were crowded, were often devoid of spirits and short of beer, which was 1s a pint and below its peacetime strength. American servicemen were warned that it 'can still make a man's tongue wag at both ends' but, judging by the number of reports of drunken Americans about the town, the warning seems to have fallen on deaf ears. The Public Morality Council's patrolling officer was loud in his condemnation of 'young American troops who unfortunately have developed a taste for alcohol': 'Day after day, numbers of these young men can be seen drunk after a mid-day carousal. They are seen in the most unexpected districts, and it is hopeless to attempt to find out where they have secured the quantity of drink necessary to get them into such a condition . . . The same practice is repeated in the evening.'

Sometimes pubs would serve only regular customers, or each customer would be allowed only one drink. In Chelsea Theodora Fitzgibbon and her friends found the pub a favourite refuge:

Generally we would meet in the evenings for a few glasses of beer or Guinness. Spirits were never on sale in a pub unless you were a regular customer, then you might be given one; only in the hotels and flossier bars. In fact in a pub where you weren't known you had to bring your own glass! . . . If it seems that undue importance is being attached to pubs it must be explained that they were the only places in wartime London where one could entertain and be entertained cheaply, and find the companionship badly needed during the war. For people of our age with no solid, regular accounts behind us, it was difficult to come by even a bottle of sherry. Food was very scarce indeed, and food for the occasional dinner party had to be hunted for and often took many hours and much traipsing about. Many middle-aged people used to drinking at home found their only source of supply was the pubs. Bombs dropping on London could not be so easily heard when one was in them, and the company lessened apprehension.

In pubs customers who did not bring their own glass had to become adept at grabbing one from the counter as soon as it was put down. Shortage of glass, cutlery and aluminium kitchenware hampered private homes and public establishments alike. Women regretted giving away the best of their saucepans to make Spitfires in the salvage drive of 1940, because it would be years before they could be replaced. In restaurants and canteens the cutlery shortage meant that customers were reduced to desperate measures, to Anthony Weymouth's chagrin: 'No restaurant, tea-shop, or canteen allows customers such a luxury as a teaspoon – they are too easily purloined. People stir their tea or coffee with the handle of a fork, or, in some instances, with a pencil. One canteen frequented by me has a none-too-clean teaspoon tied to the counter by a piece of filthy string. Most unappetising!'

To make eating out more democratic and to relieve hard-pressed housewives from some of the tedium of queuing for food and eking out the rations, the Ministry of Food encouraged local authorities to open Civic or British Restaurants to provide cheap and nourishing meals for all. As with any other restaurant or canteen, coupons were not required. They were a godsend to those engaged in war work, often working unsociable hours and unable to shop or find time to make a meal, or who lacked the facilities to cook, and to working mothers. It was hoped that the average family would be able to eat in their local British Restaurant at least once a month. To save costs, they operated on a self-service basis. Money was paid to the cashier as the customer entered the building. This was exchanged for coloured plastic discs, representing a different colour for each course. A three-course meal, of which vegetable soup, roast beef, Yorkshire pudding, roast potatoes and green vegetables, rhubarb tart and custard and coffee was a typical example, could be had for just under a shilling.

The end of the war did not stop the trend for eating out. By September 1945 the *Sunday Graphic* was reporting that with Britain's rations the lowest for six years, more food than ever was pouring into the restaurants and hotels of London's West End. 'London diners eat nearly twenty-five million meals a week.' Apparently, nearly 300 new restaurants had been opened in the year up to mid July. Housewives were complaining that too much food was going to hotels and restaurants while they had to queue. 'People who eat in the West End every night don't do it because they have to,' said one housewife. 'They'd soon stop it if they had to give up coupons.' According to the report, Londoners were spending £250 million a year eating out. There was plenty of money in circulation and with little to buy except War Savings

Certificates Londoners grasped at any opportunity to bring some cheer into their lives.

The biggest disappointment of 1945 was that the food situation did not ease up with the peace: indeed, it got worse. In the previous two years, the Government had built up food stocks of 6,500,000 tons – importing about 2 million tons more than was consumed in 1943 – but decided to sit on these stocks, rather than give the people more to eat. The Government knew that shipping would have to be diverted for military operations and they foresaw that after the end of the war the world would suffer from a pressing shortage of food. Britain's food stocks were to be diverted to the starving populations of the liberated countries of Europe and of defeated Germany. By July 1945 the total stocks of food and animal feeding stuffs under the control of the Ministry of Food had fallen to 5,500,000 tons and were still falling. At the shops, food scarcities and queues were worse than ever. Most understood the need to share scarce food supplies with the liberated countries, although inevitably there was a certain amount of resentment that the Germans were being fed too, even if in Britain the German POWs' rations were being cut. 'One certainly has to pay dearly for the privilege of winning a war these days,' Anthony Heap complained.

As early as 23 May, barely two weeks after VE Day, Colonel Llewellin, who had succeeded Lord Woolton as Minister of Food in November 1943, announced that with the issue of the new ration book on 28 May there would be cuts in rations. The meat ration of 1s 2d worth a week was to be maintained, but one seventh of it was to be taken in the form of tinned corned beef over the next five months: fortunately, corned beef hash had become a popular dish. Cooking fat was to be reduced from 2 ounces to 1 ounce per week, the butter allowance was 2 ounces and margarine 4 ounces. The bacon or ham ration was to be reduced from 4 ounces to 3 ounces per week. The present sugar ration of 8 ounces was to be maintained, including the allowance of an extra pound for domestic jam-making, but there would be no extra Christmas bonus of sugar, as there had been in 1944. Cheese was to remain at its present level of 2 ounces with no hope of an extra ounce for the winter months, as had been the case the previous year. One egg per person per fortnight might be managed and two and a half pints of liquid milk a week. The sweets ration stood at 12 ounces a month. The points allowance was to be reduced from 24 to 20 per 4-week period. By the summer of 1945, it took 12 points to buy a tin of salmon, 17 for a small tin of spam and 54 for a large one, 4 points for a tin of baked beans and 2 for a tin of sardines, so that the 20-point allowance did not go far.

In August a boatload of bacon, butter and eggs was arriving in London every five days from liberated Denmark: it did not mean more rations, but better quality rations. The fresh butter was being mixed with three-month-old dominion butter. Fine weather at home meant that there were good crops of fresh tomatoes and fruit coming into the shops and, as ever, housewives were busy bottling for the winter months. Greece had earmarked its entire crop of currants – about 150,000 tons – for Britain and ships were arriving from Greece with currants, cigarettes and olive oil. There had been an acute cigarette shortage for some months and by September the press were referring to a 'cigarette famine', warning that many customers would not get more than 10 a day and even then would have to be regular customers and take any brand. In the budget of April 1945 cigarettes went up to 2s 4d for 20.

In London, women had had enough and in July a queue revolt was initiated by a vicar's wife, Mrs Irene Lovelock, who asked the question: 'Why do we queue anyway?' Tired of standing in the fish queue and not getting anything, she drew a group of local women together to petition their MP about the invidiousness of queuing, demanding some more equitable way of distributing food that was not rationed but was in short supply. The Ministry of Food, who had been in the habit of sending its staff to stand in queues and listen to the conversation of shoppers to obtain feedback, should not have been surprised by the revolt. As early as June 1944 Robert Barrington-Ward, the Editor of *The Times*, had protested about the length of queues in south London, pleading with the Government to do something to alleviate the situation. Labour was not being released from the forces or war work quickly enough, while clearly the distributors were failing to keep pace with the return of the evacuees to London. Now, in the summer of 1945, the London queue revolt took off like wildfire and became national, only to be magnified by the worsening food situation the following year. As the *Sunday Graphic* opined:

With extraordinary official aptitude for passing the buck the Ministry of Food blames the Ministry of Labour and the Ministry of Transport. Now all three, in a kind of armed unanimity, are blaming the War Office for a delayed demobilization which keeps potential shop assistants in uniform. There remains the recalcitrant, domineering, bureaucratic shopkeeper. Not all of them, mind, but some – the man to whom a queue outside his shop is the breath of life, because it bolsters up his self-conceit.

There was little prospect of the situation improving in the foreseeable future, not least because hard on the heels of VJ Day on 15 August 1945 the United States terminated the Lend-Lease agreement, which had enabled Britain to import food and other goods on extended credit. The war had left Britain virtually bankrupt. The *Sunday Graphic* warned its readers:

We must produce a great deal more food than we did before the war, because food is scarce in the world to-day, and in any case we shall not be able to buy as much imported food as we did. In striving for others we have become a debtor nation. Britain's investments and our shipping, which helped to pay for food imports before the war, have been largely sacrificed. It is only by greatly increasing our exports and services that we can buy the imports we require and thus increase the whole vast volume of our internal trade.

The average housewife would no doubt have been incredulous had she been told in 1945 that rationing would continue into the fifties. Mrs Bell was one of thousands who had been expecting peace to bring a return to the good old days. 'Days when we would have roast beef for dinner on Sunday again. Instead of once a week, the tiny piece you got.' She had promised herself that she would soon 'have two eggs on a thick slice of gammon'. It was a hope that would be dashed and long deferred. After years of queuing and scrimping, women were already depressed enough without this added disappointment, as Anthony Weymouth noted: 'I read in the newspaper this morning that nervous disorders are on the increase, and two of the reasons seemed to me sound. They were Disillusion and Food. People expected a return to "the good things they used to enjoy" and now they are disillusioned. As to food, it was stated that lack of variety was "telling on them" mentally. Hope deferred or, as in this instance, vanished, is unquestionably a cause of emotional maladjustment.'

The euphoria of victory quickly gave way to depression as civilians faced another winter of food and fuel shortages. Already in the summer, when they were advised to start ordering in their coal, Londoners were dreading the coming winter. The coal shortages, the indignity of having to collect it by pram from emergency dumps, would continue through the hard winter of 1946 and the freak conditions of 1947, when the weather brought the country to its knees. As a final blow, in mid December 1945 Smithfield meat porters were threatening to strike, paralysing the meat trade, so that many Londoners were facing the prospect of eating their first peacetime Christmas dinner out of a tin.

A British serviceman returning from America at the end of the year was shocked at what he found in London: 'It is hard to realize that I am in the capital of a victorious nation. There is no thought of triumph. The chief thought among Londoners is food.'

Christmas 1944 had been hard, but at least people had

peace to look forward to. The first peacetime Christmas was one of gloom and despondency at the worsening shortages. A sign of the new age of austerity was a London butcher sleeping in his shop with a loaded shotgun: he had turkeys to guard.

5
Shabby Chic

'It was smart to be shabby – and we all were'
– Verily Anderson

In wartime it was considered good for morale to look one's best, yet unpatriotic to be fashionable. It was a matter of pride for London women to look smart, but after years of clothes rationing and trying to 'make do and mend', standards were not quite what they were. They were sharp-suited but down at heel – literally, as heels higher than two inches had been banned. They wore pretty floral frocks to the knee to save material, but with stockings practically non existent they covered their bare legs with gravy browning. Deprived of shampoo and dyes, their lank shoulder-length hair was gathered up into a roll sometimes stuffed with a sanitary towel and secured with pins, or else an untidy pile of curls on top of the head. A Polish diplomat in London hated to see them walking about 'hatless and dishevelled', while English men were unhappy at the sight of women in trousers. It was no longer *de rigueur* to wear evening dress and diners at fashionable restaurants wore lounge suits, while both sexes were to be seen in uniform.

When clothes rationing was introduced in July 1941 the then President of the Board of Trade, Oliver Lyttelton, told the nation bluntly: 'We must learn as civilians to be seen in clothes that are not so smart, because we are bearing yet another share in the war. When you are tired of your old clothes remember that by making them do you are contributing some part of an aeroplane, a gun or a tank.' Factories and labour were needed to make munitions, not clothes. Shopping for new clothes, just for the sake of it, was frowned upon. Another of the Ministry's cartoon characters, the swastika-infested Squander Bug, who jumped up and down gleefully every time a woman spent money unwisely, was there to remind them that they were only playing into Hitler's hands.

It was permissible for men, if not women, to look shabby. Men who did not look shabby, Oliver Lyttelton said, should be ashamed of themselves. By 1942 when American servicemen started to arrive, they were warned: 'If British civilians look dowdy and badly dressed, it is not because they do not like good clothes or know how to wear them. All clothing is rationed and the British know that they help war production by wearing an old suit or dress until it cannot be patched any longer. Old clothes are "good form".'

Women's magazines, whose whole *raison d'etre* had been consumerism, eagerly co-operated with the Government in feeding propaganda to their readers, encouraging and admonishing them by turns, in a determined effort to urge them to make do and save. The glossies like *Vogue* and *Harper's Bazaar* sought to keep the flame of fashion – the dream – alive while admitting that 'fashion is out of fashion'. The *Daily Herald* wrote, 'Fashion and the language of fashion no longer have a place in this war.' Fashionableness was to be divorced from smartness, which was still on the agenda for women, to maintain morale. Most suburban women – the wives of teachers, clerks, minor civil servants and shopkeepers – already relied heavily on *Good Housekeeping*, *Women and Beauty*, *Woman's Weekly*, *Woman* and *Woman's Own* to show them how to dress cheaply but smartly and how to manage their budget. Now those magazines devoted their whole energies to the war effort.

Although upper- and middle-class women might buy their clothes from London's stores – Harrods and Fortnum & Mason, Debenham & Freebody, Marshall & Snelgrove, Bourne & Hollingsworth, Dickens & Jones and Robinson & Cleaver, all of whom sold copies of Paris fashions at affordable prices and tried to emulate Hollywood glamour – most of these women were also used to having clothes made for them and understood the intricacies of 'fit'. Thousands of women habitually made their own and their children's clothes, using the Bestway fashion books for home dressmaking and patterns in the magazines. Women in wartime, therefore, were better equipped than they would be today to follow the Board of Trade's Make Do and Mend campaign, when 'Mrs Sew and Sew' would teach them all sorts of new tricks.

As ever, the rich were less hard hit by rationing than everybody else. They had large wardrobes of good-quality clothes to see out the war. Chips Channon, for instance, had more than 40 suits, which would last him for years. Not in this league, Harley Street doctor Anthony Weymouth quipped: 'Nearly all food and clothes are rationed, and so, as I say, there's not much advantage in being well-to-do these days. The rich man is he who has not yet spent his clothing coupons, not he who has the largest bank balance.'

The working class started the war at a disadvantage. The scant clothing they possessed consisted of cheap, shoddy goods usually bought at market stalls. Cheap clothing was not really cheap, because it had a short life. Shoes and boots, often bought on tick, were poorly made and needed frequent repair. Conversely, many young women from a poor background who joined the services gained a wardrobe the like of which they had never possessed – especially shoes. Land Girls were particularly well kitted out, with a hat, three shirts, a pullover, two pairs of breeches, two pairs of dungarees, two overall coats, six pairs of stockings, two pairs of socks, one pair of leather shoes, one pair of boots, leggings, gumboots, an oilskin or mackintosh and an overcoat.

Genuine second-hand clothing was exempt from coupons, but the problem for law enforcers was to distinguish stolen goods from the second-hand. Markets such as Petticoat Lane became a mecca for 'spivs' and a clearing house for black market goods – usually items looted from bombed shops, warehouses and private homes. The second-hand clothing business was also thriving, as East Ender Arthur Harding remembers:

The surprising thing about wartime was that the second-hand clothes trade, despite the scarcity of coupons, was very brisk. I was buying more suits than I had ever bought before in one day, good quality suits, complete wardrobes. I found that people were willing to sell their clothes more readily than before the war, especially those with men who were prisoners of war or missing. A lady at Coulsdon called me into her large house. She knew I came from the East End and gave me a large quantity of beautiful children's clothes on my promising to sell them cheaply to the poor of Bethnal Green. Then she sold me all her husband's clothes. He was a major in the army and had been missing since Dunkirk. Such tragedies were to be found everywhere in the middle-class districts.

Rating cash and food above clothes, however, the poor would often – illegally – sell their clothing coupons, and there was a ready market for such transactions among the well-to-do. Arthur Harding continues:

I knew a lot about the black market because of the old-clothes business, so I could help the Ghost Squad [Scotland Yard's squad formed to tackle black market activities] a lot. People came in to sell clothing coupons, I used to give £3 for a book, but I never sold them for money, only exchanged them for second-hand clothes. Mind you, I made a great bargain out of it, for £3 I might get £20 of clothing back. I could never understand why wealthy people risked their reputation and character in order to get something the rest of the community wasn't getting. The poorer people used to sell the coupons, because they couldn't afford to buy new clothes, so I exchanged them for old clothing. It was the better-off people who bought them – magistrates and all, one was a man sitting on the local bench somewhere Epsom way.

By the time rationing was introduced, clothes cost 69 per cent more than in 1939, partly owing to the introduction of purchase tax in October 1940. Most garments and footwear attracted tax at 16 per cent, but items like furs, silks and gloves (the materials having to be imported), veils, hairnets, belts, suspenders, shoe laces, corset laces and hair pins carried 33 per cent tax. Clothes rationing would follow the points system. The Board of Trade issued a 2d booklet, *The Clothing Coupon Quiz*, with questions and answers to explain the new system. By 1943 a clothing coupons section was issued with the main ration book, detachable so that each member of the family could look after their own, as opposed to the food ration books, which were usually kept by the housewife who shopped for the whole family. In February 1945 the Government's instructions spelt out the process of collecting the new ration books:

The new ration book (including the next Clothing Book) will be issued from 28 May onwards, for food purchases from 22 July. When you collect it you must have your present Food Book and Identity Card (giving your present address) with you. You must write your address on the front cover of the Food Book and your name, address and National Registration Number on the front of the Clothing Book. You will be told when you can use the Clothing Book. Until then none of the coupons is valid.

There was an extra piece of bureaucratic detail for women to follow: 'Every woman should write MRS in front of her name at the top of page 4 [of the old Food Book] if she is married or has been married at any time, otherwise she should write MISS.' In case she was too stupid to understand, the instruction amplified: 'Thus, Mrs Smith or Miss Smith.'

The Board of Trade received feedback on the demand for certain goods and whether the supply was adequate or short. Inevitably, fluctuations occurred when new coupons were issued or at the end of a coupon period. Clothing coupons remained valid, even after a new ration book was issued: they could be saved up and carried over. The family of someone who had died was supposed to return his clothing coupons, but the temptation to spend them often proved too much. It was no great surprise how many of the dead had apparently enjoyed one final shopping spree before their demise.

Every item of clothing was given a points value, according

to how much labour and material were needed to produce it, but cash must also be paid. For instance, a woman's winter coat, advertised at Clapham's Arding and Hobbs in 1945, cost 18 coupons and £14 7s 6d – a considerable sum when the average weekly wage was £4–£5. Items of children's clothing were given lower points value, to take account of the fact they were constantly outgrowing their clothes and needing new ones. The WVS ran clothing exchanges, where women could surrender children's used clothing in exchange for points, to be used at the store. Some private schools were not so helpful, insisting on full uniform, for which other members of the family often had to contribute their coupons. Domestic servants were required to hand over coupons for the apparel their employers expected them to wear and even nurses had to surrender 10 coupons a year for their uniform.

The initial allowance was 66 coupons per person for 6 months, but by the last year of the war this allowance had been drastically reduced. In January 1945 Anthony Heap was complaining that 'clothes rationing remains as stringent as ever. The next 24 coupons, valid from 1 December, have again got to last us six months – possibly seven.' By June 1945 clothing stocks were at an all-time low and there was concern that manufacturers would not be able to honour the nation's coupons. In August 1945 the appropriately austere Sir Stafford Cripps, appointed President of the Board of Trade by Clement Attlee after Labour swept to power in the general election the previous month, announced a 25 per cent cut in clothing coupons. The 24 coupons which were to become valid on 1 September were to last until 30 April 1946 – equivalent to cutting the ration to 36 coupons a year.

Cripps promised that this would be the last cut in the clothing ration and suggested that the longer people conserved their coupons, the better the selection of clothes that would be available in the shops. Manpower – or womanpower – was being transferred from munitions back to clothing, but this was a slow process. Cloth was needed for 'demob' suits – and they needed plenty of it, as tailors maintained that demobbed men were taking larger sizes as a result of service life – while some clothing was being donated to the liberated populations of Europe. When the Minister was asked if the people of any European country were less well clothed than the British, he had to admit that this was the case only in parts of Holland and the southern Balkans.

Obviously, the coupon ration was completely inadequate to maintain the average wardrobe, as Anthony Weymouth quickly discovered:

Until you have done a little shopping for yourself you don't realize what a short way coupons go. I was amused when Gervais Rentoul told me the other day that he had bought nothing in the way of clothes or hosiery for some time. He therefore felt rich in coupons, and went to his hosiers and ordered some collars, some socks and a pair or two of pyjamas. When, however, he produced his coupons, he was told there were not nearly enough and he must either give up a pair of pyjamas or cut down the number of collars. His look of disgusted surprise when he told me this was most amusing.

Clothing coupons had a dampening effect on the traditional January sales, as a Kensington woman found in 1945: 'Well I bought some more Savings Certificates today from the bank and then "slushed" my way through the streets of melting snow. Every now and then a shop would advertise a "clearance" of a few lines of goods, but coupons or points restrained one's purchases however low the price. Few of us had many of our twenty coupons left.'

It was illegal to give away or sell coupons, although obviously no one was going to complain about coupon trafficking in the same family. Retailers were not allowed to accept loose coupons, but sometimes they took pity on customers, as a North London woman remembers: 'We were not supposed to give our clothing coupons to others, but the shop assistants were sympathetic and if someone had a special need for a new dress or a pair of shoes we all contributed a few coupons to enable the purchase to be made. We lent each other clothes whenever possible and my wedding dress went up the aisle five times!'

Women often went without in order to clothe their families and it was usually out of their coupon ration that scarce household linen and towels – also on points – were acquired. It was often incumbent on fathers to give their coupons to clothes-conscious daughters, as Anthony Weymouth knew only too well, especially when Ave was getting married: 'I have got my coupons, or rather lack of them, carefully taped. I have twenty left, most of which I suppose will be earmarked for the bride-to-be. But I want a mackintosh (18 coupons), a new suit (26), and I *must* have a vest (4) – and I could do with some more collars, shirts and socks; but, as William [his former chauffeur] used to say, "Wot a 'ope!"' He was amused by a cartoon in *Punch*, in which a father is interviewing his prospective son-in-law. 'Young man,' he asked, 'are you in a position to supply my daughter with twenty coupons every six months, as *I* have had to do?'

Men were feeling particularly hard done by. In February 1942 Hugh Dalton, a Labour economist in Churchill's Coalition Government, had succeeded Lyttelton as President of the Board of Trade. It seems he lacked Lord Woolton's sure sense of what the public would and would not accept. The following month Dalton announced a series of measures designed to reduce the labour and cloth expended on clothing. Utility fashion was born. All men's jackets were to be single-breasted, with at most three pockets, only three buttons on the front and none on the cuffs. Waistcoats could carry only two pockets. Metal and leather belts were banned, their components being far more useful to the war effort. Thanks to the Japanese occupation of Malaya, rubber to make elastic was in short supply, so that elastic waistbands were forbidden. Trouser legs were restricted to a width of 19 inches. And, horror of horrors, trouser turn-ups were banned. Dalton was impervious to the storm of protest, even in the House of Commons, about the latter, while intrepid tailors who made trousers too long 'by mistake' so that they might be turned up were prosecuted. As a final blow against male pride, boys had to wait until they were 12 before making the rite of passage into long trousers.

Men, proving less flexible than women to wartime stringencies, were truly disgruntled. In March 1945 the *Daily Mirror* was particularly critical of Utility:

True economy would have been to make fewer things and better. Mr Dalton holds out no immediate hope of a return to the full-length sock. Yet the austerity brand has been a complete 'flop', and shopkeepers cannot get rid of them. Scarcely a man exists who would not prefer *one* pair of normal socks to two or three pairs of short ones . . . As to the pettifogging regulation about pockets, buttons, shirt cuffs, collars, etc, these have counteracted any possible usefulness by generating large quantities of public irritation.

Added to these galling restrictions, men's wardrobes were becoming seriously depleted. In January 1945 an article in the *Daily Express* outlined their plight:

Before the war a man with a decent average salary would buy three pairs of shoes a year and one pair of slippers (32 coupons). He now buys one pair of shoes and makes his slippers do. He cannot buy a double cuff shirt now. When his cuffs wear out his wife has to cut off the tail and make new ones. A man who pre-war would buy three shirts at once (24 coupons) now buys one. Twelve pairs of socks (24 coupons) before the war, now buys four. Many men go without gloves. The pre-war two-suits-a-year man has to decide between a suit (26 coupons), a top coat (18 coupons) or a raincoat not warm enough for freezing weather (18 coupons).

But women were just as deprived. Pre-war, shops claimed, women bought 2 to 18 dresses a year (180 coupons), but 'now just pop in to say "Hello".' The biggest demand was for woollen housecoats (8 coupons). 'These save stockings, overalls, corsets, tempers.'

By the end of the war, the MP Harold Nicolson's wardrobe was down to its lowest ebb. He wrote most amusingly about it in the *Spectator*:

Fortified by VE Day and the Whitsun recess, I have had the courage to perform a duty which I have long evaded and postponed. I have taken stock of my wardrobe . . . Strangest of all these phenomena of wardrobe conduct is the behaviour adopted during these five years of war by my pyjamas. The first phase of disintegration was what might be called the *replacement* phase, during which period I was able for quite a long time to maintain an outward show of decency, either by patching those that were still living from pieces of those which were demonstrably dead, or by adopting the more diverting method of wearing the trousers from one suit with the top piece of another. That happy and, as it now seems, luxurious period lasted for about two years. It was succeeded by the second phase, the *reticulated* phase, when my pyjamas ceased to be a united whole, but assumed the form of netting or lacework. And to my distress this phase, since D-Day, has been succeeded by a third phase, the *ticker-tape* phase, during which my pyjamas have ceased to resemble nets or lacework and have assumed the form of pendant strips, such as might be worn by some zany in a morality play. This phase is uncomfortable, and I am aware that when winter comes this year the spring of 1946 will seem very far behind. A serving officer recently returned from the Central Mediterranean Force was, in fact, so touched by my predicament that he offered to give me a roll of figured cotton which he had bought at Lagos and on which some Manchester cotton mill had imprinted a pattern of enormous yellow pineapples upon a background of blue. It may well be that this cold and garish material is well adapted to the needs of a Gold Coast maiden; an elderly politician should, however, take great pains not to render himself gratuitously ridiculous; and I shall have, for two years or more, to stick to ticker-tape.

The indignity of it all did not end there:

What I find so humiliating – nay, so degrading – about this sudden disintegration of my wardrobe is that it imposes upon me all manner of subterfuges, dissimulations and lies, since, although by immense application I am able to maintain some semblance of decency in my outward vesture, the tatters which it conceals underneath are truly deplorable . . . What is truly disgraceful is that, when visiting the houses of the rich and great, or even when keeping an appointment with my doctor, I take with me or wear those isolated remnants of my wardrobe which have still survived the storm.

Nicolson approached a 'leading pundit of the Board of Trade' to assure him that he would only have to 'endure this ticker-tape existence' a few months longer. Not a bit of it. He was warned that there would be a prolonged shortage stretching far into the future. Nicolson was in despair. 'I see that by 1947 all that I shall have left to wear will be my Defence Medal. Gladly will I submit to this nudity, gladly even will I don the pineapples of Lagos, if I feel that thereby I can contribute in any manner to our export trade or release to the unhappy Europeans one square inch of warmth to cover my despair.'

Nicolson's underwear might have been down to its last tattered threads, but women had long been reduced to making their own. Women's pants required two coupons, the more elaborate knickerbockers still favoured by some of the elderly and middle-aged three. Blackout material, among other unlikely bits of unrationed cloth, was pressed into service to make French knickers. Elastic continued in short supply even after the Japanese defeat in August 1945. 'Are you worried about elastic?' *Woman* asked its readers. 'Unless you're in the black market, how are you keeping your panties in the correct position, not to mention pyjama trousers now that the stuff is so scarce?' Many had replaced pyjamas with nightdresses because they cost six rather than eight coupons and did not require precious elastic, while pants were secured with string or buttons if they could be spared.

All women still wore corsets. The Board of Trade's Make Do and Mend propaganda reminded them that with rubber being scarce 'your corset is one of your most precious possessions.' The three main essentials needed for corsets – rubber, steel and cotton – were urgently needed for war purposes. Since 90 per cent of the world's rubber was in the hands of the Japanese, roll-ons were banned. The special hand-tempered steel was needed to make small arms and precision instruments. Much of the special yarn used for corset cloth was diverted to jungle equipment. As labour was engaged in more essential war work, the Board of Trade had asked the Corset Trade Association to get their manufacturers to design a simpler corset which could be made by comparatively unskilled workers, thus cutting down the long painstaking production process of high-class corsets.

Women were urged to make sure that their corsets fit properly. 'In particular don't wear one too small, as this stretches the rubber and puts too much strain on it.' The greatest enemies of the corset, the Government warned, were 'sunlight and grease. Never let your girdle get really dirty. Wash it frequently, and, if you possibly can, have at least two corsets, and wear them alternately.' Those who did not possess two corsets were advised to wear their corset over a thin undergarment, rather than next to the skin, to protect it from grease and perspiration. On no account must a corset be pulled or stretched or yanked, but always removed carefully, washed and kept in a cool, dark place, not a hot cupboard.

Naturally, women complained that the new Utility corsets did nothing for their figures, while the Board of Trade retaliated that it was doing very well indeed to produce 10 million wearable corsets at reasonable prices in the sixth year of war. By then, however, with synthetic rubber starting to come through from America and labour trickling back, the outlook for the corset was more hopeful. The Board of Trade was promising better corsets for 1946, using stronger cloth and steel supports. Surprisingly, perhaps, the corset was not abandoned, when the war was liberating women in so many ways, but continued to be worn for at least another decade.

Special arrangements could be made for women whose figures were not conventional. Anthony Weymouth's daughter Yvonne, for instance, had a long back and had to wear a specially made corset. In wartime, it could be obtained only by sending an order signed by a doctor to the Board of Trade, who had to give permission for the corsetière to make it. There was an outcry from Weymouth's feisty daughter when the Board presumed to make further enquiries:

I was thinking this evening how nice it will be when these infernal rockets stop dropping at intervals throughout the day and night, making one jump out of one's skin, when I heard Audrey say to Yvonne: 'The Board of Trade rang up this morning to know why you wanted a pair of corsets, Yvie.' And Yvonne replied: 'I like their cheek – what on earth have my corsets got to do with them? I should have thought they'd have more to think about.' Now I must say at the moment I felt inclined to agree with Yvie – impatient as she is with government departments. But the fact is that we've got so used to restrictions of one kind or another that we've come to accept them as a matter of course. It is only in a case like this, when one is suddenly struck with the absurdity of a particular restriction, that one realizes how really totalitarian we have become.

Bras were another casualty of the rubber shortage. 'Your Gossard is a priceless treasure to-day – difficult to replace,' the manufacturer advised women, stating the obvious. 'The happy possessor should handle it with great care. Always have it fitted when you buy and observe the golden rule of patient persuasion when you put it on at home. A few extra minutes in adjusting it will repay you in months of longer wear. The same flawless design and perfection of line as prevailed before the war are symbolized in the name Gossard. Still hand-cut with the flair of an artist, Gossard remain the best in "utility".' Unfortunately not all women could get their hands on a Gossard or any other make of bra and some were reduced to making their own out of spare scraps of material.

Stockings were held up with suspenders, but they too were in short supply, as a West London woman recalls: 'At first we thought we would never run short of clothes, but we were very patched in the end. One spent a lot of time darning. The worst was suspenders; there was no metal so we sewed buttons on to tape, but they soon cut the stockings.'

This was all the more tragic since stockings had virtually disappeared. Unless one was prepared to trade in the black market, it was very hard indeed to obtain them. One day in September 1945, 4,000 women queued from dawn outside a Wimbledon store when word spread that a supply of 'fully fashioned' stockings had arrived. Sales started at 9 a.m. and by 1.30 p.m. 3,500 'lucky' customers had bought one pair each. Some of the staff concentrated on crowd control, while the rest served. Women were mortified to appear without stockings, fearing bare legs would make them look available. American servicemen found the bare legs of English women, so white compared with the smooth brown legs of their sun-kissed female compatriots, singularly unattractive. Of course, it was the promise of stockings, or the newly invented nylons, that attracted some women to American servicemen, who never seemed to run short of them. Others just had to improvise as best they could, as a Crayford woman remembers: 'To help out with stockings, we went bare legged as long as we could. We used leg make-up to hide white legs. In 1942, I lasted out till 28 October before succumbing to the cold. When stockings lost their colour, we dyed them. I spent three and a half hours on one occasion, putting new toes and heels on a pair of lisle stockings.'

For those who could afford it, Cyclax produced Stockingless Cream and Elizabeth Arden Fin 200, obtainable only in the London area. They were like a fake tan, able to resist rain, mud and splashes. Others resorted to liquid gravy browning, applied with a sponge or cotton wool, or a cup of cold cocoa. They would paint black lines down the back of each leg, in imitation of seamed stockings. These expedients were not waterproof. It was particularly mystifying to American servicemen that the trousers of their crisp, well-tailored, quality cloth uniforms should become so stained when they were throwing their partners about in the jitterbug. Perhaps that was one of the reasons they were so keen to dispense nylons.

By the end of the war the underwear of the average woman was down to its last gasp. An article in the *Sunday Graphic* in August 1945, asking 'Is this going to be pneumonia winter?' touched on the problem:

It would be illuminating to know how many women have got any presentable underclothing left by now. What about that modicum of pure-wool next the skin (we won't mention silk) which we are advised to wear in the English climate? Most of us, taking for granted matters would improve after the peace, have put off replenishing our underwear; we've had all we could do to maintain a 'top-dressing', with a portion of our coupons dedicated, necessarily, to the household. It's useless to talk about women's 'folly' in sacrificing what *isn't* seen to what *is*. That isn't folly, it's morale. The woman who knows she is badly turned out starts from scratch in the social race, in the business race, in the sex race.

For all that queuing and walking home in the blackout, good shoes were required, but they were almost impossible to find. Women tramped up and down Oxford Street trying to find the right size, especially if they were not a standard fit, while a store's entire new batch of stock was often sold out within hours. Sometimes there was even a queue to win the right to join a queue for shoes. In 1943 peep toes were banned and heels were limited to a height of two inches: the ban on high heels was lifted in February 1945. The rubber shortage meant that shoes were mainly wooden-soled, known as 'woodies'. Alternatively, there were Phillips invisible stick-a-soles, which if stuck on new shoes meant that the original sole never wore down.

Reluctant mothers pressed children into second-hand shoes, as advised by the Board of Trade: 'In countless cupboards throughout the country, children's shoes are lying idle, not because they are outworn but because they are outgrown. What a help it would be if mothers would pass these shoes on to a friend, whose child could wear them. Or perhaps a local school, welfare clinic or some local women's organization may already be running a children's shoe exchange.'

Cobblers, drafted in to the services or war work, were a rarity. Later, countless women ended up in hospital receiving treatment for bunions and other disfigurements as a result of spending the war in the wrong footwear. No wonder they had

ISSUED BY THE
BOARD OF TRADE

Mrs.

SEW-and-SEW

on

Steps you can take to save your SHOES

Buy shoes wisely. Remember that fit is more important than appearance. It's worth a little search to find really comfortable shoes.

New shoes will last longer if worn first on a dry day.

Give your shoes a rest — don't wear the same pair two days running if you can help it.

When you take off your shoes, use shoe-trees or stuff them with paper to keep the shape. Always undo fastenings first.

Damp shoes should be dried out slowly—*never* near strong heat. Put wet "woodies" sole-side up.

Clean regularly — a little polish every time is better than a lot now and then. Use dubbin on boots and shoes for rough wear.

See to repairs promptly — heels especially. A 'run-over' heel spoils the shape of the whole shoe *and* tires the foot. Leather studs and 'rails' on Woodies must be replaced before worn down to the sole.

Rubber studs, rubber soles and iron tips help shoes to wear longer.

* * *

Children's Boots and Shoes

Always buy on the large side to allow for growing. Extra socks will make a slightly big shoe comfortable. Ask the retailer to advise you which shoes are most durable and suitable for your children.

Teach your children to change their shoes on coming indoors.

been advised to remove their shoes carefully on coming home and to soothe sore feet in a bowl full of water (not necessarily hot).

The war altered women's dress in a number of ways, reflecting their new active role, but also the breaking down of social distinctions. The thirties was the last time everyone 'knew their place' and dressed accordingly. Society sanctioned correct dress for each class. All that became meaningless when, as the American pamphlet *Over There* put it, 'Old-time social distinctions are being forgotten as the sons of factory workers rise to be officers in the forces and the daughters of noblemen get jobs in munitions factories.'

Before the war the upper-class and aspiring middle-class English woman relied on classic suits, which London tailors did better than anyone else, and romantic evening gowns as the main staples of her wardrobe. She needed a tweed suit which was neither country-rough nor city slicker, something to be worn with equal ease at Goodwood or in the Ritz bar. Correct dress to her was not necessarily highly fashionable dress, since it was not done to flaunt wealth and privilege – something that the American Wallis Simpson failed to grasp in her cuttingly chic and expensive Paris fashions. Hardy Amies, working at the London fashion house Lachasse before pursuing wartime adventure in the army and as a secret service agent, produced the perfect article, his style combining English restraint with Gallic chic in a way that eluded his fellow countrymen. These women might patronise the court dressmaker for their evening gowns, but they had their suits, coats and sensible winter shoes made by men. British tweeds, tailoring and craftsmanship in leather, hand-wrought shoes, belts, gloves, bags and luggage were excellent. You could tell an English lady by the quality of her accessories and, although the leather shortage meant these goods virtually disappeared from the market during the war, hers had been made to last.

When Utility was introduced – hallmarked on the garment by two abstract-looking 'C' shapes dovetailed with 41, denoting Civilian Clothing 1941 – the obvious place to start was the suit. The tweed suit, or costume, was already pared down and unfussy in a way that meant that even if it had not been such a psychological comfort – providing a sense of continuity, of country values, of quality and class – it would survive as the practical basis of wartime fashion. The tailored look chimed with the no-nonsense, efficiency-for-victory approach which was the prevailing attitude. As restrictions on material began to bite, the suit became more minimalist, until even Wallis Simpson would have approved its severity. As Colin McDowell says, 'It was the nearest thing to a civilian uniform for women in the history of dress.' The main consideration was for it to be practical. As with men's suits, lack of material dictated the details. A maximum width was laid down for belts, seams, collars and sleeves, as well as the number of pleats in a narrower skirt. Pockets were trimmed or abolished. The number of buttons was limited. The depth of the hemline was specified and rose to the knee. So assiduously was austerity fashion promoted that even Queen Elizabeth, a great lover of frills and flounces, had to comply. Her designer Norman Hartnell was forced to obey the injunction against the use of embroidery and had to paint by hand any ornamentation on to the fabric of the Queen's clothes. Although the Queen continued to wear a fur slung round her shoulders, fur and leather trims were also outlawed.

The Government had to sell Utility to women and asked members of the Incorporated Society of London Fashion Designers – including the couturiers Norman Hartnell, Hardy Amies and Worth – to produce the designs for the basic garments: a top coat, a suit, an afternoon dress and cotton overall dress. The restrictions imposed a discipline on them which meant they did away with the fussy and produced something elegant and sophisticated. Templates were available to the trade and a ceiling put on prices that retailers could charge for Utility clothes: the average price of a suit was 92s 10d, a coat 83s 7d, a cotton dress 17s 10d, a blouse 21s 5d. Utility goods were blessedly free of purchase tax, unlike furs and fully fashioned stockings. The war was a great leveller in so many ways, not least when it came to dress. For the first time the ordinary woman was able to obtain well-designed clothing. The women's magazines and the newspapers enthusiastically endorsed the Utility scheme, an early advocate prophesying: 'Before long the society woman who pays 30 guineas for a frock will share her dress designer with the factory girl who pays 30s.'

Hollywood introduced glamour to the most humdrum lives, particularly in wartime, and British women sought to imitate the dress of their favourite stars. Hollywood had taken the lead in flaunting sophisticated trousers for women, but they had been slow to catch on in pre-war prurient Britain, when it was considered 'fast' for a woman to wear trousers. The likes of Lady Diana Cooper could get away with it on a Mediterranean cruise with the Windsors, but the great swathe of 'respectable' middle-class women could not. They modelled themselves on Queen Elizabeth, whom they adored, and *she* would never be seen in trousers. The war changed all that. Even if the Queen chose to pick her way over a bomb site wearing her customary high heels, skirt, furs, pearls, gloves and hat, it was no longer practical for other women to observe these conventions.

Women were queuing for food, buses and trains, travelling to work long, unsociable hours, often trudging through bomb-damaged, unlit streets. They worked as ARP wardens, as fire-women and as ambulance drivers. They worked in the factories and on the land, drove buses and trains. Trousers were warm and practical, especially as stockings were so hard to obtain. For the duration trousers were tolerated, not least because so often the man of the house – who, according to fashion historian Colin McDowell, as 'breadwinner considered his role as that of moral, social and, indeed, fashion arbiter for the women in his care' – was away. Nevertheless, the disapproval did not entirely go away and returned with full force in 1945. An article in the *Sunday Graphic* carried the headline, 'Time Women Stopped It':

Far too many of us, for far too long, have been masquerading in public in men's clothes. If ever it was smart to wear slacks or shorts in public that time has long since passed. It has simply succeeded in being cheap . . . Women's figures do not show up to advantage in trousers and jacket – they are not built to carry them . . . Femininity is a quality we should court. It's time that women, off duty, stopped wearing men's clothes.

Hats, which were universally worn by all classes and both sexes before the war, had not been subject to rationing, perhaps in a bid to keep up women's morale. Since they were not on points, they became scarce and expensive. Many women resorted to making their own, using Amy J. Reeve's *Practical Home Millinery* or *Madame Eva Ritcher's ABC of Millinery*. With hats in short supply the President of the Board of Trade asked the Archbishop of Canterbury to reassure women that it was no longer considered improper to attend church without a hat. Young women needed little excuse to throw off the convention of wearing a hat. In the Hollywood films they so admired, the emphasis was on the woman's hair, so what need of a hat? Stars like Rita Hayworth allowed their hair to fall in soft feminine waves to the shoulder. Veronica Lake's 1943 'peekabo' hairstyle was the new, sexy look women wanted to copy, but just at this time safety rules were introduced, insisting that hair be covered when working with machinery – where there were innumerable accidents involving women. In response to a plea by the US Government, Veronica Lake changed her hair into an upswept style, but women were determined to keep their hair long in defiance of the new safety rules and in spite of their more austere, grimmer dress. For work purposes, long hair could be wrapped in a turban, made from a jersey scarf wrapped round the head and kept in the pocket when not in use. This eventually metamorphosed into a turban-style hat.

Thanks to the Princesses, Elizabeth and Margaret Rose, headscarves had become acceptable. Theodora Fitzgibbon adopted the snood:

This was a wonderful invention for wartime England, when there were so many disturbed nights, and no time to go to hairdressers; they were made of a coarse fishnet, like a bag, and threaded with elastic. You popped all the back of your hair into them and there you were. It was a mark of defiance then for young women to have shoulder-length hair, as it meant that you weren't in the forces, and therefore, not conforming. Until they became over-popular, they were both attractive and useful.

In April 1945 the *News Chronicle* announced that 5 million Utility hats, price-controlled at 21s and 25s 6d, would be released into the shops in May. But 'will women – used to being hatless for the last five years – wear them?' A Streatham woman told the paper:

Even if five million mass-produced hats were given away there would not be a rush for them. Each woman likes to be separate, distinctive, apart from her friends. On hats generally the younger woman with bright fluffy hair looks charming and attractive without a hat, but after thirty a woman is 'improperly dressed' without one. At that age the face lines begin to show. A hat care-fully – shall we say? – camouflages the wrinkles, and the woman feels happy and all is well.

Another London woman was adamant she was not going back to the old ways:

I have not worn a hat for the last seven years, and I am certainly not going to start now. Since I gave up hats my hair has improved beyond belief. I am no longer obliged to change my hairstyle to suit the caprice of the milliners, nor do I have to go through the soul-destroying business of choosing a new hat, which always ended in my being coerced by a conscientious assistant into buying some-thing which I never dared to put on my head again!

A Hampstead woman bemoaned the fact that, unlike the smart Parisienne, English women had always been too self-conscious about hats. 'Only one in a thousand will wear the kind of startling design which is an acknowledged feature of

Longchamps,' she drawled. Her final put-down was to conclude:
'I am sure the five million Utility hats will be appreciated and
eagerly sought after by the modest English business girl.'

Just as it was embarrassing to be caught out wearing new
clothes, it was considered very bad form to wear a new
wedding dress – indeed, any wedding dress – after 1943 and
for some time after the war. Even when Princess Elizabeth
married Lieutenant Philip Mountbatten RN in November 1947
the fact that she had a splendid white wedding on an envi-
able allowance of 100 coupons was a cause for criticism in
some quarters. Some brides might resort to making a wedding
dress and veil out of curtain lace, which curiously enough was
not on points, or even parachute-silk and -nylon, which went
on sale in 1945 (up to then it could only be obtained illegally
through the black market), but a white wedding, like evening
dress, was considered frivolous and disloyal to the cause. The
coupons were better spent on the trousseau and the bottom
drawer. Most women had resorted to the historical expedient
of wearing their best outfit, dressing it up with a few accessories. As for the guests, a Bexley woman recalls someone
using a trick she can only have learned from the redoubtable
Scarlett O'Hara in the wartime cinema hit, *Gone with the
Wind*: 'I can remember a friend going to a wedding, a very
posh wedding . . . But she hadn't any clothing coupons. So,
she took down the velvet curtain and made herself a dress, by
tucking it and pinning it. When the wedding was over, she
unpicked it and put it back up as a curtain.'

Old traditions died hard, at least where the more conservative male sex was concerned. Shortly after VE Day Anthony
Heap, a keen theatre-goer, was pleased to see that evening
dress was making its way back at first nights: nearly half the
men in the stalls were wearing dinner jackets again. 'At this
rate the theatre will regain its pre-war glamour,' he speculated.
Similarly, in the autumn he noted that 'the more exclusive
West End restaurants are insisting on their clientele wearing
evening dress again, despite coupon shortage. But these people
still possess presentable pre-war evening clothes and can afford

to get new ones.' Deprived of domestic staff to cook and serve them at table, it seemed unlikely that the more prosperous households would ever return to donning evening dress for dinner at home, as Anthony Weymouth was sad to record: 'The life we used to live seems an immeasurable distance away. Shall we in the post-war years sit down to a formal evening dinner? Has the pleasant custom of changing from working-day clothes into a dinner-jacket gone for ever? How far we have departed from this former custom was brought home to me this evening when, in a fit of absence of mind, our Yvie sat down to dinner in an overall.'

In fact, the pressure was already on to move away from austerity towards a softer, more feminine look. 'The frou-frou woman abandoned in 1939 is on the march again,' the *Daily Mail* announced optimistically at the beginning of 1945. A new romantic era was now about to burst upon 'a grateful masculine world'. Women had played their part in the war, now it was time for them to retire to the home, to look appealing to the returning heroes. The beauty editor of *Home Chat* duly took up the baton:

It all started with me a couple of months ago. The war news was invigorating and victorious. It set my blood leaping and my mind bounding ahead. It set me thinking, of course, of post-war problems, of post-war planning, of the immense and serious things ahead. But, because I am a woman, it also set me thinking of lovely, gay, feminine things ahead, too . . . the little more leisure, the return to gracious living, the re-furbishing of tired homes and tired wardrobes, the prettily laid table, witty conversation, brilliant evenings with 'him'.

And again, because I am a woman, it set me thinking, 'What do I wear on these evenings?' And suddenly I rebelled against the little black frock. Suddenly I wanted elegance, glamour and gaiety, and the delicious consciousness of 'changing' at night.

Yet I knew rationing was likely to remain. I knew I shouldn't have any more money. But I wanted, I wanted, I *wanted* to dress up and look pretty. And this is how I solved it all.

There followed various suggestions on how to improvise. The war might be just about over, but Make Do and Mend was still on the agenda. As late as February 1945 the Mayor of Hammersmith opened a Make Do and Mend Exhibition at the local Co-op Society department store in King Street. It was organised by the Board of Trade in collaboration with the LCC. There were talks on 'Useful Knitting Hints', 'Soft Toy Making', 'Routine Care of Clothes', 'Loose Covers and Valeting at Home' and 'Solving the Hat Problem'. The British people did not know it yet, but Make Do and Mend, like clothes rationing, would be relevant for years to come.

'To wear clothes that have been patched and darned – perhaps many times – is to show oneself a true patriot,' Hugh Dalton announced in 1943, 'even when old clothes aren't exciting, they are a war-winning fashion to follow which will speed the day of victory.'

The Make Do and Mend campaign had been introduced by the Government because it was desperate to cut a consumer demand for clothes that could not be satisfied without keeping resources – human and material – away from war production. The campaign was personified by Mrs Sew and Sew, a cartoon character used in innumerable government posters and advertisements. There was a rash of practical booklets. The Board of Trade's *Make Do and Mend*, price 3d, carried the usual mix of encouragement and instruction. 'First, I would like to thank you all for the way in which you have accepted clothes rationing,' Hugh Dalton wrote in the foreword, giving women readers the customary pat on the head. 'You know how it has saved much-needed shipping space, manpower and materials, and so assisted our war effort.'

The purpose of the Make Do and Mend campaign was 'to help you to get the last possible ounce of wear out of all your clothes and household things'. The emphasis was very much on how to *care* for clothes to make them last. Very careful instructions were given on how to wash and iron various items of clothing properly, so as not to ruin them, with the short

supply of soap available for the task. War was declared against the moth.

In addition, 'No material must lie idle, so be a magician and turn old clothes into new. For major alterations there are many good renovation patterns on the market. Many other ideas will suggest themselves to meet special circumstances.'

There were innumerable ideas for renovating children's clothes and cutting down adults' old clothes into something for the children. Plus fours, for instance, would make two pairs of shorts for a schoolboy. An old skirt would make one pair of knickers and a little play-skirt for a seven-year-old. Children's clothing should ideally carry large hems and tucks at shoulder and waist so that it could be let out and down as the child grew. Women were also advised to raid absent husband's wardrobes to convert their unwanted clothes to their own use, 'if you are sure he won't want them again after the war'.

More women then than nowadays knew how to ply a needle, but those who could not sew were urged to join sewing classes. 'Your local Evening Institute, Technical College or Women's Organization is probably running a class now. Ask the Citizens' Advice Bureau; they will be able to tell you when these classes meet.' The WVS and WI held 'Make Do and Mend' classes, as well as organising groups of women to carry out repair work for others, such as the overalls of local war workers. Those who already knew how to make do and mend were asked to pass on their ideas and to hold sewing classes where equipment could be pooled.

Newspapers like the *Daily Mail* worked hard to educate their readers. Their 'Sew and Save' column provided solutions to such problems as planning a wardrobe, home dressmaking and hints to achieve smartness. Women's magazines, as ever, were a constant source of helpful advice on everything from turning old blankets into overcoats to transforming sacking into a child's dress. Everything helped. *Woman* was at pains to remind its readers that their clothes could be preserved if they kept their elbows off the table, their hands out of their pockets and if they avoided taking their foot out of their shoes and resting it on the heel. Gloves could be preserved if they took them off before powdering their nose and a coat would wear out slower if a bag was not rubbed up against it while walking.

Darning and patching was tedious, laborious and time-consuming. 'A stitch in time now saves not only extra work in the end, but precious coupons,' the *Make Do and Mend* booklet reminded women. Gwladys Cox began the New Year of 1945 complaining: 'Coming on top of a year of incessant bombing, one feels as if one's nerve would give way, sometimes. It is so hard, so very hard, to cope with all the difficulties, hardships, and, in some respects, real *want*. Our clothes are getting threadbare. For the best part of two days, I have been darning and patching a pair of Ralph's trousers that are only fit for the rag-man.' Women were forever darning their husband's socks, repairing frayed shirt cuffs and replacing frayed collars with new collars made from the shirt tail, and even cutting out the back of the shirt to replace a badly worn front, using near-matching material for the back. On top of this they had their own mending to do – the constant battle of the stocking – as well as trying to maintain the household linen, turning worn sheets from sides to middle. Washing lines revealed the full history of a family's war on the clothing front.

At a time when civilians were running for their lives to the air raid shelters, the Government's booklet was advising: 'Always carry a needle and cotton and mending silk with you – this will save many a ladder in stockings or prevent the loss of buttons; your friends will thank you, too. How many times have you heard someone say, "Has anyone got a needle and cotton?"'

When even darning and patching no longer served, there was still another task: 'When finally discarding clothes that have gone too far to renovate, be sure to cut out any good bits of material to put in your piece bag; pieces of stockinette and old corsets in particular are invaluable for patching other garments of the same type. Odd scraps of thick wool can be unravelled for darning. Be sure to have a well-stocked work basket with all the coloured cottons and mending materials you might need.' Spare scraps of material could also be pressed into service as tea cosies, coverings for buttons, kettle holders and furniture polishers.

Old sweaters were unpicked and recycled. 'New life for old woollies' ran the Government slogan. A north London woman who worked in a Mobile Medical Unit remembers: 'Clothes rationing brought many problems, and on the unit we used to swap hand-knitted jumpers, unpick them, wash the wool and re-knit them in a different pattern in the long hours of waiting for something to happen.' The Government maintained it was 'true economy in money, coupons and material' to use large knitting needles and fine wool. 'A long-sleeved, 2-ply jumper is just as warm as a 4-ply one.'

Some London stores ran a renovation service for clothes and hats. It must have been very tempting to cheat Make Do and Mend with its hours of tedious grind and let the stores take the strain.

In January 1945 the readers of *Home Chat* received a wake-up call of sorts:

Here we are – you and I – at the beginning of 1945 . . . looking forward to a New Year that we confidently expect is going to be the most wonderful ever – because Victory is in sight . . . almost, if I'm not being too optimistic, on our doorstep. And you're hoping . . . oh so fervently, that 'he' will be home to celebrate next New Year with you.

Which makes me wonder . . . and I expect you're wondering, too . . . what kind of you is he going to find awaiting him? Are you as nice to look at as you were when he went away? It is so fatally easy – isn't it? – when the one important person in the world is away for months on end . . . maybe years . . . to let yourself slack. To neglect your figure . . . your face . . . your hair. Oh, I don't mean you don't give them any attention at all. But you're just a little less fastidious, a wee bit careless, because you're tired, maybe, or simply can't be bothered because there's no one to say lovely things to you . . . to appreciate your loveliness.

So, now, at the beginning of the New Year, with good resolutions in the air, do let me persuade you to make up those deficiencies . . . to resolve, from this moment, to make the very most of yourself, so that he will say, the instant he sets eyes on you again, 'You're lovelier than ever, my darling.'

Woman took up the same theme, anxious to jog readers into action. 'Nearly everyone's hair has gone a bit duller and darker through wartime food and worry. But special hair care in the remaining weeks or months before he arrives will make a big difference,' Helen Temple's Beauty Parlour suggested. It is hard to know what could be done, apart from a more careful diet and vigorous brushing. With shampoo and running hot water in short supply, it was impossible to wash hair regularly. Women had to resort to desperate measures. Helen Temple advocated 'a quick steaming over a basin of boiling water to put new life into hair' and 'A hard rub with the fingertips, through a clean towel, helps to remove grease and surface dirt and makes the hair springy again. While the hair is damp from the steam, curls are twirled into pins and waves are pressed in.' Hairpins were a luxury to be carefully hoarded and hairdressers asked clients to bring their own towels.

Similarly, since 'a hot bath is not always possible, a quick sponge all over with lukewarm water, to which a dash of eau-de-Cologne is added, gives a fresh glow.' After the fall of France perfume was almost non existent. Even something as basic as soap was rationed. By 1945 each person was allowed 3 ounces of soap a month, equivalent to a square of about 1 inch, or 4 ounces of hard soap for clothes washing, or 6 ounces of soap powder. Women had to make a choice and there was seldom enough to cover all needs. Women were undoubtedly still in the business of pleasing men, at least the advertisers thought so. 'Eve Toilet Soap keeps your complexion radiantly youthful . . . for him [photograph of serviceman]. Will he find you as young and lovely when he comes home again?' trilled one advertisement. Sunlight Soap, costing threepence farthing and two coupons, was promoted to preserve those precious undies and pre-war pillowslips.

Two gripes American servicemen had about English women were that their teeth were bad and they smelt. They were warned in the booklet *Over There*: 'One of the things the English always had enough of in the past was soap. Now it is so scarce that girls working in the factories often cannot get the grease off their hands or out of their hair.' Toothbrushes were very hard to come by. Deodorant was not commonly used pre-war, but wartime advertisements promoted its use. 'Girls in Air Force Blue Need Odo-Ro-No' spelt one advertisement, depicting a young woman managing a barrage balloon. Not only were deodorants a revelation, but many working-class women who joined the forces were still using rags instead of sanitary towels. In the summer of 1945 an advertisement cautiously promoted 'Lil-lets for *married* women who prefer the comfort and obvious advantage of internal sanitary protection.' Apparently 'small quantities' were now 'obtainable from chemists at 1/9 per carton of twelve'.

Cosmetics and other beauty products were limited because ingredients such as glycerin, castor oil, talc, fats, petroleum and alcohol were all needed for the war effort. Even the cosmetic manufacturers were engaged on war production. Cyclax, for instance, had been producing sun barriers and cream to protect the skins of soldiers in the North Africa campaign and working their way up from the heel of Italy. Paradoxically, the war saw women wearing make-up to an extent that they never had hitherto. Before the war, it was considered 'fast' for respectable women to wear make-up. During the war, it was imperative for morale for women to 'put their best face forward'. Looking good was a duty. Women had to improvise. Soot, charcoal and shoe polish were pressed into service as eye shadow. Lard could be used as a cleanser after cold creams and removal creams disappeared. The beautiful Theodora Fitzgibbon, who had been a model, reveals her own tips:

Make-up . . . was almost unobtainable and of very poor quality. We used Meltonian shoe cream for mascara (I had a brief week on moustache-wax which made my eyelashes look like furry spiders' legs), Trex or Spry cooking fat for cleansing cream (how many bearded ladies as a result?), calamine lotion as a powder base and sometimes even baby powder for face powder. Eye shadow was not fashionable then off the stage, but we put Vaseline on our eye-lids and lips to achieve that 'dewy' look. Often it trickled down if the room was hot, which looked as if one had been crying, and sympathy was often given as a result. We were far too sly to admit what in fact it was and sometimes pretended a sadness which did not exist. In an attempt to curl up the ends of my hair I was once surprised by Dylan [Thomas, the poet] as I was using a chunk of large macaroni, called *rigatoni*, with a hair grip. He was agog as he inquired: 'Are we going to eat it afterwards?'

Women had long been accustomed to taking their lipstick and powder cases for refills, so as not to dig too far into the quota. 'All the quotas are based on money,' the *Daily Mail* was at pains to remind its readers, 'so the more you pay for the trimmings the less you will get of the cosmetics themselves.' If 'every woman bought refills of lipstick, powder, eye black and rouge there would be more than enough cosmetics to go round'. What cosmetics there were reflected the times. Lipstick was regarded as 'a red badge of courage'. Cyclax produced a lipstick called 'Auxiliary Red' – 'the lipstick for service women' – and like all cosmetic companies linked patriotism to beauty. They doggedly advertised their products, so that their brands would survive the war in women's consciousness. Women in the services needed particular advice on what make-up would complement their uniform, such as that *Home Chat* was able to give 'Disillusioned':

Q: I've joined the ATS recently, but – oh, Vanity Fayre, I look so drab in khaki – being rather of the mousey type. Do tell me what make-up to use?

A: It has to be discreet to conform to rules and regulations. Choose a peach-tinted foundation cream, a peachy-toned powder, and just touch your cheeks with a spot of rouge. A red rouge and lipstick with a slight mauve-ish tinge looks well, but if you can't manage to buy these, get a soft rose tone.

With the end of the war in sight, in January 1945 Elizabeth Arden was bringing out lipstick in colours anticipating the gay new mood and less restrictive dress, which would surely prevail once Germany admitted defeat. They included Red Feather, a bright red to cheer the very young, and Cinnabar, a rich dark red, to be worn with 'velvets, black and furs' – very optimistic.

In spite of wartime restrictions, magazines such as *Vogue*

continued to feature clothes not available in Britain, but reserved for export, in order to keep an interest in British fashion alive and to bring in much needed dollars. Photographs of American clothes were also used to fill the pages. Hollywood had some excellent designers. American manufacturers were also far advanced in production techniques and competitively priced. Their ready-to-wear clothes were more sophisticated in fit and sizing than the equivalent in Britain or Europe. Britain could not compete in the ready-to-wear market. Its weapon was still couture, even though many of London's couturiers had closed during the war and Hardy Amies's Lachasse in Farm Street, Mayfair was being used as an ARP centre. The question confronting the industry in 1945 was who would command the world fashion trade? London, Paris or New York?

Under the German occupation Paris had existed in isolation. The couture industry had lost vital ground, while London and New York had moved on without it. In contrast to the austerity which was the keynote of London fashion, Paris had adopted frivolity as a weapon against the Germans. It was out of tune with the times. But Paris was liberated in August 1944 and French fashion, with the blessing of its Government, reasserted itself very quickly. The French Government understood, as the British Government did not, that the fashion industry was a prime asset in rebuilding the country's export trade. Besides, *haute couture* was a huge employer. When the photographs of the first post-Liberation collections appeared in the autumn of 1944 the clothes-starved British – who were about to experience some of the worst months of aerial attack and destruction of the entire war – were offended at the casual gaiety and extravagant waste of material.

In January 1945 *Picture Post* was writing: 'At the moment, Paris has lost touch with reality through its wartime isolation. Designers worked in a vacuum and their products show lavishness out of keeping with the spirit of the day. For the first time ever London fashion designers have banded together to share inspiration and views under the title "the Incorporated Society of London Fashion Designers". After all, London has a superb tailoring craftsmanship tradition and Britain makes wonderful fabrics.' Unfortunately, London was extremely short of fabric, but so too were New York and Paris hampered by shortages.

When Paris showed its spring collections in March 1945, Britain was still in the thick of the war. In London Norman Hartnell was showing 25 new models, as opposed to his pre-war 125, and his trademark bridal gown was missing. His dresses were simple crepe and fine wool with a new, very low, 'V' neckline, presumably for Victory, and three-quarter-length sleeves. Soon large London stores were selling cherry-red and violet-blue coats to suit the peacetime mood. Britain was beginning to redirect labour from wartime to peacetime production, but it would take time to re-establish skilled workers after they were demobbed and to train new recruits. The first non-austerity fashion show, 'for export only', took place in London and attracted 'highly respectable orders' in late 1945. However, the fashion industry, like the housing industry, was encumbered with red tape. *Picture Post* complained that the Board of Trade was offering 'no hope or help, so Paris and New York have nothing to fear'. This was all the more frustrating since with the abrupt end of Lend-Lease in August 1945 Britain's need for foreign currency, especially for dollars, was acute.

That same month an article in the *Sunday Graphic* was very despondent:

Paris, incidentally, talks about staging a fashion show over here. Why put the French designers to the trouble of bringing their models to a country which has no means of buying them? And why agonize us by dangling before our eyes things that not one woman in a million has a chance of buying? This may be the place to mention that I strongly deprecate the custom in some shops of displaying goods that are 'not for sale'. We've got enough to put up with without this form of pointless sadism to add insult to injury. WE WANT CLOTHING, HOUSES AND FOOD – the mere essentials of living.

Londoners might have been forgiven for thinking that with the peace all these were just around the corner. John Lewis

Gradually the Ministry of Information realised that it could rely on the good sense of the British people. Nazi-style propaganda was inappropriate in a democracy and regarded as a bit of a joke by the British. Nevertheless, this row of posters urging the public what to do and not do shows that the Ministry was leaving nothing to chance.

The Government lent its support to the establishment of wartime day nurseries, like this one in Lambeth, in order to encourage mothers to work for the war effort. As soon as the emergency was over, however, it showed no further interest in providing facilities for working mothers. After all, a woman's place was in the home, looking after her family.

A Southwark family rescuing their few remaining possessions before the looters beat them to it.

he coal shortage and lack of labour to deliver it meant that Londoners were reduced to
ollecting their meagre allowance from emergency coal dumps, carrying it away in prams
r dragging it in sacks. It was a situation that continued long after the war, despite the
ationalisation of the coal industry.

ombing was a dirty business, but mobile laundries enabled women living in damaged
omes or without fuel to keep on top of the grime.

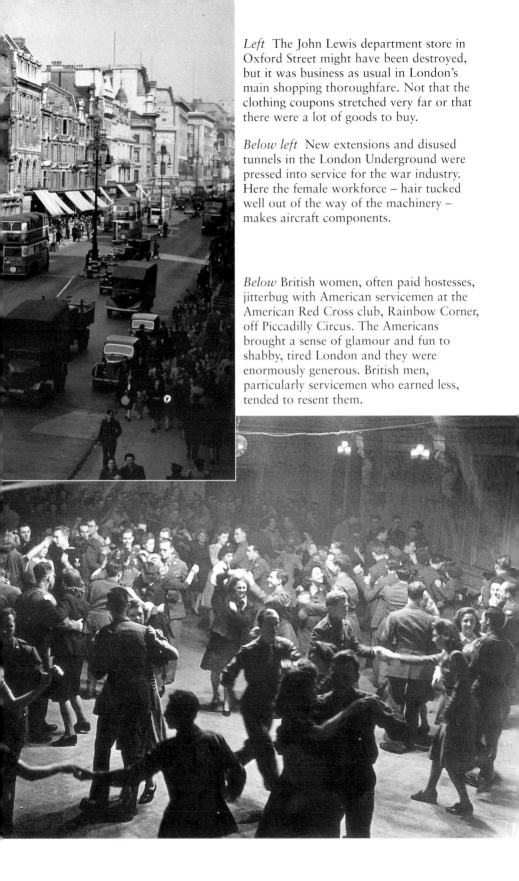

Left The John Lewis department store in Oxford Street might have been destroyed, but it was business as usual in London's main shopping thoroughfare. Not that the clothing coupons stretched very far or that there were a lot of goods to buy.

Below left New extensions and disused tunnels in the London Underground were pressed into service for the war industry. Here the female workforce – hair tucked well out of the way of the machinery – makes aircraft components.

Below British women, often paid hostesses, jitterbug with American servicemen at the American Red Cross club, Rainbow Corner, off Piccadilly Circus. The Americans brought a sense of glamour and fun to shabby, tired London and they were enormously generous. British men, particularly servicemen who earned less, tended to resent them.

Above It was a criminal offence to waste food in wartime, but every neighbourhood had its pig bin

Left No opportunity must be lost to produce food for an island under siege and here National Fire Service men rear pigs in the ruins of Lincoln's Inn Fields.

bove The 1,000-year-old fortress of the Tower of London withstood the worst the Nazis uld throw at it, while vegetables flourished in the moat.

ft Even the most unpromising ground was turned into allotments and these Bethnal reen boys are determined to do their bit.

The House of Commons might have been destroyed, but the freedom and democracy which the Mother of Parliaments stood for had triumphed.

was employing advisers to show demobbed women – who were given clothing coupons instead of demob suits – the new lines in clothes, and Selfridges was holding a services' dress parade every Friday at 3 p.m. during September and October. It began with a five-minute beauty talk, followed by a parade of Utility fashions showing two sample wardrobes, each totalling between £8 and £10, consisting of either a coat, dress and overall or a suit, blouse and mackintosh. Firms were also prepared to alter and dye uniforms. This was about as good as it was going to get for many, many years. Londoners had no idea just how long it would be before they could put away their sewing kits.

It was in vain, then, that the King told his new Prime Minister Mr Attlee: 'We must *all* have new clothes – my family is down to the lowest ebb.'

6

Off the Back of a Lorry

'In 1945 the war against Germany and Japan came to an
end and the war against crime in London began'
– John Gosling, Ex-Detective Superintendent, Scotland Yard

When the Commissioner of Police of the Metropolis wrote his
annual report for Parliament for 1945, there was no masking
the fact that crime was rampant and, worse, on the increase.
London, as ever, was the crime capital of the country. Criminal
gangs flourished. The Piccadilly Commandos and Hyde Park
Rangers – prostitutes in the West End – plied their trade with
impunity, while their less professional sisters were not above
luring some hapless American serviceman into a dark corner
and robbing him. Looting of bomb sites, sometimes while the
dead and injured lay trapped in the debris, was not uncommon.
Pilfering from employers was rife. Robberies from warehouses
and hijacking of lorries fed the black market, which was
increasing in vigour as wartime scarcities continued into the
peace. The damaged state of much of the property in the
capital – and the absence of many householders in the country
– made breaking and entering a cinch. There was a rash of
female burglars. Deserters without papers roamed the streets
preying on the public to survive. Even respectable men and
women were increasingly drawn into a dalliance with crime.
    War offered fresh opportunities for crime. Sleek in their
Savile Row suits, their molls dripping with furs and jewels,
London's underworld kings were having the time of their lives.
But there was also a new breed of criminal abroad: ruthless
young men, armed robbers, who meted out gratuitous violence
with casual ease. Criminal associates such as the Elephant Boys

of Bermondsey, who had robbed a City jeweller and run over a brave but foolhardy man who tried to stop them in December 1944, had no compunction in shooting to kill as they made off with their booty. Armed violence had been imported with the Americans, who lived in a society where guns were commonplace. By 1945 the country was awash with guns, illegally sold by American servicemen at £25 for a handgun or brought back by British servicemen from abroad.

Jewel heists and safe breakings were frequent, but at the end of 1945 criminals had their sights on an even bigger prize: 160 frozen turkeys in south-east London.

By the end of the war the spiv had made his appearance on the streets of London, distinct in his loud and garish clothing, his gait an imitation of the Chicago gangsters in Hollywood films. Regarded with a degree of tolerant affection by a public weary of official restrictions, he could be seen in the West End selling stolen cigarettes and, after June, hanging around Warren Street, where used cars with dodgy logbooks were on sale.

At the outset of war the Government had assumed complete control over the lives of the people, when authority was transferred wholesale from Parliament to ministers and civil servants. The nation would be ruled by Defence Regulations rather than Acts of Parliament. They would secure 'public safety, the defence of the Realm, the maintenance of public order, and the efficient prosecution of any war in which his Majesty may be engaged.' In theory, all existing laws, even habeas corpus, were swept aside and the Government and its bureaucrats would issue new regulations, Orders in Council, concerning all aspects of life, great and small. Any infringement of regulations brought retribution. The Government now had authority to prosecute and punish offenders, detaining them indefinitely and without trial if necessary. It had the right to seize property, other than land, and to enter and search without warrant.

For everyone, from the company director to the local grocer to the humble housewife, the rash of wartime regulations meant there were more laws to break, sometimes inadvertently.

It was very often not the common criminal but the ordinary householder who had slipped up, but there were no allowances for mistakes. In the early days of the war, when blackout hysteria was at its height, a woman was prosecuted for running into a room, where her baby was having a fit, and turning on the light without first securing the blackout curtains. Even as late as February 1945, when the blackout had turned to the dim-out and was irrelevant since most enemy air activity was robotic, a man was charged at Marlborough Street for carelessly showing a light after dark. Others were charged with exceeding the 20 mph speed limit in the hours of darkness.

A woman was fined 15s for failing to prevent her dog from 'chasing or worrying sheep in Hyde Park'. Aliens who changed their place of employment or residence without written permission found themselves in court, as did British subjects registered under the National Registration Act 1939, who were obliged to notify the authorities of a change of address. Thousands were in possession of stolen identity cards, their letters and numbers bearing no relation to the holder's neighbourhood, family or name.

With the return of the basic petrol ration in June and more cars on the road, the Commissioner of Police complained there was an increase in car crime, taking up valuable police time. 'You are nothing but a contemptible young cad,' the Clerkenwell magistrate told one of many convicted of joyriding and driving a car without the owner's permission and without insurance. Innumerable Londoners were charged with fare-dodging.

The Treasury might try to divert all excess cash into war savings, but illegal gaming and street betting flourished. Fines imposed by the law were outstripped by winnings. Restricted to afternoons while the blackout prevailed, dog racing was as popular as ever. It was a perfect venue for illegal money laundering and trading in stolen or forged papers on the part of black marketeers. Military police found a swoop on the dog tracks rewarding, since it attracted deserters, American and British. In an age of strict licensing laws and scarcity, bottle parties offered night-long semi-legal drinking – made dangerous by the use of illegally brewed hooch, which could cause brain damage, blindness and death.

During the war the population of Greater London – coinciding with the 693 square miles of the Metropolitan Police District – had dropped by nearly 2 million, to 6,908,000, and yet the number of indictable offences per 1,000 of population had almost doubled since 1938. The number of indictable crimes in 1945 was 128,954, compared with 103,804 in 1944. The Commissioner of Police, Sir Harold Scott, attributed the increase in 1945 to the general 'unsettlement' as thousands returned to the capital, including demobbed servicemen and overseas troops passing through on their way home.

He was evidently hoping that with the end of the emergency and the return of energetic young police officers to the force after demobilisation, allowing the elderly who had been holding the fort to retire, there would be a return to the pre-war level of crime and detection in the capital. But it would take time to build up the force to pre-war strength and to train new detectives, and meanwhile the black lines on the crime graphs in the map room at Scotland Yard revealed the unwelcome truth that the criminal was in the ascendancy.

John Gosling, who was to head Scotland Yard's new Ghost Squad to combat crime, his 'manor' being the notorious 'Crooks' Dormitory' stretching from King's Cross in the west to Aldgate in the east, to Highbury Corner and Stoke Newington in the north, down to Dalston and back across Islington to King's Cross, was under no illusions about the challenge he faced: 'Against the depleted ranks of the police was ranged a new type of criminal, cunning, ruthless and well-informed. Many had served in the Armed Forces – some with distinction – and many more were deserters. They were younger, fitter, harder, more resourceful and more energetic than the pre-war criminal.'

London was a thieves' paradise. It was brimming with opportunities for crime. Nearly everything was scarce or unobtainable, food and clothing were still rationed, cigarettes and alcohol were in short supply and carried heavy customs duties which had raised their prices three or four times above pre-war levels, jewellery and other luxuries carried huge purchase tax. Given a new mobility with cars and lorries, stolen or otherwise, the criminals, according to Gosling, 'swooped almost every night' and 'the pickings were good':

Lorry-loads of tea, sugar, butter, clothes, cigarettes and whisky disappeared from the streets or were stolen from warehouses. Jewellery and cash vanished from private houses into the pockets of thieves who worked liked phantoms. Furs and rings, clothing and petrol coupons, carpets, lipsticks, typewriters, razor blades, shoes – anything with a ready cash value was loot for the army of the underworld. The figures of stolen property rose to astronomical proportions: millions of cigarettes, hundreds of thousands of forged or stolen coupons, thousands of bottles of liquor, thousands of pounds worth of jewels.

Impatient with the never-ending shortages, more and more previously law-abiding citizens were complicit with the criminals in breaking the law. As a Walthamstow woman admitted: 'No one thought they was doing anything wrong buying this stuff –it was never outrageously expensive – no one had that sort of money to be exploited by these people.' They were tired of hardship and longed for those little extras that made life brighter and more comfortable. In tired, grey, dismal London, shabby from lack of paint, its people threadbare and bored with the meagre rations, scrimping and saving and making do, the black market boomed and the crooks took every advantage of it.

In the New Year of 1945 long queues formed outside the Old Bailey three hours before it opened every day and public attention was riveted on the trial being heard in Number One Court. Here was a prime example of a young woman being led astray and indulging in the sort of violent, immoral behaviour the war had fostered. Eighteen-year-old Elizabeth 'Marina' Jones, whose soldier husband was missing in action, had left a respectable home in Wales to become a striptease dancer in the capital. With her lover, the gun-toting Private Karl Gustav Hulton, a 22-year-old deserter from the 501st Airborne Division from Boston, she was found guilty and condemned to death for the cold-blooded murder of George Edward Heath, a taxi driver from Kennington. Hulton had shot him in the back at point-blank range and Jones had robbed the man of his wallet, watch, pen, cigarette lighter and propelling pencil even as he was dying. They had thrown his body in a ditch near Staines.

Just for the hell of it, the two had assaulted and robbed several others, including Violet May Hodge, a 19-year-old from Bristol, who had come to London to marry a GI, only to find that he was already married. Sadder and wiser, she was making her way to Paddington to return home when she was offered a lift by Hulton and Jones in a stolen army lorry. Near Windsor, they had knocked her unconscious and dumped her body in the river, but she survived and made her escape. The gains were out of all proportion to the savagery. They had done it merely to steal the girl's suitcase and, in fact, Jones was wearing Hodge's coat when she was arrested. The arrest itself had come about after Hulton was spotted by a sharp-eyed constable in the dead taxi driver's Ford, as he cruised the Piccadilly area in pursuit of a girl whose fur coat Jones coveted.

Ordinarily, according to the terms of the United States of America (Visiting Forces) Act 1942, American servicemen could not be tried in British courts for offences against British subjects, but sometimes exceptions were made and the Americans handed Hulton over to British justice. At the trial Hulton and Jones each blamed the other for the death of the taxi driver. Murder was still a capital offence and they both received the death penalty. She was led out of the dock screaming. Hulton was to be hanged at Pentonville, Jones at Holloway. She was unrepentant, writing from her cell: 'I would rather die than serve a prison sentence. God – what a jury! How I hate the London people. Hate them like poison. And how I hate that jury! Everything pointed to my innocence, but they found me guilty. Oh! It's horrible. Everything was so ghastly.'

Nevertheless, the Home Secretary, Herbert Morrison, had to consider whether or not to give the girl a reprieve, on account of her youth. He revealed in his memoirs that Churchill was against a reprieve and the American ambassador, John Winant, came to plead hard for Hulton's life. 'You can't hang my soldier if your British girl gets off. Both are guilty,' he told Morrison.

Morrison agreed. 'Yes, but there is only one reason for the decision; the girl was only just over eighteen at the time of the crime. Under British law we cannot hang under eighteen and this girl is only just over.'

Not all crimes reached the Old Bailey or were of this sensational nature, however. In 1945 there were only 35 murders in the capital – that is, known murders, for with Reginald Halliday Christie, the notorious serial killer of Rillington Place, serving in the wartime police and already embarked on his killing spree, who knew how many of his victims and the victims of other unknown assailants were passed off as air-raid casualties or hidden beneath the ruins? A few murders were carried out randomly in the murky darkness of a raid, such as that of 'Irish Molly', of Shoreditch, who was found strangled in a surface shelter. The hunt was on for a tall man, probably an ex- soldier, who lived 'somewhere near Cambridge Heath Road', who had been seen chatting to her on the evening she died. He was never found or brought to justice.

Some murders were what the French would categorise as crimes of passion, perpetrated by jealous or infuriated husbands, who returned to find their wives had been unfaithful. These coincided with an increase in violence in the family, brought about by the disruption of family life during the war. There was a worrying increase in juvenile delinquency. The divorce rate soared, while there was also an increase in the number of cases of bigamy going through the courts, some of them encouraged by the fact that a soldier with two or three wives could have them all drawing allowances for him.

There were heated fights between British and American or Canadian servicemen, often because the former resented the latter having a British girl on his arm. Rape was not a capital offence in British law, but American servicemen convicted of rape were likely to be hanged by their own authorities. There was an increase in robbery and assault with intent to rob, most of them occurring in the streets after darkness. In September 1945 a patrolling officer on behalf of the Public Morality Council noted that there 'are still a large number of US troops around and cases of violence and assault by these troops are on the increase, including use of firearms and murder of an Army officer for purposes of robbery by soldiers'.

American servicemen often had cause to lose their rag, as they were frequently cheated, overcharged in taxis, restaurants and clubs. They were also the innocent dupes of London women. Margaret O'Malley of Chapel Street, Camden Town, was sentenced to one month's imprisonment for stealing £2 from an American sergeant by luring him to Park West, a block of flats 'with many exits' on the Edgware Road: 'The sergeant said he gave her £2 and she took him to the flats and told him to wait while she paid for a room. He waited three minutes and as she did not return he went to look for her. He found her in a street nearby with two girl friends. She looked guilty on seeing him and offered his money back if he said nothing to the "cops". He called the police.' The accused said the sergeant molested her and she did it to get rid of him. It seems she had been making a habit of robbing American servicemen and had £12 on her when she was arrested.

A barmaid living at Royal College Street, Camden Town, the wife of a prisoner of the Japanese and mother of three, had stolen a wallet containing £8 and a driving licence from an American soldier: 'Detective Collins said the soldier met the accused in a public house, and went with her to the cinema. While there he took off his coat and put it on a chair. The woman made an excuse to leave, and he later found that his wallet was missing. He looked in various public houses and eventually found her. She then had only £4 10s in her possession.'

'I wonder what your husband would say if he knew about this?' the magistrate reproved her, while imposing a sentence of two months' hard labour – that is, whatever labour the prisoner was fit to do, and it also meant sleeping without a mattress for the first two weeks of sentence.

The presence of large numbers of troops in the capital – men who knew they could be killed imminently – and the rise in wages enabling more men to patronise them, meant that prostitutes had never had it so good. Demand exceeded supply, so that they could charge more for less time. By May 1945 American servicemen were being charged £5 for a few minutes, although British servicemen with their lower pay were on a different tariff. The parks, especially Hyde Park, were major centres of prostitution, but Marble Arch, the Edgware Road and Shepherd's Market in Mayfair were all popular haunts. Prostitutes jostled with each other on crowded pavements and some did a brisk trade in selling their beat to others. Residents complained that once respectable flats were being turned into brothels, while illicit clubs, part brothel, part drinking den, part gaming house, sprang up and moved on, just a few steps ahead of a police raid.

So great was the demand that a veteran like Marthe Watts was doing a 14-hour day. She took home 49 clients in the course of VE Day. Prostitution itself was not illegal but soliciting was, the most common method in the wartime darkness being for the prostitute to shine a torch in her face. A patrolling officer on behalf of the Public Morality Council deplored the situation:

They [prostitutes] still patrol in the usual places. They still appear to be working on the technique of inducing the men to speak to them, this ruling out any possibility of a charge of soliciting. This accounts for the apparent lack of action against them, as many magistrates now demand proof of annoyance to foot passengers before registering a conviction and unless this is forthcoming police are naturally chary of taking action.

Nevertheless, most prostitutes had a string of convictions for soliciting: by 1945 fines were giving way to prison sentences. It was easy to run foul of the law, particularly for the hundreds of amateurs who were exploiting the situation to earn some easy money. As the Public Morality Council man guessed: 'One suspects that a lot of complaints about the prevalence of brothels is really a reflection on increased promiscuity.'

Running a brothel was a criminal offence and it took only two offenders to comprise a brothel, as a south London mother and daughter found to their cost: 'At about 3am officers entered the house. Thompson (mother) and Small (daughter) were there in a bedroom with two American soldiers who said they met them in Shaftesbury Avenue at midnight and paid them £3.'

Thompson, whose children had been evacuated but who was expecting another, had already been charged on a previous occasion with running a brothel. Asked why she had broken her promise not to re-offend, she answered: 'My children were writing for boots and clothes; my husband is still inside and I was forced to resume.' She was heavily fined.

Homosexuality was a criminal offence. As the Public Morality Council officer noted in the autumn of 1945: 'Police are again conducting a campaign against those engaged in this deplorable offence. The happy hunting ground is Piccadilly and Leicester Square.' Offenders were usually charged with being 'concerned together in committing an act of gross indecency'.

As abortion was still illegal, desperate women resorted to a back-street job. It was a sordid and dangerous business, even costing them their lives.

'You killed this woman just as certainly as if you had shot or poisoned her,' Mr Justice Wrottesley of the Old Bailey told an Islington woman, passing sentence of five years' penal servitude on her. She had pleaded guilty to the manslaughter of Elizabeth Moore, a 38-year-old married woman of Hammersmith, and 'to using an instrument for the purpose of procuring an abortion'.

When a south London woman performed an abortion on a six months' pregnant woman, she tried to pass her subsequent death off as an air-raid casualty, telling police she had admitted the girl to her house suffering from bomb shock.

Looting was considered a heinous crime, a capital offence under the Defence of the Realm Act. Surprisingly, perhaps, the death penalty was never imposed. Looting was not confined to the hardened criminal or the casual thief: a proportion of men in official positions, in positions of trust, such as ARP wardens, auxiliary firemen, even police, were charged with the offence. Even something as trivial as a rescue worker picking up a bottle of liquor from a bombed site and sharing it with fellow workers after a long night's work was regarded as an indictable offence.

It was hard to define looting. A boy who found a packet of cigarettes in the street and took them home was far removed from the rescue worker who stole the handbag of a woman lying dead or injured in the rubble. And yet in wartime both these offences fell into the looting category. There were hundreds of cases of people who would consider themselves to be law-abiding citizens taking advantage of the situation created by bombing to help themselves to other people's property. Verily Anderson was one of them and had a lucky escape:

A nursery fire-guard was something impossible to find in any shop. The day I stepped out of a bombed site with one in my arms, I walked straight into a policeman. I thought instantly of the notices saying that looters might be shot. The policeman shook his head in a disappointed way, as though he expected better of me.

'I know,' I said, 'I'm ready. You can shoot me.'

'It's not that, Miss,' he said, 'I've had my eye on it to take home after dark for my own toddler.'

'Take it,' I said, holding it out to him. I knew now what thieves meant by *hot*.

'No, miss,' he said sadly. 'You got it first.' And he continued on his beat.

In Walworth the Reverend Markham noted that some looters went in the guise of fire-fighters:

The Town Hall provided them with steel helmets and armbands identifying them as members of a Fire party. During gunfire, they would patrol in pairs down the Walworth Road. If no one was about, they would heave a brick through a shop window and dash round the next corner. Another pair would follow, and, if the coast was clear, empty the shop window, and disappear with their loot to the café. On several occasions I chased them off when this was happening.

Some wanted to become ARP wardens because it offered the perfect opportunity for looting, as Markham recalled:

I tried to prevent it being done by the wardens. I remember refusing to enrol one man, who, early on in the raids, wanted to join our Post. He said, 'I am always first on the scene of any incident. I have a small van, and can be on the spot without delay.' I made a few discreet enquiries and found that he was a burglar, that his van was full of tools, and that he made a point of driving all over the borough, particularly to business premises, when they were hit, and diving straight into the ruins to find the safe. His only concern with us was that he wanted the cover of a warden's badge and identity cards.

Markham complained that, with the exception of the odd War Reserve policeman, the police were 'conspicuously absent from the scene' on these occasions.

When in January a V-2 hit a public library in Hackney, killing several children and destroying surrounding buildings, three men took the opportunity to steal tobacco from a bomb-damaged shop while the woman shopkeeper lay trapped beneath the wreckage. They were all men who had come to London to help in the repair of 'blitzed' houses and now found themselves in the local magistrates court: 'Detective Watson said he arrived on the scene of the incident a few minutes after the bomb had fallen. After helping to get casualties out of the library, which had been completely demolished, he kept observation on the three prisoners, who were digging at a tobacconist's shop. They were shovelling in the opposite direction to where the shopkeeper was trapped in her wrecked shop.'

Albert Taylor, an Essex man engaged in clearance work, had actually exercised violence on his victim, robbing a woman subsequently sent to hospital after sustaining a V-bomb injury. He had stolen cash and jewellery worth a sizeable sum from her. In court he said he had acted on impulse. It was his first offence and he was sorry. 'Sorry!' boomed the magistrate, Mr W. Blake, QC. 'Robbing a woman who is lying in hospital helpless and you say you are sorry!' Taylor was sent to prison for three months.

Time and again magistrates reiterated the unpatriotic nature of looting. When two lorry drivers employed in carrying salvaged goods from a V-bomb incident in Hackney were charged with keeping a radio, the magistrate described their crime as 'mean and un-British' and gave them three months' hard labour. When Leonard Humbley of Southwark and Thomas Turrell of Peckham were found guilty of stealing from a Clapham air raid shelter four blankets and a bedspread, the property of people who habitually sheltered there, the magistrate told them that it was an 'exceptionally mean theft'. Humbley was given a five-month prison sentence and hard labour, Turrell three months' hard labour.

In a similar case, when a Bethnal Green man employed by a firm of contractors who were removing bombed-out people's effects to store appeared on remand charged with stealing a gold ring and medallion from an area damaged by enemy action, he was told: 'These people have been bombed and lost practically everything, and then you go and rob them of the goods they have been able to save. You deserve a long term of imprisonment.'

There was a fine line between looting and theft, but when the accused tried to exonerate himself by admitting stealing by finding, he was firmly put down by the magistrate: 'What was it but looting? You knew the property belonged to bombed-out people.'

There were always pickpockets at work as people crowded into the shelters. As so many brought along their valuables, in a handbag or small suitcase, the thieves could be sure of a good haul. Some preyed on people while they slept: 'A man was sent to prison for six months at North London Magistrates Court yesterday for stealing a woman's handbag while she was asleep in a Hackney air raid shelter.' Apparently he had entered the shelter at London Fields at two in the morning and robbed the woman.

Most crimes were mundane, the perpetrators snatching at opportunities, often on impulse, and increasingly motivated by an urge to beat the system, which after six years of war now seemed onerous and pointless. During the war people generally had obeyed rules on rationing out of patriotism, but since VE Day this had changed. 'Sacrifices were no longer necessary, and had ceased to be fashionable; and then lawlessness was in the air.'

The *Daily Mail* claimed that rationing and the coupon system 'have seriously lowered standards of morality' as many were willing to pay a bit more for that coupon-free overcoat or dress or stockings. It reminded readers that goods bought 'off the ration' were stolen goods. Just as culpable was the housewife who bought goods from her friendly grocer 'under the counter' or paid for that 'little bit extra' without coupons.

Stealing or fabricating ration books and clothing coupons offered an obvious opportunity for the criminal. As they were less sophisticated in design than bank notes, they were easy to forge. Illicit printing presses were busy churning them out, although it was hardly necessary, since they were so easy to steal. Officially produced coupons could be stolen at the printers or in the post and, eventually, used coupons passed on from the Food Offices could be stolen when they were sent to be pulped. As the Post Office refused to count the coupons which were brought to them by retailers for return to the Food Office, there was every chance to cheat either by putting into the envelope less than the stated number of coupons or merely stuffing the whole envelope with newspaper cuttings. There was a brisk trade in stolen coupons, as they were passed along a network of buyers and sellers, and offloaded on susceptible members of the public. A Southwark man remembers: 'One day this old boy turns up with a big shoebox full of clothing coupons. So he said, "Want these?" for a tanner or something, so I said, "All right, I'll have them." So I did. We were all fiddling you know. It went on all the time.'

Arthur Harding, who had been in the East End rag trade and helped the Ghost Squad, recalled:

The Ghost Squad were interested in anything that was detrimental to the war – possessing coupons, or black market business. There were people who were making fortunes for themselves out of rationing. Vast quantities of forged coupons were put on the market. In one case they were selling coupons at a shilling a time and when people who bought them came to undo them, all they found were bits of paper. The crooks in the West End were raiding the town halls to find out where the coupons were stored, and pinching the whole lot. They would sell the coupons at 4d or 6d each according to the value of the coupon. The forging was done in the West End – all around Shaftesbury Avenue, but they were sold in the East End.

He concluded resoundingly: 'I knew some of the bleeding villains that was at it.'

There was an insatiable demand for black market petrol. Petrol for military use was dyed red as a deterrent to thieves. A number of people were prosecuted for siphoning petrol from the vehicles of their employers, who had official usage. While the ban on private motoring existed, it was less profitable for black marketeers to trade in forged or stolen petrol coupons, since anyone driving was liable to draw the attention of the police. But after the restoration of the basic petrol ration in June 1945, allowing the private motorist about 90 miles a month, the black market trade in petrol coupons flourished – along with the sale of second-hand cars of dubious origin. When merchant seaman Henry Westwood of Stockwell pleaded guilty to receiving 517 petrol coupons, he was left under no illusions by the magistrate: 'You took part in a sordid anti-patriotic deal in the black market and tried to make profit out of the country's distress.' Westwood received a four months' prison sentence.

It was a criminal offence to buy rationed goods without handing over coupons. Uniformed police had powers to stop and search anyone carrying what looked like a suspicious package, as a Woolwich housewife found when she was fined for 'unlawful possession of six tins of Grade 2 salmon, three boxes of dried eggs, and a cotton dress, suspected stolen or otherwise unlawfully obtained':

Evidence showed that she was stopped by a police officer in the street and asked what she had in a shopping bag she was carrying. She told him to mind his own business. He then asked her if she had her ration books with her and she said 'No'. On examining the basket he found the goods mentioned in the charge. She then said she had bought the salmon and the egg from a merchant seaman in a public house for 5s and a pint of beer, and that she had bought the frock from a woman at Woolwich. She did not know the woman and did not give her any coupons.

It transpired that she had several previous convictions and was fined. She impudently asked if she might have her property back. 'Most certainly not,' the magistrate snapped. 'It is rationed.'

Similarly, a Stepney man who was stopped and searched on High Road, Ilford, was found to be carrying two legs of lamb, which he had procured without coupons. The court was told: 'It was stated that Coutts was stopped with the two legs wrapped up in his overcoat. He refused to say where they had come from except that a butcher had given them to him because he had done the butcher a good turn. The police said they had been unable to trace the origin of the lamb and Coutts had absolutely refused to assist them in any way.'

It is interesting how loyal these people were to their suppliers. When a local greengrocer was summoned at North London Magistrates Court for overcharging for tomatoes and cucumbers, for instance, he was alleged to have told the food inspector of Hackney Borough Council that 'he would sooner be put against the wall than divulge the name of the wholesaler who supplied him.'

The Minister of Food, Colonel Llewellin, maintained there would be no black market if it were not for 'the anxiety and greed of some consumers, including restaurants, hotels and manufacturers dealing in stolen food'. After years of rationing, Londoners were obsessed with food and many were all too willing to cheat the system. There was every incentive for anyone selling food to flout the regulations – at the beginning of 1945 there were no fewer than 415 Ministry of Food Statutory Orders in force – as there was always a ready market for it.

On the outer perimeter of Greater London, market towns such as Romford, Chelmsford and Braintree were centres of black market food trading. Here hens officially sold for breeding were passed off for human consumption. Eggs were subject to a similar ruse. Dealers simply had to sign a declaration that they were being sold for hatching purposes, which exempted them from the usual regulations; the contempt in which they held the system was seen in the fact that they often signed themselves 'Winston Churchill' and gave 10 Downing Street as their address. There was a lot of dodgy meat about, and butchers could be prosecuted and imprisoned for passing off, say, horseflesh as stewing steak. Slaughtering a pig except in the presence of a representative of the Ministry of Food at a stipulated time and place was illegal, but this does not say it did not happen. All this was grist to the mill of the black market.

Many hoteliers and restaurant owners were eager participants in the black market. They simply could not afford to lose their customers and convinced themselves that if they did not provide the customer with what he wanted he would simply move on to a rival establishment that was less scrupulous. They were willing to pay the high prices demanded, obtaining illegal food in the markets out of town and from other illicit sources and by trading with crooked wholesalers at Covent Garden. These wholesalers were also able to hold retailers to ransom, blacklisting them if they refused to pay their preposterous prices – or if they merely questioned these prices. There was also a tendency on the part of wholesalers and retailers to withhold goods from customers unless other goods were bought as part of the package. It was no excuse for anyone in court to maintain they had been overcharged for goods in the first place and therefore had to pass on those costs to the customer.

To stifle inflation and consequent social unrest, the Government ran a strict policy of price and quantity control on food. The public was becoming increasingly angry about the Ministry of Food's inspectors treating themselves at the taxpayer's expense to meals in restaurants to ensure that they were not charging more than the statutory 5s for a meal and that they were not serving more than one protein course. By 1945 even magistrates were growing impatient with their methods, as seen when the New Corn Exchange Restaurant at the Mansion House was charged with selling two officials meals totalling 12s 6d. Noting that no one else in the restaurant that day had paid more than 5s, the magistrate dismissed the case, after inferring that the officials had provoked the situation, just at a time when the short-staffed restaurant was at its busiest.

Undercover men and women from the Ministry would also enter shops, sometimes provoking a shopkeeper to break the law by spinning some hard-luck story to procure goods without coupons. It was also an offence to sell rationed goods to non-registered customers. Under the Acquisition of Food (Excessive Quantities) Order, food officials had the right to raid ordinary households to inspect the larder for signs of hoarding.

Markets were a free for all, in which coupons for food, clothes and other commodities rarely changed hands. Berwick Street market in Soho benefited from the proximity of the American servicemen's club at Rainbow Corner, since the Americans could supply for cash goods scarce or unobtainable in Britain. Not surprisingly, Berwick Street was a good place to pick up women's stockings, but the Americans might also do a brisk trade in razor blades which, being rationed, were a natural commodity for the black market and sold for grossly inflated prices, not just in markets but also in the lobbies of some of London's premier hotels. East End markets such as Brick Lane and Petticoat Lane, of course, did a roaring trade in illicit goods. A visitor to the East End just after the war noted:

The wife . . . stopped at one of the stalls, which was being served by a woman who was wrapped in several layers of mufflers, great coats and snow boots and wore a knitted pirate's cap. She had just lifted the corner of a piece of sacking, part of the stall, and had withdrawn from under it a pair of silk stockings for a customer (her ostensible trade was in vegetables). Later, we saw her drive off in a taxi, after her day's work.

Markets were a perfect place to dispose quickly of illegally manufactured goods. Cosmetics were a case in point. Nothing could be produced without Government sanction, as raw materials were in short supply. Under the Toilet Preparation Order manufacturers of cosmetics were limited in the amount they could produce. A hike in the price of cosmetics by 50 per cent over pre-war levels gave an additional fillip to the black market trade. This was the era of the lipstick robbery. Thieves stole £5,478 worth of lipstick refills from the premises of Cyclax in South Molton Street. Subsequently, Arthur Gosling of Chevening Road, Brondesbury was fined £20 for receiving nine dozen lipsticks, valued at £27, knowing they were stolen. He was selling lipsticks 'marked 5s each freely among factory girls at 3s 6d'. However, the police were unable to trace the thieves or recover the bulk of the lipsticks.

Worse, it was the era of illicitly manufactured cosmetics, which could be dangerous. The Ministry of Information produced a short documentary, *Black Market Beauties*, revealing the full horror of badly disfigured faces as a result of using such concoctions manufactured by amateurs in unsanitary conditions.

Illegal cosmetics manufacturers would try to make the

goods look as authentic as possible, counterfeiting the labels of established manufacturers such as Yardley and Cyclax. Sometimes their sloppiness gave them away, as when Lea Espir was charged with unlawfully supplying controlled goods, 'to wit, forty-five gross of perfume without there being marked on the containers, or labels affixed thereto, the name and address of the manufacturer of the goods'. Lea Espir had also failed to 'place controlled goods, to wit, hair cream into containers'.

The Board of Trade was also hot on the trail of vendors of assorted items of haberdashery. William Donoghue was charged with 'unlawfully selling one dozen snap fasteners at a price, to wit 1s, which exceeded the maximum price of two pence', while Charles Brumwell had been 'unlawfully selling price-controlled goods, a bundle of twelve hairpins at a price, to wit 3d, which exceeded the maximum price contrary to Articles 1 and 4 Miscellaneous Haberdashery (Maximum Prices) Order, 1944. He had also neglected to display a notice in writing setting out the maximum price fixed for hairpins. He was fined £1 for each offence and costs of 3 guineas.

The fact that stall-holders were selling vast quantities of goods without obtaining coupons with which to replenish their stock indicated that they were being supplied from the proceeds of theft in the first place. With the profits they were making, they could also procure illegal coupons to replenish goods if necessary. The problem for inspectors was to amass enough evidence to convince a court, but they and the plain-clothes police who patrolled the markets were pretty conspicuous and stall-holders devised an early warning system when the law was approaching. As a final defence, they could always claim that the goods they were selling were defective or second-hand, since no coupons were required for them.

Market stall-holders breaking the official price controls on food were easier to pin down, as a Streatham stall-holder found when he was charged with selling, without a licence, one pound of tomatoes for 3s 6d above the controlled price and failing to display a maximum price notice and to keep a record of purchases of tomatoes. It was a typical scenario involving a tip-off and the Ministry of Food's inspectors:

Mr Lilly, for the Wandsworth Food Control Committee, said the defendant was a stallholder and ordinarily sold flowers. He had no licence to sell anything else. As a result of a complaint made to the Food Office that the defendant was charging 5s a pound for tomatoes a test purchase was made on 19 May by an assistant enforcement officer, who saw behind the stall bags containing pounds of tomatoes, which the defendant said were 5s a pound.

In mitigation, the defendant told the enforcement officer he had had to pay 4s a pound for these tomatoes.

'"That may be so," the magistrate rejoined, "but the object of the Ministry is to close this black market ring. The controlled price was 1s 6d a pound. The trader in the market was charging too much for supplies."' He imposed a £6 fine.

Time and again, Ministry of Food officials swooped on offenders selling goods illegally. There were regulations governing the smallest details. George Townshend was charged with 'selling cucumbers at a price in excess of the prescribed maximum price viz. 4s for a cucumber weighing 14 oz, the correct maximum price at the rate of 10d per lb being eight and three farthings. Contrary to Act 3: The Home Grown Cucumber (Maximum Prices) Order 1942'.

Even someone selling his produce privately could be prosecuted if he sold it above the controlled price. A 75-year-old West Hampstead man was a registered domestic poultry keeper. He obtained a few eggs a week and supplied one here and there to friends and neighbours. Izetta Freeman complained to the Food Control Committee that he was charging 6d each for eggs, when the controlled price was 2d. Telling the court that he did not know there was a restriction on the price was no excuse. He was fined the considerable sum of £4 with £3 3s costs.

Some shopkeepers were on the fiddle, selling goods without coupons or not returning the correct number of coupons to the Food Office. These retailers were obviously obtaining their goods illicitly, knowing that they could make good money out of the transactions. An East End woman says: 'I remember taking my ration book to the butcher in Hoxton. If we gave him some extra money he would give us extra meat. There was a Welsh dairy down Cremer Street. The lady there would offer me butter and tins of salmon and other things that were difficult to get.'

Food Office officials were not above selling coupons themselves. An assistant at the Food Office in Hackney, formerly a councillor in the borough, extracted coupons from the office and passed them to a businessman who passed them to a restaurateur, who sold them to customers at a massive profit, of which a proportion went to the official. He received a five-year prison sentence. Clearly, if Food Office officials were allowed to join the scam and get away with it, the whole rationing system would collapse.

Contrary to Lord Woolton's assertion that the black market was small and spasmodic, it appeared to be thriving. This was certainly the case after the war. Of course, it bore no comparison with the black market in newly liberated Paris, which in the absence of rationing to ensure fair shares for all was raging out of control. It was further stimulated by the presence of Allied servicemen running highly profitable rackets, not least in smuggling luxury items by air and sea into England. In England, where there was an ordered rationing system which had public support, the black market operated on the fringes. Indeed, a certain level of black market trading might have been seen as a useful safety valve, relieving the build-up of social and economic pressures, just as illegal gaming and betting offered another kind of outlet – whatever the Treasury might say about the need to direct surplus cash into war savings. The black market was never large enough to affect national supplies or to interfere with the housewife's daily purchase of staple foods. It needed to be kept in check, however, and officials managed this with varying degrees of leniency and severity.

In the New Year of 1945 police were trying to penetrate a black market smuggling ring in Chelsea. Foreign seamen were bringing in quantities of spirits, stockings and cosmetics and distributing them through a servant in a large house in the district. The black market had its natural home among the criminal fraternity in the East End, of course. A Hoxton woman remembers: 'We didn't go without. There was a big black market operating, especially in tinned goods and American nylons which we all wanted because they never wore out. We never went short.'

It was easy for the black marketeers to persuade others to comply. With the labour shortage, warehouses were sparsely guarded. Night watchmen often turned a blind eye, or were bribed to leave factory or warehouse gates open so that lorries could be driven directly into the yards and make a swift exit. They worked on the understanding that if they went to prison, their wives and children would be looked after while they were inside. A watchman who 'talked' was likely to suffer a 'regrettable accident' when he was released.

In the first few months of 1945 clothing stocks in shops were low, giving black market operators the chance to cash in thousands of pounds worth of goods stolen from factories and warehouses. The thieves obviously had some expertise, as they were selecting cloth according to the demands of fashion, particularly in women's wear for spring. 'We shall return. Have better quality next time!' was the message chalked on one factory wall by thieves.

Another ruse was to sell stolen clothes to a shopkeeper, then rob the shop, since the shopkeeper was hardly in a position to 'squeal' to the police.

In the freezing weather, with severe shortages of coal and coke, the black market was quick to exploit the situation. In Fulham, for instance, coal men were delivering short, retaining at the end of each journey what amounted to a number of sacks to sell to black marketeers. Given the scale of this operation, it is pathetic to read of a case at North London Magistrates Court: 'Lilian Emily Fitzjohn, 40, a housewife, of

Ball's Pond Road, was fined 20s for stealing a piece of coal, worth 1s, from a Ministry of Fuel dump.' A police constable had observed her entering the dump through a hole in the fence and emerging with the piece of coal. The magistrate was sympathetic. 'I suppose she is short of coal like everybody else. The miners don't seem to be able to produce enough.'

The blackout had always been considered by the criminal fraternity to be a present from Hitler. It was easy for gangs to approach their target and make their exit in total darkness and to clear the display window of, say, some Bond Street jeweller's shop, when it was unlit. With the introduction of the dim-out in September 1944 their activities in the West End received a slight set-back, but they could still operate in the less well-lit suburbs. The obvious target was the legion of empty or damaged houses in the areas where there had been intense V-bomb activity. Scotland Yard was perturbed at the number of removal-van burglaries of furniture and household belongings. Spies pretending to be second-hand clothes dealers would tour an area amassing details of house ownership and absentee householders. Insurance companies were wary of all new business and as a final slap in the face to victims the Government stated that if loss of possessions was owing to looting rather than enemy action, claims could not be made under the War Damage Act.

Burglaries fed the black market. By the end of the war, fur coats rather than jewellery were the most prized loot, since none had been produced during the war. There was a rash of burglaries for fur coats in the wealthy Hampstead and St John's Wood areas. A woman with a good fur coat might be followed home and the house watched until the time she was rash enough to leave not wearing it, when the thieves would go in to snatch it.

Scotland Yard decided to start the New Year of 1945 with a round-up of female crooks. A report in the *Star* said that the police were determined to put a stop to the current spate of housebreaking by women:

Figures at police headquarters show that so far women offenders in London have confined their activities to petty thefts, such as ration books, clothing coupons, and small cash, but there is evidence that they are now seeking wider fields. There is a slight upward grade in thefts by women pickpockets, who have been operating in the West End, and cases of highway robbery by women have been reported to the police. Thefts of bags and coats left on chairs or tables in dance halls are frequent and have been mainly traced to women. But women burglars are the problem, and the Yard intends to solve it.

Perhaps not all of them were women. When a 22-year-old private in the Pioneer Corps was caught coming out of the window of a Wimbledon flat, he was found to be wearing female clothing under his battledress. He told the court: 'I dressed in ladies' clothes which I took from some of the places, because I thought it would be easier to walk around at night and not be pulled up by police for my pass.'

In an era of shortages it was all too tempting to steal from one's employer. Pilfering had always been endemic, but in wartime it took on a new urgency, as thieves either stole for themselves or in order to sell. There was no problem in getting rid of the gear, because the black market was eager to buy it and, indeed, the existence of the black market acted as a stimulant. 'There was a lot of thieving going on, lots of goods for sale,' an East Ender recalls. 'People would come knocking at our doors asking whether we wanted to buy things.'

All levels of staff were involved in illegal activity, from management to the lowliest clerk and shop floor worker. There was an increase in white-collar crime and council officials were not immune. Shortage of staff meant that supervision was slack. A temporary chief clerk at Wembley Council in the spring of 1945 was found to be siphoning off a proportion of the fees from mothers of children in the council's day nurseries. In Croydon an official employed by the Croydon War Damage Chattels Department to interview householders about claims made for damage to furniture and other household goods was extracting fees to which he was not entitled. When he investigated the claim of a war reserve police constable, he was about to leave when he said, 'If it is convenient to you, Mr Harrison, there is a fee of £2 2s to be paid.' The witness handed the money over, but the game was up. It is surprising that this stunt was still being pulled so late in the war, by which time the public might have been expected to know that there was no official charge for the war damage assessment service.

In wartime companies and factories were subject to myriad regulations, so much so that one peeved owner complained: 'The government has governed my business until I do not know who the bloody hell owns it. I am suspected, inspected, examined, informed, required and commanded, so that I do not know who the hell I am and where I am, or why I am here at all . . . The only reason I am clinging to life at all is to see what the Bloody Hell is going to happen next.'

Companies had to account to the various ministries for the use of the raw materials they were allotted and for the food they were supposed to supply. If, for instance, a milk depot failed to honour the ration, the Ministry of Food would take a very dim view of it. However, there were businessmen who exceeded their quota for production, selling the surplus on the black market, or who claimed Government money for employees they did not have. The job of honest employers was made harder still by the number of employees ready to steal from them. A look at cases of theft reported in the *Hackney Gazette* illustrates the scale of the problem. Bodies and companies affected included the ARP; Ever Ready; the Ardath, Strathmore and Phillips tobacco companies; several milk depots; the London Passenger Transport Board; Shoreditch Sanitary Towels; Bovril; the Post Office; Cossor's Radio; Berger Paints; the Metropolitan Police canteens; Odeon Theatres; the London Co-Operative Society; several transport contractors; numerous small concerns, including the WVS stores of household goods donated by the provinces and the council's furniture stores.

The problem was not just confined to petty pilfering. In

spite of paying its workers good wages, Ford's of Dagenham suffered theft on a grand scale. It was amazing what thieves were prepared to smuggle out secreted about their person. When six employees of Briggs Motor Bodies of Dagenham removed American machine tools, they were so essential to production that they could not be spared from the works to be shown in court as evidence.

It was impossible to guard railway depots thoroughly, so that the chances of a parcel arriving at its destination in wartime intact or at all were slim. Millions of pounds worth of goods in transit was stolen in the course of the war. Morale among railway employees was poor. Railway pay had been perennially low, a grievance that was to lead to a great deal of strike action at the end of the war, so that railway employees were easily seduced by the black market. The call-up meant that the railway had to take what recruits it could, some planted there from the criminal underworld.

'I just took it because it is so hard to get,' Dorothy Zilkin, a railway porter, told the court, when she pleaded guilty with two colleagues for stealing six tablets of soap, value 2s 3d, from a van they were unloading at St Pancras station.

'Everybody is facing the same difficulties, but we have to observe self-control,' the magistrate rebuked her, as he imposed a 20s fine.

She was lucky. Five other women were sent to prison for six weeks for stealing five packets of shampoo powder and a pot of face cream and 'unlawful possession of the same'.

When a 24-year-old labourer appeared on remand at Old Street Police Court charged with stealing 88 torch batteries from Spitalfields Goods Depot, the magistrate expressed his regret that while thousands of honest men were performing great feats in transporting goods, they were being let down by 'this blackguardly minority who won't stop stealing'.

In May 1945 the notorious 'suitcase gang' was brought to trial at the Old Bailey. The six members of the gang would go to the guard's van of a train and simply change the labels on suitcases, redirecting them to Mrs Annie Harris of Islington

High Street. 'In that way they made Southern Railway innocently deliver stolen goods to receivers.' The leader of the gang, Lewis Bennett, was a deserter from the Royal Navy and over several months had amassed £7,000 worth of stolen property.

The London docks were notorious for theft, but as wartime shortages took hold and prices rose, pilfering took on a whole new dimension. A Bermondsey man remembers: 'We were close to the docks, and we always considered this to be the larder of London, so you had a hell of a lot of dockers walking in and out of there, and they weren't all choir boys by any means! And many a case has been dropped, and you know, "Sorry about that, it slipped!" And so there was a little source of supply coming through there, which was kept very quiet!'

Some had stooped so low as to remove emergency rations from lifeboats, but by 1945 the more common offence was to steal cigarettes from the vast quantities being shipped to HM Forces in Europe, where cigarettes were the prime, unofficial currency. Dockers loading cigarettes on to ships would be approached by black market agents to join the racket, with goods being sold through a network of receivers and 'go-betweens'.

'If we went to the dock police or the harbour master we would have to turn informer,' said one docker. 'You cannot imagine what our life would be after that. It's easy for an "accident" to happen here.' Cigarette cartons were arriving in Europe full of wood shavings, while dockers, willing or otherwise, were selling the cigarettes on the black market at 3s for 50.

Generous and open-handed as the Americans were, it obviously did not do for British employees to pilfer from the US Government. These offenders were dealt with sharply not by American law enforcement but by the British magistrates, who saw such misdemeanours as a betrayal of Britain's foremost ally. So a 59-year-old cleaner, Annie Moore, discovered when she was charged with 'unlawfully removing certain Army stores to wit two ground sheets, two pillows, one broom-head, one torch, one hatchet, one hand brush, one canvas water bucket, five kitbags, two blankets, one eiderdown and a

quantity of linen. Property of the United States Government.'
She was fined £5.

Whether it was from their employer or someone else, people
stole because they longed for what they could not obtain otherwise. There was a sharp increase in female shoplifting, particularly of clothes that could not be legally acquired except by
coupons.

Dorothy Roberts, a 43-year-old clerk, was charged with
'stealing one pair of cami-knickers, one tin of peas and two
tins of crawfish, value together 10s 4d, from Littlewoods'. She
was obviously keen on cami-knickers, because she progressed
straight from Littlewoods along Oxford Street to Marks &
Spencer, where she stole another pair valued at 7s 6d.

Housekeeper Winifred Brookes was charged with stealing
'one dress, two pairs of stockings, one belt, one box of face
powder, one jar of bath salts, value together £2 15s 8d, from
Bourne & Hollingsworth in Oxford Street.' It was hardly
worth her while, as she was fined £6 with £3 3s costs.

Dorothy Bristow and her daughter Jean obviously decided
to replenish their winter wardrobes, when in September they
stole one jumper suit, one dress, one child's dress, three jumpers
and three cardigans worth £8 13s 4d from C & A.

The Commissioner of Police noted that a great deal of stolen
property was small in value: articles which before the war
were considered to be of only nominal worth had taken on
enhanced value because of their scarcity. More than one half
of stolen property was clothing, money and food. The casual
thief was just trying to make life a little more bearable.

Failure to obey the directives of the Ministry of Labour and
National Service and being late or absent from work were
indictable offences in wartime. The Ministry had total power
to direct all able-bodied men and women of appropriate age
into work and largely controlled their working lives. When
Marthe Feldmann was charged for being 'without reasonable
excuse, persistently late for work in contravention of the
Essential Work Order 1942/44' she was fined £1 with £2 2s

costs. Daisy Arnold was ordered by the court to report to her local labour exchange to be directed into work again. She had told a National Service officer that her factory job 'had made her throat sore' and had 'taken it upon herself to quit'.

In February 1945, 19-year-old Eric Simmonds of Purley Way, Croydon, was summoned at Croydon Magistrates Court for his continued failure to undertake work as a coal-mining trainee. He told the court he was unwilling to go down the mines as he suffered from dermatitis, but that he was prepared to serve in the forces. Too bad: men were desperately needed for the coal mines. A draughtsman earning £2 12s 6d a week, he was fined £4 with £1 15s costs.

The prohibitive cost of alarm clocks was the excuse of a young Croydon factory worker appearing in court. Dora Murrell, who was employed at Briggs Motor Bodies Ltd, was apparently late for work on no fewer than 49 occasions and absent altogether on 2 days. 'I find it hard to wake up without an alarm clock and I haven't got one,' she pleaded. She had a permit to buy an alarm clock, but as this scarce commodity cost £2 9s 6d and her weekly wage was only £4 8s, she claimed she had been unable to afford it. A fine of £4 and £1 1s costs no doubt put the clock even further out of reach.

In a Bow Street café almost opposite the Magistrates Court American servicemen gathered to dispose of their property for cash. In a raid on the café in January 1945, it was found that 4 of the 15 soldiers there were deserters, while the owners, Luigi and Ernest Borzono, were each sentenced to 12 months' imprisonment for being in possession of US army clothing and unlawful possession of clothing coupons. There was a brisk trade in American uniforms, which were sometimes worn by British deserters.

By the last months of the war, there were thousands of deserters at large in the capital and these included American and Canadian servicemen, as well as British. In January 1945 there were 18,000–19,000 deserters from the US army and many of them were hiding out in London, Chelsea being a favoured stamping ground. The fact that they continued to wear uniform meant that many were not discovered unless they were challenged. The US military police, known as Snowdrops because of their white helmets, would periodically swoop on American deserters and lawbreakers, racing through central London in their De Soto cars equipped with 'wailers' and springing from them gun in hand – much to the wonder of Scotland Yard officers. There was an agreement by which they handed British offenders over to the British police, and vice versa. American servicemen arrested by their own police were consigned to the Central District Guard House in Tottenham Court Road until they could be processed. Some military trials were held in an improvised courtroom in Grosvenor Square, near the American Embassy.

At the outset many of London's criminals had found a way to avoid the call-up, eager to take advantage of the rich opportunities they saw unfolding on the horizon. There was the case of the salesman, Jack Brack, from Brick Lane in the East End, who received a genuine exemption certificate from the Medical Board for a heart condition. He quickly turned this to his advantage by impersonating other men at the board and winning them exemptions. He earned as much as £200 – a small fortune – for an exemption, which he blew gambling. Crooked doctors who sold medical exemptions were struck off. Of course, the army did not really want to recruit criminals, so that those with a record or subsequently committing a criminal offence found that crime paid. Similarly, a woman writing 'Prostitute' under occupation was unlikely to be recruited into the forces.

As under the National Service (Armed Forces) Act conscription embraced an increasingly wide circle of men and women in the course of the war, there was a corresponding increase in unwilling recruits. Some simply failed to turn up in the first place, such as Florence Evans in January 1945, who was charged with failing 'to comply with a direction given to you by a National Service officer to present yourself for interview'. For those who failed to avoid being called up, the only option was to abscond. Paradoxically, desertions increased at times when there was a lull in the fighting: more men tended to desert out of boredom or because of family troubles, than out of cowardice. The number of deserters actually increased *after* the war, among those impatient with the slow process of demobilisation. Military police, RAF Special Police and Naval Pickets were engaged on a perennial quest to track deserters down.

Many simply went AWOL, like Mary Kathleen Mancini, charged 'for being an absentee from the ATS' and 20-year-old Frances Avenell, an absentee from the WAAF. They do not seem to have compounded their offence with any other crime, unlike 28-year-old Thomas McGuire, charged with being 'a deserter from the South Staffordshire Regiment' who had 'broken into a warehouse at 142 New Cavendish Street, stealing 680 yards of suiting material, eight coats and one costume'.

A Hoxton woman remembers: 'Sometimes you would see deserters from the forces in the pubs. They would be followed by the police. Everyone could recognise the police. The deserters would go into the ladies' toilets and escape through the windows.'

Prostitute Alice May Ward, 29, was charged with aiding and assisting deserter Charles Burton Tidewell, 'knowing he was a deserter, to conceal himself'. Since Ward had come to the attention of the authorities, they also took the opportunity to prosecute her for failing to notify them of a change of address, while Tidewell was charged under the Larceny Act for stealing money.

Mrs Eileen Davies of Shepherd's Bush was sent to Holloway Prison, convicted of harbouring her husband as a deserter. Granted compassionate leave after his wife had been bombed out of their home, he had failed to return to his regiment. In going to prison, she had had to leave her eight-month-old baby daughter in the charge of the Fulham Relieving Officer. The Labour MP for Hammersmith North, Mr D.N. Pritt, and the Soldiers', Sailors' and Airmen's Families Association had written to the Home Secretary, Herbert Morrison, pleading for clemency. 'No normal woman can seriously be expected to betray her husband and the father of her child to the police,' Pritt wrote. 'It seems to offend against every human consideration.'

After serving ten days of her sentence, Eileen Davies was freed on Morrison's instructions, but, in a final twist to this tragic case, her baby Mary died. Mrs Davies, who was expecting another baby imminently, blamed herself, as a neighbour told the press: 'She does not blame the nursing home where the baby was sent, but she cannot get it out of her mind that had she not been sent to prison for sheltering her husband her baby might be alive today.'

Without identity cards or ration books, deserters had to steal to live, although they could equally be furnished with forged or stolen papers by the criminal fraternity, in exchange for their services. Deserters were readily taken up by criminal gangs if they could prove their worth. Only 10 days after deserting, Ronald Candy had managed to secure an enormous haul before he was arrested:

When an admitted army deserter, Ronald John Gordon Candy, 20, was taken to Dalston Police Station on Tuesday he made a statement under caution in which he confessed to stealing last month 2,650 cigarettes, 52 lbs of butter, 24 lbs of lard, 20 boxes of chocolates, and clothing to the total value of £53, from a lock-up shop at King Henry's Walk, Mildmay Park. None of the property has been recovered. The accused said he had stolen it for £14. He had two accomplices.

On 10 December 1945 military police launched a round-up of deserters in the capital. Four nights later, 2,000 uniformed police, CID men and British, Canadian and American military police took part in the biggest raid ever, when the West End was sealed off to trap 'wanted' men. The hunt went on all night for 20,000 deserters and other wanted criminals. Directed by radio from Scotland Yard, the police swooped on pubs, dance halls, pin-table saloons, restaurants, cafés and clubs, demanding identity papers. In the streets anyone carrying a parcel or a case was stopped and asked to open it. Billy Hill, one of London's most notorious criminals, scoffed at the police effort:

They questioned every living soul they saw within the boundaries of Mayfair and Soho . . . they checked thousands upon thousands of service passes and identification cards. From eight o'clock at night they worked until the early hours. I think they might have tumbled about half a dozen deserters . . . Identity cards? They were as pieces of paper we could get any day we liked. Army passes? We could print them if you wanted them . . . which all goes to show how organised we were, and handicapped were the law in trying to fix us.

In perhaps the most dastardly crime of all, as demobilisation gathered pace, racketeers took to lurking at London's railway terminals to lure bewildered ex-POWs to a drink, when they would rob them of their money and papers. Without proof of identity, there was every chance these hapless victims would be picked up as deserters.

In June 1945 a group of London housewives waited outside Bow Street Magistrates Court to catch a glimpse of the notorious William Joyce, alias Lord Haw-Haw, who had been captured in northern Germany and flown back to England for trial. The charge was the most serious of all: 'For that he committed High Treason in that he between September 2, 1939 and April 29, 1945, being a person owing allegiance to His Majesty the King, adhered to the King's enemies elsewhere than in the King's Realm, to wit in the German Realm, contrary to the Treason Act of 1351.'

It was a moot point. Joyce was born in America of Irish parents who had taken American citizenship. During his time in Britain, Joyce had never taken British citizenship, but the case against him rested on the fact that he had fraudulently obtained a British passport in 1933, and used it when he escaped to Germany in August 1939. He took German nationality in

September 1940 but, meanwhile, he had been broadcasting hostile propaganda to Britain on German radio while holding a British passport – albeit one to which he had no entitlement. In reality during the period before he took German citizenship, Joyce as an American had been the citizen of a neutral power and therefore innocent of the crime of high treason against the British monarch.

In the case of John Amery, son of Leo Amery, a member of Churchill's War Cabinet, there could be no doubt. In wartime Germany, Amery had been actively persuading British prisoners of war to join the British unit of the SS, 'The Legion of St George'. He was motivated by a genuine fear of the Bolshevik menace from the East. As his father put it, 'He never worked to help Germany as others had, who had such light punishment. He had worked *against* Communism.'

After Amery was hanged, his father wrote to Robert Barrington-Ward, the editor of *The Times*, at Christmas 1945 to plead for the lives of others of his son's persuasion:

'Now that my dear son has paid the penalty for his sincere, if misguided, beliefs, may I plead at this season of Peace and Good Will, through you, for the life of the few others who have been selected for trial under the Act of 1351.'

Barrington-Ward was sympathetic but demurred from printing Amery's letter. 'Your son's courage and dignity on the final day of the trial have been attested publicly by impartial witnesses of the proceedings. They have spoken for themselves,' he told the grieving parent. To plead for these others, he excused himself, 'inevitably involves presumption of their guilt'.

As an unoccupied power, post-war Britain saw none of the passion for vengeance against traitors and collaborators that was so rampant in the liberated countries of Europe, particularly France. When the Government decided Joyce should be hanged on 3 January 1946 at Wandsworth Prison, after his appeals to the Court of Appeal and the House of Lords had been turned down, it was to misjudge the public mood. Far from being seen as a danger to Britain, Joyce's wartime broadcasts, heralded by his trademark 'Jairmany calling, Jairmany calling . . .' had been regarded by the average English man and woman as a good laugh.

As wartime shortages gave way to post-war austerity, there was little to laugh about. Wartime restrictions continued and rationing became stricter. With the national emergency over, the public had become resentful of authority with its lecturing and hectoring, its do this and don't do that, its battery of regulations governing the smallest details of life. Compliance was turning into outright hostility. Sacrifice made sense when invasion or defeat was possible: it was irksome when it was being demanded simply to close a 'dollar gap' in the post-war balance of payments.

The wartime community spirit was replaced by a selfish Me First mentality, and general lowering of the moral climate. The new Labour Government projected its forthcoming plans for the welfare state not as a vision for living for which the country would need to work hard, but, naively, as the first great chance to get something for nothing. It was an attitude that seeped into the very fabric of life. Fiddling expenses and ripping people off were typical examples of the new, post-war British disease.

It was the heyday of the criminal, the racketeer and the spiv, and as more and more ordinary people joined the scam, the notion 'nudge nudge wink wink . . . it fell off the back of a lorry' entered the national consciousness.

7
A Brief Period of Rejoicing

'In all our long history we have never seen a greater day than
this'
> – Winston Spencer Churchill, 8 May 1945

Shortly after midnight, in the first minutes of 8 May 1945, a
great thunderstorm with sheets of lightning raged over
London, almost in imitation of the one that had been a prelude
to hostilities in September 1939. 'Heard that thunderstorm in
the night? God's wrath, that was!' one Londoner commented.
It was only fitting that after the storm Tuesday, 8 May – VE
Day – dawned fresh and bright with the promise of sunshine
and temperatures in the seventies.

After months of waiting, the day began quietly. Only a few
weeks before a woman who worked in the City had recorded
in her diary: 'The war news is so wonderful that it almost
passes belief – can we really hope we are at the end of this
ghastly business? Dare we?' There was a feeling that the long
struggle could not really be about to end. 'Wouldn't it be lovely
if it was true?' a Londoner told Mass-Observation. 'Do you
really think it could be? Just think of it, to go to bed and to
go to sleep and know that you will be safe all night long.'

William Hall, working in Civil Defence in Hackney, noted
that even confronted with impending peace, the British were
showing the characteristic restraint that had seen them through
the war: 'Now the war is ending it's almost unbelievable, like
a fantastic dream – not much gaiety and outward emotions
showing – but an undercurrent of excitement.'

Others felt that the end of the war had been so prolonged
that it was impossible to anticipate it with any sense of joy:

Well, I don't know. I'd have felt more excited if it had finished last summer, when we all thought it would. Somehow I don't feel so excited now. I feel sort of deadened, as if when I see the headlines 'Germany capitulates' I shall just think 'So what?' I mean, everything will go on as before, and there will be less food than ever, and I don't suppose my husband will be coming home for months and years, and they will nag us about winning the peace or something, just as they nagged us about the war. No, I'm afraid I don't feel in the least exhilarated – not the way I did last summer.

Nevertheless, preparations were under way for the big day. As early as the first week of March Gwladys Cox had noted that, 'The tobacconist in West End Lane has Union Jacks for sale, and says they are going like hot cakes, people buying them up before the final rush.' London stores were busy stocking up on red, white and blue flags and bunting, Selfridges having the best selection, and on the eve of VE Day the Board of Trade was at pains to announce: 'Until the end of May you may buy cotton bunting without coupons, as long as it is red, white or blue and does not cost more than one and three-pence a square yard.'

On 29 April there was an Associated Press news flash from San Francisco declaring, 'Germany has surrendered to the Allied Governments unconditionally.' It was just the sort of false report Intelligence chiefs dreaded, because it meant that the fighting forces relaxed and lost their edge. After an hour of jubilation, the report was firmly denied by President Truman and by the Supreme Headquarters of the Allied Expeditionary Force (SHAEF) in Europe. Hitler shot himself on the afternoon of 30 April, but his death, announced on the evening of 1 May in a news flash on the Forces Programme before a resumption of *Music While You Work* and in the newspapers next morning, did not bring an immediate end to hostilities. When James Lees-Milne heard the news of Hitler's death he felt nothing: 'Somehow, I fancy, none of us was very excited. We have waited and suffered too long.'

Under Hitler's successor, Grand Admiral Karl Dönitz,

Germany continued to fight, determined to resist the Bolshevik menace to the last, although hundreds of thousands of German troops were being captured or surrendering all over Europe. On 4 May the wealthy MP Sir Henry 'Chips' Channon was dining at the Ritz when he stumbled on the news of the surrender of a section of the German forces to Field Marshal Montgomery at Lüneburg Heath:

After dinner, I went along the corridor of the Ritz, being, like everyone else, in a restless mood (all London has been on edge these last few days, waiting for the final announcement) and went to read the latest news on the tape machine. There I read that at 9.13 a communiqué had been issued at SHAEF that the Germans had capitulated in Holland, Western Germany and Denmark, and that the cease fire will begin tomorrow at 6 am.

The British army's war in Europe was effectively over, but for three more days the war on other fronts dragged agonisingly slowly to its close and the tension of the last days was unbearable.

At 2.41 a.m. on 7 May, at a schoolhouse in Reims, General Alfred Jodl signed the unconditional surrender of all German land, sea and air forces, wherever they might be. General Walter Bedell Smith signed for the Allied Expeditionary Force and General Ivan Susloparov for the Soviet High Command. General François Sevez signed as a witness for France. The surrender was to come into effect at 59 minutes to midnight on 8 May. The Supreme Commander, General Eisenhower, then telephoned General Sir Hastings Ismay, the head of Churchill's Defence Office, with the news. The general, known as 'Pug', recalled:

At about 3 am that morning, I was awakened by my telephone bell and told that the Supreme Commander was on the line. These nocturnal calls had never brought good news and I was afraid that something had gone wrong. But my mind was soon put at rest. 'Is that you, Pug?' 'Yes, Ike. What has happened?' 'They have signed on the dotted line. It's all over.' My wife heard what had been said and her eyes filled with tears. I too felt a lump in my throat and could scarcely voice my congratulations.

Mindful that Churchill had asked never to be woken during the night unless Britain was actually being invaded, Captain Richard Pim, the Royal Naval reservist who ran the map room in Churchill's bomb-proof bunker beneath Whitehall where the Prime Minister also slept, waited until Churchill awoke on the morning of 7 May before giving him the news. 'For five years you've brought me bad news, sometimes worse than others,' Churchill told Pim. 'Now you've redeemed yourself.'

It should have been a straightforward matter of making a public announcement at 6 p.m. that evening London time, this being noon in Washington and 7 p.m. in Moscow. By this time the orders to the German forces to lay down their arms would be public knowledge anyway. Accordingly, Churchill alerted the War Cabinet and the Chiefs of Staff to be ready to accompany him to Buckingham Palace that evening, from where he would make the official announcement. But this was to reckon without Stalin's refusal to recognise as conclusive the American-dominated Reims surrender, at which only the obscure Susloparov had represented the Soviet Union. Stalin insisted that the final surrender of the German forces on the Eastern Front should take place in Berlin, with Russia's foremost soldier, Marshal Zhukov, as the senior Allied witness both to this and to the surrender that had been agreed at Reims. Stalin was adamant that VE Day could not be proclaimed until this had happened on 8 May. He therefore proposed that the announcement of the end of the war take place at 7 a.m. Moscow time on 9 May.

All day on 7 May frantic negotiations took place between London, Washington and Moscow with telegrams passing back and forth among Churchill, Stalin and Truman. Kay Summersby, Eisenhower's English secretary and lover, noted that Churchill rang the Supreme Commander eight times in the course of the day. General Sir Alan Brooke attended a small lunch party that day at Downing Street, which was frequently interrupted. Probably unaware of the tension between their respective countries, on the Baltic Field Marshal Montgomery was lunching convivially with the Soviet Marshal Konstantin Rokossovsky and toasting 'Churchill, Stalin, Truman and the memory of Roosevelt'. Nothing had been agreed among the victors when in the early afternoon the new German Foreign Minister, Count Schwerin von Krosigk, confounded the situation. He broadcast from Flensburg, the headquarters of the German Government, that the German forces had surrendered and the war was over, incidentally putting a good glow on Germany's ignominious war record and resounding defeat:

After a heroic fight of almost six years of incomparable hardness, Germany has succumbed to the overwhelming power of her enemies. To continue the war would only mean senseless bloodshed and futile disintegration. The Government, which has a feeling of responsibility for the future of the nation, was compelled to act on the collapse of all physical and material forces and to demand of the enemy cessation of hostilities.

Meanwhile in the homes and streets of London tension was building. The newspaper headlines that morning had been non-committal: 'End of War in Europe in Hand', *The Times* prevaricated and 'It may be Today', opined the *Daily Mail*. Twelve elderly bell-ringers at St Paul's were standing by for the signal to ring out the victory peal, a signal that never came. Everyone had bunting ready, but was it right to put it up? A Chelsea woman admitted, 'I don't know whether to start putting out my flags or not. I don't want to be the first and make a fool of myself.' A woman standing at Euston station remembers the crowd suddenly falling silent as the words came over the loudspeaker: 'Here is an important announcement . . .' The railway official went on to inform them that the 4.09 p.m. for Northampton would be leaving from Platform 7 and not the platform shown on the board. There was a mighty roar of indignation from the disappointed crowd.

Most uncharacteristically, Londoners were actually talking to strangers, as the pent-up excitement threatened to burst. A woman walking along Kingsway was assailed by streams of (scarce) lavatory paper cascading from windows. At four o'clock RAF planes were doing victory rolls over the City, watched by an admiring crowd at the Mansion House. The headline in the *Evening News* that afternoon, 'It Is Over', jumped the gun. Everyone waited in vain for an official announcement.

A Chelsea resident summed up the frustrations of the day:

It has been a day of expectancy. Ridiculously enough I felt it imperative to call for the laundry, which wasn't ready, then had a good macaroni stew at the Cheyne Walk Londoners' meal service. People were saying, 'Yes, they called themselves cultured' and 'Guess they won't want war again'. Then I went to Kensington, seeing through the still netted bus windows how flags were already appearing at windows and doors, and being tied to the railings of houses. Quite a lot of women were standing about and elderly men sitting on now useless air raid shelter covers. The suspense rather awful, expecting some person to rush up and say, 'It's over!' Or loud-speaker vans to come round, or the promised pealing of all the bells of all the churches. It didn't happen. The sun had poured on a happy and expectant London all day . . . Long queues waited for the evening papers; streets were enlivened by girls with red, white and blue bows in their hair. So attuned to war that peace wouldn't sink in; it's coming, it's coming, all the world said.

Indeed, Schwerin von Krosigk's broadcast, reported phlegmatically and without comment on the BBC News at 3 p.m., had flashed round the world, acting as a catalyst to what happened next. While the victors argued as to the timing of the peace, it was ironic that it was one of the vanquished Germans who told the world that the war was over. A small group of journalists had been invited to witness the historic moment at Reims, but there was an embargo on the news. In the event, one American reporter, the seasoned Edward

Kennedy of the Associated Press agency, broke the embargo by telephoning his report to his Paris office, which relayed it to London, from where it was transmitted without censorship, since it emanated from overseas, to New York – a scoop that made Kennedy an object of controversy for many years. Kennedy reasoned that the public had a right to know, especially after Schwerin von Krosigk's announcement. At 9.36 a.m. New York time, 3.36 p.m. London time, his report clattered off the teleprinters: 'GERMANY SURRENDERED UNCONDITIONALLY TO THE WESTERN ALLIES AND RUSSIA 2.41 AM FRENCH TIME TODAY.'

Ironically, there had been so many false alarms that no one knew whether or not to believe Kennedy's report and a further dampener was put on the news when SHAEF announced that it had made 'nowhere any official statement for publication . . . concerning the surrender of all German armed forces in Europe and that no story to this effect is authorized'. Nevertheless thousands ran out into the streets of New York shouting, 'It's over! The war's over!' while paper and cloth rained down from every window as the city embarked on an orgy of premature celebration.

Harold Nicolson heard of Schwerin von Krosigk's broadcast through the BBC News and, after running the Union Jack up the flagpole at Sissinghurst, hurried up to London: 'When I get to London there are flags everywhere. At Cannon Street I see the BBC's Chief Engineer, Noel Ashbridge, escaping exhausted from London. He says that everything is completely tied up, that we cannot get Moscow to agree to a time for a simultaneous announcement and that everything is to be postponed until tomorrow.'

The American Government and General Eisenhower at SHAEF were still anxious to comply with Stalin's request for the peace to be delayed, but Churchill was less compliant. He telegraphed Washington to tell them that the London crowd was already thronging the streets in anticipation and that he could not hold up the official announcement much longer, while he told Stalin that after Schwerin von Krosigk's broadcast it was advisable to make the announcement at 6 p.m. London time that evening, 7 May, as otherwise it would seem that 'it is only the Governments who do not know'.

Ignorant of the difficulties Churchill and the Americans were facing behind the scenes with a truculent Stalin, there was grumbling among the waiting crowd in Whitehall and Piccadilly: 'The mess they're making of it! First they've surrendered, then they haven't; then peace will be declared in a few hours, then it won't . . . It's tearing people's nerves to shreds . . . it's just like the ending of the blackout, then the dim-out; then more muddles. They miss the dramatic moment every time.'

Another Londoner told Mass-Observation:

People look pretty cheerful. So they damn well ought to be. V Day? God alone knows when. I think everyone's got to such a pitch of saying 'You can't believe this' or 'You can't believe that' that when peace *is* declared they won't be able to take it in. Oh, I do think it's a muddle. Good thing we can keep our heads. Not like those Americans. They say they've finished all their peace-night tanks of liquor already, and it was all a rumour.

Early that evening Churchill informed the War Cabinet of the day's exchanges between London, Washington and Moscow. He sincerely regretted that the delay in announcing VE Day had spoiled the spontaneity of the occasion, but he had not wanted to risk antagonising Stalin. However, it was now decided that the Ministry of Information should inform the public immediately that the following day, Tuesday, 'will be treated as Victory-in-Europe Day and will be regarded as a holiday'. The day after that, 9 May, when Britain's 'Great Russian ally' would be celebrating its VE Day, would also be a public holiday. The Ministry would also announce that the Prime Minister would broadcast to the nation – he had dictated his speech to his secretary Elizabeth Layton late on the afternoon of the 7th in the hope of delivering it that evening – at 3 p.m. British double summer time on 8 May, allowing President Truman in Washington to broadcast simultaneously at 9 a.m. Washington time. Churchill despatched telegrams to Stalin and Truman informing them of his decision.

The BBC made the announcement just as in Piccadilly the police were asking the waiting crowd to disperse: 'Move along now, it's all off.' In delaying the official announcement of peace, every anticlimax added a little to people's slowly increasing apathy and frustration. Their hopes were raised and dashed so often, disappointments were so frequent, that it became safer to feel nothing at all. 'The war's ending in just the same phoney way as it began,' someone complained. People returned dejectedly to their homes. 'Official or not,' one of hundreds of excited GIs crowded into Rainbow Corner told the *Stars and Stripes*, 'It's all over now. They were licked long ago.'

A prolonged sounding of sirens and hooters from tugs, motor boats and other small craft on the Thames that evening left no one in any doubt that the war *was* over. It was too much to expect Londoners to wait until the next day to celebrate. They started immediately. Those who had gone home made their way back to the West End. Piccadilly, decked with red, white and blue ribbons and rosettes and the flags of the Allies, quickly became the hub of a gyrating, hooting, whistling crowd exceeding 10,000, dancing the conga and the jig round the boxed-up pedestal of Eros and singing 'Knees up, Mother Brown' at the tops of their voices. Allied servicemen and -women and civilians halted the traffic and followed the lead of a New Zealand sailor who climbed on to the bonnet of a bus. Others clambered on to the roofs of private cars. A huge bonfire in Shaftesbury Avenue lent a glow to the celebrations, while in derelict basements in Soho and Mayfair bonfires were lit and merrymakers danced, their shadows flickering wildly on the scarred walls. A woman in Chelsea noted: 'Chelsea was not mad but glad that night; children up late, youths singing and a bonfire blazed in Carlyle Square. Well might we all be happy, millions of us had come through without a scratch or without losing anything. This was the night to sing. We still had London.'

Late-night revellers making their way home just after midnight were caught in the thunderstorm and drenched, while those who were already in bed and asleep awoke with a start, so conditioned were they to air raids, before they remembered that it was all over and sank gratefully back to sleep. As ever, Churchill was working into the early hours. Wrapping up the day's work with his secretary, he heard the thunder and muttered, 'What was that? Oh, thunder. Might as well have another war.' It was 3.45 a.m. before he retired for the night and 4.30 by the time she finished her typing.

The early editions of the newspapers hit the streets with the news everyone had waited so long for. 'It's all Over', pronounced the *Daily Mail*. The *Stars and Stripes* stated simply: 'Germany Quits!' Passes and furloughs for all military personnel in the United Kingdom, it announced, would be extended for 48 hours. Best of all for fans of Jane, the cartoon character who had been such a morale booster to the fighting men through the war, the *Daily Mirror* fulfilled its promise to have her naked on this day of victory.

JANE . . .

From early in the morning to late in the evening on VE Day, a series of services was held at St Paul's. At noon the cathedral was packed for a victory thanksgiving service, but many private worshippers slipping in and out in the course of the day meant that 35,000 visited the great cathedral to give thanks to God for their deliverance. Many who did not go to St Paul's flocked to their parish churches. Not all the bells were rung, since many of the bell-ringers were still away. It was noticed that there were more women than men in the congregations.

'We're from Tooting. We've come to see the sights, but Vi and I thought we'd like to start off with a service of thanksgiving and join in,' one girl told a reporter as she emerged from the noonday service at St Paul's. 'We're glad we did. We thought it was very impressive. No, I don't go to church very often, but this is an exception. I was determined to go to a thanksgiving service and even if I hadn't come to this I'd have gone to our local church service next Sunday.'

'It didn't surprise me to see it so crowded,' another woman said. 'It's the way people feel. We've got so much to thank the Almighty for. My boy was taken prisoner at Singapore. I've had one postcard from him from the Red Cross and since then nothing. I'm hoping he's alive – you have to keep on hoping. I couldn't stay at home today – it'd choke me if I did. I had to get out and be with the crowds.'

After a quiet, even lethargic start to the day, by midday crowds were gathering in the West End. The American journalist Mollie Panter-Downes was there to witness the scene:

The desire to assist in London's celebrations combusted spontaneously in the bosom of every member of every family, from the smallest babies, with their hair done up in red-white-and-blue ribbons, to beaming elderly couples who, utterly without self-consciousness, strolled up and down the streets arm in arm in red-white-and-blue paper hats. Even the dogs wore immense tricolored bows. Rosettes sprouted from the slabs of pork in the butcher shops, which, like other food stores, were open for a couple of hours in the morning. With their customary practicality, housewives put bread before circuses. They waited in the long bakery queues, the string bags of the common round in one hand and the Union Jack of the glad occasion in the other. Even queues seemed tolerable this morning. The bells had begun to peal and, after the storm, London was having a perfect, hot, English summer's day.

In the parks families were sitting with their picnics, munching sandwiches. Mollie Panter-Downes continues:

The girls in their thin, bright dresses heightened the impression that the city had been taken over by an enormous family picnic. The number of extraordinarily pretty young girls, who presumably are hidden on working days inside the factories and government offices, was astonishing. They streamed out into the parks and streets like flocks of twittering, gaily plumaged cockney birds. In their freshly curled hair were cornflowers and poppies, and they wore red-white-and-blue ribbons around their narrow waists. Some of them even tied ribbons around their bare ankles. Strolling with their uniformed boys, arms candidly about each other, they provided a constant, gay, simple marginal decoration to the big, solemn moments of the day.

The crowds milled back and forth between Buckingham Palace, Whitehall, Trafalgar Square and Piccadilly Circus. In Piccadilly American servicemen were throwing streams of lavatory paper down from the windows of their club and people were laughing. Everyone was determined to see the King and Queen and Mr Churchill at least once. One small boy, holding on to his father's hand, was more interested in seeing the trench shelters in Green Park. 'You don't want to see the shelters today,' his father told him. 'You'll never have to use them again, son.' 'Never?' the child queried. '*Never!* Understand?'

In Trafalgar Square every seat round the fountain was soon occupied, while others sat down wherever they happened to be – on doorsteps and on the kerb. Hawkers in front of the National Gallery were doing a brisk trade in victory rosettes, blowers, hats and little flags. One selling Churchill button-hole-badges yelled, 'Churchill for sixpence. Worth more!' A notice on a hawker's stand read: 'God has been good to us. It's up to us now.' Another reminded onlookers: 'There'll always be an England! We have beaten them three times – including once at Tottenham!'

A little after one Churchill emerged from his headquarters at Storey's Gate, opposite St James's Park, and was driven to Buckingham Palace for a congratulatory lunch with the King.

At the Savoy diners were being treated to a special victory lunch – still for the statutory five shillings, with a three-and-sixpence house charge, plus wine: *La Tasse de Consommé Niçoise de la Victoire, La Volaille des Iles Britanniques, La Citronette Joyeuse Déliverance, La Coupe Glacée des Alliés* and *Le Médaillon du Soldat*. Tom Pocock was sent to report a lunch being held at the Guildhall, where Ernest Bevin, the Minister of Labour, was addressing the Institute of Wallpaper Manufacturers. '*Wallpaper!* Nobody had talked about wallpaper for six years, let alone covered their walls with it. This *was* an omen of peace,' Pockock remarked. Wartime habits died hard, however: 'A waiter was carefully dropping one small lump of sugar into each cup of coffee, when he accidentally dropped a second into mine, then dredged for it with a spoon and removed it to my neighbour's cup.'

By 1.45 the lower end of Whitehall was crammed with people. A thousand extra police had been brought in to control the crowds at key points – Buckingham Palace, Whitehall, Parliament Street, Trafalgar Square, Piccadilly, Regent Street and Oxford Street – their brief being not to stop people enjoying themselves, but to prevent excess. Thousands – the Met were to estimate the crowd at 50,000 – lined the pavements along Whitehall and as they streamed in police were calling, 'Now move along there, please – keep moving!' A bus passing down Whitehall had chalked across it, 'Hitler missed this bus' – perhaps in parody of Chamberlain's unfortunate words back in 1940. A lorry filled with barrels of beer raised a mighty cheer and cries of 'Now don't go further, mate' and 'Now *that's* what I call priority.'

Mass-Observation had its spies in the crowd, reporting snatches of conversation. 'I bet Churchill's pleased with himself,' said one. 'So he should be. He's done a grand job of work for a man his age – never sparing himself.' 'Pity Roosevelt's dead,' commented another, echoing a general sentiment on this day of rejoicing. The underlying worry and cynicism about the post-war world also crept into conversation. 'It was just like this after the last war and twelve months later we was standing in dole queues.' 'Shut up!' was the response. 'No one's going to make me miserable today. I've been waiting for it too long.' A Cockney was telling her small son dressed in a Union Jack and howling with excitement and exhaustion, 'You shouldn't have come if you wanted to sit down.'

The Mass-Observation reporters also picked up the resentment felt by some at the way the announcement of VE Day had been handled. 'The way they've behaved – why, it's an insult to the British people. Stood up to all what we've stood up to, and then afraid to tell us it was peace; just as if we was a lot of kids. Just as if we couldn't be trusted to be'ave ourselves.' And, more ominously for Churchill and his party: 'Do 'em no good in the General Election – the way they've gone on over this. People won't forget it. Insult's just what it was. No more and no less.'

At 2.40 servicemen appeared on the balcony of one of the buildings opposite the Ministry of Works. A naval officer with lots of gold braid started imitating Hitler, waving and gesticulating and repeating, '*Und der Reich, und der Reich*', while the crowd applauded wildly.

Harold Nicolson lunched at the Beefsteak. By the time he emerged, the crowd was waiting expectantly for the key event of the afternoon – Churchill's speech:

The whole of Trafalgar Square and Whitehall was packed with people. Somebody had made a corner in rosettes, flags, streamers, paper whisks and, above all, paper caps. The latter were horrible, being of the comic variety. I also regret to say that I observed three Guardsmen in full uniform wearing such hats: they were *not* Grenadiers; they belonged to the Coldstream. And through this cheerful, but not exuberant, crowd I pushed my way to the House of Commons. The last few yards were very difficult, as the crowd was packed against the railings. I tore my trousers in trying to squeeze past a stranded car. But at length the police saw me and backed a horse into the crowd, making a gap through which, amid cheers, I was squirted into Palace Yard. There I paused to recover myself, and seeing that it was approaching the hour of 3pm, I decided to remain there and hear Winston's broadcast which was to be relayed through loud-speakers.

At three o'clock Big Ben struck the hour and the vast crowd fell silent to listen to Churchill, speaking, as Chamberlain had done on that Sunday morning war was declared on 3 September 1939, from the Cabinet Room at 10 Downing Street. There was total silence as they hung on Churchill's every word:

Yesterday at 2.41 am at Headquarters, General Jodl [he mispronounced the name, sounding the J], the representative of the German High Command, and Grand Admiral Dönitz, the designated head of the German State, signed the act of unconditional surrender of all the German land, sea and air forces, in Europe, to the Allied Expeditionary Force and to the Soviet High Command. Today, this agreement will be ratified and confirmed at Berlin . . . Hostilities will end officially at one minute after midnight tonight, Tuesday, 8 May [this would in fact be 9 May], but in the interests of saving lives the 'Cease Fire' began yesterday to be sounded along the fronts . . .

There were wild cheers and whoops of joy from the crowd at this and at the news that 'our dear Channel Islands', the only part of the British Isles to be occupied, would be free from 'midnight tonight'. After Churchill's brief résumé of the years of struggle, the crowd gasped when he came to the words: 'Finally almost the whole world was combined against the evil-doers, who are now prostrate before us . . . The German war is therefore at an end. Our gratitude to all our splendid allies goes forth from all our hearts in this island and the British Empire.' Loud clapping ensued as he paid tribute to General Eisenhower and to 'our Russian comrades'.

We may allow ourselves a brief period of rejoicing [Churchill continued], but let us not forget for a moment the toils and efforts that lie ahead. Japan, with all her treachery and greed, remains unsubdued. The injustice she has inflicted upon Great Britain and the United States, and other countries, and her detestable cruelties call for justice and retribution. We must now devote all our strength and resources to the completion of our task both at home and abroad. Advance Britannia! Long live the cause of freedom! God save the King!

As the Prime Minister finished, the haunting notes of the Cease Fire, sounded by the buglers of the Royal Horse Guards, rang out. Everyone stood smartly to attention for a hearty rendering of 'God Save the King', followed by loud cheers.

The speech was, perhaps, not quite up to the standard of Churchill's best wartime oratory, although the actor Noël Coward, in benevolent mood, was happy enough with it: 'A wonderful day from every point of view. Went wandering through the crowds in the hot sunshine. Everyone was good-humoured and cheerful. In the afternoon, the Prime Minister made a magnificent speech, simple and without boastfulness, but full of deep pride . . . I suppose this is the greatest day in our history.'

After receiving the congratulations of his personal staff, Churchill had to make his way to the House of Commons, but it was no easy matter. The crowd was solid. There were shouts of 'Good old Winnie!' Churchill's detective, Walter Thompson, recalled that, 'The car was literally forced through the crowd. No engine power was necessary. Everyone seemed determined to shake him by the hand. In Parliament Square the cheering crowds closed right in. Mr Churchill came forward to stand on the front seat of the car with me while mounted police cleared the way.'

After a quick tour through a 'beflagged and decorated' Ritz, where he had been kissed by the aged Mrs Keppel, 'Chips' Channon had gone to the Commons:

At the House, Questions lasted interminably, and there was an atmosphere of expectancy in the crowded Chamber. Every seat was occupied; the Ambassadors were all present, peers queued up. At three o'clock, in the Whips' Room, I heard the PM make the official announcement over the wireless that the war in Europe was at an end. I then returned to the Chamber, but owing to the ovation

Winston was having in the streets, he was delayed, and for a few embarrassed minutes we had nothing to do. Members, amused, asked desultory questions, keeping their eyes on the door behind the Speaker's chair.

Harold Nicolson observed Churchill's delayed entry:

Then a slight stir was observed behind the Speaker's chair, and Winston, looking coy and cheerful, came in. The House rose as a man, and yelled and yelled and waved their Order Papers. He responded, not with a bow exactly, but with an odd shy jerk of the head and with a wide grin. Then he started to read to us the statement that he had just made on the wireless. When he finished reading, he put his manuscript aside and with wide gestures thanked and blessed the House for all its noble support of him throughout these years.

After paying tribute to the House of Commons for being 'the strongest foundation for waging war that has ever been seen in the whole of our long history', Churchill proposed that 'this House do now attend at the Church of St Margaret's, Westminster, to give humble and reverend thanks to Almighty God for our deliverance from the threat of German domination'. He was echoing the words he had heard at the Armistice ending the First World War in November 1918. The motion was carried and the Serjeant at Arms put the mace on his shoulder and, following the Speaker, the Members filed out into the sunshine of Parliament Square. Nicolson expected the crowd to titter at the sight of politicians attending church en masse but, on the contrary: 'Cheers were what we received, and adulation. The service itself was very short and simple, and beautifully sung.' The Chaplain to the Speaker read out the names of the 19 MPs who had lost their lives in the services and as the Speaker and the Prime Minister emerged at the end of the service the bells pealed in celebration.

After the House was adjourned for the day at 4.30, Churchill was passing through Central Hall when a small boy broke away from the crowd and asked for his autograph. 'Winston took a long time getting out his glasses and wiping them,' Nicolson noted. 'Then he ruffled the little boy's hair and gave him back his beastly little album. "That will remind you of a glorious day," he said, and the crowd clapped louder than before.'

Discovering that he had forgotten his cigars, Churchill made a brief detour to pick them up, telling his detective, 'I must put one on for them. They expect it.' He stopped to light one theatrically before continuing his journey to Buckingham Palace. Soon afterwards, he made the balcony appearance with the royal family which the crowd, standing for hours outside a battle-scarred palace with its blackout still in place and its bricked-up windows, had been anticipating. The King appeared bare headed and in naval uniform, the Queen in soft powder blue, Princess Elizabeth in the uniform of a second subaltern of the ATS and Princess Margaret Rose, a 14-year-old school-girl, in blue.

A rumour that Churchill was next going to speak from the balcony of the Ministry of Health in Whitehall meant that the crowd started to drift in that direction. It was stifling in the crowd and people were already missing the WVS and the wartime mobile canteens, whom they had come to rely on to dole out tea. There were very few tea rooms open and huge queues for those that were. While people fanned themselves with newspapers and handkerchiefs, others were fainting and being passed over the heads of the crowd by the ambulance teams. Up in Trafalgar Square a band was playing Gilbert and Sullivan. Outside the Ministry there were shouts of 'We want Winnie! We want Winnie!' and 'One, two, three, four, what are we waiting for?' A voice from the back of the crowd shouted, 'Why don't 'e come out?' to which another replied, ''E's 'aving a drink, dear!'

When Churchill finally made his appearance the crowd roared itself hoarse. He began, 'God – God bless you all!' Cheers. 'This is *your* victory!' to more cheers. 'It is the victory of the cause of freedom in every land. In all our long history we have never seen a greater day than this. Everyone, man or woman, has done their best. Everyone has tried. Neither the long years, nor the dangers, nor the fierce attacks of the enemy, have in any way weakened the deep resolve of the British nation. God bless you all!' Standing on the balcony with the rest of Churchill's Coalition Government, Ernest Bevin led with three cheers for Winston and the end of the war, then in singing 'For He's a Jolly Good Fellow'.

The crowd then drifted aimlessly about, always ordered and good-humoured. Even after the pubs opened there was little drunkenness, not least because so many of them quickly ran dry. People derived enough intoxication just from being in the crowd. In Trafalgar Square a girl in a red dress frolicked in the fountain with three officers of the Royal Norfolk Regiment. While bystanders cheered, she kissed all three of the men. 'I've never shown so much leg in my life,' she shouted, to male cries of 'Don't mind us!' As luck would have it, British Movietone cameramen were on hand to capture the scene. 'I bet she'll catch it when her mother sees it all in the pictures,' a woman commented wryly.

Just before 8 p.m. someone was letting off fireworks and lines of girls and servicemen were singing, 'Oh, you beautiful doll'. A jeep went by in the direction of the Haymarket full of GIs. A girl sitting on the bonnet was waving the Union Jack and the Stars and Stripes. In Piccadilly Circus a sailor stripped and climbed to the top of the Eros box, plastered with its war savings posters, while in Coventry Street a GI did a striptease up a lamppost, whirling each item around before throwing it down, starting with his wristwatch. He was left wearing only a tiny pair of pants. In the parks people danced and played silly games and some made love. Anthony Heap noticed a group of young people dancing round the arthritic figure of the *Daily Mail*'s theatre critic and singing 'Ring a ring o' roses' as he tried to cross the road.

At 9 p.m. it was King George VI's turn to address the nation. His audience had always felt tense on his behalf, as he struggled to overcome his speech impediments, but on this occasion the King spoke for the whole thirteen and a half minutes with confidence and without his usual hesitation. He captured the popular mood, as he unerringly did, when he asked the nation to 'join with me in thanksgiving':

Today we give thanks to Almighty God for a great deliverance. Speaking from our Empire's oldest capital city, war-battered but never for one moment daunted or dismayed – speaking from London, I ask you to join with me in that act of thanksgiving . . . Let us remember those who will not come back . . . the men and women in all the Services who have laid down their lives . . . Then let us salute in proud gratitude the great host of the living who have brought us to victory . . . Armed or unarmed, men and women, you have fought, striven and endured to your utmost. No one knows that better than I do; and I as your King thank you with a full heart . . . With these memories in our minds, let us think what it was that has upheld us through nearly six years of suffering and peril: the knowledge that everything was at stake, our freedom, our independence, our very existence as a people . . . We knew that if we failed the last remaining barrier against a world-wide tyranny would have fallen. But we did not fail. Let us . . . on this day of just triumph and proud sorrow . . . take up our work again, resolved as a people to do nothing unworthy of those who died for us and to make the world such a world as they would have desired, for their children and ours.

An unusually jovial BBC News followed the King's broadcast, recapturing the key moments of the day for all those listening at home. As an indication that peace had really arrived, the newscasters had ceased to introduce themselves by name and announced, 'as a tailpiece to Victory Day news . . . something you haven't heard since the war began . . . Britain's weather on the day it happened . . . most of the time it's been sunny and very warm.' Rain was forecast.

Outside Buckingham Palace, the crowd waited excitedly for the royal family to appear on the balcony. 'We want the King,' they were chanting. 'He'll come out with the floodlighting,' someone predicted. 'Just like a cuckoo clock,' one wag responded. 'Come on, George, come on!' someone urged. 'He's shy!' Lights went on in the room behind the balcony. As darkness began to descend – it was not fully dark until 10.30, astonishingly late, as Britain was still on double summer time, introduced during the war so that the hard-pressed farmers could extract the maximum advantage from the hours of daylight – there were gasps as the floodlighting came on, illuminating Buckingham Palace. 'He's coming, he coming!' someone yelled, and at last the slight, solitary figure of the King, the ordeal of a live broadcast behind him, appeared on the balcony, waving shyly to the crowd. As he retreated and returned with the Queen, resplendent in a diamond tiara, and the two princesses, the cheers were deafening.

A young girl in the crowd later wrote to her mother describing the scene:

We didn't really think we would see anything because other people were so much taller, and there were some in front lifting children up, and added to all this we were in our flattest of flat heels in preparation for walking home . . . then the floodlights went on . . . and then out they came on the balcony and I just wish Hitler had heard the cheering – the King in naval uniform and the Queen in white evening dress with a tiara, the two princesses . . . They stood waving for several minutes and we sang 'For they are jolly good fellows'.

Altogether the King and Queen were to make eight balcony appearances that day. It was to be a momentous night for their daughters. Nineteen-year-old Princess Elizabeth and her younger sister begged their parents to allow them to go down to join the throng outside the palace. Fifty years later, as Queen Elizabeth II, she recalled the occasion:

I remember the thrill and relief after the previous day's waiting for the Prime Minister's announcement of the end of the war in Europe. My parents went out on the balcony in response to the huge crowds outside. I think we went on the balcony nearly every hour, six times, and then when the excitement of the floodlights being switched on got through to us, my sister and I realised we couldn't see what the crowds were enjoying. My mother had put her tiara on for the occasion, so we asked my parents if we could go out and see for ourselves. I remember we were terrified of being recognised, so I pulled my uniform cap well down over my eyes. A grenadier officer amongst our party of about sixteen people said he refused to be seen in the company of another officer improperly dressed, so I had to put my cap on normally.

We cheered the King and Queen on the balcony and then walked miles through the streets. I remember lines of unknown people linking arms and walking down Whitehall, all of us just swept along on a tide of happiness and relief. I remember the amazement of my cousin [Viscount Lascelles], just back from four and a half years in a POW camp, walking freely with his family in the friendly throng. And I also remember when someone exchanged hats with a Dutch sailor, the poor man coming along with us in order to get his cap back. After crossing Green Park we stood outside and shouted, 'We want the King', and we were successful in seeing my parents on the balcony, having cheated slightly because we sent a message into the house to say we were waiting outside. I think it was one of the most memorable nights of my life.

In the crowd, playwright Harold Pinter, then 15, pinched the bottom of the girl in front, only to be knocked unconscious by her soldier boyfriend.

Churchill reappeared on the Ministry of Health balcony again soon after 9.30. The crowd was packed tight from the Cenotaph to the House of Commons. This was to be an impromptu speech, not for broadcast. It turned out to be a dialogue with the people, as they interjected with cheers and jeers and boos, dismal groans and cries of 'No' and 'No bloody fear'.

'One deadly foe has been cast on the ground and awaits our judgment and mercy, but there is another foe who occupies large portions of the British Empire, a foe stained with cruelty and greed – the Japanese.' Loud boos.

'We were the first, in this ancient land, to draw the sword against Germany,' he told them. 'After a while we were left alone against the most tremendous military power the world has ever seen. We were all alone for a whole year. There we stood. Did anyone want to give in?' 'No!' yelled the crowd. 'Were we downhearted?' A long drawn-out 'No fear!' was the emphatic response.

'The lights went out, and the bombs came down' – dismal groans – 'but every man, woman and child in this country had no thought of quitting the struggle. London could take it.' Cheers of agreement. 'So we came back after long months, back from the jaws of death, out of the mouth of hell, while all the world wondered. When shall the reputation and faith of this generation of English men and women fail? I say that in the long years to come not only the people of this island, but from all over the world, wherever the bird of freedom chirps in human hearts, they will look back to what we have done, and they will say, "Don't despair, don't yield to violence and tyranny. March straight forward, and die, if need be, unconquered."'

As the cheering died down, Churchill led the way in singing 'Land of Hope and Glory'. His secretary Marian Holmes remembered the moment fondly: 'This was Mr Churchill's hour. Whatever was to come, nothing could take it from him.'

Being in the crowd was the most exhilarating experience, but people were celebrating at private parties, too. Harold Nicolson dropped in at 'Chips' Channon's open house party, but regretted it:

Why did I go to that party? I should have been much happier seeing all the flood-lighting and the crowds outside Buckingham Palace. But I went and I loathed it. There in his room, copied from the Amalienberg [a palace in Munich], under the lights of many candles, were gathered the Nurembergers and the Munichois [the appeasers of the thirties] celebrating *our* victory over *their* friend Herr von Ribbentrop [he was to be tried and executed for war crimes]. I left early and in haste, leaving my coat behind me. A voice hailed me in Belgrave Square. It was Charles, seventh Marquess of Londonderry, Hitler's friend. As we walked towards his mansion in Park Lane, he explained to me how he had warned the Government about Hitler; how they would not listen to him; how, but for him we should not have had the Spitfires and 'all this', waving a thin arm at the glow above a floodlit Buckingham Palace, at the sound of cheering in the park, and at the cone of search-lights which joined each other like a maypole above our heads.

Enraged by this, I left him in Park Lane and walked back through the happy but quite sober crowds to Trafalgar Square. The National Gallery was alive with every stone outlined in flood-lighting, and down there was Big Ben with a grin upon his illumined face . . . I walked to the Temple and beyond. Looking down Fleet Street one saw the best sight of all – the dome of St Paul's rather dim-lit, and then above it a concentration of searchlights upon the huge golden cross. So I went to bed. That was my victory day.

Verily Anderson had left her children in Sussex to come up to London to celebrate with her husband. After seeing the King and Queen on the balcony of Buckingham Palace they made their slow way back to his lodgings in Bloomsbury:

Licensing hours were extended, and it was good to see the doors of restaurants and bars and pubs left open with their lights shining out onto the pavement. It was good to be able to saunter in without having to disentangle oneself from the folds of a flapping blackout curtain, which I once heard a soldier describe as like getting mixed up in the skirts of a nun. By now bonfires had been lit at street-corners. We walked through Soho. There the celebrations had a pattern of their own. Traditional dances of central Europe were being performed with all the skill and seriousness of Highland reels. Foreigners, as grateful for victory as any of us, if not more so, advanced and retired and turned and skipped to their own thin mournful chants. Their old people stood round in the firelight clapping the time.

All over London from the West End to the outer suburbs, people celebrated by the age-old tradition of lighting a bonfire. In Hoxton Reg Neal remembers, 'They was grabbing every-thing they could to burn . . . talk about going mad!' At World's

End, Chelsea, the mayor lit the bonfire at 10 p.m. and danced gleefully round it to the accompaniment of 'Knees up, Mother Brown'. In every neighbourhood and street, residents and their children foraged for firewood and gathered round the resulting glow. Pianos were dragged outside for the singing and dancing. From Walthamstow, the elderly George Britton described to his daughter in California the amazing sight of 'Your mother! dancing till midnight round a bonfire in the road.'

No self-respecting bonfire was complete without an effigy of the defeated dictator on the top. Stella Freeman noted:

No school today as this lousy war with the Germans has ended at last. Went out with Dad and bought some flags. Everywhere there are bread queues. Mum came home and we turned out the rubbish to make Hitler a bonfire. At 9 o'clock we burnt a lovely effigy of Adolf complete with helmet. Then the fun started. We had a street party until two in the morning. The boys worked hard keeping the fire alight and we burned a lump out of the curb and ate roast potatoes. After dancing my feet felt like lead. June [her friend] came round about 12 o'clock. The street looks lovely with lights and flags. A wonderful day. Jimmy [the budgerigar] has seen the war out. Yippee.

A local paper recorded:

They ranged from modest piles of timber, old rags and bomb debris to elaborately and cunningly created funeral pyres on which life-like representations of the fallen Fuhrer were perched. In Apsley Road, South Norwood, Hitler swung grimly from a huge gibbet which almost completely blocked the roadway. Balfour Road, South Norwood, boasted a life-size model of the German dictator, one of whose hands clasped the pole of a German swastika flag, and above whose head was a neatly printed sign reading, 'I have no further territorial claims in Europe', with the 'No' faintly crossed out and the word 'Hell' substituted for 'Europe'.

Others had Hitler's effigy dressed in his original employment garb as a painter and paper hanger, with a swastika on his arm. Flames consumed the effigy, more often than not, to the accompaniment of 'Roll out the Barrel'.

Many children had never seen London lit up, or at least could not remember it alight, other than with the angry flames caused by enemy bombardment. Now, on the night of VE Day, floodlights illuminated the surprising number of public buildings that had survived the bombing: from Buckingham Palace to Big Ben and across the river to County Hall, from the National Gallery to Somerset House to the Tower of London. In Trafalgar Square floodlighting cast an eerie glow on Nelson's column, as one of Britain's great heroes gazed down on the jubilant crowd celebrating at his feet. A row of flaming torches lit up the austere gentlemen's clubs along Pall Mall. An ATS battery was using its experience in a happier cause, directing its powerful beam on to the golden cross atop the dome of St Paul's and to shining a huge V for Victory against the night sky behind the Cathedral, which in the Blitz had been illuminated by anti-aircraft flares and the raging fires consuming the City and docks. Searchlights danced madly across the sky, reminiscent of the dark days of 1940 and 1941 when they had been seeking enemy aircraft, while the smell of bonfires was also an uncanny reminder of London under fire.

Blackout regulations had prohibited the celebration of Guy Fawkes' Night during the war, but now children were able to make up for it as fireworks were brought out of storage:

Some men had procured an enormous number of fireworks, including pin wheels, roman candles and plenty of bangers, and as quite a number of children had no memories of fireworks at all, they were intensely excited. The residents vied with one another in providing refreshment, and round came cakes, tarts, biscuits, parkins, and tea and lemonade. The children roasted potatoes in the fire, still a big affair, and eventually the last of the fireworks were set off.

Elizabeth Cole remembers the thrill of it all:

Well, there was a bombed area in Shadwell Road, and we spent all day, us kids (because we had two days off from school – I'll always remember it, I didn't have to do my maths homework!) and we went everywhere we could, to find wood and stuff, you know, to build a bonfire. And my father actually found some fireworks in the shop that we'd had since before the war. The sparklers and a couple of revolving ones – they worked! And I was allowed to stay up till eleven o'clock. We were singing and there was a pub opposite, so they opened all the doors and the piano was sort of drawn towards the door. And I'll always remember the next night, my mother and I took the bus and walked up to St Paul's. And when we got up there, the lights were all focused on the cross above St Paul's and it was reflected in the sky behind. It was a marvellous sight! And all the lights were on along the embankment, and we weren't used to having them like that, you see, like a necklace of pearls, all the way down to St Thomas's Hospital, all the way down the river. And I saw Piccadilly, and it was the brightest lights! God, I'd never seen anything like that!

For the children of Mrs Bell and her neighbours in Mortlake, peace was something of a novelty:

Some of the kids that had been born during the war were mystified by all the lights, many cried in bewilderment. The winding snake of a conga got longer and longer. No one was left out. The off licence across the road did a roaring trade. Bill bought a bottle in, we toasted ourselves and our neighbour whose husband had been captured at Dunkirk – we promised a real booze when he came home. As the night wore on some of the kids were put to bed, asking why not the shelter. One woman said, 'Can't say as I blame 'em, it will take some getting used to, sleeping with the old man again.' Only then did we realise how sex-starved we had become.

One of the best treats of all was the prospect of Daddy coming home. A Wandsworth woman, who was only one when the war broke out, recalls that special moment: 'For years I had prayed, "God Bless Daddy", not really knowing who Daddy was, and now there he stood, smiling, his face lit, eyes twinkling in the light of the bonfire . . . Bells rang, fires blazed and people sang out their emotions of the past horrific years. I had never seen so many men all at once.'

Rosie White remembers:

Our house and next door had the alleyways, so you had a sort of round arch between, and you went through to the back gardens. Over the gate we wrote up VE Day and Victory and Welcome Home, Dad, and put up all the flags. We had a lovely party. One of my aunts and her four daughters and friends came up from Deptford and had their party with us in our road. Our fire burned a big hole in the corner of the street. All the wooden garden gates went on the fire. In the morning when it all died down, the tar road had melted and we had a great big crater. The council came along and repaired the road. Nothing was said. Everybody was happy. The war was over, what was there to complain about? We had roast potatoes and a girl brought her piano right out and played on her steps. It went on until the early hours of the morning. It was lovely. No more bombs and Dad coming home.

For all the rejoicing and plain relief that the war was over, some declined to celebrate, mourning loved ones who would never come home. A witness recalls the poignancy of a woman who had just put up the bunting when she received the dreaded telegram: 'My pal's dad did not come home. He had been a prisoner of war. On VE Day, the flags were up at her house but then the telegram arrived and her mother took the flags down. A year or so after that they received a photograph of a white grave stone. It had been taken somewhere in Poland.'

A young mother was also reflective on VE Day:

That evening, after the children were asleep in bed, I went outside and sat on the low front wall before the house – the wall from which the ornamental railings had long since been taken for the 'war effort'. It was a warm, still evening and the long street was quiet. But from almost every window light streamed out, splashing onto the pavement. Curtains had been pulled aside and blackouts had been removed. For the first time in nearly six years we were released from the necessity of hiding out in darkness and people were reacting by letting the lights of their homes shine out.

Too tired to move, I sat thinking of those six years . . . the war had stolen from us the simple ordinary joys of a young couple shaping a shared life. Our first home had been burnt to rubble . . . We had known the agony of separation and the too rare, too short, too heightened joys of reunions . . . I thought of those who had been dear to us who had not lived to see this . . . Of John, who had stood at the altar with us on our wedding day, John who had . . . been trapped in his cockpit when his plane sank beneath the waves . . . Of Ron, constant companion of my brother since school-days . . . who had vanished without trace when the troopship he was on had been sunk by the Japanese; of Peter, my girlfriend's gay, kind brother . . . who had been shot while trying to escape from the prisoner-of-war camp . . . They were all so young. The youngest died at nineteen, the oldest at twenty-four. I sat thinking of them . . . and then went indoors to stand looking at the sleeping faces of my two little sons, whose lives lay before them in a world at peace.

Even without mourning, some chose to spend VE Day quietly at home, as this phlegmatic account indicates: 'Rose shortly before 8 am, made tea, took wife a cup, listened to wireless, went down to shops early. Place a seething mass of people, large numbers of men with shopping baskets, but no food to speak of. Came home and pottered about, had lunch and forty winks. Got on bike and visited aged parents. Tea, read paper, listened to wireless, had a drop of Scotch, bed.'

Many held their street party on VE Day, although street parties – strangely denuded of men – took place over several weeks. Somehow women scraped together from the rations the makings of a victory tea of sandwiches, cakes, trifle and lemonade – and ice cream, if refrigeration could be found – and devoted themselves to giving the children a good time, as Arthur Welch remembers:

In 1945 I was fourteen and I'd just started work down Towlers. I wasn't there long because then I went on the building. At the end of the war everyone had street parties all day. All the mothers used to make lemonade and sandwiches. Everything was still on the ration but they made it. Even the coppers used to come out of the police station to pick up some sandwiches. We had a bonfire. We didn't go up to town, we all stopped at home.

The residents of Putney Road, Enfield waited until 26 May to hold their victory party, as reported with typical British understatement in their local newspaper:

A very pleasant Victory tea party . . . Owing to the inclement weather the tea was taken (by the generosity of Mr G. Waller) in his large workshop, which he had decorated for the purpose. This was followed by games and races for the children for prizes, some in kind, others in cash. A large bonfire with an effigy of Hitler was lighted at 9.30 pm and a display of all kinds of fireworks lasting two hours gave the children (and adults) cause for excitement. Dancing was the order of the night for adults until 11.30 when 'Auld Lang Syne' and 'God save the King' were sung. The music was provided by radio loaned by the residents and Mr Fletcher (accordion). The Committee – Mrs Stevens, Mrs Bush, Mrs Crutchley and Mrs Fletcher – wishes to thank the many donors and helpers for making the show the success it was.

Meanwhile, at the close of VE Day, it fell to Stuart Hibberd to read the midnight News with its momentous opening line: 'As these words are being spoken, the official end of the war in Europe is taking place . . .'

By now the crowd had squeezed into Parliament Square, where the Houses of Parliament were floodlit and coloured lights were strung out along the riverside terrace. All eyes concentrated on the illuminated face of Big Ben as the minute hand reached the hour. The great chimes of the clock began to usher in the peace. Just before the last stroke it had reached one minute past midnight. Peace. A great cry went up and people clapped and cheered and the craft on the river hooted.

After all the revelry many elected to sleep out in the parks – finding it was not such a comfortable experience, even on such a warm night as this. Servicemen did not need to report back to camp by 23.59, as they usually did, and many of them took to the dance-halls and clubs until three or four in the morning. Pubs were allowed to stay open until midnight, but many closed once they ran out of drink. The last tube train left at 11.15, after which a huge queue – this wartime habit being now well ingrained – stretched from Leicester Square back to Cambridge Circus for the first train in the morning. Others sat about in the railway stations waiting for transport home.

On 9 May there were no evening papers, nor would there be any the next morning. While a military band played outside Buckingham Palace, the royal family spent the day touring the bomb-stricken East End. They would visit the southern suburbs in succeeding days. On 10 May the House of Commons reassembled and cheered Herbert Morrison's announcement that the long list of Defence Regulations had been revoked, including the one making it an offence to spread alarm and despondency. The next day, Anthony Heap was happy to note in his diary:

The transition from total war to partial peace begins in grand style with the scrapping of no less than eighty-four of the emergency wartime regulations restricting civil liberties, including the iniquitous '18' that authorised the arrest and imprisonment of suspected persons without trial. A further twenty-five have been modified. I never realised there were so many. And how pleasant it is to see weather reports and forecasts in the newspapers again.

It also ceased to be illegal to foment a strike, an encouragement, if any were needed, for a spate of them. The House cheered the Prime Minister's announcement that the basic petrol ration for 'inessential' private motoring would be restored on 2 June, when cars up to 8 horse-power received 4 gallons a month and those from 10 to 13 horse-power, 5.

On Sunday, 13 May morning services of national thanksgiving were held all over the country. 'Chips' Channon was at St Paul's for the occasion:

I went to St Paul's for the great Thanksgiving Service, very hot in my morning clothes: the great cathedral was crowded, and I watched all the notabilities of the earth come in, and listened to the cheers of the crowds outside. At length the procession of clergy moved to the door to receive the Sovereigns who then proceeded up the aisle. Their Majesties looked young and smiling – though the King looked drawn. But he has the Windsor gift of looking half his age. Behind him walked Queen Mary whom I had not seen since before the war. She looked magnificent – even beautiful, and was gloriously arrayed and bejewelled in a pink-heliotrope confection. . . . Then came the young Princesses, shy and uninteresting, and the Kings of Greece and Yugoslavia, the Duchess of Kent in uniform with her two elder children, making their first State appearance, and behaving beautifully . . . The service was impressive but long – Winston all smiles and Mrs Churchill, safely back from Russia, bowing and gracious. At last it was over – and after tripping over several Field Marshals, I walked to the Savoy.

Also at St Paul's were 50 ordinary London women, representatives of the thousands who had stood up so bravely to the worst bombing of London. The St Paul's Choir School was brought back from Truro just in time.

On 12 June London had a chance to show its gratitude to General Eisenhower, when he came to receive the Honorary Freedom of the City of London and the Sword of Honour 'as a mark of appreciation of the distinguished part played by him in effecting the defeat of the German armed forces'. The Lord Mayor and Sheriffs in ceremonial dress, the Aldermen in their scarlet gowns, the blue-gowned members of the Common Council, together with past and present members of the Cabinet and leading representatives of the law, banking and the professions were all gathered at the Guildhall for the presentation. Afterwards Churchill and Eisenhower waved to cheering crowds from the balcony of the Mansion House.

Very slowly, London was beginning to pick up the threads of peacetime life. In mid June there was a dinner at the National Gallery for Dame Myra Hess, in recognition and thanks for her lunchtime concerts at the gallery, which had done so much to sustain morale and give pleasure in the darkest days of the war. The gallery's collection was being brought back from its wartime hideout and already the walls of two rooms were adorned with Rembrandt's self-portrait, Titian's *Bacchus and Ariadne,* Rubens's *Judgement of Paris*, El Greco's *Agony in the Garden*, Renoir's *Parapluies*, a nativity by Piero della Francesco, Jan van Eyck's portrait of *Arnolfini and his Wife* and Hobbema's *Avenue*. Visitors to the gallery, led by the King and Queen, said that it was like greeting old friends, startled anew by their beauty.

That same month the Sadler's Wells Opera Company returned to its Islington home and opened with *Peter Grimes* by the young British composer, Benjamin Britten. It was the first new opera to be produced in Europe since the outbreak of war. Critics were impressed that Sadler's Wells could stage an opera of such complexity within a month of the end of hostilities. Music lovers were also looking forward to the Proms, although for the first time they would not be directed by their creator, Henry Wood, but by Sir Adrian Boult and Mr Constant Lambert.

August Bank Holiday on the first weekend of the month saw a massive exodus from London to the coastal resorts, which had been out of bounds for most of the war. There had been a threat of rail strikes – something that Vere Hodgson considered astounding since 'now the railways are to be nationalised, surely the railway men will get all they want' – and vast queues snaked round London's railway stations. At Paddington queuing began at midnight for the early morning trains to Devon and Cornwall. Nine thousand trains passed through Clapham Junction bound for the Sussex coast, but at Victoria a lightning strike by firemen and drivers at a local depot meant that most of the steam trains for Dover, Margate and Ramsgate were cancelled. After waiting for hours, many went home disappointed. At Brixton Bus Depot, angry scenes took place as 2,000 people scrambled for 256 seats in 8 coaches. They mobbed the booking office and police were called to disperse the crowd.

In London as elsewhere there were soaring temperatures and hours of sunshine. On 6 August a record crowd of 34,000 watched the Test Match at Lords. Local authorities were still laying on their holidays-at-home events. In St Pancras a travelling theatre toured the streets: there was a ventriloquist, a clown, a Punch and Judy show, a children's talent competition and community singing.

Those who did manage to reach the coast were either sleeping four or five to a room or were turned away by seaside landladies, the 'No Vacancies' sign smugly pinned to hotels and guest-houses. Many slept rough on the beaches. Restaurants and cafés, still ensnared in rationing, were completely unequal to the task of feeding the crowds.

'The whole affair has been an unseemly scramble, and the scramble continues,' the *Spectator* complained. 'For good and obvious reasons, mingled with some bad ones, the foreseeable public demand has not been met; it has been let down by the utter inadequacy of transport, of accommodation and of public catering – tired crowds, well trained by five years of queuing in their towns, have patiently lined up for trains, for restaurants, for beds and for a chance to look at the waves.'

Granted, the demand for holidays was rather sudden, 'before the dislocation, damage and requisitioning could be cleared up'. For the first time the full effect of the 1938 Holidays with Pay Act was being felt. In 1938 only 15 million people had been able to take a week's holiday, but now the legislation meant that the number being able to afford to get away had doubled. So great was the increased demand that even maximum use of all pre-war resources would have proved miserably insufficient.

The war with Japan was expected to go on for a year and more, but suddenly, with the dropping of atomic bombs on Hiroshima and Nagasaki on 6 and 9 August respectively, it came to an abrupt end. On the 8th, James Lees-Milne expressed the disquiet felt by many at this startling new development: 'All day I have been made to feel despairing, careless and numb by the atom bomb. Nothing has a purpose any more, with these awful clouds of desolation hovering over us. I am shocked, shocked by our use of this appalling bomb . . . it is horrifyingly and utterly damnable.'

Noël Coward expressed his feelings in more flippant terms: 'The papers are full of the atomic bomb which is going to revolutionize everything and blow us to buggery. Not a bad idea.' A member of the Foreign Office confided in his diary: 'I must say I feel shocked and ashamed . . . I don't think humanity will think it was a very creditable action.'

In the *Daily Mirror* Donald Zec drew a cartoon showing two apes reading the headlines: 'ATOM SPLIT – CONFER-ENCE SPLIT – UNITED NATIONS SPLIT – CIVILISA-TION SPLIT – MANKIND WIPED OUT – ALL THIS, UNLESS!' The paper speculated that the atom bomb would either end war or end the world.

On the morning of the 10th the Japanese Government agreed to an unconditional surrender. The news was quick to leak out. Harold Nicolson was in town that day and met fellow Tory Harold Macmillan. They had both lost their seats in the recent general election, when Labour had won a landslide victory and, to the amazement of the world, the great wartime leader Winston Churchill had been swept from power:

After luncheon I go with Victor Cunard to buy some socks at Simpsons in Piccadilly. I leave the shop at 2.20, and as we walk down the street, we see some idiot girls leaning out of the window of an office and sprinkling passers-by with torn-up paper. 'They think the war's over', says Victor. 'No', I answer, 'I expect they have been demobilised.' We part outside Hatchard's, and I walk on and bump into Harold Macmillan who is without coat or hat. He says, 'What a pity that we could not have kept on the old House and the Coalition until today. Then we could have had a final cele-bration.' 'Is there any news? I have heard nothing', I say to him, feeling foolish. 'Yes', he answers, 'the Japs have surrendered.'

Well, that is very odd. I have no feeling of elation at all. It seems remote. There is no sign of jubilation, and I observe that the newspaper vendors have stacks of evening papers unsold and unasked for. How different it all was on VE Day! On going back to KBW I meet a small procession of American soldiers carrying Old Glory and followed by a very few urchins. It is not inspiring at all.

At midnight on Tuesday, 14 August the BBC asked listeners to stand by for a special announcement. Most people were in bed, so that they did not hear the news until it was repeated at seven in the morning. Again, Lees-Milne expressed his concern: 'I am strangely unmoved by this announcement. The world is left a victim of chaos, great uncertainty and heinous turpitude.'

A Southwark housewife, Doris Pratt, was relieved the war was over, but reflected the view of many when she said: 'At least the whole thing was finished then. But there was also the bomb and that . . . I think that was quite a shock. Yes, I think that made us feel a bit different.' In the Dulwich home of children's author Irene Byers, they could not bear to mention the atom bomb: 'We do not talk about it.' Harley Street doctor Anthony Weymouth was appalled, confiding in his diary:

I was shocked by the news that this frightful new weapon had been dropped on Hiroshima, even though I realised that it saved many Allied lives . . . When I read that we had wiped out an entire city by an atom bomb I asked myself whether we had not by this act lowered our principles to the level of the Germans. Could we not have warned the Japanese that we possessed a weapon capable of causing more widespread devastation than the largest bomb ever dropped? Could we not have added that we intended to use it on one of, say, six towns at the expiration of a certain time? To destroy one town after due warning would at least have mitigated the act; for the deaths and disease caused by the bomb would have lain at the door of the Japanese . . . That the use of the atom bomb brought the war against Japan to a speedy end cannot be disputed. But could not its use have been tempered by a little more humanity?

The end of the war with Japan meant that there were to be two days' holiday. Housewives queued in their thousands for food to tide them over, as the shops would be closed. As usual, they were beset by shortages. One Hammersmith mother of five even went as far as Baker Street to procure a loaf of bread. Thousands who had not heard the news set off for work as usual, probably wondering why the trains were running a Sunday service, and had to return, in a reverse rush hour, when they heard that it was a public holiday. They added to the chaos of thousands heading for the West End. A clippie said she had given up collecting fares or regulating the numbers on the bus. There were no taxis and some were afraid to go into the tube because of the unwieldy crowds.

That morning the King and Queen set off from Buckingham Palace in an open carriage in light drizzle for the State Opening of the new Labour-dominated Parliament. 'Chips' Channon attended the State Opening as a member of the Opposition:

Up betimes, wearing morning clothes and top hat. I drove through immense crowds to the House of Commons, which met in St Stephen's Hall. I went at once to the Lords, where I had an excellent place. It was crowded with peers and peeresses. The Ambassadresses, all wearing extraordinary hats, sat on the right with the Duchesses . . . There was a wait; the many new Socialists looked dazed and dazzled, and I was sorry for their sake that the peers were not in robes. At last the royal procession entered, led by the Heralds, the King in an Admiral's uniform and with his cap on. The Queen, in aquamarine blue, though dignified and gracious, was dwarfed by her Mistress of the Robes, the Duchess of Northumberland, who looked far the more regal of the two. The Crown was carried on a cushion. HM read out his speech, which announced the end of the war, and mentioned the nationalisation of the mines and of the Bank of England. His voice was clear, and he spoke better than usual and was more impressive. But they say that the word Berlin had been substituted for Potsdam which he could not have articulated.

Apparently Mrs Churchill had not been able to squeeze into

the crowded Chamber. 'How are the mighty fallen!' Channon concluded.

Later, in the House of Commons, the new Prime Minister Clement Attlee paid tribute to the King's courage throughout the war and to the Queen. Winston Churchill, now Leader of the Opposition, gave thanks for Britain's 'crowning deliverance'. Once more the members trooped out to St Margaret's Westminster to offer thanks for victory and the end of the war.

Towards midday the sun came out. Anthony Heap noted: 'The inevitable crowds gathered en masse in Trafalgar Square, Piccadilly Circus and Buckingham Palace listening to music emanating from loud speakers. But otherwise the rejoicing seemed to be rather subdued. Just thousands of weary looking people wandering around the streets or sprawling on the grass in the parks.'

Sir Alexander Cadogan noted in his diary: 'London not at its best, with scores of thousands of morons wandering about.' As the *Daily Mail* reporter Harry Proctor described it, London 'went crazy celebrating'. He took an hour to press through the crowd from Long Acre to Great Windmill Street. It was impossible to penetrate the crowd from there to Eros. He made a wager of £1 to two policemen to do it and they came back utterly defeated. There were groups dancing the cancan and 'Knees up, Mother Brown'. It was impossible to get into or out of a pub, but supplies were anyway low – so much so that an American sergeant was heard to say that it was worse than Prohibition. Hawkers were selling flags for as much as seven shillings and Victory whistles for five.

The day lacked the surge of spontaneous relief and joy that had erupted in May. John Lehmann was in the crowd at Piccadilly Circus:

One longed for bands and music everywhere; but it was, after all, a totally unrehearsed occasion, and people found their own haphazard way of giving vent to their feelings, as if scarcely able to believe that the long, long horror was over at last, bemused in their joy, with exhaustion suddenly coming over them. There were sailors giving girls endless, passionate kisses in the middle of the street; here and there people threw fire crackers; climbed lamp-posts; occasionally burst out singing, exclaimed to one another delightedly at the display of the searchlights; and most extraordinary of all, suddenly made dancing rings, performing strange, impromptu, atavistic steps, as they might have when the news of Waterloo, or of the Armada's defeat came through; then wandering on again.

Of course, the celebrations might have been more muted because, in the words of Tom Pocock, 'the war in South-East Asia and the Pacific had been a distant nightmare; a dark cloud on the horizon of young men who expected to be drafted there. But it had never gripped the popular imagination.' Pocock was alone in London and sad about the many contemporaries who had lost their lives in the conflict:

I wandered alone through the crowded streets to Buckingham Palace where the King and Queen were again appearing on the floodlit balcony. Probably due to solitary drinks in packed pubs, I was in a maudlin mood and began to think of contemporaries who had been killed. Until now, they had not seemed far away; it was almost as if they had been posted to some infinitely remote, but glorious, theatre of war. But today they suddenly seemed to belong to the past, fading swiftly into pale sepia images like old school photographs. Most had been my elders and news of their deaths in bombers over Germany, in torpedoed ships and in unspecified violence on various battlefronts had arrived over five years. It had often been difficult to accept because these worshipped heads of school houses, and immortals of the Upper Sixth, had seemed indestructible.

In the evening the King made a broadcast. Then the leaders of the new Labour Government, Clement Attlee, Herbert Morrison and Ernest Bevin, appeared on the balcony of the Ministry of Health, just as Churchill had done over two months before. Attlee was making a speech, but no one could hear what he was saying and he was continuously interrupted with shouts of 'We want Churchill!'

Throughout the day boys had dragged wood from bomb sites to light bonfires. After dark effigies of the still living Emperor Hirohito of Japan found himself perched beside the dead German dictator on top of the bonfires. London was lit up as it had rarely been lit up before. There were dances and fun fairs in local parks. Clapham Common had a massive fair with dodgems and helter skelters, although the authorities forbade the lighting of a huge bonfire on Streatham Common, in case the participants resorted to ripping out the fences surrounding the allotments for firewood.

After the relief that the war was over, there was the inevitable reaction at the end of a colossal task – a deep feeling of anticlimax. When on the brink of peace Mass-Observation asked one Londoner if he felt optimistic about the future, his reply summed up the prevalent mood: 'No, I don't, I feel it's going to be the beginning of dreadful problems – it'll be something for the fighting to stop, but it's going to be a terrible time.'

Around the victory celebrations there was a general feeling of relief – relief from the blackout and the bombing, relief on the part of servicemen that they would not, after all, be sent to the Far East to fight the Japanese island to island in a blood-drenched path to Tokyo. There was an upsurge of hope for the future with minds fixed on impending reunions, the return of pretty clothes and ample meals. But this feeling of relief was short-lived. As early as mid June, when Mass-Observation asked a selection of Londoners how they felt about the peace, only one in seven said they were happy or elated. A third said they felt no different from during the war, while a quarter were worried – about everything from the international situation to the prospect of the coming winter with its inevitable fuel shortages.

Days, even hours after the last victory bonfire had died down, hope gave way to doubt, distrust and bewilderment. Mass-Observation noted that people were regretting the disappearance of the camaraderie of wartime life and a resurgence of ill will and backbiting among all classes. Dominating everything was the feeling of sheer blind weariness, as well as irritation at the continued shortages, discomforts and uncertainties of life. People expected the benefits of peace to be immediate and, of course, they were not. A 40-year-old London man said: 'Oh, it does make you fed up with it all. All we've stood, and all the women of London have stood, and then having to line up now at the baker's and green-grocer's and cut down on the milk because of the evacuees coming back. And when you can't get a glass of beer nor a packet of cigarettes – why, I'd sooner have the war back again, if this is the peace!'

It was hard to pick up the threads of life hastily dropped six years before. After the nation had devoted all its energies in a sustained campaign to waging total war for so long, there was a general feeling of lethargy. As one young woman expressed it, 'I just don't feel interested . . . I've had no interest in anything since VE Day.'

Nor did victory bring a sense of well-earned relaxation. There was a fear that peace would be short-lived, that there would be another war before long. As Noël Coward, who like Tom Pocock was 'feeling desolate remembering all the people who have gone', expressed it: 'I wonder how many years of *soi-disant* peace lie ahead of us . . . I wish I had more feeling about it. My mind seems unable to take it in . . . We shall see how sweet the face of peace looks. I cannot help visual-izing an inane, vacuous grin.' There was unease and uncer-tainty about the intentions of the Soviet Union, who had gobbled up most of Eastern Europe, including Poland, the country whose independence the British had gone to war to uphold in the first place. Most menacing of all, perhaps, was the fact that mankind now had the capacity to destroy itself.

Closer to home, when the lights went on again, it was to reveal a shabby, run-down country. People were only too aware that there were huge problems to be tackled, the most pressing of which was housing. Vast tracts of the country, its cities, its industry and its infrastructure, needed to be rebuilt, and it would take years.

No wonder the popular comedian Robb Wilton quipped in the radio sketch, *The Day Peace Broke Out*: 'Well, there's nothing to look forward to now. There was always the All Clear before.'

8
Vote for Him!

'Fancy Mr Attlee as Prime Minister – am simply furious at the unthinking ingratitude of the public . . . Felt so strongly about this that I wrote a letter of thanks to Mr Churchill – it's the least one can do'

– Miss N. V. Carver of West Norwood

When news of the Prime Minister Winston Churchill's defeat in the General Election and the Labour landslide victory began to emerge on 26 July 1945 there was widespread shock that the British people could so casually cast aside the wartime leader who had saved them from the Nazi tyranny. As Churchill himself said, there had been no other candidates for the job when he had taken it in May 1940, when Britain stood alone, with the victorious German army just 20 miles across the Channel. Now the world was amazed and incredulous at the nation's lack of gratitude.

Vere Hodgson expressed it succinctly when she noted in her diary: 'I have been stunned by the news of the Election. This country, three months after the end of the German peril, has thrown Mr Churchill on one side, as if he were a worn-out glove, and we have a Socialist Government under Mr Attlee.' Whoever voted Churchill out, she added, 'ought to be ashamed of themselves'.

There was surprise at the results, but all the signs had been there to read for a long time. Since 1942 the Gallup poll had shown a clear Labour lead, but politicians placed little credence in these allegedly scientific findings and preferred to rely on their own intuition. Even though there had been a truce between the main parties for the duration of the war, there had been by-elections where the Conservatives had suffered rebuff after rebuff, being defeated by independent left-wing candidates. The memories of unemployment in the thirties and, to some extent, the failure to eradicate the Victorian slums quickly enough despite a massive housing programme between the wars, worked against the Conservatives.

Thanks to Chamberlain's pre-war foreign policy, the Conservatives were associated with appeasement, which was now regarded as weak and shameful. *Guilty Men* by Michael Foot, Frank Owen and Peter Howard, published by the left-wing Victor Gollancz in 1940, held Chamberlain and the 'old gang' responsible for everything that had led to the defeat at Dunkirk. The message was 'never again' and it had not been forgotten. What the Conservatives, in their myopia, failed to understand was that the 1945 voter was casting his vote not so much in judgement of the last five years, but in denunciation of the ten years before that. The British people were already anti-Conservative in 1939 and nothing happened in the war years to lessen that dislike.

The Conservative majority in a Parliament elected in 1935 had been in power too long. They were complacent and out of touch with the public mood. In the wake of the disastrous Conservative results of 1945, Kenneth Lindsay, MP, wrote an article for the *Spectator* entitled, 'Why It Happened'. His view was that 'with few exceptions, the Conservative Party was made up of well-to-do young men drawn from the better-known public schools or from self-made business men. To the electors they represented a class and a privileged class.' The conduct of the Conservative campaign, such as it was, was 'put in the hands of men who were curiously inept for the colossal and imaginative task'.

It had been dubbed the people's war and now it must be the people's peace. They were to be rewarded for their participation in the war with a new, fairer social order. Plans for post-war reconstruction, growing out of the need to declare what Britain was fighting for, had come to be treated as an integral part of the war effort. As early as 1940 the

Conservative Duff Cooper, as Minister of Information, had written a paper proposing a federal Europe and the adoption of domestic policies to prevent unemployment and to promote educational opportunity. But it was the publication of the Beveridge Report in December 1942 that was the real spur. Beveridge proposed a comprehensive system of compulsory social insurance to provide for all classes a minimum standard of living 'from the cradle to the grave'. For the scheme to be viable there would have to be family allowances, a National Health Service, and policies to prevent mass unemployment. Needless to say, the report became an instant bestseller, giving war workers and the armed forces the incentive to bring about this better, post-war world.

The Conservatives' reaction to the report was divided. The innately conservative Churchill, who described Beveridge as 'an awful windbag and dreamer', at first seemed lukewarm. He was cautious, preferring to postpone any definite commitment until it was clear whether or not the plans could be afforded, especially after Britain's post-war defence needs were taken into account. Although Churchill was perhaps more in favour of the proposals than many other members of his party, he was inclined to wait upon events. If he went to the country as leader of another Coalition Government after the war, then these reforms would be vital to guarantee Labour support. The Labour Party, on the other hand, eagerly grasped Beveridge's proposals from the outset. They were keen for the Coalition Government to make a definite commitment to the reforms at once, fearing that Churchill and his party would be returned to power after the war and the opportunity lost.

The general feeling was that the Coalition Government had dragged its feet over post-war reforms and that the Conservatives were to blame. Yet Conservative ministers such as R. A. Butler at the Board of Education and Henry Willink at the Ministry of Health had worked hard at formulating post-war reforms. Butler's Education Act was passed in 1944 and Willink had prepared a White Paper on the future National Health Service. In the King's Speech in November 1944 12 bills were announced for the coming session of Parliament, including the National Health Service Bill, the National Insurance Bill, the Industrial Injury Insurance Bill, and the Family Allowances Bill, which gave every family in the land an allowance of five shillings a week, without a means test, for the second and each subsequent child under school-leaving age. All parties were pledged to this social legislation, although there was certainly some reluctance among the Conservatives at backbench and grass-roots level. When it came to the 1945 election, the electorate felt it could not trust Churchill and the Conservative Party to give their wholehearted support to the post-war welfare state with the same confidence it could Clement Attlee and the Labour Party.

Churchill was a world statesman rather than a party politician. During the war his mind had understandably been on the bigger picture, on questions of strategy, and much of his concern now was taken up with the new Soviet threat in Europe. He had enjoyed being at the head of a national government and was reluctant to return to party politics. He flirted with the idea that the Coalition Government might continue through a transition period well into the peace. Like Attlee, he would have preferred not to have an election in the summer of 1945. The Conservative Party, however, wanted to press ahead with an election as soon as possible, while their greatest asset, Churchill, was still the hero of the hour. As Roy Jenkins expressed it in his biography, the Conservatives 'wanted an early cashing in of the cheque of Churchill's victory popularity'. The Labour Party feared that Churchill would be forced by his party to call a snap election, although Churchill had promised Attlee that he would not dissolve Parliament while Attlee was away at the San Francisco Conference discussing the inauguration of the United Nations Organisation. Herbert Morrison was eager to gauge Churchill's intentions:

'Three days after VE Day I went with Bevin to see Churchill to discover exactly what he was planning. It was clear that the Prime Minister was personally in favour of prolonging the life of

Parliament until after the war with Japan was over, but he confessed that he was under heavy pressure from his Party to have what amounted to a snap election some time in June. The pressure, I believe, came principally from Lord Beaverbrook and Brendan Bracken, both of whom could rely on being able to exert far more influence on the Prime Minister than most of his political friends and colleagues. There was his promise to Attlee, still out of the country, and a June election would have meant an almost immediate dissolution.

I told the Prime Minister that, all things being equal, I felt that late October would be the appropriate time. That would be a month before the life of Parliament was due to end. A new register would be in operation. Considerable numbers of troops and mobile workers would have returned home. The holiday period would be over. I added that these points in favour of an October election were made in order to enhance the chance of a fair contest adequately prepared and free from as many emotional factors as feasible.

Attlee returned from San Francisco on 16 May and immediately headed off to the party conference in Blackpool. Two days later Churchill sent messages to the leaders of all three parties – Clement Attlee of Labour, Sir Archibald Sinclair of the Liberal Party and Ernest Brown of the National Liberals – a message repeating the proposal he had already made in his meeting with Morrison that the Coalition should continue for 2 years or until the end of the Japanese war, which it was generally believed would last for another 18 months, or accept an immediate election. Unlike Attlee, Churchill knew about the atomic bomb, although the fact that he had given Britain's consent to its use, without reference to the Cabinet, does not mean that it was influencing his decision about when to hold the election. In fact, it may have slipped his mind altogether. There was no certainty that the atom bomb would succeed in bringing about a speedy end to the war, although the chances were that it would. While Attlee and Bevin seemed inclined to accept Churchill's proposal, Morrison now argued strongly that 'it would be better for the country to have a strong Party government than a wobbly coalition'.

Only Ernest Brown was willing to postpone the election until the end of the war with Japan. In his official reply to Churchill on 21 May, Attlee made a counter proposal to serve in the Coalition until the end of October. This at least would allow time for the electoral register, which had closed on 31 January 1945, to be updated. As it stood, many evacuees who had lost their homes and men and women who had been directed to work in other parts of the country would not be able to vote, because they had not been included on the register of the area to which they were now returning. The counter-proposal was not acceptable to Churchill and the Conservatives.

On 23 May Churchill resigned and disbanded the Coalition. The King asked him to head an interim government, which the press dubbed a 'Caretaker' government, and Churchill quickly appointed a new team of ministers. He announced that Parliament, which had sat continuously since 1935, should be dissolved by Royal Proclamation on 15 June, with polling day to take place on 5 July. Nearly three weeks would elapse before the services' overseas vote could be counted, so that the results were not expected to be finally confirmed until Friday, 27 July.

The Labour Party was well prepared for the fray and there was an immediate plunge into party politics, with each side trading insults. Most people could not understand why there was suddenly such a rush. Gwladys Cox wrote in her diary: 'I could not see why we could not continue with a National Government, this would check the hot heads on both sides. It was distressing, too, to hear the disparaging remarks the candidates themselves addressed to each other. Coming so soon after the team spirit in the war years, once again the bickering began. Surely we were not going to fight among ourselves.'

To the Conservatives, it was inconceivable that the nation would vote against the man who had won the war, and it has to be said that to a considerable degree the Labour Party shared this view. It was ironic how dependent the Conservatives were on Churchill, who had been something of an outcast in the party during the thirties and who even as leader seemed more interested in the politics of the Coalition, balancing the Labour and Conservative elements, than he was in the organisation of the Conservative Party or in defining its policy. The Conservatives were gambling everything on Churchill, but they were wrong. The electorate sussed what the politicians – with the notable exception of Lord Woolton, who expressed doubts to Lord Beaverbrook about Churchill's suitability – failed to recognise. Churchill was undoubtedly a great war leader to whom the nation owed its gratitude, but he was by no means the right man for the peace. At over seventy he might reasonably be considered to be too old to be Prime Minister. There was no doubt that by the end of the war he was mentally and physically exhausted, which was only too obvious in the run-up to the election and during the campaign.

With the exception of the *Daily Mirror*, the *Herald* and the *Manchester Guardian*, the press seemed to see the election as 'some sort of Roman triumph for the conquering hero'. Among the middle and professional classes, Churchill's ascendancy was assumed to be absolute, but as results would show, this assumption was outdated. Labour had broadened its class appeal very considerably. In his book, *The Middle Class Vote*, John Bonham sought to chart the growth of Labour support in the higher, middle, and lower-middle income areas of London, which he dubbed 'Westendia', 'Suburbia' and 'Blackcoatia'. There was a 19.8 per cent swing towards Labour in 'Westendia', 18 per cent in 'Suburbia' and 8.5 per cent in 'Blackcoatia'. There were also increases in the working-class areas of 17.1 per cent in 'Artisania' and 14.6 per cent in 'Eastendia'. For Churchill and the Conservatives embarking on their 1945 election campaign in the bomb-damaged streets of London, with its chronic, desperate housing shortage, allegiance was anything but certain.

The war had radicalised people. They had not made all these sacrifices to return to the same old way of life as before the war. For sacrifices, they had been led to believe, there would be rewards. The war had been a democratising process. Rationing had succeeded in instilling in people's minds the idea of fair shares for all: as Churchill's daughter Sarah pointed out to him, the socialist policies that had been introduced in wartime had proved to be a force for good, not harm. People of all classes had mixed and worked together, in the forces, the Home Guard and Civil Defence, the Land Army, the fire and ambulance services, the WVS and on fire-watching duty. The services had encouraged a certain amount of social mobility, with young men of ordinary background becoming officers. Evacuation played its part in opening the eyes of the comfortably off to the deprivations of life in the urban slums. There were few who did not want to see a fairer, more equitable society after the war.

The key issues, as far as the electorate was concerned, were housing, full employment, social security and international co-operation. The Conservative manifesto, *Mr Churchill's Declaration of Policy to the Electors*, simply rehearsed the principal promises of the Coalition White Papers: full employment, social security and a National Health Service. The priorities listed in each of Churchill's broadcasts were markedly different from those expressed by the electorate. The five great tasks as he saw them were the completion of the war against Japan, demobilisation, the restarting of industry, the rebuilding of exports, and the four-year plan of 'food, work and home'. Thus, housing came last on Churchill's agenda, whereas for the electorate it came first. Labour treated the war as done and dusted and focused on the future, in particular on the material needs of the average family, making the exaggerated promise that it would build 5 million houses in quick time.

Where the Conservatives and Labour drastically diverged was over the question of public versus private enterprise. As an advocate of the free market, Churchill could not wait to remove the wartime restrictions which had governed every aspect of trade and industry. The Labour Party, on the other hand, was wedded to the idea of economic planning and argued for the retention of the controls that were so conveniently in place. In its policy document, *Let Us Face the Future*, Labour pledged itself to nationalise the Bank of England, fuel and power, inland transport, and iron and steel. So inured had the British public become to state control, that opinion polls showed that the majority were largely in favour of its continuance, at least while the country made the long transition from war to peace.

Herbert Morrison maintained that the election was fought before a 'mature and thoughtful public' who had 'an honest and determined awareness of the issues at stake'. The evidence of this is less than convincing. Through ABCA, the Army Bureau of Current Affairs, servicemen had long been practised at examining and discussing the issues, but even then there was a remarkable degree of ignorance. Helen Bentwich, who had given over 400 talks to men and women in the forces about citizenship and the British Way and Purpose, told the *Spectator* in March 1945:

When these young men and women, typical representatives of their generation, are seen as voters in the next election their political ignorance is alarming. Being wholly uninformed about the working of the present system, they are ready to adopt any catchwords or slogans which may be in the air. Very few know anything of the local political parties in their home districts; they have little idea how a Government is chosen or of the functions of an Opposition. Many of them are unable to distinguish the work of an MP from that of a civil servant.

The servicemen and -women of 1945 had been children at the time of the previous general election in 1935. It was not altogether surprising, therefore, for a young woman to ask Bentwich, 'What's a Tory and what's a Socialist? Nobody has ever told me, and I don't know how to find out.'

Bentwich felt that the electorate's ignorance of the political system was understandable but worrying:

There are some among the younger men who have a knowledge of politics through their Trade Unions, or through some specialised study. But, within my experience, the majority of the young men, and practically all the young women, know nothing of the subject. The machinery for political education in the past has been the elections; we are paying the penalty of the political truce and of the nine-year-old Parliament. Those in the Forces are helped in their political thinking. What is happening to those in civilian life?

Writing after the Labour victory, Anthony Weymouth was also aware of the electorate's confusion, some believing that Churchill would head whichever party won power, as he had during the Coalition:

I don't for one moment believe that the twelve million people who returned Mr Attlee to power really desired wholesale nationalisation. There was an appalling ignorance as to the points at issue. I know of one soldier who told his commanding officer that he was determined to keep 'them there socialists out' so he had voted for the Labour Party. A working man gave as his reason for supporting the Socialists that he thought Churchill would have a better chance as Prime Minister with them in power than if he led the Conservatives!

General ignorance and confusion were apparent in a survey carried out in London by Mass-Observation. According to its findings, the electorate was also exhibiting profound apathy, exhaustion and cynicism. A 35-year-old working-class woman told them: 'Churchill's all right for the war job, but he's getting too old. He ought to step down and let a younger man take charge. I don't know if I'm going to vote. They've done nothing about the housing . . . I can't make up my mind what to vote for, I'll have to talk it over with my husband and I know what he'll say – he'll say they're all out to suit themselves. I don't think they do care, that's my opinion.'

There was also criticism of the timing of the election. There was a widespread belief among supporters of all parties that it was bad to have an election so soon and before the war with Japan was over. People didn't feel ready, it was all too hurried: 'Well, it's my honest opinion that the whole thing shouldn't have taken place until October. Or else after the cessation of hostilities. I don't think it was fair to rush it to this extent,' a Chelsea resident told Mass-Observation. 'The men in the fighting forces haven't had a chance to think about it, they don't know what's going on here; and a lot of them won't be able to vote, through no fault of their own. After all, they have been fighting the war; they ought to have some say in the matter.'

'I think the trouble is we're all so dog-tired that we just can't face the prospect of voting Labour,' another admitted. 'We've not got the energy to do anything against all the old racket and face a new form of government – and that's why we've all been so terribly depressed since VE Day.'

'I don't want to vote at all. I'm very much against the election, and I've never understood who foisted it on the country, and why,' someone else said. 'I simply haven't made up my mind how to vote.'

Mass-Observation's survey found that 39 out of every 100 young men and women in London were undecided about who to vote for: 'Of course I shall vote, but I don't know how yet. I think I shall go to one or two meetings and just see. My mum keeps talking against Morrison; says he was a conchie in the last war and this war he tells women of fifty to "go to it". She says you can't trust a man like that.'

'I've not taken as much interest as I should in this election, especially as this is the first time I'm using my vote, but I feel as I don't understand politics, I don't want to use my vote. The war's got us down, what with the bombing and the blackout, and the worrying about coupons and queues women like me haven't the mind to take to politics. We want to be left alone for a bit – not worrying about speeches!'

Predictably, there were complaints from people who were not on the electoral register:

I found I wasn't on the register and it was too late to have it rectified. It's quite extraordinary, because we've lived in Chelsea for fifteen months and my wife's on it all right. However, in one way I don't mind so much. It does relieve one of a certain responsibility. I feel the issues at this election are so very important, and against the dread of a Labour-controlled country and all the dreariness that would come with it or the muddle and racketeering of the Tories, I honestly feel it's very difficult to choose, so I don't altogether mind that I haven't got a vote. I'd expect to regret it whichever way I voted.

Many people were vague about what the parties stood for and let likes and dislikes of the personalities come into play. George Beardmore, who was to serve as a polling clerk in north London, had every reason to think things did not look good for Churchill, whom some considered a warmonger:

Overheard two workmen talking in the Harrow Weald teashop, a favourite rendezvous for the Council workers. Plumbers or gasfitters, I'd guess. 'Don't want him again.' A long look at the other man – so much is conveyed by looks and glances! He replied: 'Enough battles for one lifetime.' After a long pause and a sip of tea, the first man said: 'Bloody Russia', and this time looked down at the table, interested in a drop of tea that had fallen on his donkey-jacket. The second man said: 'The old cock's just aching to wave us up and at 'em again', to which the first man replied, having waited to see if the other was of the same mind: 'Catch me.'

They had been talking about Churchill and had thus agreed not to vote for him. Now multiply their little chat by tens of thousands and one gets the result of the Election. Those men weren't *for* Attlee, they were *against* Churchill who in other circles is known as the Happy Warrior.

This was long before the dawn of electioneering on television and, anyway, television did not make its reappearance until 1946, and then only in London. Radio ownership was universal, however, and listening to the radio – wireless, as it was called then – had become a national habit during the war, as families gathered round the set to hear the latest news. The BBC had won a reputation for first-class reporting and impartiality. The 1945 election would be fought very much on the radio. The BBC suspended programmes such as the highly popular *The Brains Trust*, which had frequently discussed what the post-war world should or would be like, during the electioneering period and night after night presented a series of 20-minute party political addresses after the nine o'clock News. The two main parties, the Conservatives and Labour, were allotted ten, the Liberals four, and two other groups, the Communists and the short-lived Common Wealth Party, one each. Churchill decided to do four of the Conservatives' ten, including the first and the last.

Strangely, Churchill had been slow to realise the power and reach of radio and his performances had often been lacklustre, compared with his superb and moving renditions in the House of Commons: the famous wartime speeches 'blood, toil, tears and sweat' and 'we shall never surrender' had been delivered by Churchill in the House of Commons first and read by someone else on the radio afterwards. On 4 June Churchill opened the talks with his unfortunate 'Gestapo' speech, which appalled his wife Clementine and even some fellow Conservatives. Their strongest card, the personal loyalty and respect felt for Churchill by a large proportion of the electorate, was destroyed by this speech. It certainly decided the vacillating voters to vote against him and probably lost some of those who had been loyal to the man if not the party. Churchill had never made any secret of his loathing of socialism and all manifestations of state control and now he chose to frighten voters away from Labour rather than woo them with a convincing programme of his own. In the belief that people wanted to throw off the government controls and accompanying bureaucracy which had been necessary but regrettable aspects of war, Churchill played on his well-worn libertarian card. In doing so, he went too far: 'No Socialist Government conducting the entire life and industry of the country could afford to allow free, sharp or violently worded expressions of public discontent. They would have to fall back on some sort of Gestapo, no doubt very humanely directed in the first instance.'

As Kenneth Lindsay later wrote, 'The people were looking for a policy, for a star and for hope, and they were offered dark fears and apprehension and a bogus appeal for unity.' It was hardly worthy of the great statesman, whose wartime oratory had held millions enthralled and inspired the people of occupied Europe. There was a belief at the time that Lord Beaverbrook and Brendan Bracken were behind the speech, but Churchill's Private Secretary John Colville, who had been at Chequers with the Prime Minister the weekend he wrote the speech, denies this in his memoirs. The speech might have been influenced by what Churchill had gleaned from a book published in 1944, *The Road to Serfdom*, by Professor Friedrich von Hayek of the London School of Economics. It argued that economic planning necessitated the apparatus of tyranny.

The broadcast provoked surprise and disgust and was not helped by the headline next morning in the right-wing *Daily Express*, the newspaper owned by Churchill's crony, Lord Beaverbrook: 'Gestapo in Britain if Socialists Win'. The Opinion column asked its readers: 'After ripping the Gestapo out of the still bleeding heart of Germany, will you stand for a Gestapo under another name at home?' The *Daily Herald* countered the *Express* headline with one of its own: 'A Vote for Churchill Is a Vote for Franco'.

The *Express* also made much of the notion that Attlee was a mere puppet controlled by the party chairman, Harold Laski, who happened to be chairman of the National Executive, an un-parliamentary committee. Laski had put out an unhelpful statement to the effect that Attlee's presence at the Potsdam Conference did not bind the Labour Party to the decisions reached there. Beaverbrook pounced on this evidence of the left dictating to the parliamentary Labour Party, depicting Laski as some sinister communist bogeyman, and Churchill tried to make something of it in his speeches. But the electorate did not understand what he was talking about and it only added to the woolly, confused nature of the Conservative campaign.

In the immediate aftermath of Churchill's Gestapo speech, 'Chips' Channon completely misread the reaction: 'The PM delivered a broadside against the Socialists over the wireless last night: it was a heavy pounding, certainly; and today the

Labour boys seem very depressed and dejected by Winston's trouncing. I met Attlee in the lavatory, and he seemed sunken and terrified, and scarcely smiled, though Bevin seemed gay and robust enough . . . Everyone [meaning the Conservatives] is cock-a-hoop.'

Not for long. The modest and quietly spoken Attlee was quick to retaliate with a stinging rebuke:

When I listened to the Prime Minister's speech last night in which he gave such a travesty of the policy of the Labour party, I realised at once what was his object. He wanted the electors to understand how great was the difference between Winston Churchill, the great leader in war of a united nation, and Mr Churchill, the Party Leader of the Conservatives. He feared that those who had accepted his leadership in war might be tempted out of gratitude to follow him further. The voice we heard last night was that of Mr Churchill, but the mind was that of Lord Beaverbrook.

When Mass-Observation canvassed public opinion about the speech it was obvious that Churchill's references to the Gestapo had turned voters against him and won sympathy for Attlee. 'Everyone I meet is angry and resentful and glad all at once – angry that he dare speak such lying statements into the microphone, resentful that he can make such allegations against his own countrymen, and glad that he has shown up Tory tactics, and that by one speech of abuse he shows that he has no real policy,' said a Watford man.

'I didn't think much of it,' another said. 'I'm afraid he didn't state a definite programme. He seemed to be relying on the fact that he's been a great war-leader, which isn't fair. The secret police part was rubbish. Of course, what he means is that if industry and other concerns do get nationalised we'll have so many inspectors and officials poking their noses into our affairs. But when we think of Gestapo we think of the Buchenwald and Belsen horrors and the association isn't too happy.'

'The fact that a national hero should stoop to make such public utterances as Mr Churchill has done – is all very disturbing.'

'I thought he spoke a lot of nonsense,' another stated.

'Well, what could I think of it. That a great man like Churchill should have spoken like he did.'

'It sounded childish to me. Surely he couldn't expect any grown-up person to believe what he said.'

'Scurrilous abuse if you ask me.'

'I thought that was just daft.'

The most charitable explanation for Churchill's misjudged speech was that he was obviously 'old and tired' and that 'he had too much to do, having to go off to see Stalin, etc.'

After Churchill came a series of speeches from the key figures in all parties. Attlee's straightforward and factual approach struck the right note. 'Far superior to Churchill's,' someone told Mass-Observation, 'more statesmanlike.' 'I thought he was very good and most of what he said was true,' another said, adding, 'In my opinion this election is being rushed.' Listeners told Mass-Observation that they thought Attlee, Ellen Wilkinson and Ernest Bevin all sounded 'impressive', 'sensible', 'reasonable', 'clear' and 'constructive'.

Vita Sackville-West was surprised and disappointed by Churchill's election broadcasts, writing to her husband Harold Nicolson: 'What has gone wrong with him? They are confused, woolly, unconstructive and so wordy that it is impossible to pick out any concrete impression of them. If I were a wobbler, they would tip me over to the other side.'

The joy of VE Day was short-lived. The public mood quickly turned resentful, angry even, and these feelings were focused squarely on Churchill and the Conservatives. Public opinion seemed to ignore the fact that a Coalition Government with a strong Labour contingent had been in power until just recently and was equally responsible for the miserable situation in which most Londoners were living. In working-class Fulham the mood was dark:

You ought to hear the women in the queues in North End Road – they say it's worse now than when the war was on. You've got to spend half the b—— day queuing to make a meal, and then they'll only let you have one pound of potatoes *and* they make it a condition you buy the greens as well. That ought to be stopped. Things are getting harder instead of getting easier, all because it's going abroad to feed them b—— Germans to make them strong again so that they'll plot another war. Churchill makes me sick – I've got no time for him. He says there's plenty of fish about, and then the fat ration goes down. How the hell does he expect us to fry the fish? I bet there's a purpose behind all this election business. It's all the same to me which party gets in. They all make fine speeches and do very little.

On 25 June the *Daily Mirror* took up the cause of servicemen overseas, who were complaining of a rushed election. Some of them had also been deprived of their votes owing to the confusion in the Service Register. The *Mirror*'s campaign cleverly tapped into the discontent of soldiers frustrated by the slow pace of demobilisation and the fact that many of them had no homes to return to. The paper's correspondent with the Army of Occupation in Germany claimed that soldiers had decided to write home to their wives and mothers to tell them to 'vote the soldiers' way'. The ingenious slogan 'I'll Vote for *Him*!' appeared for the first time on the front page on the 25th and was repeated every day in the run-up to the election. The newspaper also used a letter from a soldier's wife:

To the Editor
Daily Mirror

Dear Sir,
My husband won't be home to vote. He is in the CMF. He has fought against the Fascist enemy in Italy and North Africa for a better Britain – now he is denied the chance of hearing candidates give their views for a better Britain.

I shall vote for him. I know what he wants.

He wants a good house with a bit of garden. He wants a job at a fair wage, however hard the work may be. He wants a good education for his children. He wants to feel they won't have to go through what he has gone through in this war. So he wants a Parliament that will be faithful to our alliance with Russia and America.

How my husband would despise these politicians who are trying to scare us and stir up our fears. I can hear him laughing at those who think the world holds no promise for Great Britain unless we return to the bad old pre-war days.

If he and all his pals had not had the courage to laugh and have faith in each other after Dunkirk where would we be now?

My husband would say, 'Vote for Courage'. I shall. I shall vote for him.

(Mrs) C. Gardiner, Ilford, Essex

The *Mirror* used the letter to galvanise large numbers of women, many of whom had never voted or taken any interest in politics before, to vote: 'Is your husband in the Forces, your son, your brother, your sweetheart? Then vote for HIM. Look at his letters again. Make up your mind what, in the circumstances of a General Election, he would have been likely to do if he had been at home. And vote for HIM!'

'MORE THAN 200,000 BRITISH FIGHTING MEN DIED TO MAKE THIS FREEDOM AND THIS ELECTION POSSIBLE' the paper thundered a few days later.

No hint was given in the 'Vote for Him' campaign as to which way the soldier would like his women to vote, but from reading the *Mirror*'s other pages the stance was obvious. Five points were consistently stressed: This was a trick election; many voters would be disenfranchised; the Tory stunts were obscuring the real issues of housing, full employment, social security and international co-operation; the Tory Party was not fit to rule – it wanted to go back to the 'good old days'; controls might be tiresome, but there was no other way in which the public could be sheltered from 'the avarice of profiteers and monopolists'.

The *Mirror*'s political cartoonist, Zec, whom Herbert Morrison – his past differences over the seaman on the raft cartoon forgotten – had hired to draw propaganda cartoons for the Labour Party, portrayed Churchill looking at two empty picture frames headed 'Our Great Prime Minister'. One continued, 'who led us back to the good old days of Tory domination, money-grabbing, etc' and the other, 'who led us to victory in the cause of a brave new world'.

Churchill canvassed in the London constituencies on 2, 3 and 4 July, meeting the Conservative candidates as he passed through north and west London on the Monday, east London on the Tuesday evening and south London on Wednesday. More often than not the crowds were hostile. On the night of 3 July he was booed and heckled when addressing an audience of 20,000 at Walthamstow Stadium. Ironically, he was thanking Londoners for their staunch courage in a war in which 1 in every 130 Londoners had died: 'The triumph which this great city has gained by her conduct in the war – Greater London – is without parallel in the whole world.'

There was a strong opposition element in the crowd at St John's Hill, Clapham. As Churchill pledged the Conservatives to a great programme of social reform, a heckler interrupted with, 'You haven't got one.'

At Ernest Bevin's constituency at Central Wandsworth, Churchill told the crowd that he felt in his bones that he was going to win. 'I think you must settle this matter now,' he told voters. 'We want a definite decision. We want a strong united government with a substantial, trustworthy majority. How else are we going to get the houses built, the peace made, the Japanese war finished?'

'By voting Labour,' came the response.

The mood was ugly, even violent. At Tooting Bec in south London a boy threw a firework at the Prime Minister, which narrowly missed his face. As the boy was led away by the police, Churchill called, 'Don't hurt him.'

In north London John Sweetland remembers: 'I watched Churchill campaigning at Mornington Crescent, Camden Town, his open car surrounded by a rather hostile crowd. The great man was standing, raised hat in his left hand, cigar in his right. From an onlooker came a cry, "'Ere, Winston, try one of *our* fags!" followed by a Woodbine packet hurled at Churchill, who turned the other cheek as his car drove on.'

At Norwood, Churchill was greeted by his daughter Diana and son-in-law Duncan Sandys. There was a mixed reception and when Churchill mentioned housing there was loud booing.

At Lewisham High Street near the Clock Tower, the scene of one of the worst V-2 incidents of the war, people stood on ruined buildings to see the Prime Minister. Cheering was loud, but there was considerable booing when Churchill referred to Herbert Morrison:

I am going to say a word about the tragic event which occurred here. I understand that Mr Morrison has made a statement to the effect that I am responsible for it. All I can tell you is that, as Minister of Defence, I take full responsibility for everything that has happened in the course of the defence of London. Don't you think it rather a cowardly and un-British thing for a Cabinet Minister, sitting with his colleagues and taking part in the proceedings, to try to throw the blame of a particular incident on someone else, but it is thoroughly characteristic of Mr Morrison himself. Of all the colleagues I have lost he is the one I am least sorry to have seen the last of. I hope that Lewisham will throw this intruder out. He only came here because he ran away from a Communist [at his Hackney constituency].

Morrison described the remarks as spiteful and petty and unworthy of the leader of a political party, let alone a Prime Minister.

Churchill was still making unfortunate references to the Gestapo. At Lewisham he repeated that if socialism were established in Britain in a totalitarian form, it could be defended only by some sort of Gestapo. When a man standing near him objected, Churchill retorted: 'I see an ugly look on your face. It looks just like what a *Gestapo* would resemble.'

Camberwell Green, a Labour stronghold, gave him a hostile reception. Thousands of people massed in the roadway and yelled and jeered as his car came into view, and it was unable to make any headway until uniformed police intervened to force the crowd back. Outside the Central Southwark Conservative headquarters on the Walworth Road he made an impromptu stop, but there again the crowd was hostile and he was refused a hearing. There was a terrific din of catcalls and boos. The police had to come to the rescue again. It was only as he approached Downing Street that there were cries of 'Good Old Winnie' and he raised his hat to shouts and cheers.

On 4 July the *Daily Mirror* printed across the whole of its front page a final message from the editor, Harry Guy Bartholomew:

> Tomorrow the future of Britain and of yourselves is at stake, your hearths and homes, your families, your jobs, your dreams. Vote for Them!
>
> For five long years the lusty youth of this great land has bled and died.
>
> Vote for Them!
>
> You women must think of your men. For five years you have depended on them. Tomorrow they depend on you. The choice is plain: to march forward to a better and happier Britain or turn back to the dangers that led us to the brink of disaster.
>
> You know which way your men would march.
>
> Vote for Them!

The slogan tapped into the camaraderie of the troops and the sense of wartime collectivism that still prevailed. Voting for 'them', for someone other than oneself, was a vote against the selfish capitalism of the past, which had benefited the few rather than the many.

On 5 July the *Mirror* repeated a cartoon by Zec which had originally appeared on VE Day. A war-scarred soldier, depicted against a background of blasted houses, dead citizens, and the ruination of modern warfare, held in his hand a laurel wreath labelled, 'Victory and peace in Europe'. The caption read: 'Here you are – don't lose it again!' It was a subtle reminder that after the last war the fighting men had been let down: the promised homes fit for heroes had not materialised.

"Here you are! Don't lose it again!"

To impress the message further the inside pages ran stories under headlines such as 'Says They Must Give up Unborn Baby – They Can't Find a Home' and 'Wife and DCM Husband Room Two Miles Apart – Grandma Has Rest of Family'.

It was polling day and, still impervious to the mood of the electorate, Beaverbrook's *Daily Express* was already proclaiming a Conservative victory: 'They Have Won'. Nothing could be further from the truth.

On the morning of 26 July it was already apparent to Churchill that he had lost, but the massive scale of the Conservative defeat only began to emerge later in the day. Labour secured its biggest victory in London, polling a total of 754,531 votes against 504,568 for the Conservatives and increasing its representation from 28 to 49 seats. The Conservatives retained Chelsea, Hampstead, Holborn, Kensington South, Paddington South, St George's Westminster, St Marylebone, Streatham, Abbey Westminster, and one of the two City of London seats. Labour took 21 seats from the Conservatives, including Balham and Tooting, Battersea South, Camberwell NW, Clapham, Fulham East, Greenwich, Hackney North, Hammersmith South, Islington East, Kensington North, Lewisham East, Lewisham West, Norwood, Paddington North, St Pancras North, St Pancras SE, St Pancras SW, Stoke Newington, Woolwich West and Dulwich.

On a national scale, more than 33 million people had been entitled to vote, including nearly 3 million servicemen whose officers had managed to arrange for their names to be placed on the service register. Of these, 1,700,653 voted either directly, by post, or by proxy and constituted just over 7 per cent of all votes cast. Many of them voted Labour and the Conservatives were only saved from further defeat by the fact that over 1 million service people did not bother to vote. Many young servicemen and -women were casting their votes for the first time: 61 per cent of them voted Labour.

All told, 12 million voted Labour and 10 million Conservative. In the House, the Conservatives' seats were reduced from 358 to 198 and the number of Labour seats increased from 164 to 393, giving them an independent majority of 159 over all other parties and groups combined. The Liberal Party suffered a crushing defeat, emerging with only 12 seats. Even the architect of the great plan for the welfare state, Sir William Beveridge, who had thrown in his lot with the Liberals, lost his seat. The Labour and Liberal parties did not oppose Churchill in his own constituency at Woodford, but 10,000 votes were cast for an Independent there; Churchill won with a 7,000 majority. His foreign secretary, Anthony Eden, retained his seat, but 29 Conservative ministers of the Caretaker Government were defeated, including the First Lord of the Admiralty, the old Churchill crony Brendan Bracken, Churchill's son-in-law Duncan Sandys, who had latterly been Minister of Works, and the future Prime Minister Harold Macmillan, who had held his first Cabinet post in the Caretaker Government as Air Minister. In what was left of his bomb-shattered constituency of Limehouse in the East End, which he had held since 1922, Clement Attlee won with a comfortable majority of 16,000.

It was the third Labour Government of the century but the first with a clear majority. When the results were announced the mood was one of elation, surprise and bewilderment. A Tory lady in the Savoy Hotel was absolutely stunned: 'But this is terrible – *they've* elected a Labour Government and *the country* will never stand for that.'

A *Daily Mail* reporter went out to hear the people's reactions to the momentous news. 'Quite right too,' a taxi driver from Kennington told him, 'now perhaps I shall get a house. I was bombed out in 1941 and my wife and I have been living in one room ever since.'

Someone in a pub told the reporter: 'The country's seen daylight and about time too. Now let's get the boys home again, and carry on where we left off.'

An engineer from Mill Hill was cynical: 'It won't make any difference, but I hope the Socialists bring the income tax down!'

A clippie hoped: 'Now perhaps we shall get more money.'

The manager of a big West End restaurant was confused: 'I can hardly believe it yet. Everyone told me the Conservatives had got in. What on earth happened?'

A newspaper vendor in the Strand said, 'I don't care who won. I sold all my papers like hot cakes,' while a barmaid in Leicester Square was equally indifferent: 'I was not on the register, so I had no vote and I don't understand what it is all about anyway.'

An officer in a cinema queue was equivocal: 'I voted Conservative, but if these Labour fellows can speed up demob more power to their elbow. Good luck to them!'

An officer in the Ritz was confident that it wouldn't last: 'It's only temporary. When the Socialists have made a mess of it, the Tories will be back stronger than ever. It happened before, and it will happen again.'

A flower seller in the Strand: 'Ernie Bevin ought to be Prime Minister. There's a man for you.'

A housewife from Ealing expressed regret: 'What a shame to treat Mr Churchill that way. It must be breaking his heart.'

At 7 p.m. Churchill, cigar in hand, arrived at Buckingham Palace in his chauffeur-driven Rolls, giving his trademark V sign to the people waiting at the gates. He tendered to the King his resignation as Prime Minister, First Lord of the Treasury and Minister of Defence. The King wanted to offer him the Order of the Garter, which Churchill refused, saying that he could hardly accept it when the nation had just given him the Order of the Boot. Shortly afterwards, Mr Attlee arrived at the palace, driven by his wife in a Standard Ten – the sharply contrasting style heralding in a greyer, more proletarian face of government. As Attlee entered the King's presence to kiss hands, the King noticed that 'He seemed very surprised indeed.'

Dining at Number 10 that evening Churchill, according to what Harold Nicolson learned from friends, had uttered, 'Not one word of bitterness; not a single complaint of having been treated with ingratitude; calm, stoical resignation – coupled with a shaft of amusement that fate could play so dramatic a trick, and a faint admiration for the electorate's show of independence.'

As he told Captain Pim: 'They are perfectly entitled to vote as they please. This is democracy. This is what we've been fighting for.' He was not inclined to blame the people for their decision; indeed, he made an excuse for them: 'They've had a very hard time.'

Hot on the heels of Churchill's defeat, millions of pounds were wiped off share values in the worst slump the London Stock Exchange had known since the fall of France in 1940. The heaviest losses were in the industries the socialists planned to nationalise, such as the railways, coal and steel, as well as in radios, cars and breweries. However, a few days later 'Chips' Channon, whose shares had dipped £5,000 in value, reported that the market had rallied: 'Evidently it does not fear the Socialist Government, now that the first shock has worn off.'

The Labour Party was fortunate in that its leading players had five years' experience in administration in the Coalition Government behind them. Labour had come to look like a truly national party. Within 24 hours of his victory, Attlee made the key appointments in the new Government. In spite of his trade union background and experience as Minister of Labour and National Service, Ernest Bevin became Foreign Secretary. Herbert Morrison, formerly Home Secretary and Minister of Home Security, replaced Lord Woolton as Lord President of the Council and Leader of the House of Commons. Arthur Greenwood was to be Lord Privy Seal. Hugh Dalton, formerly at the Board of Trade, became Chancellor of the Exchequer, while Stafford Cripps took the Board of Trade. Sir William Jowitt, whom Bevin had entrusted with the demobilisation plans in 1942 and which had latterly been the responsibility of R. A. Butler, was to be Lord Chancellor.

On 1 August 'Chips' Channon took his seat as the Member for Southend, 'stunned and shocked by the country's treachery, and extremely surprised by my own survival'. As well he might be. A man who could boast a royal duke and duchess and an assorted coterie of European crowned heads among his close friends was obviously going to be out of sympathy with the new regime:

I went to Westminster to see the new Parliament assemble, and never have I seen such a dreary lot of people. I took my place on the Opposition side, the Chamber was packed and uncomfortable, and there was an atmosphere of tenseness and even bitterness. Winston staged his entry well, and was given the most rousing cheer of his career, and the Conservatives sang 'For he's a Jolly Good Fellow'. Perhaps this was an error in taste, though the Socialists went one further, and burst into the 'Red Flag' singing it lustily; I thought that Herbert Morrison and one or two others looked uncomfortable.

The note of nervous levity was maintained when the new Speaker, the Conservative Colonel Clifton-Brown, announced that he hoped he had been elected as Speaker of the House of Commons and not as director of some musical chorus.

The problems facing the Labour Government were immense. On the evening of his defeat Churchill said, 'The new Government will have terrible tasks. Terrible tasks.' They were not made any easier less than three weeks after they came to power by the abrupt termination of the Lend-Lease agreement with the United States right after VJ Day, while British forces were still in the Far East and without the consultation that might have been accorded Britain if the two old allies, Churchill and Roosevelt, had still been around. It has been described as Britain's financial Dunkirk. It was certainly 'the cold douche to awaken the dreamer'.

While appreciating that Lend-Lease had been a life-line in the darkest hour of the war, most British people were surprised by its cancellation without notice. They told Mass-Observation that it was 'a bit too businesslike' – shoddy behaviour on the part of a former ally: 'Well, I shouldn't say we wanted charity from the Yanks. But it's come a bit suddenly and a bit hastily; they might have held it over for a month or two – given us a little warning in advance. Pity Roosevelt's dead. It wouldn't have happened like this in his time. I think it is very serious for us.'

Another voiced a fear that enemy propaganda had been right after all:

Well, now, do you recall what they kept saying on the German wireless earlier on in the war? They were always saying we'd sold out to America and we'd find ourselves bankrupt at the end of the war. And it looks to me as if they were right. People didn't believe it at the time they thought it was just propaganda. Well, I think the people at the top must have known, but they kept the country in the dark. I don't know why they're pretending to be so surprised now.

There was a popular suspicion that capitalist America had terminated Lend-Lease so suddenly because it would have no truck with the Utopian vision of Britain's new Labour Government, with its socialist principles and promised – expensive – welfare state. 'As for America,' commented a London woman, 'I think they're behaving disgustingly. I'm not up to the details, but everybody is saying they've done it against our Labour Government – that's the long and the short of it.'

The Lend-Lease Act had been passed by Congress in 1941 and entitled an 'Act to Promote the Defence of the United States'. When the United States entered the war in December 1941 Lend-Lease became the instrument by which America was to make a contribution proportionate to the resources and capacity of the United States to the common war effort of the Allies. It presupposed equality of sacrifice, resting on the principle that every ally should contribute the utmost of which it was capable in the common cause. Up to March 1945 Britain had received Lend-Lease supplies amounting to £3,194 million and in reciprocal Lend-Lease had contributed £838 million by the end of 1944.

The Lend-Lease agreement had enabled Britain to shut down the manufacture of goods for export which it would otherwise have had to continue in order to pay for imports, and to concentrate its whole effort on the war. According to Roosevelt's successor, President Truman, Lend-Lease enabled

Britain to put 91,000 more men in the field, which was just as valuable to the common cause as the shipments of food across the Atlantic.

The war transformed Britain from a creditor to a debtor country. Up to 1941 Britain had paid America £1 million for war supplies on a cash and carry basis and in the course of the war as a whole sold foreign assets amounting to £2 million. In addition, Britain had incurred £3,500 million of short-term debts to its dominions and other countries, India being its biggest creditor with well over £1 billion owing to it.

The Government also borrowed from the British people. Aggressive campaigns ensured that surplus cash was siphoned into National Savings Certificates: savings weeks became regular fixtures in wartime life, drawing attention to their cause – building a Spitfire or a warship, for instance – by public parades and civic events. Surprisingly large amounts of money were raised from the least likely sources. In September 1945 thousands of people converged on Trafalgar Square, where a German rocket was on display, for the opening of Thanksgiving Savings Week; the money was 'to win the peace'. The target was £125 million but by the end of the week this had been exceeded by £15 million, the people of seven south London boroughs alone raising £5 million.

What the Government could not secure in the more kindly form of National Savings it took in compulsory borrowing in a system of post-war credits. Cuts in personal allowances to increase the amount of tax people paid – and by now 12,500,000 people were liable to pay income tax at 50 per cent of earnings – would be reimbursed by the Government some time after the war. By 1945 the sum the Government owed the people was £765 million and it was not until the seventies that it could bring itself to pay everyone back.

An article in the *Spectator* outlined the immediate problem: 'We have exhausted a great part of our gold reserves, we are overdrawn on foreign accounts, we have to re-equip and get going our export industries, and meet the huge expense of bringing back and demobilising our overseas forces.'

It was no accident that the Americans invented the term 'VE Day' to signal the moment when their industry would switch to peacetime production. The United States had anyway kept up a steady stream of civilian production during the war, ready for the day when they would capture the world's export markets. It knew it must export to avoid the mass unemployment which had dogged it through the twenties and thirties. Britain was slower off the mark, taken by surprise by the sudden end of the war, to which for the last four to five years it had directed *all* its efforts. Industry and business were finding it hard to make the turnaround, hampered by acres of red tape, and the slow pace of demobilisation.

'America is a going concern,' the *Spectator* article continued, 'fully equipped for peace enterprise. We are not, and cannot be till we have brought back our men, imported raw materials, and switched over our industry to productive enterprise. Against outgoings, which Mr Attlee said were £2,000,000,000 a year on the eve of Japan's defeat, we have only exports today at the rate of £350,000,000.'

Food, tobacco, petrol, machinery, raw materials such as cotton for clothing and wood for housing were all pouring into the country and adding to the debt mountain. Putting a curb on demand by rationing and imposing restrictions on house building would help only so far. Somehow imports had to be paid for. Exports would have to increase by 50 per cent – eventually 75 per cent – over the 1939 level, against increased competition and an uncertain shipping situation. For civilians working all hours, therefore, there could be no immediate rewards. Give or take some tinkering in the budget to take effect in April of the following year, income tax would remain at wartime levels, while the cost of living was getting dearer. Almost everything Britain produced was now to be for export, to bring in much needed dollars and to close 'the dollar gap'. And, meanwhile, the Labour Government was under intense, immediate pressure to relieve the housing shortage – the first great problem of the peace – and was committed to an expensive programme of social welfare.

The renowned economist John Maynard Keynes was despatched to the United States to negotiate a massive loan for Britain. As Sir Alexander Cadogan, who had just seen his report on the financial prospects of the country, commented, 'It is certainly grim reading. There are terrible times ahead for any government in this country.' Opinion was divided about Britain going as a beggar to its former ally. The terms of a loan were bound to be vigorous and restricting, with British and Commonwealth markets having to be thrown open to American goods and American paymasters clipping Labour's proposed spending on health, housing and education. Would Britain not do better to manage alone, or find some other way? Anthony Weymouth confided his worries in his diary:

Opinion in Britain is divided on the question of the American loan. Some say that it will place us in an unfavourable position with regard to our dominions and colonies and, at the rate our government is spending, we shall not be able to repay it. The 'anti-loaners' are positive in their conviction that had we refused the terms offered, in a very short time the Americans would have come to us cap-in-hand asking us to accept a loan on almost any terms so as to find a market for their manufactured goods . . . If the loan is refused, we shall have increased austerity and an even greater shortage of goods. Several business men have expressed to me the hope that it will not materialise, saying that we shall gain more in the long run through self-denial now than by accepting the loan and disturbing inter-Empire trade.

After tough, prolonged negotiations – which probably contributed to Keynes's death five months later – it was agreed in December 1945, and debated in the House almost on Christmas Eve, that the United States would lend Britain £1,100 million, of which the amount required to discharge Britain's Lend-Lease obligations was £162,500,000, leaving an available sum of £937,500,000. Interest at a rate of 2 per cent was to be charged after 31 December 1951 and Britain was given 50 years to repay the debt. Sixty years later, it has still to pay off the last of the loan.

The loan still had to be sanctioned by Congress. In Washington with the British Treasury delegation, R.H. Brand deplored the whole business, writing to Robert Barrington-Ward, the editor of *The Times*:

The North American public, not fully understanding the strength of the British case, look upon the whole matter with a very different eye from the British who regard it as perhaps the last great act in the partnership of the war. They [the Americans] regard it . . . as a request for a loan more or less on commercial terms. They do not realise what it means for the UK to be burdened for thirty, forty, fifty years with a huge debt to their Allies for the part they played in this war.

Barrington-Ward was already resigned to the inevitable: 'I think it is accepted by most people here, even by those who would have preferred (as you would yourself) a different kind of settlement that the negotiators got all that they could have got . . . The argument is virtually over here. Prevailing opinion accepts the loan as a necessity and knows that it has no practicable alternative to offer.'

In spite of post-war gloom, Labour swept the board at the local elections in November, when Labour councillors were elected in Westminster for the first time in 40 years. At by-elections before Christmas Labour actually increased its majority in the House. But as the old year gave way to the new, the first of peacetime recovery, Labour was going to have to fight the battle of the shortages against a backdrop of increasingly restive public opinion.

9
Little Hooligans

'It is a fact today that the majority of children lack parental control'

– Metropolitan Police report

'We all got the idea of these hold-ups from the pictures,' a member of a gang told the magistrate when they appeared at Clerkenwell Magistrates Court. 'Seeing the gangster films we thought we might try the same.'

The six boys had been hiding at night in the churchyard of St James's, Pentonville Road, Islington, and holding up American soldiers in the vicinity of King's Cross with dummy revolvers, relieving them of their money and valuables. Detective Sergeant Titmuss said the gang had been brought to the notice of the police as a result of several complaints made by members of the United States armed forces.

It was ironic that the boys had derived the idea of holding up America's finest from Hollywood films, the chief conveyors of a culture which the magistrate, in common with others, considered a seriously bad example to Britain's youth.

'You and your friends attribute what you have done to seeing gangster films. This is a matter which those who are agitating for children to go to the pictures on Sunday afternoons might bear in mind,' he pontificated. 'They would be so much better occupied in trying to get a better type of pictures into cinemas instead of those which put ideas into your heads.'

The youths were sent to approved school. The mother of the youngest, whose appeal against the sentence was dismissed, maintained that her John had always been a good boy and she could not understand how or why he had got mixed up with such undesirable lads.

It must have been a question which many parents, police, probation officers and magistrates were asking themselves at the end of the war. A police report explained the problem succinctly:

During the war years children have lacked fatherly control and restraint and in a large number of families mothers have obviously tended to allow too much freedom to children. It will be understood, of course, that in these cases the child was left to the care of nurseries, etc, finding invariably that when he or she returned home that some time must elapse before mother returned. This must have tended to mould the children into gangs, crime following before the child had realised the position. It is a fact today that the majority of children lack parental control and in nearly all the cases the parents are to blame.

There is no question that juvenile crime in the capital was on the increase. In 1944–5 103 boys and 260 girls were brought before the courts as being in need of care and protection. All of them were cases of neglect by the parents, often by the mother while the father was serving abroad. Ninety one boys and 90 girls were brought before the courts by their parents as being beyond control and committed to approved schools or to the care of the LCC.

The overwhelming proportion of offences for boys and girls were thefts of property, half of them by breaking into premises. There were 93 cases of theft or attempted theft of motor cars, 221 thefts of bicycles, 316 thefts from parents or employers, 84 thefts from gas and electricity meters and automatic machines. A large proportion of offenders were around 13 years of age. The incidence of juvenile delinquency among girls had risen from 11 to 20 per cent of cases, although this still represented a relatively small proportion of the population of girls under 17 in London.

The rising tide of juvenile crime was not altogether surprising. London's children had had a raw deal during the war. They had been sent back and forth between London and the reception areas in successive waves of evacuation according to the intensity of the bombing. Some never got over the 'trauma of being picked . . . a bit like a cattle market' when they first arrived in the reception areas in September 1939. The fact that some London children were verminous and had unhygienic habits grabbed the headlines. If this was a generalisation resented by the rest, it at least served to open the eyes of comfortable, middle England to the conditions in the slums. This in turn made them more receptive to the Beveridge Report when it was published in 1942. Complaints came thick and fast about the behaviour of the children and their visiting parents, but also about the grudging attitude shown by some householders – often the better off, who could use their influence and position to dodge their obligations – in the reception areas. As late as the summer of 1944 the vicar in the Somerset village where Irene Byers was staying was holding out against London evacuees being billeted on him. She was delighted to hear that he had been forced eventually to take in a group from the East End: 'I hope they give him hell!'

It has to be said that London teachers who were evacuated with their pupils did a valiant job in safeguarding their interests. They had to do a great deal more social work than the role usually entailed, keeping an eye on the children's moral welfare but also taking care of practical details, such as making sure they had adequate clothing and that their footwear was in good repair. It was up to them to liaise with the children's care organisers in London to obtain the necessary remuneration from the parents for replacement clothing and shoes. Sometimes teachers came into conflict with billeting officers, whose priorities were not the evacuees' welfare so much as safeguarding local interests and keeping in with influential people.

The phoney war and the return of 35 per cent of evacuees to London by January 1940 gave the LCC a chance to investigate the complaints emanating from the reception areas and make the necessary improvements. In future, doctors would examine children the day *before* they left London, to ensure they were free from infection and 'from vermin, nits, abrasions, lesions or scratches of any nature'. Billeting households had the right to expect that evacuees would be properly clothed, so that they did not have to dip into their own pockets – although many generously did so. The poorer London schools, prior to the first evacuation in September 1939, had distributed charity clothes to the needy, but householders in the reception areas were generally appalled at the patched and threadbare state of the children.

Whereas middle-class children could write home requesting a parcel of clothing confident that it would be forthcoming, many poorer parents were finding it difficult to supply clothing for their evacuated children. They were not used to the number of clothes regarded as normal by householders in the reception areas and, of course, it was much more expensive to clothe children when they were away from home. At home they could patch garments and hand them down from one child to another. If boots needed mending, father could do the job, saving five shillings. From 1941 the London Clothing Scheme, organised by County Hall and manned by the WVS in a series of regional depots, ensured that evacuees whose wardrobes were found to be deficient would receive the necessary clothing. The cost was met by the Exchequer from the Evacuation Account, but the evacuating authority could recover the cost from parents who could afford to pay – as a civil debt if necessary.

More efforts were made to cement friendly relations between Londoners and the reception areas. A number of the LCC's children's care officers were seconded to the Ministry of Health – which was responsible for evacuation, even though the local authorities were in charge of the detailed planning – and allocated to regional offices to organise this work and to control it centrally from Whitehall. Other organisers were lent to local education and billeting authorities. It was the beginning of systemised child-centred welfare work, which would possibly not have been forthcoming if it had not been for the war and the evacuation of London children.

Hostels were provided for 'difficult' or 'problem' children – constant bed-wetters, for instance – in big houses commandeered for the purpose, as well as for mentally and physically handicapped children. London's social welfare residential schools, approved schools and remand homes were moved as bodies to safer areas. In due course, residential nurseries were set up for children under five, whose mothers volunteered for the forces, nursing, or were engaged in war work. Mothers had to pay 10s 6d a week for their keep.

Experiences of evacuation were as varied as the number of children involved. Of course, many of the better off had evacuated their children privately, sending them to stay with friends in the country, so that they were spared the trauma of being billeted with strangers. Some had a succession of foster homes, contributing to the disruption and uncertainty of these years. Some were fortunate in finding kind and responsible people to look after them, people with whom they and their parents sometimes forged life-long friendships. Others were abused and exploited.

Householders with evacuees received billeting allowances varying from 8s 6d for under-fives (10s 6d for one child only) to 16s 6d for young persons aged 17 or over. Parents were subscribing 6s, while the Government contributed the rest. Those who could not afford 6s a child were means tested and paid accordingly. Sadly, there were cases where the householder was pocketing the billeting allowance, using the child's rations and underfeeding the child. Two little girls who were billeted on an old lady were subjected to a reign of terror:

Arriving [after a long train journey] tired, cold and very frightened all the old dear had to give us was a plate of cold mutton, mint sauce and dried bread. Very timidly we refused to eat the mutton making the excuse that we didn't eat meat anyway. We made do with the dried bread and mint sauce. From that day on for all the time we were there we never saw a piece of fresh meat again. On

Sundays if we were very lucky we had corned beef or tinned pilchards – an absolute luxury. However, this was supposed to be a great secret and the old lady warned us that if we told anyone she would turn us into frogs! We actually believed her for after all we were only young! Even when school health inspectors called to find out how we were and why we looked so undernourished not a word passed our lips for we really did think the old dear was a witch with powers to carry out her threat!

There are accounts of evacuees being driven to steal food from others at school, just to survive. Some householders were also unscrupulous in making the child work, either doing the housework or working out on the farm. Strong boys were in particular demand, but one girl evacuated to a rural hamlet in Devon got her own back for being exploited:

This foster mum thought she was on to a very good thing with me and the other eleven-year-old girl billeted with her. I think she regarded it as a business transaction. We were expected to shop and wash up and look after a whining three year old. The locals thought of us as devilish, street-wise kids from London which was regarded as the centre of all evil. Being a resourceful child, I got my own back by teaching the three-year-old some fruity London street terms. This was one way of repaying the lady of the house for all the drudgery she was subjecting me to.

Parents who discovered their children were being exploited removed them, but parental visits were few and far between and there must have been many children who suffered in silence.

A vestige of sympathy has to be reserved for those who had difficult children foisted on them. Not all of them had the sense of humour of the couple who attached to their charge a label reading: 'Returning one small boy. Please send doodlebug instead.'

Evacuation from Greater London, known officially as the Metropolitan Evacuating Area, was never compulsory, except in the case of children – usually the under-fives – certified to be suffering or likely to suffer in mind and body as a result of enemy attacks. Ministry of Information posters urged parents to leave their children in the reception areas, where they would be safe from the bombing. The posters implied that to bring the children back to London was to play into Hitler's hands. Pressure was put on parents through leaflets to register their children for evacuation, while the LCC Education Officer directed head teachers to visit the homes of unregistered children and persuade the parents to register them for evacuation.

Evacuation ensured the preservation of the next generation. It also secured the removal of 'useless mouths' not engaged in the war effort from the front line. Those children who remained in the capital had to endure all the fear, danger and noise of air raids, nights of disrupted sleep in the shelters, possibly being bombed out, as well as witnessing death, maiming and destruction all around them. As Bernard Kops, a Jewish boy living in Stepney, described it:

And we went underground to get away from the sirens and the bombs. Yet they followed me and I heard sirens until the world became a siren. One endless cry of torture. It penetrated right into the core of my being, night and day was one long night, one long nightmare, one long siren, one long wail of despair. Some people feel a certain nostalgia for those days . . . They talk about those days as if they were a time of true communal spirit. Not to me. It was the beginning of an era of utter terror, of fear and horror. I stopped being a child and came face to face with the new reality of the world.

Fathers were very often absent on active service and their mothers involved in war work, so that there was less parental supervision and, in a few cases, actual neglect.

In the reception areas babies rescued from the bombing and life in the shelters in London in 1940 and 1941 and taken into the residential nurseries grew into healthy children 'with beautiful teeth, hair and skin and delightful manners'. All of them had individual care and were brought up in small 'families' of eight or ten children with their own permanent nurse or 'mother'. Children were having their horizons widened through opportunities that were denied them in London. They were often living in better home conditions, affecting their behaviour, deportment, culture and vocabulary. In some cases, such as the actor Michael Caine, who was billeted with the squire, it instilled a taste for the good life, an ambition to live such a life themselves. Audrey Sparks had come from a home without books and now a whole new world opened up for her: 'My foster-parents had masses of books and I'd literally never seen one. I can remember the smell of snapping open a book they gave me at Christmas and inhaling its exotic aroma. And this old couple gave generous Christmas presents. I'll never forget the smell of the Christmas tree – the pine needles! What did it matter to me that they were old when they were so kind?'

London children were experiencing country life, benefiting from the fresh air, nature walks and open spaces. They were helping with the harvest and growing food. Whereas in London, the more unruly, unsupervised children were running wild on the bomb sites. In Fulham and Chelsea boys vandalising bomb-damaged houses were described as 'Little Hooligans' in the local paper. Some were stripping houses of valuable material. Richie White was one of them:

On one trip to Beckenham there were four of us. I don't know how, but we knew lead or metal was worth money, so we went up on the roof of a bombed-out house. We got a big box out of the shed and we filled it with lead – square bits of flat lead. We carried it home and as we got into the turning Peter's brother Bobby come out and said, 'What you got there?' He went 'Lead', and his brother belted him and said, 'You get in, you'll get nicked, you'll get put away.' So he disappeared and then Reggie, David's big brother, heard and gave him a whack and made him go in. So that left me and Charlie. We were panicking a bit. When we got to Charlie's house he didn't want to know, he was worried. So I dragged it down to my house, I took it in and my mum said, 'What you got there?'

'I got some lead, Mum.'

'You little bugger, where'd you get that?'

'Off a roof.'

'You could have killed yourself.'

We put it on a pushchair, rags on top, and took it to Wilson's, the scrap metal dealer down at Lower Sydenham. We got four pounds, which was a lot of money. Wilson never asked no questions. I went to Charlie and I said, 'We got two pounds.' So I gave him a pound and me and mum had three. That must have lasted us for ever, three pounds! We never went back for more, though. We were scared after that.

Inevitably, lack of supervision led to accidents. Several children were drowned in the static water tanks holding emergency supplies for the fire service. Just before the tanks were emptied at the beginning of May 1945, two boys of 13 and 11 were drowned in one at Poplar. They had been using a door from a ruined house to sail across the tank and had been tipped into the water when it tilted. Three building workers and two locals attempted to rescue them, but it was too late.

The Chief Inspector of Education in London admitted that it had been no secret that the war had made a casualty of London's education. At the time of his report in July 1943 he reckoned that although some of the ground lost in the earlier years of the war had been recovered, the average retardation was probably between 6 and 12 months, and that stable conditions were essential to enable teachers to recover lost ground. It was unfortunate that the V-weapon attacks which began in June 1944 should have interrupted an organisation that was approaching peacetime standards. This was only the last in a series of reversals which had dogged the education of London's children throughout the war. Teachers had to make strenuous efforts to maintain morale. While they had to work hard to attain pre-war standards, this was not a period in which any educational advances could be made.

It had never been anticipated that two systems of education, one in London and the other in the reception areas, would be in operation concurrently. It had been assumed at the outbreak of war that the majority of London's 450,000 children in full-time education and their teachers would spend the duration of the war in the reception areas. But with a proportion of children coming back to London each time the bombing diminished and others refusing to send their children away from London at all, schooling had to be provided in both places. Teachers, who were originally evacuated to provide 1 for every 30 pupils, had to follow the drift of their pupils, but there was inevitably a time lag and periods when children back in London had no formal schooling, while teachers could never be sure how long they could expect their pupils to remain with them.

Some of the fee-paying schools such as Westminster, St Paul's and City of London removed themselves en bloc to the country at the outset of war, so that their pupils' education was not disrupted, and of course many parents who could afford to do so evacuated their children privately and arranged for them to continue private education out of London. Over 1,000 London schools were damaged in the course of the war and some had to be demolished. In a private school such as Dulwich College which had incurred serious damage, it was estimated that reconstruction would cost £250,000, and parents were warned that tuition fees would be increased from £15 to £18 a term from September 1945 to pay for it.

Children returning to London at Christmas 1939, swelling the numbers of schoolchildren in the capital to 192,000, usually found that their school had closed. Emergency schools were opened as fast as the necessary air-raid shelters could be provided for them, but many children fell through the net. Twelve-year-old John Sweetland returned to a block of flats in Marylebone in the late autumn of 1939: 'Back home after five weeks of evacuation and filled with the elation of perhaps a never-ending holiday, for schools were closed. Maybe the war wouldn't be so bad.' He spent the days in Hamleys and looking into the windows of other toy shops. His school remained closed, so that after a year's absence, he continued his education at a technical college which his father had found for him.

By December 1940, 3 months after the onset of the Blitz, the number of schoolchildren in London was estimated at 80,400, probably the lowest at any time during the war, with the exception of the period immediately after the evacuation in September 1939. There were also 39,000 children under 5 in London at this time. With the end of the Blitz in 1941 the drift back to London resumed, but now many children found that their schools had been given over to other purposes, such as British Restaurants, the National Fire Service, Civil Defence and rest centres. School could not be compulsory while few schools existed and attendance grew slack. Teachers, like Civil Defence workers and so many others in wartime, had to improvise. Sporting an official armlet, they would go from house to house gathering the remnants of different schools and classes to offer some formal education in any premises that could be acquired. Some gave private tuition or held small classes in the homes of pupils.

Once more, emergency schools reopened, but the capacity only afforded half-time attendance. A teacher working in an emergency school near Dalston Junction found that she had 50 children in the morning and the same number in the afternoon, each class taking one shift. Her old school at Church Street, Stoke Newington, reopened in 1941 on the top two floors of its premises, while the rest centre continued to operate downstairs. Half-time schooling did not end until March 1945.

Children who should have started school at five, but instead were starting at six or seven, were some of the biggest casualties of the crisis. In a school containing up to 400 pupils at West Ham towards the end of the war, for instance, there was not a single child of 7 who could read. There were also behavioural problems in all age groups. Teachers found that the disruption of war had dealt a serious blow to the children's powers of concentration. They were easily distracted and showed little application for hard work. They were restless and noisier than usual.

The situation was hardly better in the reception areas. Some local schools were unable to accommodate all the London evacuees, while some school groups were disappointed to find that they could not remain together, particularly after some began to drift back to London. London schools had been well equipped, far more so than the great majority in the reception areas. London teachers again had to improvise, often sharing the local school building but holding their classes at odd hours. Children of varying ages and abilities would be thrown together in the same class, as they were in the emergency teaching groups in the capital.

A woman whose father was a fire fighter in Clapham recalls that when she returned home from the country at Christmas 1939 her school had closed, so that she had no schooling at all. Returning to the country after October 1940, she found that school was 'a haphazard affair' with 'overflow' classes held in the village hall. There was a constant turnover of teachers, many of whom had to follow their pupils back to the capital. Her disrupted education meant that she received no groundwork in maths and never caught up.

London children in the reception areas would find they were discriminated against in small ways. Joyce Barrett, evacuated from Shoreditch to Luton, remembers that local children were 'favoured over the evacuees – from parts in the school play to the price of a cup of Ovaltine'.

The V-1s arrived just as education in London was stabilising and returning to pre-war standards. In June 1944 there had been 237,000 schoolchildren in the capital, but this number rapidly dipped to 136,500, before creeping up to 173,000 in December 1944 and 192,000 in March 1945. Stella Freeman had been evacuated in 1939, but returned to Shepherd's Bush in January 1944, just in time for a recurrence in conventional aerial attacks the following month. In June the V-1 onslaught brought a renewed exodus, but Stella stayed: 'Lessons were somewhat disrupted by the newly arrived doodlebugs. Indeed, at one point letters were sent to parents asking if they would prefer to keep us at home as shelters were inadequate. I forged my father's signature on the reply and spent three happy weeks playing Monopoly in my friend June's air raid shelter.'

As the exam she had taken as an evacuee in Somerset was not recognised by the LCC, she had to resit to get into grammar school. She passed, but Kensington High School had been bombed, so that she and other children had to squash into a big house in Upper Phillimore Gardens for lessons:

So began the daily journeys on the 49 bus, often late, sometimes non-existent, as West London suffered badly at this time from buzz bombs and rockets. The White City flats, Peabody Buildings, Westway and the Pavilion on the Green, all were hit about this time. Strangely enough, I can't remember being worried about the bombs. The cold, the queues and coming home to an empty house after school, because my mother was working at Pritchard's the bakers on the Green seemed much more important. Trying to do three hours homework at night in the same room as a radio tuned to *ITMA* or Vera Lynn's *Hello Boys* was not very easy either.

Irene Byers, who had left Dulwich to accompany her children down to Somerset during the V-1 period, regretted that it meant another disruption to her son's education: 'I worry about Chris's continued lack of schooling and his refusal to go to the local headmaster for private tuition. But he dislikes him so heartily, and I dare not send him to the village school because he has made many enemies amongst the local boys by so cleverly imitating their Somerset drawl from the safety of this side of the hedge.'

As if examinations were not bad enough, children in London often had to take them under aerial bombardment. In March 1945 Lewis Blake was sitting his entrance examination for selective secondary education:

The form master had just given out the English language papers when a distant rumble roared across the heavens. It did not distract us unduly, not after months of far bigger thunder crashes. The paper before us was a more immediate cause for panic, as with trembling fingers and anxious eyes we scanned it for a question we could attempt without too much head-scratching.

The essay topics transported us to a world far removed from the reality of our own lives. The war fell away behind a halcyon mist of an eternal peace-time summer with topics like 'My Favourite Sport or Hobby'. Perhaps the only game I knew how to play was truancy. 'A School Outing in the Countryside'. More promising. We had had a few of those, only we called it evacuation. 'An Evening Spent at Home'. Gripping stuff. Did they mean the air raid shelter?

Two hours later a great bang smacked the sky outside the classroom windows and subsided with a heavy thump somewhere to the north. We looked up momentarily from our ink-stained pages. The teacher, a tall, spare man in a ginger suit who never smiled in our presence, turned from the window to face us. His eyes met ours impassively. 'You have one hour left,' he said, without a change in his expression. To finish the paper, or to live? Never mind. Back to the excitement of adverb clauses.

He was telling us our time was nearly up just as a mighty crack seemed to arc over the heavens and rend them apart. A giant thud shook the floor and windows. Our time *will* be up if they come any closer. He did not bat an eyelid. A slight questioning look, perhaps, but nothing more. We took our cue from him and showed no reaction. It sounded as if the next street had caught it. It hadn't, of course. The windows would not have survived so close a hit. Incredible to think that the crash emanated from Blackheath Village, nearly two miles away, as some of us later learned.

That afternoon, during the maths paper, there was another loud report, but this time six miles away in Sidcup. By then the day's ordeal was nearly over – the examination, that is. The happy prospect of an early release from the confines of that torture was in no way blighted by the ever present threat from above. We thought the rockets were something which happened to others, never to us. We unknowingly lived in a charmed rocket-free oasis in central Catford. Around us, within a radius of a mile or so, something like twenty rockets must have come down already. So close, yet so far. Had the campaign gone on for but a single day longer than it did, who knows if our luck would have held out?

On Wednesday, 2 May 1945, 1,500 local authorities in the reception areas received a telegram from Henry Willink, the Minister of Health: 'Operate London Return Plans.' It was the signal to put into action the meticulously planned return of 500,000 London evacuees, including mothers and babies, the aged and handicapped, as well as schoolchildren – but the latter could leave only if they had suitable homes to return to. If not, they were to stay in the reception areas.

On 16 May all London schools closed, so that 7,000 teachers, cards in hand, could make a week's survey of the children's homes, noting bomb damage, serious illness, imminent confinement on the part of the mother, lack of sleeping room (although not of beds or bedding, which could be provided from government sources), and other reasons that might prevent the child's immediate return. Teachers were to mark the card 'Home' or 'No Home'. 'No Home' evacuees were to stay in their billets in the reception areas until further notice.

A reporter from the *News Chronicle* accompanied a teacher up and down the bomb-damaged New North Road in Islington as she did her survey of the evacuees' homes. At Number 156 Gracie and Freddie Wilkinson's father had bought them a black kitten, to greet them on their return from Lancashire. There were two rooms in which the whole family, including a two-year-old baby, had to live. However, the rooms were 'dry, light and airy and there were two good large beds and a cot and the parents were longing to have the children back'. The teacher wrote 'Home' on the Wilkinson children's cards.

At Number 180 the three-storey public house, the Kenilworth Castle, had been partly destroyed by a V-1. Only one bedroom remained. The publican's wife was in sole charge, as he was lying seriously ill in the bedroom after being injured by the V-1. The couple's only child, 14-year-old Moyra, was in Bath. 'We want her back,' her mother said, 'but this is no place for her. I sleep in the office and it's not fit for a child.'

The teacher listened sympathetically, made a tour of the damaged house and wrote on the card, 'No home as yet.' The girl would remain in Bath for the present.

At Number 170 the mother of Derek and Raymond, evacuated to Northumberland, was just putting the finishing touches to their bedroom. They were to share a big double bed near a window overlooking the garden. One glance round, one question as to whether there were any infectious diseases in the house, and down went 'Good Home' on the boys' cards.

By the end of the day 29 teachers had reported on 83 homes to the principal at Shepperton Road School. Most houses had been accepted as good enough, at least for the time being. Six had been turned down for lack of accommodation and six others were found to have been destroyed. The parents had disappeared, leaving no forwarding address to which their children could return: shocking, but not uncommon.

Elsewhere in London the returns show the consequences of the bombing:

1. Home destroyed – parents living in one room in mother's flat – four adults in three rooms.
2. Mother living in one room.
3. Father in two attic rooms – mother deceased.
4. Father in Forces, stepmother in two rooms. There are four children (three boys and a girl).
5. Home destroyed by a rocket – present address not known.
6. Mother shares one room with a sister – was previously bombed out at Stoke Newington.
7. Husband POW, mother living with mother-in-law. No accommodation.
8. Family bombed out of Loughton. One boy of fourteen and brother reside with mother in one bedroom and the sitting room. No bed available.
9. Mother is war widow living in semi-basement bed-sitting room. Has another child in Queen Mary's Day Nursery. No accommodation. She is asking foster parents to keep the boy.

In a paper on the return of evacuees prepared by the LCC

Education Officer's department, it was understood that some children would have to remain in the reception areas for the time being, as both parents were serving in the forces and not yet demobilised, while others had mothers who were still engaged in war work. Some had parents who had died or disappeared, or who were unable or unwilling to resume care.

Whatever the reasons, every unaccompanied child evacuee had to be accounted for. Of 56,000 cards sent by the authorities in the reception areas to London for marking up, 37,000 children had homes deemed fit to return to. Of the remaining 19,000, some had already returned home privately, while others had given the wrong address. Some could not return because of a temporary difficulty at home or for educational reasons. The grammar schools, for instance, had been evacuated as self-contained units and would return en bloc after the end of term. Secondary school pupils who were not part of self-contained units and who were taking their school certificate or Higher Schools certificate in June or July were advised to remain in the reception areas to complete them. The rest were unable to return because of some long-term problem.

A cross-section of reasons for children unable to return home obtained by evacuation officers for the LCC starkly illustrates the disruption and tragedy of war and its impact on the family:

1. Father killed on active service and the foster parents are prepared to keep her. The mother is making the necessary arrangements.
2. Father in Forces and does not want children to go back to mother.
3. Parents separated. Two children are in service locally. Employers want to keep them. In same family are two other children whom foster mother would like to keep.
4. Three children. Parents are living at different addresses and seeking divorce.
5. Two illegitimate children. Parents separated.

6. Parents cannot be traced.

7. Father living alone, mother in mental home.

8. Father living alone, mother dead.

9. War orphans.

10. No mother, ignored by father and stepmother.

11. Mother deserted the family, father in ill health.

12. Mother deserted the family, father in HM Forces.

13. Father a returned POW. Divorce and custody of children pending.

14. Mother killed in an air raid and father in RAF. Home destroyed. Grandmother unable to look after the child.

15. Father killed (RAF). Children expected to go to Reedham Orphanage.

16. Mother dead – father living with another woman. Married sister will care for the child if the father contributes.

17. Mother war widow and working.

18. Mother dead, girl of 15 keeps house.

19. Both parents dead, two elder brothers in HM Forces.

20. Mother dead, father in Army mental asylum.

21. Parents living apart and responsibility for care of children not clear.

22. Mother dead. Father living in a lodging house for men only.

23. Mother has been admitted to hospital, being seriously ill with tuberculosis.

24. Children accepted at Dr Barnado's Home.

In the borough of Stratford, 254 children were unable to return as there was no suitable accommodation for them; 14 sets of parents had disappeared without trace; 10 children had fathers in the forces, but had lost their mothers; domestic problems prevented another 29 from returning; 2 had been orphaned.

In Kilburn, 95 children were unable to return because their homes had been bombed or were overcrowded, or a parent was living in one room; another 37 could not return owing to the desertion of a parent, to impending divorces and disputes over custody and adoption proceedings. Forty-five could not return because there was no one to care for them, the father still being in the forces or the mother being at work, or the mother being insane or not in control. The parents of 18 children could not be traced.

Some parents disappeared in order to avoid paying the billeting charges for their evacuated children. Others simply did not want them back. The Public Assistance Authority had the power to put in motion the necessary machinery, using National Registration as an aid, to locate parents and compel them to resume responsibility for their children. The question to be decided then was, 'Will it be in the child's interests to remain apart?'

War had thrown the focus of attention on the welfare of children as never before. Had it not been for the war, the conditions these children were living in and the neglect and abuse some of them had to endure would probably never have been brought to public attention.

Children were not to be returned to their homes in London if there was clear evidence that they would be exposed to risk of serious neglect or physical or moral harm. An article in the *News Chronicle* drew attention to the plight of children in a residential nursery in Bath. There were the twins, Daisy and Lil, six, from Bermondsey, buried under their home by an early bomb, brought out from under the debris, badly injured and shocked. 'The parents want the twins back, but they have never been to see them and have appeared before the courts for neglect,' the *News Chronicle* reported. 'What should be done about Daisy and Lil? No one knows.'

There were two other sets of twins in the nursery with much the same history. 'The mother of one pair has disappeared. The father of the other pair is a wife beater and a child beater.' Then there was a six-year-old Indian girl, 'found in a shelter with nothing to indicate how she came into the world. An attempt to billet her has failed because of her colour.'

It was disturbing to find, through the follow-up visits paid to children who had already been taken home by their parents before the V-1 attacks, how quickly some of these children's welfare was thrown into jeopardy again: 'Phyllis, 6, who in three years had been built up from "a shadow" into a sturdy, sociable girl, was found a month after her mother took her away, in a dirty basement and suffering pangs of hunger.'

Some private individuals had volunteered to foster children who had been considered 'unbilletable'. A Mrs S in Caversham had taken in 15 evacuees, of whom some half-dozen were 'orphans or as good as orphans'. Bill, who had arrived at five years of age with 'all the bad habits of a neglected child', was now 'a delightful youngster with charming manners'. He had received only 'three letters each with a different postmark, but no visits, no gifts, no clothes from his parents in three and a half years'. His foster mother was praying that his parents would not turn up to claim him, telling the *News Chronicle*: 'I've hardly had a wink of sleep since the return-home scheme was announced. Bill loves us as much as we love him and it will break our hearts to part. He is a grand little boy and our ambition for him is to get him into a Navy training college as he has developed a love for the sea and ships.'

Twelve-year-old Sam was unwanted at home. 'My father says he doesn't want the children of my mother and my mother says she doesn't want the children of my father, so no one wants me.' His parents had now vanished. 'This is my home and I'm happy here, and I don't know what I'd do if they take me away,' he added, trying to keep back the tears.

Jack, 11, who had lived with Mrs S for 2 years, told her: 'I've got four fathers, and I don't like any of them. I'd rather have you. Please don't send me away, ever.'

Arthur, now 12, had been brought before the courts as 'unmanageable'. Now his mother was saying that she wanted him back, but his father had written to say he did not want him back. 'It's not because of the bombs, I'll have you know, that we evacuated him. It was only because we couldn't do anything with him.'

The Minister of Health hoped to avoid bringing children back to London to an institution or children's home, especially if they had settled down in a good foster home in the reception area. Public Assistance Authorities were to liaise with the billeting officers to find out whether the householder was willing to continue to care for the child or, failing that, whether an alternative foster home could be found in the area. Where a child's home had been broken up by separation or divorce or desertion of a parent, this was considered a good reason for leaving the child in its foster home in the reception area, subject to recovery of the cost from the parents.

If a child had been orphaned as a result of enemy action the Ministry of Pensions would bear the responsibility of making proper provision for the care of the child. If only one parent had died, the pension would be paid to the surviving parent. If the child's parents had died other than by enemy action the child would come under the care of the Public Assistance Authority of the area of settlement, unless that authority could find some relative to take charge or provide for the child.

Some residential nurseries would remain open for the time being, until alternative arrangements could be made for children without parents or a home to return to. At least, in the eyes of the LCC Education Officer's Department, there was some comfort to be drawn here: 'The difficulties of disposing of those who cannot be reunited with their parents may be mitigated by the fact that they should have formed good habits in their nurseries, and young children with good habits are usually attractive to potential foster-parents or to those who wish to adopt a child.' It was a slightly rosier picture than that depicted in a memo from the LCC Chief Officer of Social Welfare concerning an abandoned female child – perhaps the offspring of some brief wartime liaison:

<u>Abandoned female child</u>
With reference to your memo of 30 October about the naming and registration of the above mentioned infant, enquiries have been made at the various establishments at which the child has been since she was found on 9 July 1945 at Paddington Station. It appears

that the child was transferred from South Eastern Hospital nursery to Hutton Residential School Nursery on 16 July as an unknown foundling. While at Hutton she became known as Barbara Hutton, for convenience sake and in that name was transferred to Eastern Hospital on 27 July. The movements of the child since then are as follows: on 12 September she was transferred back to Hutton Residential School nursery, on 6 October she was transferred to St Andrew's Hospital, on 25 October she died in hospital.

Immediately after VE Day there was a rush back to the capital. Some children had been evacuated privately and, of course, parents were at liberty to bring them back when they wanted. But those requiring government funding for their return journeys were advised to stay in the reception areas until organised transport was ready for them. No expenses would be paid for those ignoring the order.

The first trainload of mothers and babies was due in early June. Unaccompanied schoolchildren with escorts provided by the LCC – usually 1 teacher for every 12 to 15 children, which meant that the schools would have to close again over the period – would follow a fortnight later. Children with disabilities were to be returned after the main parties had been dealt with. Evacuees in residential nurseries would be the last to return. They would be sent in the first instance to WVS receiving nurseries at Regent's Park before dispersal to their homes.

Eight trains a day each carrying 6,000 evacuee mothers and children and later 10,000 unaccompanied children were scheduled for London in a process that involved tight co-ordination between the Government, the LCC, the local authorities in the reception areas and the railways. The process would be carried out seven days a week over a period of four to five weeks. Trains were to depart from the reception areas no sooner than 11 a.m., to allow time for all parties to reach the terminals, while railways were to try to ensure that returning evacuees would reach London no later than 8 p.m. The WVS would distribute food during the journey. About

200 extra porters were to be laid on at London stations to deal with the extra luggage; as labour was short, they were to be drawn from NFS and former Civil Defence personnel. Schools were needed as reception centres for returning evacuees, while at the same time they were required for use as polling stations for the general election.

Every child must come home with their personal belongings, identity card, ration book, clothing coupons, and food for the journey. A complex card system with cross-referencing was devised to keep track of each child and ensure that they eventually ended up at the correct dispersal point for their home. Trainloads made up of groups from each reception area were returning to a number of different London boroughs spread over a wide area. Children and their luggage were to wear coloured and coded labels, according to the location of their home. On arrival at the London terminals, they were to be divided into the relevant groups and London Passenger Transport buses would carry them to the first of two dispersal points until they eventually arrived in their own locality. Here, evacuation officers would make an accurate and final check against his list. The children were then given a meal and every effort would be made to ensure that they reached home that same night.

In May 1945 a Ministry of Health paper entitled *Notes on the Return of Unaccompanied Children* warned of the difficult adjustments families would have to make once the children came home.

Parents were warned that children had had to become self-reliant and could not be expected to make a sudden switch to being 'docile, obedient, considerate and helpful'. Parents were urged to be patient and understanding. There were bound to be problems if a child returned to find another born during the war years, a sibling who now seemed to hold the place in the home and in their parents' affection which the older one remembered as theirs.

Comparisons would inevitably be drawn between the billet

and home, making it difficult for the child to settle down. 'Some children will exaggerate the treatment and conditions in their billets to win sympathy and attention.' Thousands of children would find coming home an anticlimax. Teachers warned that children had often been living in far superior accommodation in the reception areas to their own homes. Some children were shocked at the darkness and meanness of their home. 'It was hate at first sight,' one recalls. 'I let it be known loudly and persistently that I wanted to go back to my "real home".'

A woman who was evacuated with her school at the outset and who had had five foster homes, including one much grander than her own home, remembers: 'It wasn't the joyous homecoming I'd waited for over all the years. Our school building had been bombed and we had to make do with inadequate patched-up classrooms. Our homes were shabby with war damage and neglect.'

A child might even want to go back. 'If he wants to he should be allowed to maintain contact with his foster family and friends in the reception area.' Those who found it most difficult to settle were the children who had been evacuated overseas, to America, Canada and Australia, where they had often experienced a far higher standard of living and a different culture. A girl who had been evacuated to Australia was 15 when she returned to London and found it impossible to come to terms with her new existence. Her mother told her sadly but bravely that if, after a year, she had failed to settle, then all right, she could return to her 'other family' in Australia. 'What it must have cost her to say that,' she recalls, 'having just got back a daughter after five years' absence!'

Some evacuated children had received generous gifts of clothes and footwear, toys and books from their wartime foster parents. 'Parents will need to remind themselves that these gifts belong to the child to whom they were given, who may set great store by them, and should not be divided up among other members of the family.'

It seems evident today that many evacuees repressed their

feelings of loss and rejection and bewilderment at the time and only came to terms with them later in life, if at all. Parents were advised that children showing signs of strain should be referred to the school doctor and to a Child Guidance clinic, but many children who probably needed help must have fallen through the net. Health visitors were to help parents and children make the necessary adjustments, while the welfare authorities were to arrange a follow-up visit immediately after the return home of children under five and frequent visits in the following weeks.

Children under five presented a special problem, as most of them would have been living in residential nurseries and would have forgotten – if they ever knew – what life in an ordinary family was like:

Life in a nursery is arranged so that hazards and dangers are reduced to a minimum. They will not be used to heavy traffic, a fire not well guarded, boiling kettles, teapots, etc. They will be used to a well-ordered daily routine with regular well-balanced meals, early bed, a midday rest, no sweets or snacks between meals, daily doses of cod liver oil and orange juice, and so on. Many parents will be tempted to be indulgent in the first few weeks to a degree which they cannot maintain and which might, in any case, be harmful.

Whatever the adjustments to be made, these children had parents and a home to return to. But, of course, many children were not so fortunate. Their homes and family life had been irredeemably shattered by war. For them there was charity. As the first peacetime Christmas drew near, it was decided that something must be done for the 5,000 London children still billeted in the reception areas and the 700–800 in the residential nurseries. It was initially agreed that the LCC's Christmas Treats Fund would give a 5s allowance to each child. Subsequently, this was revised to 2s 6d a head for the older children and 1s each for those in the nurseries, leaving a substantial £3,000 in the fund. Parties, it was felt, would place 'an unnecessary burden on local authorities'.

As for those naughty boys on the bomb sites, the little hooligans who were running out of control, things were about to change. There might be some discipline at last. Daddy was coming home.

10
Reunion of Strangers

'Back in "Civvy Street", the demobbed soldier stares unbe-
lievingly at the beflagged house, at the motto picked out in
coloured beer tops over the fanlight, "WELCOME HOME
GEORGE", and suddenly he is on the other side of his
dream! The door is opened by the wife he hasn't seen for
years . . . he is introduced to his family . . .'
                    – BBC General Overseas Service, *Civvy Street*

After nearly six years of war, long separations, and their varied
and extraordinary experiences, men and women had grown
apart. Women, in particular, had changed beyond all recognition. They had inevitably developed a degree of independence and gained confidence in abilities they did not know they
possessed. Husbands and wives found they were virtual
strangers. They had to learn to live together again. It was not
easy and some parted. Fathers had to get to know their children, and children had to learn to share their mother with the
strange man who had returned from the war. For some, the
relationship was too fractured ever to be repaired.

Servicemen returning from a long period overseas were
unprepared for the changes the war had wrought. Many
retained a rosy picture of their wife and children, which they
discovered bore no relation to the reality when they came
home. They expected everything to be the same, and it was
not. It was the difference between the reality and their dreams
that was so hard to reconcile. As the BBC's *Civvy Street* put
it: 'That is a very large part of his trouble – expecting life to
be as it was. His gallant womenfolk, not wishing to under-
mine his morale, wrote cheerful letters, suppressing the more

379

tedious details of life, and although he gathered there were trials and shortages, in his heart he treasured a romantic picture of his wife with the firelight on her hair, and a laughing chubby baby in her arms.'

The image had sustained the men through the bad times, but the reality came as a shock or a disappointment. 'The girl-wife had grown up, and perhaps become "tough" from factory life, while the husband may have acquired more refinement in the Officers' Mess. The housewife and mother, becoming a huntress for food, had given up glamour for a time-saving turban and stout-soled shoes. The charming baby is a boy with hostile eyes, very resentful at first of the much needed firmness of a father.'

Some found they had grown too far apart ever to be reconciled. A WVS worker gives a poignant description of one such reunion, where the husband had been wounded and captured at Dunkirk. He had spent many years in the prison hospital, in pain, but he comforted himself with thoughts of his wife, with whom he was desperately in love:

He saw, as is natural in a dream, their little home slightly glorified. He saw his wife running her house and looking after her babies and, of course, always looking as he loved her most. All through his suffering he was comforted by the knowledge that one day he would get home again, that then everything would be perfect . . .

And the wife? She had to leave the little house to take the children away from the air raids. She shared a house in the country with another woman and her children for two years. At last, unable to bear sharing any longer, she brought the children back to London. Her furniture and curtains had suffered damage from neglect. As a sergeant's wife she had not much money, but she did not want her husband to come home to a shabby house. She took the children daily to a war-time nursery and got a part-time job in a factory. She put the children in the nursery by seven am. She worked in her factory until mid-day, had dinner in the canteen, came home past the shops to get her food and about three began her housework and cooking. At half past four she fetched her children. After a little play she bathed them and put them to bed. As soon as they were asleep she got down to washing and mending their things. In between these chores she paid the rent and the insurances, filled in Government forms, got new ration books and all the other odd jobs that fall on the householder. She grew more tired and dragged-looking each year; just one thing kept her going. Some day her husband would come home. She had her dreams too. He was coming home the gay, strong young man who went away. He would hate to see her tired and worried and he would kiss her and pull her head on to his shoulder and say: 'You relax and leave everything to me.'

The end of this particular story is a tragedy. I heard it from the man's side. 'It was if we were strangers. We sat night after night facing each other across the fire. We seemed to have nothing to say. It was as if a wall had grown between us. We couldn't go on like that. We're getting a divorce.'

In a series of programmes on the Home Service, *Can I Help You?*, covering the whole gamut of problems likely to be encountered by the newly demobilised, John Morgan was at pains to warn those about to be reconciled:

We've got to remember that civilians have been shifted about a bit as well – that the war's made a mess of some of their lives, too. First of all about home. That's the place that every single member of the forces is looking forward to – home – but home isn't just a place – it's people – it's you and me, and you and I are not the same individuals we were two, three, four or more years ago – and we mustn't expect men who've been fighting over half the world to be the same either. But I do think we shall have to meet them more than halfway. It's much more difficult for them to realise that we've grown a bit older, a bit wiser, perhaps a bit tougher and almost certainly a bit shabbier. So it seems to me that somehow we've got to scrap the idea that any of us is 'Coming back' to something we left, or that there's any real difference between the serviceman and the civilian. Then there's the children. It's been grand to have photographs and to hear all about them in letters – but it's quite a different thing to live with them after living for years with other men, in ditches, in barracks, in jungles or in ships. How much do the children really know about Daddy? Is he just a strange man who comes home on leave sometimes – if he's lucky? Mind you, I don't believe in being all solemn and high-hat about all this – I'm just saying – really – it's worth planning for – *this* is resettlement just as much as jobs or training – and it's the part of resettlement which no one can do for us – we've got to do it for ourselves.

Women, too, were targeted with advice. As if they weren't tired enough, they were now going to have to prepare for a difficult period of reconciliation with their husbands, learning to make allowances for the stranger who had returned to them, soothing their homecoming. Newspapers and magazines carried articles on the subject of 'When Your Man Comes Home'. In the *Sunday Graphic*, the Reverend Elliott told women readers:

All these years they have been dreaming of home, living for letters, solacing their lonely hearts – even in the midst of a most wonderful comradeship – by looking at well-thumbed photos. All the same, the war has taken it out of your man. Inside himself he may be very weary, perhaps wounded, in spite of his bronzed face and his hearty manner. There is something in him to be healed. He has seen things that he won't talk about. He has been in Hell, though he may pretend that it was a grand time. Maybe he has helped to clean up one or other of those beastly concentration camps, or fought through tropical jungle in the monsoons, or tramped the high Alps, or sailed in convoys when no man's life was safe for a single moment. . . There is always something strange and new in the eyes of a man home from the wars. Such experiences as these change men and change them quickly . . . Don't expect him to settle down in a month – or less. Don't expect him to look at life as he used to look at life. And don't worry if for a little time he seems disillusioned, even with his home, even with you. It will all come right, believe me, but it will need a lot of mutual adjustment – and a great love and a great patience.

In October the *Daily Mirror* ran an article entitled 'Advice to Nervous Returning Servicemen from the Wife of one of Them'. She began briskly:

So, servicemen, you're coming home. You and 320,000 like you are being demobbed this month, and the next and the next. Many of you married ones may be feeling rather scared about the homecoming, because you know it isn't going to be so easy to pick up the threads of married life again. Many people have taken it upon themselves to tell your wives how to welcome you. I think it's about time someone gave you a word of advice.

Be glad to be back. Say so as often as you can. You simply cannot overdo this, however much you repeat yourself.

Be prepared for civilian restrictions. Many of you will have little idea of what has been going on in English homes. So don't expect too liberal a welcome – in material things at any rate. If your wife greets you in a new dress, be surprised and delighted, and, if she produces a home-made cake or a roast dinner, ask her how on earth she managed to do it. Do the shopping for her one morning, too, and decide for yourself whether a piece of fish for supper is worth all the queuing.

Be appreciative. Life has just dragged on, becoming harder and more lonely with each successive month. So tell her she's wonderful, that you're proud of her, and all the rest of it.

Take over some of the family responsibility. Don't forget that for a long time she's been mother and father in the home, and maybe part breadwinner too. She may have been tied to the home and the children day and night for years, perhaps without a chance of an occasional evening out. Take over your fatherhood at once and help a little with the mothering too. See that young Tommy toes the line and doesn't play his mother up too much.

Be prepared for changes in her. I don't mean in her looks. In fact you should be prepared not to notice any war-weary lines in her face or her clothes. But you should expect to find a more independent woman, who has matured in the hard school of war.

Be affectionate. She'll be shy, the same as you. Don't rush her off her feet, or try to woo her too ardently at first. Don't forget that however much she's changed, however self-sufficient she may seem, she's darn glad to have you back.

War brought massive disruption to family life. It broke up not only families but also neighbourhoods. In Greater London there was wide-scale movement among the population, the less fortunate being bombed out and changing their address many times. From the outbreak of war until the end of 1945, there were 60 million changes of address nationally in a civilian population of 38 million. Housing conditions, the separation of families and the effects of the mobilisation of women, were perhaps the most severe strains on the family in wartime.

Nationally, at least two and a half million women were deprived of the presence and support of their husbands, who were serving in the forces: to give an idea of what this meant for London, about 15 per cent of all men were enlisted and just over half of these were married. Men and women were not only called up into the forces, but might also have to leave home to work in, say, the munitions industry. They might also have to leave home if they were working in some of the government offices or departments of the BBC which had been moved out of the capital. It was rarely practical to take family or elderly dependents with them. Family life was further fractured by the evacuation of women with children under five and by the evacuation of children on their own. Between the wars, families had been getting smaller, so that in times of crisis there were fewer close relations who could be called on to help: the onus was on the Government to do so. For the first time, the state took an

n all our long history we have never seen a greater day than this' – Churchill's hour of ctory.

or years Vera Lynn had sung of when the lights would go on again in London and now the oment had come. On the night of VE Day, 8 May 1945, floodlighting revealed that a rprising number of famous landmarks, such as Big Ben, had survived the bombing. Children ho had never known anything but the blackout were dazzled by the sight of London lit up.

Left VE Day saw a spontaneous outburst of joy and mad antics with Londoners and servicemen of many nationalities dancing and singing in the streets. The boxed-up empty plinth of Eros in Piccadilly was a magnet to revellers.

Below Londoners celebrated Victory in Europe by the age-old tradition of lighting bonfires. Effigies of Adolf Hitler fed the flames or were hanged in gibbets in the streets.

With its dome rising miraculously above the smoke and flames during the Blitz, St Paul's had become the symbol of London's long struggle and survival. On the night of 8 May 1945 young women of the ATS shone their Victory beams behind the dome in a sky gloriously free of enemy aircraft and missiles.

VJ Day, 15 August 1945. It's all over at last. American servicemen and British girls step out in triumph along Piccadilly.

Street parties, such as this one in Southwark, took place in the weeks after VE Day, when women scraped together their rations to give the children a tea to remember. Few men were present, as most of them had yet to be released from the forces.

...addy comes home to his prefab – and lucky to get it. Reunions were not always an ...alloyed joy. Husbands and wives had grown apart and children often resented the ...anger's intrusion.

The Labour leader, Clement Attlee, electioneering in what was left of his Limehouse constituency. In July 1945 he replaced Winston Churchill as Prime Minister after a landslide victory for the Labour Party.

Sir Patrick Abercrombie and other planners envisaged the revitalisation of the South Bank and Docklands, but recognised that it would probably take 50 years to complete. So it has proved. Today this site boasts some of the capital's smartest apartments and restaurants.

Not even in their wildest dreams did Londoners imagine that rationing would continue for years after the war. But here they are in Tottenham in May 1951 queuing at a mobile food office for new ration books.

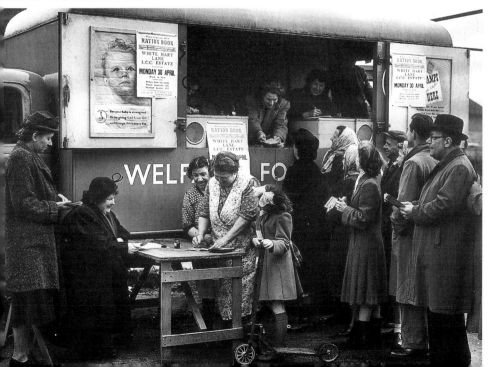

Vast tracts of bomb-damaged London remained untouched for years after the war. The Barbican, seen here in 1956, was completely devastated. The high-rise flats and cultural centre which now occupy the site were not built until the sixties.

interest in and intervened in the family. Subsequently, it was never to withdraw.

The mobilisation of women – and the absence of many women from the home for long hours of work – was perhaps the most radical and disruptive factor. At the outset of war, the Government was reluctant to change the established pattern of life. The place of a married woman was in the home, looking after her husband and children. The Government feared that servicemen would resent their wives being conscripted and that this would have an adverse effect on morale. It ignored the recommendations of various women MPs, a cross-party group of whom sat on the Woman Power Committee later succeeded by the Women's Advisory Committee, to extend conscription to women. However, after 1941 the need to harness labour to carry on the war effort from such a small population as that of Great Britain became imperative and the Government realised that it had to bow to the inevitable and squeeze every ounce out of the available 'woman power'.

The Minister of Labour and National Service, Ernest Bevin, had complete authority under the Crown to direct personnel into the armed forces, industry and war production, to 'freeze' people in essential jobs, and to prosecute those who failed to comply. As everyone in the country had to register for an identity card and ration book, it was very difficult to avoid conscription. From March 1941 onwards, successive groups of women were called upon to register at their local labour exchange – an announcement giving the registration date for a particular age group would appear in the newspapers to alert them that their time had come – and in due course the net encompassed all women between the ages of 18 and 50. Any woman up to the age of 60 with nursing experience had to register, as there was a desperate shortage of trained nurses, as did former textile workers up to the age of 55. So desperate did the need for cloth become that some textile workers who had gone into munitions were ordered back into lower-paid textile jobs.

Women with children under the minimum school-leaving

age of 14 who were living with them or women who were shouldering a domestic burden such as elderly, invalid parents were exempt, as well as those above the age limits. In practice, a high proportion of these 10 million 'immobile' women – out of a pool of 17 million women between the ages of 14 and 64 — volunteered for war work of some kind. This is where the Women's Voluntary Service was so clever and adaptable, as it allowed women to contribute what hours they could. It had 1 million volunteers. The wives of men serving in the armed forces were exempt from any form of national service that took them away from home, but single women were categorised as 'mobile' workers and could be ordered to leave home and go where labour was needed. The Government would pay their travelling expenses to the place of work and there would be help in finding them digs. Women under 18 were permitted to attend university for 3 years – 2 years if they were 19 on entry – provided they undertook to do work of national importance, such as teaching or social service, when they left.

The Government had come a long way in a short time, but under no circumstances was it prepared to allow women to take up arms. The Labour MP, Edith Summerskill, pleaded long and hard to join the House of Commons Home Guard and to obtain the right for women to join the Home Guard, but they could do so only as auxiliaries. They were not to use weapons. Similarly, women who volunteered for the Women's Royal Naval Service, the Women's Auxiliary Air Force and the Auxiliary Territorial Service were engaged only in non-combatant duties, thereby releasing men for combat. Women working on anti-aircraft sites would work out by the use of scientific instruments where the gun was to be aimed, but only the men were allowed to fire the shell.

Smart upper- and middle-class girls opted to join the armed services, the WRNS being the most exclusive and the ATS the least – until Princess Elizabeth joined and gave its reputation a boost. Within these services there was a strict hierarchy, usually based on class. Upper- and middle-class girls were less commonly seen in the factories, where most of the workers had received only an elementary education. Mary Beazley, an admiral's daughter who worked in a parachute factory in Tottenham Court Road, admitted she had nothing in common with her working-class colleagues and felt lonely. For a girl with her educational background she also found the work tedious and repetitive and 'quite soul destroying'. In Inez Holden's novel, *War Factory*, the middle-class girl on the factory floor, Feather, stood out as 'the sort of girl who would have been "ladying it" at a First Aid Post attached to some auxiliary service'.

The normal working week under the Factories Act was 48 hours, but during the war women such as those in the Royal Ordnance factories making guns, shells and explosives were working a 55-hour week, which meant a 10-hour day for five and a half days. It was found, however, that long hours did not increase production, which began to lag behind owing to worker fatigue. Fatigue led to accidents and fatigue coupled with lack of time to give to other chores led to absenteeism and a general deterioration in women's health. Employers had always been opposed to the idea of part-timers, but now the Government prevailed on them to reconsider. It was a good deal for employers, who were able to save on bonuses, insurance and holiday money, while ensuring a high level of productivity with an eager and reliable workforce. The Government threw in the final carrot by offering certain exemptions of married women's earnings from income tax.

Part-time work was perfect for women with heavy domestic commitments and it was better for production too. Monotonous, repetitive work lent itself well to five- or six-hour shifts. Any longer than that and output would start to flag. Two women could work half a shift each. Alternatively, there were outwork schemes, which brought the work home to small groups of workers. For instance, several aircraft firms set up branch establishments in the London suburbs to do just this. Any woman between the ages of 20 and 45 without household responsibilities and who worked less than 55 hours

a week was required to do compulsory fire watching at her place of work.

To keep women workers fit and productive, the Government ordered improvements in factory medical and welfare facilities and cloakrooms for women. Safety measures were to be installed around machinery, where the accident rate – getting their hair caught in the machinery, for instance – was extremely high. For Mary Beazley and her colleagues in the parachute factory, however, little could be done to reduce the acute eye strain they suffered from looking at the bright white silk under lights, short of reducing their hours and productivity. Women factory workers whose health was deemed to be at risk could be sent to a rest home for a short break. Others had to make do with one week's holiday a year, which, in common with everyone else, they were urged to spend at home so as not to put unnecessary strain on the railways.

Any factory with more than 250 employees engaged in war production had to provide a canteen. Generally, they provided a meal of meat and two vegetables for about 10d and workers were to be given a reasonable time off to eat their meal in peace. This facility reduced absenteeism. Over half of all factory workers were in factories employing fewer than 250 people, however. They depended on British Restaurants run by the local authorities for their meals.

Sporadic efforts were made to arrange shopping facilities for women working unsociable hours in the factories. It was found that giving employees unpaid leave in which to do their shopping cut down on absenteeism. Some shopkeepers agreed to take a list and allow women to pick up the goods after work, although this was generally unpopular with other shoppers, many of whose lives were just as harassed as the factory workers'. Sometimes the WVS would help out, doing the shopping for several factory workers. The shopping problem was never satisfactorily resolved, however. Laundries were set up to cut down on some of the chores in homes that lacked machines and detergents and often even hot water: so essential were they, that workers in the laundry industry were frozen in their jobs.

The noise and the stuffiness on the factory floor were often unbearable, especially during the night hours when the blackout was up and there was insufficient air in the place. Kathleen Bliss, who was working in Morrison's aircraft factory in Croydon, noted: 'Because of the blackout, all doors and windows are tightly closed, and everyone soon becomes a bit drowsy through lack of ventilation.'

Music from loudspeakers kept them awake and relieved the hours of tedium. The BBC's *Music While You Work*, often featuring dance music by orchestras led by Jack Payne, Harry Roy, Geraldo, Joe Loss, Victor Silvester, Billy Cotton, Mantovani, Jack Jackson and Henry Hall, had been launched with the factory workers in mind, but singing was popular among women in all walks of life, as a former ATS member recalls: 'We never stopped singing. We knew all the words. That played a very big part in our lives . . . We could lose ourselves. We could forget the horrors of the war. And it was marvellous that we could do that.'

The most popular songs were the romantic and sentimental ones, such as those sung by Vera Lynn, the plumber's daughter from East Ham who had become 'The Forces' Sweetheart'. Her 'We'll Meet Again' and 'The White Cliffs of Dover' had a wistful appeal, while 'Faithful for Ever' and 'There's a Boy Coming Home on Leave' expressed an ideal of constant and faithful love.

One of the main purposes of Basil Dean's ENSA – Entertainments National Service Association – was to entertain factory workers: its first dinner-hour show was at Woolwich Arsenal in July 1940. The shows varied in quality and were not always a great hit with the audience. Concentrating exclusively on serious music and drama, CEMA – the Council for the Encouragement of Music and the Arts – provided 4,500 half-hour concerts in factory lunch hours or midnight dinner breaks, with audiences up to 7,000. CEMA also brought opera and ballet to people who had never seen them before and definitely won some life-long fans.

Trips to the local cinema maybe twice a week, where they

could see the main film and a B movie as well as the Pathe News and trailers for 1s 9d, were the main form of escape and relaxation for hard-working women. They also flocked to the dance halls for a few precious hours of hectic gaiety. In what little spare time she had after long hours at work and fire watching, Nancie Norman, a civil servant in the Home Office, would frequent the Strand Ballroom. Tired nurses could still summon up the energy to go to the Hammersmith Palais, where dance bands such as the late Glenn Miller's (he was killed in 1944), Benny Goodman's, Tommy Dorsey's and Joe Loss's were all the rage. For the really intrepid the Paramount in Tottenham Court Road held jitterbug marathons and swing contests: by 1945 dance halls had long given up on trying to ban jitterbugging. There were jazz clubs at Mac's Rehearsal Rooms in Windmill Street and 100 Oxford Street.

On the whole, women welcomed the opportunity to work and found it a rewarding experience. When asked what they enjoyed most about work, most said it was the companionship. Work alleviated loneliness while husbands were away. Many were driven by patriotism, but it was also useful to have the money. The wives of the lower ranks of the armed forces were especially hard up, but for any woman unaccustomed to having money of her own, this was something of a novelty. As one middle-aged woman on part-time work told Mass-Observation: 'When you get up in the morning you feel you go out with something in your bag, and something coming in at the end of the week, and it's nice. It's a taste of independence and you feel a lot happier for it.'

Nevertheless, they were at a disadvantageous position in the workplace. As the former Chief of the Transport and General Workers Union, Ernest Bevin had been able to persuade the trade unions to allow women into jobs hitherto done by men. Women's trade union membership doubled during the war, rising to 2,200,000 in 1944, or just over a quarter of all women workers, despite the fact that many of them were classed as 'dilutees' because they were diluting the skilled, male, workforce for the duration only. In theory, women were to receive the same pay for the same jobs. Women's average pay rose from £1 12s 6d to £3 3s 2d a week during the war. In an exceptional week in, say, a Royal Ordnance factory with lots of overtime and bonuses this could be bumped up to as much as £8; against this a first-year nurse's salary was only £5 a month, although she would also receive board and lodging. In spite of being better off, however, women were paid only 52 per cent of men's average earnings.

All sorts of ruses were employed to short-change women and to ensure that they did not encroach too far into the male preserve. They were considered to be doing the same job as a man if they could do the job without supervision or assistance, but the foreman's usual practice was to interfere in some way, so that the woman could be deemed 'unskilled' and paid accordingly. Some men even stooped so low as to tamper with the machinery, so as to hinder the progress of the woman who succeeded him on the next shift. Many women had undergone government training for the job, but found that they were not being allowed to do that job. Lots of jobs, in skilled engineering or the higher echelons of the civil service or just plain factory work where strength was required, were considered 'men's jobs'.

Young women who would normally have stayed at home until they were married left to join the forces or work in munitions factories. Some were evacuated with their offices from London, but as ever many came into the capital to work. Away from family and familiar neighbourhoods, they enjoyed unprecedented freedom, which in turn resulted in a relaxation of moral codes and an increase in promiscuity. The results were inevitable: a rise in the rate of illegitimate births and in sexually transmitted diseases.

In his annual report at the end of 1944 Sir Philip Game, Commissioner of Police for the Metropolis, stated: 'One of the most distressing social consequences of the war is the growth of professional prostitution among young girls and the promiscuous association with servicemen of girls who are adrift from homes or parents.'

In January 1945 the newspapers were reporting that girls under the age of 18 – too young to be mobilised – were frequenting the West End, attracted by the idea of getting off with GIs and other Allied servicemen. No doubt their fathers were away on war service or had absconded and their mothers were engaged in war factories and the girls were not sufficiently supervised. One way or other, their family life had been fractured under the stress of war. Given the age of the girls, they were perhaps evacuated children whose experiences had been unfortunate; the children who had gone without schooling for long periods; the ones who had endured the terror of the bombing and been bombed out at least once.

A report in the *Sunday Despatch* noted that 'Fifteen- to eighteen-year-old girls, not yet within the scope of the Ministry of Labour control, throng the streets, particularly near troop centres, in the hope of "picking up" with Allied servicemen and having a good time.' They were tempted by the pleasures and excitements that would normally have been way beyond their reach. As one report put it:

One of the most remarkable features has been the way in which girls of about fourteen seem to attract Allied servicemen – all that seems to be necessary is for the girl to have a desire to please . . . Those girls who are misfits at home or at work, or who feel inferior for some reason or another, have been very easy victims. Their lives were brightened by the attention . . . and they found that they had an outlet which was not only a contrast, but was a definite compensation for the dullness, poverty and, sometimes, unhappiness of home life.

The article revealed that women police were swooping on selected areas of the West End to check identity cards. Those dodging mobilisation were to be dealt with accordingly but under-age girls would be taken by van to the nearest police station. Their parents would be informed of their whereabouts. Apparently, these 'good time' girls did not need to use their ration books, as they were sleeping in air-raid shelters and eating in cafés.

The patrolling officer of the Public Morality Council deplored the lax moral climate in which the girls were operating:

I must again refer to the very large proportion of girls of about 16 to 18 years of age, always looking for a good time at somebody else's expense. These girls, a large number of whom travel from the East End and usually in couples, throng the amusement and sports arcades, often undoubtedly for the warmth and light offered, but principally to get off with the American troops who seem to use these places for a like purpose. There is no solicitation, but they easily get into conversation whilst playing with the various machines, and then they are on a very slippery slope, which in many instances ends in disaster.

Immediately before D-Day there were 1,421,363 Allied, dominion and colonial troops in Britain, and even after the D-Day landings, thousands of them would spend their leave in the capital or pass through. American servicemen were particularly numerous in London, a popular belief being that if they stood to attention the wall they were leaning on would fall down. Many – especially men – found them irksome.

Their bold confidence, unfettered by traditional English conventions of class and respectability, had a strong influence on the women they drew into their orbit. They had no inhibitions about, say, wandering into the Savoy for a drink and taking an English girl who, in normal times, would not have dared venture through the door. Odette Lesley was one of many who would dance with 'GIs, Canadians and boys from other foreign countries' at the Hammersmith Palais. 'I felt a strong sense of independence that I'd never felt before,' she recalls. 'It was so exciting. I felt that anything was possible.' Such women had had their whole outlook on life changed and their behaviour with it: they would never be able to fit back into the restricted confines of their previous existence.

These were men about to go into battle, knowing they could soon be dead, so that they were determined to extract every ounce of pleasure from life. Men going to war are not easily refused and they can be very persuasive, even to women who normally would have said No and meant it. The Americans were fun and intent on enjoying themselves and for many English girls they held an irresistible attraction:

To girls brought up on the cinema, who copied the dress, hair styles and manners of Hollywood stars, the sudden influx of Americans, speaking like the films, who actually lived in the magic country, and who had plenty of money, at once went to the girls' heads. The American attitude to women, their proneness to spoil a girl, to build up, exaggerate, talk big, and to act with generosity and flamboyance, helped to make them the most attractive boy friends. In addition, they 'picked up' easily, and even a comparatively plain and unattractive girl stood a chance.

Attracted by the glamour, the smart uniform and the amount of cash the Americans had at their disposal, some English girls made themselves only too available. James Lees-Milne noted: 'American soldiers speak with surprise about the familiarity of English girls, none of whom decline to sleep with them. They are convinced all English women are tarts, and despise them accordingly, just as English soldiers despised the French girls during the last war.'

The distraught mother of one of them 'too ashamed to give her name' wrote to the Public Morality Council:

I ask you as a mother to take notice of the following. As God is my judge this is the truth. My daughter has returned home to me after two years. Ran away to get married to an American. To cut a long story short, she became a prostitute, selling her body day in and day out. She has now been removed to a home in the country ruined for life at the age of 23. She has told me of her experiences with these Americans. I shudder when I think of them. They are responsible for many of our foolish young girls getting VD. She told me that there are three houses run as brothels and that girls infected go there every night . . . The girls arrive at the houses at 10.30 to midnight. Drunk.

During the war, the incidence of venereal disease increased alarmingly, especially in London and the major ports, rising steeply after the arrival of US troops in 1942. Hitherto the subject had been taboo, never discussed publicly in deference to strong religious and moral objections, so that there was a high level of ignorance about the disease. In 1942 the Ministry of Health launched a campaign to educate the public. A typical VD advertisement ran: 'The increase of venereal disease is one of the few "black spots" on the nation's wartime health record. A very important cause is ignorance.' The advertisement goes on to explain how VD is contracted and how it can be cured by early treatment. 'Any man or woman, boy or girl, who has sexual relations with a casual acquaintance risks picking up syphilis or gonorrhoea. Clean living is the real safeguard.'

The Government was concerned that the efficiency of servicemen was being impaired through their infection with venereal disease. Under Defence Regulation 33B, which came into effect in 1942, any person suspected of passing on VD to more than two patients could be compelled to undergo examination and treatment. Servicemen returning on leave or after demobilisation were warned to finish their course of treatment before resuming sexual relations with their wives.

Unfortunately, the VD campaign was slightly hampered by the shortage of rubber to make contraceptives, until the Chief Medical Officer urged that an exception be made and the relevant companies given a rubber allocation. Hot water bottles were almost impossible to obtain and teats for babies' bottles were scarce, but contraceptives were back in production.

The rise in the number of illegitimate births, among women of all ages and classes, to more than twice the pre-war level was not in itself an indication of greater moral laxity. There had always been a high proportion of pre-marital conceptions, but in peacetime there had been more opportunity to legalise the union and legitimise the offspring before the birth. In wartime, a man might be sent abroad before he could marry the mother of his child. Some of these unions were legalised in due course, but as many neglected to legitimise their

Venereal VD Diseases

"The alarming increase in these loathsome diseases makes it imperative that accurate knowledge should be given to the public and the simple facts frankly discussed."

SIR WILSON JAMESON,
Chief Medical Officer.

QUESTIONS ANSWERED

Why are Venereal Diseases a growing menace?

Wartime conditions have brought about an increase in venereal diseases which are spread through free and easy sex relations. Many sufferers put off seeking medical advice and meanwhile spread the disease to others.

Why does this problem concern everybody?

Venereal diseases damage the nation's health, threaten the future of the race, cause wasted hours and reduced efficiency in the factories and Services. They are highly contagious. Husbands infect wives (and vice versa) and the infection may be passed on to unborn children, condemning them to a life of misery and ill-health.

Can Venereal Diseases "just happen?"

No. They are caused by germs which cannot grow in the human body of their own accord. Usually they enter the body during intercourse with an infected person.

What are the Danger Signals?

Syphilis first appears as a small ulcer on or near the reproductive organs from 10 to 90 days after infection; usually 21 days. The first sign of gonorrhœa is a discharge from the reproductive organs 2 to 10 days after infection.

offspring retrospectively – as they were entitled to do – it is impossible to gauge the proportion: the figure of irregularly conceived maternities later regularised by marriage fell from 70 per cent before the war to only 37 per cent in 1945, before beginning to rise again in subsequent years.

Daughters were often away from home, so that their families were unable to police their courtships. It was far easier for men, removed from family pressure and neighbourhood disapproval, to dodge their obligations altogether. Some illegitimate pregnancies were the result of single encounters, perhaps on the part of inexperienced and naïve girls, and probably under the influence of drink. There were certainly more illegitimate babies than in peacetime and many of them might not have happened but for the peculiar circumstances of war.

It was one of the social consequences of war that the state accepted new responsibilities for the welfare of unmarried mothers and their babies. They could no longer be left to the mercy of the voluntary societies and the poor law. Attitudes were changing. An article in the *Spectator* in the spring of 1945 suggested: 'The first reaction of all concerned is so often, "How can we get rid of the child for the mother's sake?" when the question should be, "What are we to do to help this child and this mother to make the most of their lives?"'

The stigma of giving birth to an illegitimate child and illegitimacy itself could not be wiped out overnight, however. Every effort was made to enable single mothers to keep their babies, although in practice it would be very hard for them to support themselves. Some remained determined to give up their babies for adoption and the National Children's Adoption Association tried to find good homes for them, although they had to be wary of people with ulterior motives: 'Would-be adopters have given as their reasons a desire to escape from national service, ARP, or even fire-watching, while the child's clothing coupons are another source of temptation.'

Curiously, it was very difficult to find adoptive parents for the offspring of Allied soldiers. 'Most couples are very particular on this point,' the secretary of the Adoption Association said, 'they want nothing but British.' Nevertheless, in the years 1945–7 55,000 adoption orders were made nationally, with a peak of 21,000 in 1946.

Long before they reached the adoption stage, however, some young women panicked. Some opted for an abortion, which was still illegal unless the mother's life was endangered. They therefore had to resort to 'back-street methods', putting their lives on the line. Anyone procuring an illicit abortion or conducting one was liable to prosecution.

Alternatively, the woman might give birth and then find she could not cope. There are innumerable mentions of abandoned babies in the press. 'A pleasantly spoken young woman called at a house in Bessborough Street, Victoria,' ran one such report, 'carrying a baby and asked the occupier if she would be kind enough to look after the baby while she went to look for lodgings. She did not return and the baby was taken to Ladywell Institution, SE.' Another report described an 18-month-old boy abandoned in a restaurant in Limehouse. He had been well looked after and was 'fair with blue eyes, he was dressed in a light blue woollen jersey, pink woollen jacket and hood, and had on leather walking reins'.

Worse than abandoning the baby was actually doing away with it or leaving it to die. When the emergency water tanks which were dotted around London for the fire services were emptied at the end of the war, some were found to contain the tiny corpses of babies; it is impossible to know whether they had been dead when they were put there or if they had been deliberately drowned.

Women who had abandoned their babies were often traced and brought before a court of law: 'You must have no more of these fleeting affections which land you with babies,' a magistrate told a 22-year-old charged with abandoning her 6-week-old baby in an air raid shelter on Clapham Common. As ever, it was a pathetic situation. 'She said she had left the child because she had no money and was desperate. The father, she stated, was an American soldier, whom she only knew as Frankie.' She received scant sympathy from the magistrate:

'You have made a plaything of yourself, and it is always the woman who suffers in the end.' She received two months' probation. 'Now remember'– he wagged his finger at her – 'no more monkeying about with men!'

When a 27-year-old Stepney dressmaker, Sally Solomons, abandoned her son Victor, not yet 2 years old, at Moseley Buildings, Camlett Street, Bethnal Green, it was obviously a plea for help: 'She seems to have completely lost her head and acted without commonsense at all. I think she was actuated by terrible shame.' This was the opinion of Miss Rosenthal, the probation officer who accompanied her to Old Street Magistrates Court. 'The child was born as the result of an American soldier taking advantage of the girl after a casual meeting, added Miss Rosenthal. She put the baby at the entrance of a flat on the ground floor of some buildings, believing that it would be rescued within a few minutes and this, in fact, happened.'

The magistrate said he wanted the public to understand that children could not be left in that 'haphazard fashion' to risk the chances of fortune. 'You have been penalised already,' he told the accused, who wept during the proceedings, 'while someone else goes scot free. Some of you people ought to think about this before.'

Occasionally, a baby was not abandoned but abducted. Frustrated motherhood and a woman's anxiety to present a son to her soldier husband on his return from the war were the reasons given for the abduction of Maurice Jakubowicz, who disappeared from his pram outside an Oxford Street store in April 1945. The abductor, Mrs Faith Crogham of Earl's Court, had had a miscarriage after her husband had gone abroad. 'I hadn't the heart to write and tell my husband about it,' she confessed. Instead, in July she wrote to tell him she had given birth to a boy. When he came home on leave and there was no baby she told him the child was with friends.

A week later when she was in Oxford Street she saw a baby crying in his pram and picked him up to comfort him. Then she took him home, pretending to her husband he was theirs.

The baby was found through a tip-off in an anonymous letter. He had been well cared for. In a curious twist, it transpired that Faith Crogham was a bigamist, who had left not just a husband but a child. Obviously, she was emotionally disturbed and it cannot have helped that she was sent to prison for 18 months for child abduction and 6 for bigamy, the sentences to run concurrently.

What is perhaps surprising is the number of older, married women who were having affairs and giving birth to illegitimate babies. They at least should have had some understanding of and access to contraception, which was often denied to single women. The affairs in themselves are perhaps not surprising, taking into account the strain and the loneliness these women were under through long years of separation from their husbands.

Films such as *Waterloo Road* and *Since You Went Away*, released early in 1945, attempted to diagnose the effects of wartime absence upon the hearts – and behaviour – of those left behind. 'Does absence make them grow fonder?' asked the *Spectator*'s critic in a rave review of 'the tear compeller' *Since You Went Away*. 'Or do they falter in their loneliness? Or does absence make the heart swell and swell until it fairly brims over with every synthetic sentiment, every device that has ever been invented for the marketing of tears in the guise of entertainment?' The content of the films would certainly resonate with everyone in the audience.

If they were not tied to small children, almost all the women with absent husbands were working and life was hard: it was understandable if they occasionally went out to enjoy themselves at a dance or over a few drinks. It was easy to form attachments under the emotional stress of war. For some, going out with other men became habitual, but there were always cases of married women who had lapsed only once and found they were pregnant or that there was no turning back.

The romantic novelist Barbara Cartland was a wartime marriage counsellor:

It is very easy to say what a woman should do or should not do when she hasn't seen her husband for four years . . . They were young, their husbands were not fluent letter-writers – they started by not meaning any harm, just desiring a little change from the monotony of looking after the children, queuing for food, and cleaning house with no man to appreciate them or their cooking. Another man would come along – perhaps an American or an RAF pilot . . . He is lonely, she is lonely, he smiles at her, she smiles back, and it's an introduction. It is bad luck that she is married, but he means no harm, nor does it cross her mind at first that she could ever be unfaithful to Bill overseas. When human nature takes its course and they fall in love, the home is broken up and maybe another baby is on the way, there are plenty of people ready to say it's disgusting and disgraceful. But they hadn't meant it to be like that, they hadn't really.

The post-war booklet, *Living Together Again*, noted that women who thought they were happily married now had their eyes opened to other possibilities: 'They had only a stereo-typed experience to go upon, and in many cases had never so much as realised that their knowledge of sexual love was imperfect. Before the war they went on contentedly with their husbands, unaware that they were not really satisfied.'

German propaganda had been at pains to point out to British servicemen in the desert and then in Europe that while they were fighting, the Americans were seducing their women back home. The Government was concerned at the effect such propaganda and, indeed, such knowledge would have upon the morale of the fighting troops.

The *Daily Mirror* complained that lurid statements concerning the morality of servicemen's wives made by judges, magistrates, social reformers and the 'eternal busybody' was giving a cumulative picture which was 'false and distorted and likely to cause great pain and distress to our soldiers in foreign lands'. The article stressed that cases that drew publicity were isolated ones and 'bear no relation to the majority of service wives who have carried bravely on'.

The *Star* agreed: 'The exemplary conduct and courage of women in so many lonely homes fully justify the faith of the great majority of men overseas. Giddy and feather-brained women exist in war as in peace. War-time gives loose wives and loose husbands more opportunities for infidelity.'

This was certainly true. War and separation and dislocation from their usual surroundings seem to have totally altered some women's character and behaviour. Irene Byers, evacuated from Dulwich to a Somerset village where there were a lot of black GIs and a great deal of racial prejudice, noted: 'Crowds of them haunt the village in the evenings and gossips say that there will be many half-caste children born after the war. It seems that the married women are more open to temptation than the single girls.'

A London schoolteacher who was evacuated to the country with a group of mothers and young children recalled:

There was only one of the London mothers evacuated, out of a possible forty I know personally, that was not going the pace in this little village with soldiers. The one exception was a mother who had had an illegitimate son before she was married, and possibly knew the game was not worth the candle. I think not so much that standards have changed, but that people have been uprooted from their home surroundings. Evacuation, joining the Forces, Mother going out to work in strange surroundings. This has put morality to the test. It is difficult to have an affair at home, there are too many checks.

In a paper entitled 'Sex, Morality and the Birth Rate,' Mass-Observation noted that evacuation and loneliness, as well as opportunity, prompted promiscuous behaviour. It quotes the case of Mrs J, 30, mother of two boys of six and four: 'She became a flagrant wanton; lived with one soldier after another. Took her six-year-old boy out to cafes while she solicited. Looked like a first-rate tart. Child never had enough sleep, kept awake by mother's affairs. In the end started shop-lifting. Baby was born in prison. Now, this is the strange part of it. A mother said to me: "She was such a nice respectable woman in Camberwell; never looked at a man."'

Then there was the case of Mrs D, aged 36, mother of five:

In London I admired her tremendously. She was a devoted, unselfish mother. Starved herself between '31 and '33 when her husband was on short time. Evacuated to country, working on munitions. Began having affairs with soldiers. Left home, lived with her lover. Returned home owing to sickness of five-year-old girl. Started off again, husband discovered letter in bag from Canadian soldier, giving her away. Later caught her out having a motor ride with a Canadian on a dark night. At Easter she left her family of five for good.

It is not known how many illegitimate children were born to married women, but generally during the war the illegitimacy rate seems to have been three times the pre-war figure. A married woman's child is believed to be her husband's, unless she states otherwise when registering the birth, but of course a lot of husbands came home to find a child that could not be theirs. The consequences varied. Some marriages broke up; other women were compelled by their husbands – as was their right – to give the child up for adoption; some men kindly accepted the illegitimate child as one of the family. Ironically, a married woman could not offer a child for adoption without her husband's permission, so that there was little or no possibility of her concealing her infidelity.

Home Chat, that most conservative of women's magazines, was anxious to encourage women to be faithful to their husbands. As late as February 1945 it was advising:

You are urged to be like Caesar's wife, above suspicion. Imagine being hundreds – perhaps thousands – of miles away from home, with mud or sand everywhere, insects, bullets, fear, loneliness, and the only link with home letters from the loved one – and news of our families. How pitifully easy under such conditions to become jealous, to imagine the worst!

You must have read official stories of the effect on the men in an entire company when one man's wife has "gone off the rails".

However much the other men love and trust their wives, little doubts creep in. Letters are re-read anxiously – as they try to read something between the lines that isn't there.

Suppose, then, that your man reads of the dances you have been to and notices the way 'Jock' and 'Pete' is so often mentioned. Can you blame him if he begins to wonder? Then too, there will always be people with diseased minds who delight in writing anonymous letters to men away from their wives. Suppose one wrote about you . . .

It seems hard to have to forgo innocent pleasures just in case of unjust scandal, doesn't it? Yet think what our men are giving up for us. It makes our sacrifices seem infinitely small. And there is another aspect we must consider. Can we trust ourselves to mix with the opposite sex without becoming emotionally involved? Times are not normal, and the woman accustomed to the love and companionship of her husband finds it hard to do without it.

The article concluded: 'A few more months of loneliness and sober living and we shall be the more eager and happy to greet our men. Let us seek our amusements in the company of our own sex for a little longer.'

The *Star* could not resist a little levity, warning readers: 'Unless you can prove you bought it yourself, don't chew gum when he's home.'

Unfortunately, some women did not trouble to hide their infidelity or were caught unawares by their husband's return. There was a spate of murders and violence as trigger-happy servicemen found their wives *in flagrante delicto*. In January 1945, 32-year-old Alfred James Morgan from Camberwell came home on leave unexpectedly to find another man in the house. In the ensuing row he shot his wife in the head saying, 'If I cannot have you, nobody else shall. You've had it.' Morgan later claimed he had produced the gun to frighten his wife and that it had gone off by accident. Fortunately, the shot was not fatal and Mrs Morgan forgave her husband and asked him to do the same.

There was a surprising amount of sympathy for the man in this situation, no doubt prompted by the age-old disapproval of the erring wife or immoral woman. On passing sentence on Morgan at the Old Bailey, Mr Justice Charles commiserated with him, saying it must have been a bitter blow to come home on leave and find his wife with another man. 'But,' he added, 'if soldiers come back home and find that their wives have not been faithful to them it must be known that they cannot resort to violence, particularly with firearms, under the stress of these circumstances.'

Morgan's was by no means an isolated incident. 'It is another of these cases which, unfortunately, are becoming common, of a man who comes back from the Army, finds his wife has been unfaithful, and takes the law into his own hands,' opined a barrister at Old Street in September, when Frederick James Hooker of Shoreditch was committed for trial at the Old Bailey, charged with the murder of his wife, Lilian May. He had been demobilised in July and returned home to find his wife had been 'carrying on and had lost all affection for him'.

He had used a knife and told a passer-by: 'I have killed my wife and stabbed her. If I had not killed her, she would have killed me. She had been carrying on with other men. I begged her not to for the sake of the children. That is why I have done it.'

He had promised his wife he would forgive her if she gave up her lover. 'She told me to get out. I stabbed her in the neck. I think more than once. I did not know what I was doing. I have been going crazy for the last three weeks. I could not eat or sleep. I kept asking her to be fair to me, but she would not. I idolised her and thought the world of her. There had been no other women in my life. I just longed for the time I could get back to her. It was the other man that drove me to do this. I kept thinking about my children.'

She had died from a throat wound but there were cuts on her hand, where she had tried to ward off the attack.

The end of the war saw an increase in the number of marriages taking place: the rate had risen and dipped according to the fortunes of war, from the summit of 22 per 1,000 in 1940, through a slump to 14 per 1,000 in 1943, to 19 per 1,000 in 1945. There had been a wartime trend towards younger marriages. Of women marrying for the first time during the war, 30 per cent were under 21. The wartime birth rate roughly corresponded with the rise and fall of the marriage rate, although it faltered slightly in 1945 – possibly, in London at least, as a result of the disturbance and uncertainty caused by the V-weapon attacks from June 1944, while in 1945 itself many women were giving the housing shortage as their reason for restricting the size of their family.

A marked feature of the war was the number of marriages of British women to members of the armed forces of the dominions, colonies and Allies. Londoner Betty Weiner, whose father ran a club for lonely GIs, was one of 80,000 British women who became GI brides. She married quickly in March 1945, when he had a week's leave. 'Looking back on it now, we didn't know our husbands . . . there was no way of knowing their parents, their friends.' On the other hand, 'you didn't know if you were going to be alive tomorrow, you didn't think too much therefore.' Before the wedding she had to take a Wasserman (blood) test and be vetted by his commanding officer. When she went to obtain her visa from the American Embassy in Grosvenor Square she encountered a degree of hostility. 'They didn't make you feel welcome – "taking our boys". You were made to feel like a bit of a slut – as if you had to find a man.'

Given their attitude, it was understandable that the Americans were not in any rush to transport these women across the Atlantic. Some of those who were left to languish in England well into 1946 went on protest demonstrations at the long delay in being reunited with their husbands. Betty Weiner was fortunate in that her father was willing to pay the astronomical sum of £100 for her air fare to New York – it took 23 hours – and a further £100 to the person who 'fixed' the flight. When she arrived, in common with many GI brides who had been misled by the brash confidence of the American men, she was 'slightly disappointed' by her husband's living conditions. She found the Americans 'didn't somehow speak the same language'. Feeling desperately homesick, she would go down to the quay to watch the ships leaving for England and cry. Not surprisingly, a proportion of GI brides returned to England.

Those GI brides who were waiting for an assisted sea passage across the Atlantic could while away some of the time at the School for Brides at Rainbow Corner, the American servicemen's club in the West End of London. Classes were held on the first Sunday of the month, when they could learn about the US system of government, education, public health, cooking, housewifery, shopping, clothes, customs and currency. They could also pick up all sorts of handy tips. For instance, they were told that it was better to spend $25 on a jar of 'restoration cream' than the same sum on four new hats. The extremes of the American climate would not be kind to English skin, inured to moderate temperatures and soft rain. They must get into the habit of drinking eight glasses of water daily to make up for the lack of moisture in the American air.

In contrast to the publicity given to the GI brides, Britain's war widows were receiving little attention and certainly not enough sympathy and support. Edna Bucknill recalls:

As a young war widow, I was among the ranks of the 'walking wounded'. Almost ignored, as if one had a dread disease that no one wanted to know about. War widows were disregarded. You couldn't get accommodation easily. War Widows' Pensions were treated as 'unearned income' for tax purposes and, therefore, taxed at the highest rate possible. How about that for losing my husband, three brothers, my home and a baby?

While the war was a stimulus to marriage it was an even more powerful stimulus to divorce. The number of divorce petitions filed in England and Wales rose from 9,970 in 1938 to 24,857 in 1945 and to a post-war peak of 47,041 in 1947. In addition to divorce, there were also about 25,000 legal separations in 1945-6, a 150 per cent increase over the pre-war level. Even without the war, there might have been some increase owing to the liberalisation of the divorce laws in the Matrimonial Causes Act in 1937. Whereas before the war over half the petitions had been filed by wives, in 1945 58 per cent came from husbands. Adultery was the most common cause cited. For the sake of morale, the Forces' Welfare Services enabled service personnel to obtain divorces more cheaply and expeditiously than civilians. It may be that some servicemen were pretending they were the injured party to enable their spouses to save the full costs of proceedings.

It was hard for the courts to keep pace. Divorce was still sufficiently novel for newspapers to include short notices of divorces granted, naming the parties concerned and outlining the reasons. In 1945 the London *Evening Standard* tended to list the numbers as some sort of score which grew ever more fantastic. On 15 January alone, Mr Justice Hodson in the Divorce Court made absolute the record total of 1,124 decrees nisi – the proceedings for which took 10 seconds.

Many wartime marriages had been rushed affairs between people who hardly knew each other. After long absence, they felt little or no responsibility towards each other. Odette Lesley was such a case:

Like a lot of girls, I really married in quite a hurry in wartime. The men were in the services. We knew they were going away, going abroad, and we felt we wanted to get married. I was married when I was 18, and I got married on the Tuesday, and Wednesday I was saying goodbye to him. I saw him very briefly after that, and then it was three years before I saw him again. And, of course, because I had changed through the war, through the experiences, meeting all sorts of people, I'd got this sense of independence, which coloured everything I thought about. Then I started to think about my husband. I had awful guilty feelings because I was sure that there was no way when he came home that I'd be able to settle down, into the rather dull, domestic routine which was what he would have expected. I thought to myself, 'I can't stay with him, because I can't do what he wants, I want more out of life now, I want to have more experiences.' In fact, when he was sent back to his unit for demobilisation I ran off to the Channel Islands, because I knew I couldn't cope with that sort of marriage and that was the end of it. This, of course, was the effect of war.

In other cases, couples who had once loved each other found they were no longer compatible. It was hard to sustain a relationship over years of separation: a commanding officer noted that it was often all right for the first two years, but troubles and infidelities tended to occur in the third year of separation. The Government had established an efficient and cheap postal system serving the troops overseas and their families at home. However, the overwhelming proportion of the population had left school at 14, so that they were not necessarily the most articulate letter writers; letters are often inadequate or misunderstood. Although divorce was still not done in 'respectable' families (and in the higher echelons of society divorcees could not be received at court or enter the Royal Enclosure at Ascot), the increase in earnings during the war must have facilitated divorce for some for whom it would previously have been unthinkable.

Inevitably, where strangers were meeting outside their own neighbourhoods and where hasty marriages were taking place, there were cases of bigamy. Between the wars, about 350 cases reached the courts annually, but by 1945 the national level exceeded 1,000 a year. In 1944 a printed warning against bigamy was included in every civil notice of marriage. The following year there was a spate of articles in the press about the increase in bigamy. 'The vast majority of these bigamy cases are committed not by criminals,' the *Daily Mirror* suggested, 'but by ordinary people who have drifted apart from their legal partners through war conditions.'

A former ATS girl, Ethel Barnes from Clapham, was bound over for a year for making two false declarations for the purpose of procuring a licence for marriage. She declared that her intended, John Hudson, was a bachelor and that she was 21. When the couple turned up at Lambeth Register Office she produced her army pay book as proof of her age. The date of birth was given as 6 June 1923, but it had obviously been doctored. The superintendent registrar ascertained from Somerset House that her correct date of birth was 6 June 1926. As she was under 21, she would have to obtain her parents' consent to the marriage. They refused to give it, as they suspected that the man was married. Inquiries revealed that Hudson had married in 1935 and had a wife and three children in Newcastle.

He said, 'The marriage would have been a bigamous one, as I was already married. I didn't know until I went to the register office that Miss Barnes was only eighteen. In any case, I didn't want to marry her when I knew her age.'

Unfortunately, Miss Barnes had had to leave the ATS when she discovered she was pregnant – as all service women were bound to do. Hudson was responsible for her condition. The magistrate told him he was lucky not to be charged with bigamy and fined him £10 for making a false declaration.

'Monotony, Rationing, Queues, Make Wives Moody', proclaimed a *Daily Mail* headline. War took its toll on women's health, looks and youth. There was an increase in prematurely grey-haired women. It didn't need an Edinburgh professor – who reported his findings in February 1945 – to tell women they were suffering from the strain of trying to do too much for too long. They had had to manage the household and the children without the support of their husbands. Many of them had lost their homes and been separated from their children, at least for some of the time. The majority had done some sort of war work, either working very long hours or just a few hours a day in the local Civil Defence force or the WVS. After work, there had often been compulsory firewatching at night. For all of them, there had been hundreds of nights of interrupted sleep and always the strain of knowing that they or their loved ones might be killed at any time.

In addition to all this, they had had to endure years of queuing for food and trying to stretch monotonous wartime rations into appetising meals; they had spent what little time they had left after work and the completion of household chores in faithfully following the Government's dictums to 'make do and mend' and 'dig for victory'. On top of all this, there were innumerable wartime innovations – the complexity of the rationing and points system for one thing – for them to contend with. No wonder they were flagging under the 'double burden'.

The Harley Street doctor Anthony Weymouth noted:

Most people are agreed that women have had an extremely hard time in this war. Have I not seen dozens of women patients in the last two years who have told me that they are mentally and physically exhausted by the cooking, cleaning, and queuing? Only the other day one explained to me that she was able to carry on her life while the war was on only because she believed that it was 'for the duration'. Now, she added, she can see no end to her life of hardship and the hope which buoyed her up during the war years has left her.

With the traditional support in family and neighbourhood withdrawn, the state had had to intervene in many aspects of life which had hitherto been managed privately. It was bad for morale among the forces if their families were not being taken care of when they were in trouble. If women were engaged in war work, they could not also be on hand to look after children or elderly relatives. War exposed the many gaps and shortcomings in the existing welfare system, which was based on the old poor law and workhouse tradition. These casualties of war were not asking for charity in the old sense and could not be treated with the same lofty disdain as the poor and needy had had to endure hitherto – being made to feel ashamed because they were asking for help.

War necessitated an expansion of the social services and created the rationale for the post-war welfare state. During the emergency, the state was ably supported by voluntary organisations, not least the Women's Voluntary Service, who with female initiative and common sense were able to suggest many practices which the Government adopted. The key to the WVS was its flexibility and it also brought a much needed human touch when helping families in crisis. In the case of the forces, SAAFA (the Soldiers' Sailors' and Airmen's Families Association) did invaluable work helping servicemen's families in need.

Maternity is a prime example where women actually derived some benefit from wartime conditions. Bomb-blasted London was no place to give birth. At the outset of war, many of London's maternity wards – there had been a shortage of beds with only about 2,100 spread across the whole range of voluntary and municipal hospitals and homes – closed and expectant mothers were encouraged to have their babies in the country, where emergency maternity units had been set up. In quiet periods, where there was little or no bombing, many of them were refusing to leave their homes and give birth in unfamiliar surroundings. The arrival of the V-1s and V-2s quickly changed their minds. In the summer of 1944 there was a mass evacuation of London's hospitals and their maternity wards were closed again. The Minister of Health was urging expectant mothers to 'please register for evacuation now and make sure that your baby will be safe and have a good start.'

At the peak of the V-weapons crisis about 750 expectant mothers a week were leaving London under the Government's evacuation scheme and maternity units were being hurriedly reopened or established in the country to meet the extended requirements. The poor state of the capital's housing after the V-weapons period ensured that an exodus of 200-300 a week persisted even after VE Day. London hospitals were slow to reopen their maternity wards or bring them up to speed again after the end of hostilities, but in July 1945 the Ministry announced that the cost of the emergency maternity homes could no longer be borne by the Exchequer's Evacuation Account. As from 31 August, the woman's local authority in London would have to bear the cost of her travel expenses and the 14s daily rate for the 5 weeks she would spend lying in at the unit.

In October 1945 an LCC paper on the financial situation reported a further tightening of the screw: 'The Metropolitan Borough Medical Officers of Health have been asked to look at the home conditions of all expectant mothers in order that only those for whom arrangements for confinement at home are out of the question shall be registered for accommodation in these emergency maternity homes.'

Generally speaking, these maternity units offered a better standard of care than most women had been used to in the more common practice of pre-war home deliveries. Betty Hill, who was evacuated to Ruskin College, Oxford, to have her baby, remembers the good ante- and post-natal care she and the other women were receiving under the new system, whereas before the war very little of this had been available or encouraged. At the end of the war, the Minister of Health declared that he was proud to have held office at a time when it was possible to report in the fourth year of the war that the infant mortality rate was the lowest on record; the neo-natal mortality rate was the lowest on record; the birth-rate was the highest for 15 years; the stillbirth-rate was the lowest on record and the chances of a stillbirth were only three-quarters of what they had been even 5 years previously. There was now a growing demand for institutional confinements by expectant mothers. The precedent for special maternity clinics and safer births had been established, ironically through the exigencies of war.

The state also intervened to save the vulnerable – expectant and nursing mothers, babies and small children – from some of the deprivations of the wartime diet. The National Milk Scheme ensured they had one pint of milk a day for 2d (the current price being fourpence halfpenny), or free if the family income was below a certain level, while they could obtain free cod liver oil and orange juice from the local food office or welfare centre.

Preventative medicine took a step forward with the Ministry's widely publicised scheme for diphtheria immunisation, which became vital in London in 1940 when so many were sleeping in crowded air raid shelters and there was a high risk of contagion. The cost would be borne by the Ministry, although local authorities were responsible for operating the service. It was a great success, cutting the number of deaths from diphtheria to one-quarter of the pre-war level.

As soon as the emergency was over, the pressure was on for women to forget any notions of independence and return to the home. The country owed women an immeasurable debt for their wartime contribution – as Ernest Bevin acknowledged when he declared 'our women tipped the scales of victory'– and yet now it seemed that everything they had achieved was to be eradicated from the popular consciousness and they were expected to slip back into the pre-war mindset. It was considered fine for women to work when the country needed them, but with peace came the return of the old mores.

The Women's Advisory Committee on Post-war Reconstruction was indignant: 'Women have established their claim to a share in the economic life of the nation. By having shared equally with men the tremendous task of producing for the needs of the war, they have an equal right to employment after the war.'

That was the theory, but it was hardly likely to be borne out in practice. Indeed, the position of women made little advance as a direct result of the war, despite the magnitude of their wartime achievements. Progress was stunted by Government policies, the opposition of the trade unions and, it has to be said, by the attitudes of some of the women themselves.

A Mass-Observation paper, 'Will the Factory Girls Want to Stay Put or Go Home?', includes this revealing summary of the typical patronising attitude:

It is more or less true also that the average human considers the bearing and rearing of a family, combined with looking after a house and husband, a full-time job for a woman, leaving her little time to go out to earn an independent living. In general, therefore, the ranks of female labour have always been recruited on a short-term basis from young unmarried women who wished to keep themselves for a few years with marriage in view, and from a minority of women who for one reason or another had been left without a provider.

Women's magazines were some of the loudest advocates of a woman's true place. Images of domestic femininity were stressed in the media under the pressure of consumer marketing. An article in *Home Chat* was most emphatic: 'The moment you say "I will" you belong to the Wives' Repertory Company, for to be a good wife you have to play a variety of parts. Like a good actress in any Repertory Company, it is essential for a wife to make a success of each and every one of her "roles". If not, she will fail in her chosen career – marriage and home-making.'

Biddy, the 'heroine' of this article, says that after the war is over she is perfectly willing to let her husband play the 'male lead' once more, for, as she points out, has she not already 'a star part of her own – that of leading lady in her home? And although she has proved, beyond all manner of doubt, that she is quite capable of understudying for her man, she says her heart will always lie in the star role of home-maker she played so well before the war.'

Both Mass-Observation and the Wartime Social Survey collected evidence showing that large groups of women wanted to continue their wartime jobs. One-quarter of women questioned by Mass-Observation in 1944 said that 'women should be allowed to go on doing men's jobs' and 28 per cent said 'depends on the post-war conditions'. Some women undoubtedly welcomed the chance to retreat to the home. Mary Beazley noted that most of her colleagues in the parachute factory in Tottenham Court Road lacked ambition: they worked hard and had a sense of responsibility about what they were doing, but their interests were limited to the cinema, clothes, their families and the man they would marry. They were working only for the duration of the war and marriage was their ultimate goal. Ignoring the fact that their findings showed that a large proportion of women would like to carry on working, or would if post-war conditions permitted, Mass-Observation concluded that 'even in the Services and overwhelmingly so in the factories, marriage and domestic life remains the almost universal post-war hope.'

It is significant that when each of the women's services ran refresher courses on how to be a civilian, domesticity took pride of place. There were courses on cookery, rationing, budgeting, household repairs, making loose covers, rug-making, dress design and embroidery. There were visits to gas and electricity showrooms to learn comparative fuel values. They obviously expected most of their personnel to marry and become housewives as, indeed, they did.

'Of course when we get married I shan't want to work,' a factory girl told Mass-Observation. 'I shall want to stay at home and have some children. You can't look on anything you do during the war as what you really mean to do; it's just filling in time till you can live your own life again.'

A married part-time piece-worker: 'I've got a home and a husband and a child of fourteen still at school. I only came as a war-time thing – I wouldn't say I disliked it; it's a change from housework, but I hope I'll go back and lead a peaceful life when the war's over.'

On the other hand, the money was useful. A part-time radio valve maker from Wembley admitted: 'I hope the return of women to the home will not be made a grave issue after the war. Speaking for myself, I shall be sorry to leave my job, and the part-time hours I work could be continued ad infinitum as far as I am concerned. I have not enough to do to occupy me intelligently in the house, and after years of voluntary "good works" a small regular pay packet is very welcome.'

Many felt there were bad times ahead and that the jobs would go to the boys. 'I don't think things look too good for after the war,' a factory worker told Mass-Observation. 'A lot of the girls would like to stay on, and the boys will come back and want the jobs. I think it's going to be just as bad as the last time, or even worse.'

It is extraordinary that in a bankrupt Britain, which was

going to have to produce exports 75 per cent over the 1939 level just to survive and close the dollar gap, in a country that required total reconstruction and modernisation, the prevalent notion seems to have been that there was only a finite amount of work available – and that men must be given priority when it came to jobs. Women were given to understand that by staying on they were taking the work that would otherwise be available to men coming out of the forces. They were also put under pressure by returning husbands, many of whom felt uneasy about having a working wife. A North Kensington woman recalled wistfully:

Then I went to Rickard's the motor coach firm. They had a factory round by the Wesleyan Church in Lancaster Road. I did mostly arc welding on tanks. My husband was one of the first to go into the Army so he was one of the first to come out. I didn't stay long at Rickard's. The men were all coming back and they wanted the jobs. Anyway, my husband didn't like me doing this welding – he didn't like the blokes there – he thought they were looking at me! I went back into machining and made soldiers' uniforms on a conveyor belt. But I enjoyed the welding and I reckon I could still do it.

Of course, a proportion of married working-class women had always worked in manual jobs. Many middle-class women were still conventional enough to accept that once they were married husband and household took priority, while the average middle-class man considered it shaming to have a wife who worked. War had opened many cracks in the edifice of convention, however, and people were now more inclined to question the norm. A 45-year-old London secretary, who was married, felt that it should be up to the individual to decide:

I do not think any woman who is married should have to go out to work; I think those that really wish to, and have no small children (or can put their children in a nursery school if they are little), should be able to. A man should be paid sufficient to support a wife, and there should be adequate family allowances. If the wife really wants to do some work which is of interest to her, I think it is a good thing for her to feel free to do so, provided she doesn't neglect the home too much, and that her husband really feels happy about it. (Husbands are getting used to it in wartime, and may be educated to agree to it in peacetime!) I am sure *every* married woman needs at least some interests outside her home if she is to lead a full life.

Although there were only 15 women MPs in the wartime Parliament, this number was pushed up to 23 with the Labour victory in July. More women of higher educational attainment were infiltrating the professions, as doctors, dentists, barristers and solicitors, architects and accountants, although the numbers were still small. It had been the practice for middle-class women in white collar jobs – civil servants, teachers, bank clerks and office workers – to leave work on marriage. That was fine if it was voluntary, but more often than not it was compulsory to do so and an increasing number of women resented the fact.

Many employers removed the marriage bar for the duration of the war, only promptly to slam it back again once the emergency was over. In London the more far-sighted LCC had removed the marriage bar for women teachers in 1935 and after that the numbers leaving on marriage had declined significantly, showing that an increasing number of women wished to reduce their dependency in marriage. The 1944 Education Act which came into effect in April 1945 was a landmark, in that all female teachers could now stay on after marriage, partly because there was a shortage, but also because once the provisions of the Act came into force children would be staying on at school for an extra year and R.A. Butler, who framed the legislation, did not feel it was to their benefit to have a 'sex-starved spinster' as headmistress.

There had so far been no such concession to civil servants, even though the Government had had no compunction in recalling some of the women civil servants who had been sacked on marriage to ease the extra workload generated by wartime bureaucracy. In the spring of 1945 there was hope that the marriage bar for women civil servants might be removed 'some time in the future'. Meanwhile, there was a continuing demand for their services. The bureaucracy did not vanish with the peace and, soon, the welfare state was to generate even more, necessitating a fivefold increase in the army of women clerks and typists in national and local government service over the pre-war level. Similarly, the raising of the school leaving age under the Education Act and the introduction of the National Health Service in 1948 demanded an increase in the numbers of teachers, nurses and midwives.

Ernest Bevin threatened to resign and Churchill said it would force a vote of confidence in the Government – the only one of the war – if equal pay for women teachers was written into the 1944 Education Act, despite the motion having been carried in the House. For civil servants there was no question of equal pay in the foreseeable future. Those who had been recalled during the war had been paid the rates of temporary staff – about half the level of their previous earnings. With the exception of women doctors in the Army, who received equal pay, women in the forces had received two-thirds of the men's pay, as had women in Civil Defence and in the Auxiliary Ambulance service. The exception to this sorry tale was transport. Women bus and tram conductors were granted equal pay with men by an industrial court award in April 1940, although men continued to hog the better paid driving jobs. There were 7,500 women bus conductors in London during the war and in 1945 they were top of the women's pay league with average weekly earnings of £4 1s 7d.

The Equal Pay Campaign Committee had lobbied hard to achieve equal pay for women and the amount of Parliamentary support for the campaign was a source of concern to the Cabinet. In 1945 a Royal Commission – consisting of five men and four women – was set up to 'examine', 'consider' and 'report' on the question of equal pay. Surely, women were asking, equal pay was a matter of simple justice, so why did it need a commission to decide the matter? It was obviously a delaying tactic. The commission dithered about until 1946, by which time much of the wartime pressure for reform had evaporated. It was clearly going to be an uphill struggle against entrenched attitudes.

'I am strongly against equal pay for women,' said one man expressing the general opinion of his sex, 'not because I feel that women are inferior, on the contrary. The man is usually the wage earner, and as such should not be in competition with women for his job . . . The main thing is to see that a man has ample to keep his family and should also have first claim on all jobs before a woman, then let women have an equally advantageous system of wages and conditions and all other amenities.'

Unfortunately, some women felt the same way. 'I do feel that equal pay will upset the relations between the sexes,' one woman twittered. 'Personally I like a man to have much more money than me. It gives me twice as much pleasure to have a book or dress bought for me by a kindly male than to buy it for myself – and this is not because I am a gold-digger, but because I am feminine.'

At a debate held in the Hampstead Citizens' Society one of the participants expressed a similarly regressive view: 'If women were given equal status, it might mean buying one's own chocolates and paying for one's own seat in the cinema.' She agreed that male workers should be paid more, 'which in a way is really assisting women'.

Fortunately, another woman retaliated with an argument that won the day for the equal pay lobby: 'It is not enough for women to look forward to a life of housework. They should seek that equality which will mean emancipation from drudgery and monotony. Marriage should not be a barrier to advancement.'

Woman magazine was clearly on the side of equal pay:

Many of us who would support the battle for equal pay hesitate to do so because we think it right that a man supporting a family should earn more than a single woman. But this argument does not hold water unless bachelors and spinsters are paid the same lower rate. Even in that event it is a bad argument, for wages

should be paid according to skill, not according to family responsibility. An employer cannot give his best-paid job to a man just
because he is the father of six!

If most men could not contemplate women earning equal pay,
they certainly were not ready for their wives to earn more than
they did. One woman wrote to *Home Chat* pleading for help:

When my John was in the Army his firm went out of business and
on his discharge from the service he had to take a much inferior
job. Meanwhile, I had been put in charge of an important department at my factory, and am now earning twice as much as my
husband. He feels this very much and will not go out with me to
the theatre, pictures, etc, because he can no longer afford to pay
for both and will not let me pay for myself. The same difficulty
occurs if I buy anything extra for the house. He is so hurt and
unhappy. What am I to do?

In one respect, there could be no going back to the pre-war
situation: the employment by the upper and middle classes of
domestic servants. There had been around 1,590,000 male
and female servants in Britain at the outbreak of war, but
many of them had been conscripted or taken up better paid
war work. There was little or no incentive for them to return
to their former servitude when the war was over. If they did,
they were in a position to demand high wages. Harley Street
doctor Anthony Weymouth, who felt that his wife had
managed heroically without servants during the war,
complained: 'Wages are very high and domestic help is scarce.
A "daily" demands half-a-crown an hour, while living-in
servants receive as much as £3 10s 0d a week and all found.'
The crux of the matter was that 'incomes, as opposed to wages,
have not risen.' As a professional man Weymouth's fees were
the same as they had been before the war, but he had to pay
more for services, food and other scarce goods.

There was much discussion about the 'domestic servant
crisis' in 1945. The *Sunday Graphic* told women not to despair,
as there were plenty of war widows, for whom the prospect

of a live-in job enabling them to keep their baby was their only hope. It amounted to sheer exploitation: 'They will accept £1 a week, run a house single-handed or look after your children. They want frequent times off during the day to look after their own babies. There are more of these women than there are jobs for them!'

Readers were informed that young girls released from war work might be persuaded to come in as dailies, but at an exorbitant 2s an hour. 'All very expensive, but that's the position.' The girls had had their heads turned and considered the work tedious and demeaning. 'If girls would only take a little more pride in their work, they would find it interesting enough,' a resident of Neville Terrace SW7 sighed.

It is understandable that many women, if they were in a position to do so, preferred not to work after marriage, since housework was in itself so laborious and time-consuming. With or without domestic staff, women in 1945 might be well advised to invest in a copy of the newly published *Housework Without Tears*, with a foreword by Lady Beveridge, whose husband's plans for the welfare state incidentally seemed to assume that women would return to the home after the war. 'There cannot have been any time in the history of our country at which the attention of all the people has been so much engaged by the problem of housekeeping without tears,' she wrote. 'It is not only that so many houses have been destroyed or damaged but also that the remainder have been discovered to be all too frequently of a sort designed for a social system which is a thing of the past.'

The book described some of the labour-saving appliances and equipment which would be available once Britain had dug itself out of its post-war financial pit. It was intended as a guide for the housewife 'when she makes her choice, and' – of course – 'for her husband, as he thinks about the cost.' As women would find out in due course, the gadgets facilitated housework, but did not make it disappear.

* * *

One way to ensure that married women with children would return to the home was to pull the rug from under them by closing the wartime nurseries. When the first nurseries were opened in 1941, the thought behind them was that although the Government could not compel women with children to work, they would be very much more likely to do so if there was nursery provision for their children. Even so, there was only provision in 1,500 nurseries for 71,000 children nationwide. These included residential nurseries in the countryside for bombed-out babies who had lost their homes in London and other cities: these nurseries had been set up largely with the help and initiative of voluntary organisations such as the WVS and with generous funding from charitable organisations in the United States before it entered the war.

At the beginning of 1945 the rumour that the nurseries were to close was worrying women and questions were raised in the House, with Edith Summerskill asking the Minister of Health: 'In view of the fact that the Minister of Labour has indicated that as many women workers as possible will be needed after the war, how does the Right Honourable and learned gentleman propose to provide for the care of small children?'

She received no satisfactory reply and as soon as the emergency was over, many of the nurseries closed abruptly, as a group of munitions workers later told *Woman's Hour*: 'The day after armistice was declared we went out, children in tow, to drop them off at nursery while we went to the factory. Only the nursery doors were barred and we all had to go home. [Childcare provision] was finished just like that, overnight.'

The Minister of Health justified the action by explaining that wartime nurseries, which had charged women 1s for a full day including meals, had been financed by the Exchequer to enable women to participate in war production. This was no longer required. He hoped that some would be taken over by local education authorities as nursery schools. However, these would be for children between the ages of two and five only, while wartime day nurseries had taken babies under two. Wartime nurseries had been open all the year round, unlike nursery schools which were an adjunct to elementary schools and kept normal school times.

The Minister's last word on the subject reflected the widely held view that the best person to look after a young child was its mother, a notion that was increasingly stressed through the late forties and fifties. Significantly, when the *Daily Mirror* asked what was to become of all the young women currently employed in the nurseries as nursery nurses, the Ministry of Health's response was: 'Oh, they'll be able to get jobs with the Waifs and Strays perhaps, or some of the local authority homes for children. Of course, the training will help them when they marry and have babies of their own.'

He then wiped his hands of the problem.

As early as 1943 Major Cyril Nathan, the chairman of the National Society of Children's Nurseries, had written *A Four Years' Plan for Children's Nurseries*, recommending that nursery provision should be an essential part of post-war reconstruction planning. He remarked on the irony that 'the most effective stimulus for nursery provision has been not so much the desire to promote the welfare of mothers and young children in peacetime, as the necessity in wartime of enlisting married women with young children as industrial workers.' He urged that at the end of the war nursery provision 'is not reduced but increased'. He argued that the housing situation in the post-war period would be so bad that babies would need nurseries. It would be a period of adjustment for all.

The country's birth rate, he continued, 'is falling in a dangerous measure [at the time of writing in 1943, this was the case, but the post-war campaign to increase the birth rate also put pressure on married women to stay at home with the children], because of economic fear on the part of parents and because young mothers fear a life of unrelieved domestic drudgery'. Nurseries would help spot any health problems or other deficiencies in the children before they started school. There was lots of evidence, he said, of 'the improvement in the physical and mental development of children regularly attending nurseries'.

He was careful to add that nurseries should be regarded as 'an extension of and not a substitute for the home'. They were also beneficial for mothers, suffering from the strain of wartime life and its aftermath. 'If there are to be more children, and happy children, happy mothers and a happy family life, some relief from this strain is imperative.'

Opposed to Nathan's argument was John Bowlby, a child psychologist whose studies were conducted among a narrow sample of evacuees and children in institutions during the war. He claimed that maternal deprivation led directly to juvenile delinquency, a questionable finding which was eagerly grasped by the large and powerful lobby which felt that a mother's place was in the home.

The closure of the wartime day nurseries, as with so much social policy concerning the family, took no account of the women who were sole breadwinners, as Marian Cutler, *Woman's Hour*'s social affairs expert, explained: 'For instance, there's the young widow who must work to supplement her pension, the unmarried mother who wants to earn enough to make a home for her child, the wife with a disabled or invalid husband or where work keeps the home together, the woman separated from her husband. Without her earned money the care of the child might become the responsibility of the State.'

Work was a necessity for these women, many of whom could be classed as casualties of war, but it was all the harder to obtain if they could not place their children in daytime nurseries. To be fair, they were given priority in the few remaining nursery places which now became the responsibility of local authorities. Otherwise, they had to resort to the pre-war system of leaving their children with minders. Some war widows were reduced to placing their children in children's homes – poor recompense for the families of men who had died for their country.

Instead of nurseries, women were to be offered a new incentive to have larger families and stay at home. In the early spring of 1945 the Family Allowances Bill providing 5s a week for the second and each successive child after that, subject to income tax, was passing through Parliament. There was an outcry when, typically, the legislators decided that the amount should be paid to the man of the family, rather than direct to the mother. Eleanor Rathbone, MP, protested loudly:

We who are urging this change know very well that the great majority of British husbands are decent, kindly men who will do the right thing by their wives unless they have good reason to distrust them. We also recognise that mothers are not all 'plaster saints' and that some of them deserve distrust. But there is a minority of men who, if they once get the allowance, will spend it on drink or betting, and neither wife nor child will benefit.

It was a small triumph when in May it was agreed that the allowance would be paid direct to the mother.

But perhaps the 5s family allowance would prove less of an incentive to family growth than the Government hoped. A series of papers by ten experts on population, *Rebuilding Family Life in the Post-War World*, revealed that five in every seven couples were now making some attempt to plan the size of their families and nearly half of all children born were wanted and deliberately brought into the world by their parents. Only a month after VE Day an article in *The Times* suggested: 'The transition to voluntary parenthood is clearly in full swing in Britain, and the replacement of population will come increasingly to depend on the extent to which people want children and consciously decide to become parents . . . the advent of voluntary parenthood has brought with it the danger that the family will be, not planned, but planned out of existence.'

As early as 1942 Ernest Bevin started planning the demobilisation process, but when it actually happened three years later it was a mess. The plan had rested on the Japanese war continuing for up to two years after the end of hostilities in Europe, allowing time for an orderly, staggered demobilisation of 4,243,000 men and 437,000 women from the services and into the job market. Everyone was taken by surprise by the sudden end of the war with Japan, throwing Bevin's plan into disarray. From then on, the new Labour Government was under huge pressure to demobilise as quickly as possible. Mass-Observation noted that there was widespread frustration at the slowness of demobilisation and a feeling that the Labour Government had better hurry up, since it was – erroneously – considered to be owing to the forces' vote that they were in office at all. The Conservative Opposition did not neglect to fan the flames of dissatisfaction. In the event, demobilisation started on 18 June 1945, a third of them were out by Christmas and the remaining two-thirds by the following Easter.

Age and length of service were to determine the order of release, with special cases – those with rare skills, returning prisoners of war, married women and personal hardship cases – circumventing that rule. Class A represented the oldest and longest serving; Class C comprised the compassionate cases; Class B comprised the people whose skills made them urgently needed for reconstruction. They were subject to recall if they left the jobs to which they were directed, and were to receive three instead of eight weeks' paid leave as a gratuity. Unfortunately, there were by no means enough men in Class B to fulfil the needs of reconstruction and the plan generally failed to take account of the fact that ex-servicemen had had enough of rules and regulations and being told what to do. It looked fine on paper, but took no account of human foibles. Inevitably, there were grumbles about 'unfairness' and resentment of those responsible for the scheme.

The plan had been for demobilisation to be linked closely to the employment requirements of critical industries, but so abruptly had the war ended that British industry was caught in the time lag and a web of bureaucracy, as it creaked and ground its way from wartime to a peacetime production. In August 1945 it was announced that 1 million men and women were to be released from the munitions factories over the following two months 'to take part in Britain's great export drive and in reconstruction'. But employers complained that with the best will in the world their factories could not be turned round quickly enough, not least owing to government obstruction. Some were even facing the prospect of having to lay off workers – who would receive unemployment pay – during the period of transition. At the same time, there was no automatic transfer of the whole munitions workforce into peacetime industries. Dock workers and others had all earned high wages – sometimes as much as £36 a week – under the stress of wartime necessity and were in for a shock at the inferior wages peacetime would afford, while many women munitions workers, indignant at the low pay offered by the textile industry, opted not to bother.

In late August the *Croydon Advertiser* picked up on the fact that some of the local factories were still on wartime production or gradually terminating war contracts. Others were finding the Board of Trade would not grant licences for carrying out peacetime orders, while there was insufficient labour available even if the licences were forthcoming. For example, Mr Percy Harper of Harper Automatics Ltd, which had been turning out intricate cutting tools for making ammunition, sent out a letter to his employees thanking them for their co-operation during the war and warning them that unless permission were soon obtained to switch over to the manufacture of peacetime automatic machines he would have to let people go or close altogether. Similarly, the Standard Steel Company had been producing heavy engineering machinery, but now wanted to revert to making structural steel – desperately needed for house-building – but was unable to do so while the Board of Trade dithered about granting a licence. These problems were almost certainly universal.

Servicemen were taken to various demob centres, where they received their civilian outfit, courtesy of the Government. The wardrobe was based on that of a middle-class family man dressed for church, so that there was a hat, a three-piece suit, a shirt with two collars, a tie (in many patterns), two pairs of socks, one pair of shoes (brown or black), a raincoat, two studs and one pair of cufflinks. They all looked remarkably similar. 'Three young men in new suits came in. The suits were blue, grey and brown; but were alike in being severely, even skimpily cut, and in being very new,' J.B. Priestley quipped in his novel about demobilisation. Servicemen were advised that on their return home – 'after shaking hands with your wife' – they should 'go upstairs without delay and see what you have in the way of pre-war clothes'. On no account were they to throw any out, thinking they had outgrown them. The extra build they had acquired through good food and exercise in the forces would soon disappear in Civvy Street.

No sooner were the ex-servicemen out of the gates than they were besieged by spivs – those who had been able to dodge conscription and profit from the war – offering wads of cash for their demob clothes, which had a ready sale on the black market. It was not an auspicious return to civilian life.

Resettlement offices were set up all over the country to help the 8 million demobilised servicemen, Civil Defence personnel, factory workers and others who had been directed into war work away from home to settle into civilian life again. Their scope was very narrow. The whole focus was on the practical side of life – jobs – when many of the returning servicemen desperately needed counselling. It was not forthcoming. They were not encouraged to talk about their experiences. Very often they had no one to talk to. They felt that they could not burden their wives and families with their problems. They missed their pals and the camaraderie of service life. Those who were lucky enough to meet up with others at the British Legion felt better when they found that they were not alone, that others were experiencing the same feelings of disenchantment.

The Reinstatement in Civil Employment Act was supposed to guarantee servicemen their old jobs back: perversely, it embraced only those who had been compulsorily called up, not volunteers. However, many servicemen did not want to return to their old jobs, even if they still existed. Many of them had been no more than boys when they left. They had matured. War had changed them. Possibly they had been promoted and held responsibilities way beyond what they could ever have hoped to achieve in their former civilian existence. Those who wanted to return to their old jobs had to fill in the appropriate form. The rest were advised to start looking for work or take training while they were still in the forces.

As his last act as Minister of Labour and National Service, Ernest Bevin had introduced a Control of Engagement Order, requiring all jobs to be filled through the Ministry's employment or labour exchanges. The idea was to guarantee all employers a fair share of local labour. There was conscription into the forces for men between 18 and 30 and, indeed, the services were a rather popular option at this time. New recruits enabled older men in the forces to return to civilian life.

Men who had been brought out of retirement – in the Metropolitan Police, for instance – to fill posts vacated by those who had joined the forces were gradually being replaced by the returning servicemen. Doctors in civilian practice, often like Anthony Weymouth putting their retirement off until after the war, were said to be suffering proportionately more illness and nervous breakdowns than their patients. In August 1945 there were still 17,000 doctors in the forces: the BMA wanted 5,000 of them out before the winter to ease the load on those who were flagging after their wartime burden.

There was a huge well of dissatisfaction among servicemen after their experience of demobilisation. This was the moment cynicism set in, a cynicism which was only exacerbated by a whole series of disappointments they encountered in civilian life. It is not as if their expectations were that high. In the spring of 1945 the British Legion had run an essay competition, in which servicemen were invited to describe their hopes for the post-war world. The overwhelming desire was for security, plenty of jobs, adequate wages and pensions for all.

'My hopes for the post war are similar to those of Sir William Beveridge,' said one. 'The things I desire from the peace are things which thousands of normal people want – a home, employment, and a reasonable amount of security,' another confirmed.

In order of priority, the men wanted:

1. Employment for all at good wages.
2. Adequate housing at controlled rents.
3. A state health service.
4. Improved education, including higher education and vocational training for all.
5. Adequate pensions for widows, dependents and the disabled, and subsistence allowances for the unemployed.

In a similar survey Mass-Observation also found the men's post-war hopes modest and reasonable: 'A man asks only a very little when he finally leaves the hell of battle; he asks only for some kind of paid employment, a home and comfort for his family and himself at a cost within the compass of his wage, and the right to enjoy his leisure time.'

Although many of the wishes expressed by the men in the British Legion essay competition were to be embodied in the welfare state, few of them were to be forthcoming in the immediate future. Servicemen underestimated the difficulties they would encounter in civilian life.

First of all, they were shocked and surprised not to be greeted as returning heroes. They had been warned that civilians had had a tough war and would be too wrapped up in their own problems to take any account of theirs, but it took a while for many ex-servicemen to appreciate this. They were confused, angry and resentful, especially as even their wives did not seem to be offering the sort of sympathy and understanding they felt they deserved. As one of them explains: 'We disembarked, not expecting any particular acclamation, but at least we hoped to find the work of the fighting forces overseas had been realised and appreciated by our womenfolk. What did we find? That any expectations we had of picking up the threads of our domestic life were lost in a wild fandango of pleasure-mad, sensation-seeking civilians. And somewhere in this chaos were our womenfolk.'

Tired civilians saw well-fed servicemen with tanned faces and their gratuities in their pocket and compared it with their own grim lot. Only prisoners of war had had a worse time than they had, civilians felt, and merited their sympathy. In fact, servicemen had received no great financial benefit for putting their lives on the line. By 1945 a private had been earning 3s a day. If he was a married man, a proportion of his pay would be stopped to go to his wife, leaving him with 1s a week. On leaving the army, a major with five years' service, three of them abroad, would receive release pay, allowances and a gratuity amounting to £324 12s 8d, while a private with three years' service would receive £78 16s 2d. Each would receive a civilian outfit worth £12. It might be some time before they found a civilian job.

Servicemen resented the disparity in financial reward between themselves and civilians and the money 'lost' while they were waiting to be demobilised. Now that he was about to be demobilised, the prospect before the ordinary serviceman looked far from rosy, as one young soldier told the *News of the World*:

I have been in the Army since the beginning. By the look of things I shall be out before Christmas. I am sick to death of reading about my gratuity, my 56 days' [paid] leave, my reinstatement rights, and all the rest of it. I should like you to know the sort of world I am coming back to. First of all, I have no job waiting for me, nor do I know a trade. I have done fairly well in the Army and am a corporal, but I am no good at office work. During the war I have married and I have a baby, but no home. My wife lives with her parents. Last leave we did not get on too well together. Well, there it is. No job, no home, no trade, and a wife and baby. The only answer I can think of is emigration, but I know nothing about it. Demobilisation is not going to solve my difficulties. It puts me right into the thick of them – and there are thousands like me.

Servicemen were unprepared for the shabbiness of the homes they returned to – that is, if they still had a home – and the chill greyness of life in bomb-damaged cities. A land fit for heroes? one of them queried. You had to be a hero to live in it. Hard on the heels of peace, an overwhelming apathy had set in and after the excitement of actually being demobbed and coming home many servicemen felt this profoundly. There was a feeling of anticlimax and dislocation. The service was not there to support them any more, to tell them what to do, to provide meals and accommodation. 'I woke up one day and looked into the future and saw . . . nothing,' one of them admitted. 'For the first time in five years I was on my own, no comrades, no system to support me. I felt worse than I did when I sat on top of a 200-pound bomb.' Civilian life, with its unfamiliar bureaucracy and restrictions, its meagre rations, queues and shortages, was tough. So much so that some men regretted their demobilisation and wanted to return to the services.

Resettlement offices found that the biggest worry of the demobilised serviceman was finding a home. In August the *Daily Mail* cited the case of a Mr R.C.S. of Hayes, Middlesex, discharged from the Royal Marines owing to an extremely painful duodenal ulcer. With his wife and nine-month-old child, ill with enteritis, he was sleeping in an under-surface air raid shelter, because they could not obtain accommodation, despite their doctor writing to Hayes Council saying the case was urgent. His case was by no means unique.

The housing shortage meant that many couples had to move in with their in-laws or share accommodation, sometimes for years. As one woman who had been in the ATS and was now working as a clerk in London recalled: 'We lived with my parents when we got married. We thought it would only be for a year but it ended up being nine years. They were hard years because my husband was quarrelling with my mother . . . they just couldn't live together. So I was like a referee, really, for nine years before we got our own home.' Most young couples were in the same position, which was particularly hard if they had young children.

One exasperated young ex-serviceman postponed his marriage plans because he could not find anywhere suitable to live, as he told *Picture Post*:

I am 27 years old and have just been discharged after five years in the service. I intended getting married in May and settling down to start a family. For the last six months I have been trying to find a house, a flat, anything, where we could live. But nothing doing. The best we have been able to get so far is our name on a never-never council list, an offer of a furnished flat at four guineas a week, and a house, bomb-damaged, at £1,500. All this out of my wages, £6 a week as a clerk, before deductions. Well, I have decided with my fiancée that after being engaged for three years, we are going to keep on being engaged till we get somewhere to live. We don't want to live with her parents or mine. We have seen too many marriages go wrong that way. And we aren't going to bring up our children living in furnished rooms. What's happened to the better Britain that you promised us a couple of years ago? When we needed guns, the Government found them. When we needed planes, the Government found them. We want houses. So what about it?

There was disappointment, too, about the difficulty in finding a job, as one demobbed officer explained to the *Spectator* in December 1945:

Sir – When I started job-hunting towards the end of my time in the army, I expected to find my war service some slight advantage. After all, as I'd entered my home town on leave, I'd seen an enormous notice to the Forces, "Welcome Home", and later when I went to the Demob Centre we'd been greeted by an even bigger placard, "You saved the world". And so it seemed fair to hope that one's own part of the world would be reasonably grateful.

The facts are very different. First I went to the Appointments Board of the Ministry of Labour. They were most enthusiastic, but the net result of the visit and two subsequent letters was NIL, not a solitary job of any sort to try for, not even a temporising letter, although a courteous chief had promised to ring up constantly with suggestions. After four months of unbroken silence I got a very faint response by asking a friend in the Ministry to prod them. Meanwhile, I approached the firm I have been with before the war. Though I had left several months before the start, I thought they might at least be glad to see

me. But so far from being keen, they were not even enthusiastic towards their employees who had gone direct to the war.
They were taking them back at their pre-war salaries, while
those, who for one reason or another had remained behind,
were flourishing in their stead.

Next I tried the Situations Vacant columns. For a short time
at the end of the European war there was quite a spate of ex-
officers and ex-servicemen required, but now it is very rare to
see any preference for them; the last I saw in *The Times* did
not mention ex-servicemen. The people asked for are those
already in civilian jobs.

There is no need to elaborate the simple point that in general
there is no welcome home for the returned warrior. Even drink
and the better un-rationed goods are denied him in favour of
the civilian customer who has dug himself in under the counter
for the past five years . . . I realise the employer's hesitation:
if we were too young before the war for the job, we are too
old now to start. But many managed to learn the trade of
arms pretty quickly, luckily for the employers at home. In
return, let the employers give them a chance to prove themselves in peace. And for heaven's sake stop telling us 'You've
been lucky. You've been in the army away from the flying
bombs and rationing.'

Getting reacquainted with the wife and vice versa was one
of the hardest adjustments for the returning serviceman. Kit
Beasley on the Isle of Dogs had married in 1941 and then
waited four years for her husband to return from the war.
Her experience was pretty typical, but she was lucky in that
they managed to overcome their difficulties rather than split
up:

I can remember my husband coming home from Egypt. I was
in bed and it was early in the morning, about 7.30, and he
was knocking at the door and I looked out and I thought, oh
my God, he's home . . . It was a mixed feeling because I'd
made so many friends and I knew very well that from then
on I was going to be at home. At first we used to argue – but

gradually we worked it out. We had to – we just had to work
it out. You had to learn all about one another again because
obviously we'd both changed in that time. I was more grown
up, I'd gone around.

When he came out it was very, very difficult to get to know
him again. I think it was a time when we could have easily
split up. He came home and no way did I feel I could settle
down with him. You had to go all through a sort of courtship
again. Four years is a very long time to be apart, but gradually we got together, though things were very, very difficult
because we had nothing. Our money from the army was very
little and we had just the necessary things like a bed and a
chair – no carpets or things like that. The island was just like
a bomb site after the war. My home was bombed during the
war. We finally found an old flat. It had an outside toilet, no
bathroom. Times were very hard.

Many women felt that their husbands had changed beyond
recognition. Like their wives, they were suffering from overwhelming war weariness. Many of the men were depressed
and angry and without special help these feelings poured over
into ill health or antisocial behaviour, which was particularly
hard on their wives and families. It was especially problem-
atic if the returning serviceman had been a prisoner of war,
as Dorothy Richards discovered:

I was very happy to have him home and then you realise that you've
not got the same man back. His mother, as well, couldn't understand how he'd changed and how difficult he was. He was ill, you
see, and it took him two or three weeks to really come around and
then he began to feel better. He still had a lot of the prisoner of war
in him. Even now you can't touch his things. In the prison camp
they only had a certain limited space and what was theirs was their
own and nobody touched it. It's continued all his life and I have to
be very, very careful. He wasn't like that at all before he left.

Joan Pender remembered a different man from the one who
returned from the prison camp:

We all went down to meet him. Mum dressed us all up and we all had to stick together . . . Everything was wonderful that first day. Then the drinking started. I was the only one, being seven when he went away, who could remember Dad the way he was. The war changed him. And what I still remember was him butting his cigarettes out on the floor like he was still in the prison camp. He was just a completely different person to what he was. It was terribly hard for Mum.

Men were shocked at how much their wives had changed. Those who had left a young, pretty wife behind had to conceal their dismay at how old and careworn she had become, but servicemen generally were appalled to find how exhausted their wives were. Worst of all, however, was the extent to which women's personalities and behaviour seemed to have changed. They were no longer the quiet, simple housewives, shop assistants or office clerks the men had left behind. They had managed the household and the children in their absence and even earned a living. It was difficult for men to come to terms with their wives' new-found independence.

Women had become sophisticated in all sorts of ways. Naturally, they had developed some sort of social life of their own – perhaps meeting foreign servicemen who had widened their horizons. Women were used to going out to the cinema and dances or just down to the pub – during the war women started going to the pub either alone or with other women, whereas this had rarely been the case before the war – and men found it hard to accept this. Very often they resented the new network of friends the wife had made and were very possessive and selfish, as the son of one of them remembers: 'Mum had got used to doing things differently. She had neighbours and they would pop in, not a lot, but they were nice ones. When he come home he started objecting to them coming in, objecting if they called out or came round. He didn't want her to go round there, didn't want them to come here. He wanted her to be in all the time.'

A wall had gone up between many couples. They found it

impossible to pick up where they had left off and no longer knew how to talk to each other. Some sought help from the Marriage Guidance Council, but many others never recovered or split up. There were also quarrels over how to manage the children, who had been used to having Mummy to themselves and now had to get used to Daddy's discipline.

When fathers came home, they had to get to know their children. They were warned that they might seem rather 'out of hand' and to go easy with them. Some had been born after their father's departure, while others were too young to remember the man who had been away for two, three or four years. Even the few who had been lucky enough to hear their father's voice on a specially made gramophone record sent from overseas might have had a problem recognising the man himself. He did not always look the same as the man in the photo on the mantelpiece. One small child exclaimed when she met her father: 'But you've got legs!' The photo she had kissed every night had depicted him only from the waist up. Others remember seeing a soldier walking up the street and asking, 'Is that my daddy?' or waiting at the railway station with their mother and straining for the first glimpse of him:

My mother and I stood at the barrier watching a stream of khaki-clad soldiers pouring from the train. I remember asking my mother, 'Is that one Daddy?' over and over again as I had no idea what he looked like. Then suddenly one of them stopped and clasped my mother to him. My feelings were of surprise and disappointment – he was my father, but he seemed more interested in my mother – and she in him. I felt somehow I'd lost them both.

'If I close my eyes I can still feel the rough khaki uniform and the strange new sensation of being kissed by a man,' another recalls.

Some resisted all approaches from the strange new man, refusing to acknowledge his presence or communicate with him. 'Mummy, Mummy, tell this man to put me down!' was the hurtful but understandable cry heard in many households. Even those who had regularly said goodnight to their father's picture had trouble coming to terms with the man in the flesh, as one mother recalls: 'When my husband came home, my boy was absolutely petrified of him. He wouldn't stay in the same room with him. If I went to the loo he would come and wait outside the door for me. He used to keep saying to me, "Mum, when's that man going?"'

Even with the best of intentions, the equilibrium in the household was altered by the arrival of this unfamiliar stranger. 'The atmosphere did change afterwards,' one Londoner who was a boy at the time remembers. 'Things started getting back to normal. Kids had to go to school, the husbands came back and I suppose there was a lot of tension at home. The way I feel, when there's just one parent at home, there's no tension. When you get two there's conflict.'

Often mothers were torn, trying to keep the peace and to reconcile fathers and children to each other's presence. One such anxious mother wrote to *Home Chat*:

When my husband went abroad our little boy was only four. Now he is eight, and he does not seem at all pleased at his father's return, although all the time my husband was away I spoke continually of him to the child, so that he would not forget his daddy, and he seemed interested and proud of his achievements. I was especially shocked and hurt this morning when he whispered to me: 'When is Daddy going away again?' My husband notices this unfriendliness, and he is rather upset by it.

The magazine's agony aunt advised her to talk to her husband about it, suggesting the boy might be jealous. It is 'up to the father to win the boy round by being friendly and taking an interest. You have to be careful not to show too much interest in your husband when the three of you are together.'

Inevitably, children who had shared the fear and horror of the bombing with their mothers had formed an unusually close bond with them. 'I always felt resentful towards him for coming back and spoiling what had seemed to be such an idyllic mother-daughter relationship,' one woman confessed – a feeling that must have been common.

Many children had shared their mother's bed during their father's long absence – for warmth, for companionship, and perhaps because it would be easy for her to scoop them up if they had to make a dash for the air-raid shelter. Now those children resented being turned out and relegated to their own room: 'They embraced; he seemed utterly foreign, no part of me or her. When he gathered me up his face was rough and his khaki was harsh with an alien smell. I wriggled to escape, not wanting to be held. What followed was worse: I didn't sleep with Mummy any more.'

If some children resented the intrusion, fathers could also be jealous of their children. A woman caught in such a situation asked *Home Chat*'s advice:

When my husband went away our baby was three years old. Now he has been invalided out of the Army after three and a half years out East. Though I'm thankful to have him home, I'm bitterly disappointed because he takes no interest in our little girl, who is rather grown up for her six and a half years and a most fascinating child. He resents the attention I give the child and is irritable because I cannot go out with him in the evenings as I did before. The child, on the other hand, seems equally to resent him and asked me this morning when I am going to send 'that man' away. You can imagine how shocked and hurt I was. What am I to do?

Some men had become too inured to army life to make the necessary concessions to their family, as a woman whose husband had returned from Burma recalls:

When he came back home our little girl was ten and didn't know who this overpowering man in uniform was and he, of course, didn't know her. He still thought he was in command of men and treated us like army personnel, spitting out orders that must be obeyed and, consequently, we became quite afraid of him and all that aggression within him. It really had a devastating effect on our lives, as my little girl and I had been so close because of all the trauma of bombing, air-raid shelters, etc. We both resented this man who dominated our otherwise close and loving relationship. It did something to us all . . . it didn't make for a very happy time for many years, or ever again, if I am honest.

When fathers had been absent from a child's life for many years, they often found it impossible to establish a relationship with that child. There was an additional danger that a child would feel left out and alienated when he or she gained new siblings after the war: 'Life for me changed totally,' one woman recalls sadly. 'From being the cherished only child of my mother who had all her attention, I was now part of a growing family with a stranger for a father and two baby brothers who took all my mother's time. I was part of that other life "before the war".'

Indeed, for everyone life would henceforth be divided into 'before the war' and 'after the war', so traumatic had the intervening years been. In a war that had torn families and neighbourhoods apart on a vast and dramatic scale, what is perhaps remarkable is not the number of families who were irredeemably damaged, but the social stability of the great majority of families, who perhaps grew stronger and closer as a result, and of the nation as a whole.

EPILOGUE:
A Planner's Dream

'The value of victory is what we make of it. Peace is not an end, but a beginning'
  – Lord Latham, Leader of the London County Council,
May 1945

'Before VE Day had actually happened, I remember going to the County Hall to see a plan for London for after the war. It was the Abercrombie Plan. I can remember going to see it and feeling that it had all been worthwhile, and it'll be wonderful when it's all built. I came back, sort of full of the joys of spring as it were, thinking that after all this terrible tragedy we've been through all these years – now we've got a chance to build a proper London, you know. And I remember telling my father and he said, "Yes girl. I've heard it all before." Now I've got to the age he was then, I can quite understand why he said that to me. What a shambles they've made of it! What a shambles!'
  – Southwark resident

At the outbreak of war London was ripe for reconstruction; by the end, it was presented with an almost unprecedented opportunity. Large swathes of unsightly, poorly planned housing, business and industrial premises had been destroyed by the Luftwaffe. Their demolition was long overdue. Now was the moment to complete the task and build a bright new modern metropolis. That the result did not quite match up to the planners' visions was perhaps inevitable. There is no question that opportunities were missed. But to dismiss the achievement of the planners is to forget what existed before in large areas of the county: dilapidated Victorian back-to-back tenements without adequate indoor sanitary facilities; overcrowding; housing indiscriminately jostling with factories belching out pollution; lack of green spaces; the unchecked expansion of dreary suburban ribbon development. It is also to overlook the difficulties of finding the necessary money and labour for reconstruction and the pressure the authorities were under to apply quick fixes, to get the people housed and the metropolis up and running again.

Even in the square mile of the City of London, the oldest municipality in the world and arguably the richest, it was high time for change. The City was totally given over to commerce, comprising banks, offices, warehouses and markets, with a few eating houses for the midday meal and a sprinkling of shops for necessities. Much of it comprised narrow, twisting alleyways bordered by tall buildings dating back over several centuries. Natural daylight was a rare commodity. The war destroyed one third of the City's building accommodation and one quarter of its rateable value. Suddenly, large tracts of land which had previously held buildings with a multiplicity of ownerships, making concerted schemes for the development of more practical modern offices on larger sites impossible, were there for the taking.

At the height of the Blitz the Government turned its attention to the reconstruction of London after the war. In March 1941 Lord Reith, as Minister of Works, asked the London County Council to prepare a plan for redevelopment. The council appointed Sir Patrick Abercrombie, Professor of Town Planning at University College London, and its own architect, J.H. Forshaw, to produce the plan. Working with a surprisingly small team, they were able to utilise the maps showing the bomb-damaged areas that had been prepared from the onset of the Blitz by the LCC's architect's department. The result was the *County of London Plan, 1943*. A year later Abercrombie followed this up with the *Greater London Plan 1944*, which was actually published in 1945: it complemented the first, showing how development plans in the County of

London (117 square miles) were to be co-ordinated with those in Greater London (693 square miles).

The County of London's two-tier system of government meant that the plan had to be submitted to the 28 metropolitan boroughs for their approval and comment, as well as to the London Passenger Transport Board and railways, the utility companies and others with a vested interest: a long period of negotiation began. The book of the plan, complete with maps, sold out immediately and a simple edition was compiled for schoolchildren, since they would be the inheritors of the new metropolis: indeed, they would be middle-aged before many aspects of the plan were realised. Exhibitions with models illustrating the proposed improvements were held at County Hall and the Royal Academy, attracting 75,000 visitors. Like the Beveridge Report which preceded it, Abercrombie's Plan instilled hope for a better post-war world, a world in which poverty and squalor would be eradicated – a world worth fighting for.

The plan won the backing of the Coalition Government, which introduced legislation to facilitate its implementation. The Town and Country Planning Bill became law in November 1945. It gave local authorities powers of compulsory purchase over blitzed and derelict sites at 1939 prices and the right to designate them reconstruction areas. The 1945 Redistribution of Industry Act enabled the Board of Trade to refuse planning permission for new factories or large factory extensions. In practice, there were ways for companies to get round this and, anyway, the trend for the future would be away from manufacturing towards office work and the service industries. The New Towns Act of 1946 empowered the Minister of Town and Country Planning to designate the sites and to set up Development Corporations to purchase and plan the land. A massive and more complex Town and Country Planning Act in 1947 drastically reduced the number of planning authorities in London and their decisions were to be made in accordance with government-approved local development plans. All development and

change of land use was now subject to local authority planning permission.

Abercrombie seconded the proposal to develop the South
Bank, a squalid, run-down area between Westminster and
Waterloo Bridge, which had first been mooted in 1935 when
Herbert Morrison was Leader of the LCC. 'This development
of the South Bank is the opportunity for the greatest spec-
tacular effect of the new London,' Abercrombie decided. There
would be a picturesque riverside embankment with a cultural
centre housing two new theatres, a concert hall, an assembly
hall, sports facilities including a swimming pool, one or two
hotels, cafés and restaurants, offices and shops. Further along
between London Bridge and Blackfriars Bridge, there was to
be a Shakespearean quarter with a new Globe Theatre on the
site of the original. Southwark Cathedral would be enhanced
by a more worthy setting. Fortunately, the LCC was the freeholder of most of the land running along the river, although
much of the finance for the development was to come from
the Exchequer – eventually.

'When possible the river, London's most beautiful and most
neglected open space, will be revealed,' Abercrombie promised.
He recommended that the railway bridges spanning the
Thames should go underground and be replaced by two new
road bridges at Charing Cross and Temple. The river, as in
the seventeenth and eighteenth centuries, was once more to
become 'a highway for pleasure'. This would not affect the
activities of the Port Authority further east, although there too
he envisaged something different: 'Many of the warehouses
and similar buildings have been destroyed or damaged. Many
of the remaining ones are antiquated and need rebuilding.
Here seems an opportunity for a great scheme of replanning
and rationalisation which will lead not only to vastly increased
efficiency and economy, but also to interesting architectural
effects.'

In the West End Abercrombie deplored the jumble of architectural styles. General shabbiness had prevailed even before the
war: the proliferation of 'To Let' signs, he believed, indicated

that the buildings had outlived their useful purpose. Markets such as the one in Covent Garden were an anachronism, adding to traffic congestion: he advocated its decentralisation, something that did not take place until the 1970s. Similarly, he recommended the overhaul of the coal distribution system, although that would eventually be taken care of by the switch to central heating.

Abercrombie was a leading advocate of decentralisation. Outside the square mile of the City of London – the original Roman city – London had grown up from a series of individual villages which had long since congealed in a featureless mass. The identity of these villages and communities had not entirely disappeared, however, and Abercrombie wanted to enhance and formalise them. Each would be distinct, with 60,000 to 80,000 inhabitants within the villages and within them communities of 6,000 to 10,000, each with its housing served by its own elementary school and shops, its homes separate from places of work, which would be placed in their own compact space. Above all, there were to be adequate open spaces in direct proportion to the size of the population, both within the community and separating it from the rest. Children would no longer play in the street but in playgrounds. These neighbourhoods would be untroubled by the noise of continuous through traffic because an ambitious new system of four ring roads with a series of sub-arterial roads would divert all but the necessary local traffic away from the area.

Housing densities were to be strictly controlled. London's historic propensity towards unplanned, unchecked expansion and overcrowding was to be quashed. The plan envisaged three housing density zones, with height limits on residential buildings of 80, 60 and 40 feet respectively: a high-rise West End zone, where an upper limit of 200 people per acre would allow a large number to enjoy a central location with the benefit of the royal parks as open spaces for recreation; a mixed sub-central zone, encompassing the East End and south London riverside boroughs, was to have a maximum of 136 people per acre; the suburban parts of the county were to have 100 per acre. Beyond the boundaries of the County of London housing densities in Greater London were to be still lower, with about 50 an acre in the suburbs and 20 in the existing Green Belt developments.

To house a smaller number of people in lower density housing with more open spaces would necessitate a far larger number of flats than had existed before the war. Several of the metropolitan boroughs expressed disquiet about the number of flats the plan entailed as opposed to the single-dwelling houses which the majority of people infinitely preferred. 'Families would be packed like oranges,' Stoke Newington Council complained, warning prophetically, 'This method of living is not conducive to family life.' Abercrombie himself would probably have been appalled by the sixties' high-rise estates with their accompanying social disadvantages, which were the ultimate manifestation of his plan.

For Abercrombie's plan to work, over 600,000 people from the County of London were to be relocated, along with the gradual decentralisation of an equivalent number of jobs. The removal of this surplus population, he argued, would be facilitated by the fact that so many had already been forced to leave during the war and had found temporary housing and jobs elsewhere. There was the added consideration that many no longer had homes to return to. If his plan of providing more space per person was to work, all the people could not be put back into the homes they had left. The figure for dispersal was only about one seventh of the pre-war population of the county: it stood at 4,063,000 in 1938, declining to 3,245,000 by 1947, by which time everyone who was coming home had done so. But Abercrombie's percentage for removal is misleading. It is to ignore the impact it would have on the most crowded, industrial boroughs – Stepney, Shoreditch, Bethnal Green, Finsbury, Bermondsey and Lambeth – which were to lose between one third and half their populations.

The drift of population out of London had begun before the war. About 345,000 people at the rate of 58,000 a year had removed themselves from the County of London to the outer suburbs and beyond, many of them filling those new semi-detached houses and bungalows which Abercrombie so deplored lining the routes out of London and creeping ever onwards into the countryside. These middle- and lower-middle class people had not been able to afford the houses with gardens they wanted in central London, but they depended on transport to bring them into London to work and for entertainment. They were the sort of people for whom Abercrombie now envisaged affordable flats in the West End: democratisation, he felt, should be reflected in the plan, which 'provides for a greater mingling of the different groups of London's society'.

Abercrombie's plan represented a radical new departure from the earlier trend of moving to the edges of London but commuting in to work. For one thing, his target population tended to be the working class of the East End who had enjoyed tight-knit community life before the war and, generally speaking, had not been part of the exodus to the new private housing which had grown up in the suburbs. Now these old communities were to be broken up, with relatives who had lived in the same street as a sort of mutual support system often dispersed to different locations. The decline in Bethnal Green's population had started before the war, but it accelerated with the bombing. It collapsed from 90,000 at the outset of war to 47,000 in 1941, although it would be back up to 60,000 in 1948, before the arrival of the municipal bulldozer. This was to be the trend across most of London's overcrowded working-class, industrial boroughs which had already been decimated by war.

Unlike the pre-war developments, Abercrombie's new communities would be self-sufficient. There would be adequate jobs for them in the locality, without them needing to spend several hours a day commuting – 'strap-hanging' as he called it – into London. They would have their own shops and places of entertainment. The London County Council had been buying up land far outside its borders for housing estates, hospitals and residential schools before the war, but now Abercrombie wanted to take this further. A great admirer of Ebenezer Howard's Garden City movement, Abercrombie proposed that London's excess population be relocated not just in expanded old towns within 50 miles of the capital or 'wholly outside the Metropolitan influence', but in new satellite towns in Essex, Hertfordshire, Kent, Surrey and Berkshire. The idea was for them to develop an economic life and community spirit of their own.

Abercrombie loathed the urban sprawl on the outer edges of London and wanted to stop it in its tracks. He reiterated the importance of the already existing Green Belt, a circular belt of preserved countryside about 10 miles thick, with its outer limits about 20 miles from Charing Cross. Development in this area would be subject to strict planning controls. Between the Green Belt and the metropolis, Abercrombie's outer road, the D road, taking traffic round the capital in a massive circular sweep, would not be realised until the opening of the M25 42 years later.

This was London's last chance, perhaps, to solve its traffic problems – before reconstruction took place and before vested interests would make it too disruptive and too expensive. Traffic was already a problem in the thirties, but Abercrombie seems to have had little inkling of the enormous surge in private car ownership after the war. London has almost 10 times more cars today than it had when Abercrombie found these same roads inadequate. Most of his inner circular road schemes – one of them with cars sweeping along the Embankment before disappearing into a tunnel under the riverside terrace of the Houses of Parliament – were never realised. But he recommended that a start should be made on projected roads that had been in hand before the war: the east–west connection along Marylebone Road; northern and southern approaches to the Blackwall Tunnel; approaches from the north to London Docks; improvements at Elephant and Castle, which had been badly bombed and was part of the hinterland of the South Bank development scheme; an

Old Street bypass. He also recommended a rationalisation and co-ordination of the traffic around London's main railway stations – most of which were long overdue for modernisation even before being bombed – and an expansion of the Underground system.

Abercrombie's plan did not cover the City of London, although by the time a plan for the City's reconstruction was ready to be implemented the corporation had lost its planning powers to the LCC by the 1947 Town and Country Planning Act. The scale of destruction in 1940–41 had encouraged the Royal Academy Planning Committee, chaired by the elderly Sir Edwin Lutyens, to take another look at Sir Christopher Wren's original map for the planning of the City after the Fire in 1666. Could Wren's great vision, which had been rejected by Charles II as too sweeping and impractical, or something just as bold be realised after all? *London Replanned*, which the Royal Academy team published in 1942, showed St Paul's revealed as never before. From the west it would be approached by a triumphal way up Ludgate Hill, remodelled into a straight, tree-lined avenue leading up to the cathedral set in a vast piazza. To the south, St Paul's was to be opened up to the Thames, by way of a broad staircase bordered by classical villas. There was to be a monumental vista from New Oxford Street all the way to the British Museum, necessitating the destruction of Museum Street. Covent Garden, like the South Bank, would become a cultural centre.

Obviously the ideas recommended in *London Replanned*, as indeed other schemes dreamt up by architects more in touch with fantasy than reality, would require an unthinkable amount of demolition and expense. They were no more realisable in 1945 than they had been in 1666. The corporation turned with relief to the only practical plan for the City of London, one that took account of the cost. The challenge was immense. Finance would have to come from the City itself and the corporation demanded a high return for its capital. Like the plan for the County of London which required more space per person, the City plan had to provide accommodation for half a million commuters in lighter, more spacious conditions than before. The best of the old had to be preserved, yet it had to coexist with the new.

The beauty of Professor W.G. Holford and Dr C.H. Holden's Plan of 1944 was that it recognised that diversity was an essential ingredient of the City's charm. Most of Wren's churches were to be rebuilt, preferably with small forecourts to emphasise their intimacy. They proposed that the skyline around St Paul's should be protected; that high-rise buildings should be more strictly set back so as not to impede the light. The desolate ruined space stretching from London Wall up to Cripplegate – the Barbican – was to provide working-class housing. Restaurants, cafés, pubs and shops were to be encouraged.

The City was a place of work but it was also a place of beauty, with a rich past and, hopefully, a thriving future. To improve traffic flow there were to be widened roads, some on several levels, such as those on London Wall, Farringdon Road, Thames Street and New Bridge Street, but there should be places for the pedestrian to enjoy the City's wealth of contrasts without the interruption of heavy traffic. New emphasis was to be laid on the river, with steps running down from St Paul's to the embankment. The south-east view of St Paul's, opened up by the bombing, was to stay open.

Throughout its long history the building of London has so often been *laissez-faire*. Plans are only paper and yet Abercrombie established the basic principles for London's post-war reconstruction. By the time the LCC and the various local authorities were ready to act, up to six years after the end of the war, most of them followed the outlines of his plan, even if some aspects of it were never implemented. Compromises had to be made on the road system. In other respects, the plan was to be overtaken by trends which Abercrombie could not have been expected to anticipate. He could not know that the post-war population would increase, rather than stagnate, making nonsense of his population ratio per acre. He could not know that the loss of London's manufacturing would be quickly replaced by a boom in office work and the service industries, encouraging the ever-increasing flow of commuters back into London from greater distances. He could not have foretold the demise of the Port of London and the growth of docklands as a location for smart offices and apartments, let alone of the development of Canary Wharf as an alternative business arena. He probably would not have guessed at the rise in home ownership and buy-to-let and spiralling prices, although he would have applauded the regeneration these trends are at last bringing to neglected inner-city sites.

At the time, it was recognised that the new London would take 50 years to build, and so it has proved. Standing on the Millennium Bridge with an unimpaired view of St Paul's and a revitalised embankment on the south side, enjoying the full sweep of the river from a top-floor balcony in the Shell Building or in a boat trip from Westminster to Greenwich, and capturing the excitement of the ever-changing, thrusting City skyline from the vantage point of the new City Hall, it has been worth the wait.

RESURGAM

Notes

ABBREVIATIONS
TNA: The National Archives
LMA: London Metropolitan Archives

Prelude

The main source for what London looked like, giving a detailed account of what historic treasures had been destroyed or preserved, is William Kent's *The Lost Treasures of London*. Other sources are *St Paul's Cathedral in Wartime* by the Very Reverend W.R. Matthews, Dean of St Paul's, Robert Hewison's *Under Siege: Literary Life in London 1939–45*, Mollie Panter-Downes's, *London War Notes 1939–1945*, Mrs Robert Henrey's *London Under Fire 1940–45* and Tom Pocock's *1945: The Dawn Came up like Thunder*. Information about the arts is drawn from the *Spectator* and Howard Ferguson's *Dame Myra Hess by her Friends*. The first impression of how tired and drawn Londoners looked, through the eyes of a newly arrived American, comes from the papers of Mrs E.H. Cotton in the Department of Documents, Imperial War Museum.

'Through the long war'. *Picture Post*, vol. 27, no. 7, 19 May 1945.

Chapter 1. Rockets Fell like Autumn Leaves

The key secondary sources for this chapter are Norman Longmate's *The Doodlebugs* and *Hitler's Rockets*.

17 'Rockets Fell like Autumn'. James Lees-Milne, *Prophesying Peace*, 15 January 1945, p.151.
18 The Dean worried there would be panic. Very Reverend W.R. Matthews, Dean of St Paul's, *St Paul's Cathedral in Wartime*, p.62. The book describes in detail the damage done to St Paul's and the methods by which it was protected.
19 'We are suffering'. George Beardmore, *Civilians at War*, p.187.

19	'Just as all these wonderful'. 'A Day and Night Diary of Kensington during the War kept by Vere Hodgson, 25 June 1940–2 September 1945', in future referred to as Papers of Vere Hodgson, Department of Documents, Imperial War Museum.
19	The state of morale is summed up in TNA/INF 1/292, Home Intelligence Weekly Reports, no. 221, 29 December 1944. It is also described in the *Stars and Stripes* in the first week of January 1945.
18–20	The behaviour of the V-1s and V-2s is described in the paper 'Lessons from Recent Raids – Long Range Rockets', TNA/HO 186/2299.
21	Joyce Barrett, Imperial War Museum Sound Archive, 9563/2.
21	Women's Voluntary Service. It added 'Royal' to its name in 1966 to become the Women's Royal Voluntary Service (WRVS).
21	'grabbed each of his small children'. Charles Graves, *Women in Green*, p.226.
22	'makes you feel'. 'Letters from George and Helena Britton to their daughter Florence Elizabeth Britton Elkus in Berkeley, California during the Second World War 1938–45', in future referred to as Papers of George and Helena Britton, Department of Documents, Imperial War Museum.
22	'He dreads the doodlebugs'. Papers of Mrs Irene Byers, Department of Documents, Imperial War Museum, 88/10/1.
23	'You accepted a plane'. Odette Lesley in Joanna Mack and Steve Humphries, *The Making of Modern London*, p.135.
23	'The doodlebugs kept us busy'. Stanley Rothwell, *Lambeth at War*, p.32.
23	Mary Beazley in Imperial War Museum Sound Archive, 18266/4.
24	the man who missed the bus is mentioned in Leonard Moseley, *Backs to the Wall*, p.365.
24	two elderly spinsters . . . their Pekinese. Charles Graves, *Women in Green*, p.225.
24	the baby wrapped in linoleum is described in *News Chronicle*, 21 February 1945.
24	'to see the beastly thing'. Papers of Vere Hodgson, Department of Documents, Imperial War Museum.
25	the trees had lost their leaves. Tom Pocock, *1945: The Dawn Came up like Thunder*, p.27.
25	'Nasty, dirty, noisy chimney man'. Charles Graves, *Women in Green*, p.225.

25 'the familiar splutter'. John Lehmann, *I Am My Brother*, p.180.

25 'a doodlebug comes over our bus'. Harold Nicolson, *The War Years*, p.384.

25 'You didn't complain'. Nancie Norman, Imperial War Museum Sound Archive, 16705/4.

26 'I can still remember my horror'. Odette Lesley in Joanna Mack and Steve Humphries, *The Making of Modern London*, p.132.

26 'Viti has been kept up'. Harold Nicolson, *The War Years*, p.380.

26 'On June 15th we go to bed'. Papers of Mrs Irene Byers, Department of Documents, Imperial War Museum, 88/10/1.

27 Evacuation of the sick, aged and infirm, TNA/HLG 7/534 and 535.

27 Making the Underground safe is described in Charles Graves, *London Transport Carried On* and the capacity of the tube shelters in Nigel Pennick, *Bunkers under London*.

31 Major Brock-Chisholm in Nigel Pennick, *Bunkers under London*, p.24.

35 The country was divided into 11 regions roughly corresponding to those of Cromwell's major-generals in the 1650s.

37 'Actually the V-2 began'. William E. Hall, Diary, Hackney Archives, M4472.

37 'One Friday evening'. Papers of Mrs P. Bell, Department of Documents, Imperial War Museum, 86/46/1.

37 'At 7.20 am on Saturday morning'. TNA/HO 192/1134.

38 'The silence of the authorities'. Stanley Rothwell, *Lambeth at War*, p.33.

38 'We catch a much earlier train'. Papers of Mrs Irene Byers, Department of Documents, Imperial War Museum, 88/10/1.

39 'Since the Government's admission'. Mollie Panter-Downes, *London War Notes 1939–1945*, p.357.

39 George Orwell was exasperated. *Tribune*, vol. III, p.280, December 1944.

40 'The rockets, if less frequent'. Papers of Mrs Gwladys Cox, Department of Documents, Imperial War Museum, 86/46/1.

40 'We don't stand a chance'. Papers of Mrs P. Bell, Department of Documents, Imperial War Museum, 86/46/1.

40 'The rockets, dearie?'. The Trustees of the Mass-Observation Archive, University of Sussex, FR 2207 'V-2 Bombs – SE London', 19 February 1945.

40 'It is no good worrying'. Papers of George and Helena Britton, Department of Documents, Imperial War Museum.

41 'It was like putting you in your coffin'. Reg Neal, Imperial War Museum Sound Archive, 9573/1.

41 'Lessons from Recent Raids – Long Range Rockets', TNA/HO 186/2299.

45 'Audrey told me afterwards'. Anthony Weymouth, *Journal of the War Years and One Year Later*, 7 December 1944, p.365.

45 Incident Report, Mackenzie Road, TNA/HO 186/2400, ARP Incident Reports (Islington).

46 'He knows that the steel joist'. J.H. Forshaw, LMA/LCC/AR/WAR/1/29.

47 'We cut a hole'. Papers of Reverend J.G. Markham, Department of Documents, Imperial War Museum, 91/5/1.

47 Typical was the old woman. George F. Vale, Bethnal Green's Ordeal, p.8.

51 'I pulled the chain'. Described by Miss Geering in Shepherds Bush Local History Society, *Around the Bush – the War Years*, p.54.

51 'on the pavement people ducked'. Tom Pocock, *1945: The Dawn Came up like Thunder*, p.25.

52 'I walked down to St Leonard's Terrace'. James Lees-Milne, *Prophesying Peace*, p.158.

52 'One grew hard'. John Lehmann, *I Am My Brother*, p.281.

53 The cinema provided the people's great escape. See Guy Morgan, *Red Roses Every Night*, pp.53–55.

53 Report on the Forest Road Library incident in Hackney Archives.

53 'Some, especially the clever'. *Daily Express*, 9 May 1945.

54 'Arrived home from office'. William E. Hall, Diary, Hackney Archives, M 4472.

54 'I know he was in the library'. *Daily Express*, 9 May 1945.

54 'It was *sick*!'. Reg Neal, Imperial War Museum Sound Archive, 9573 1/1.

55 'The day, Saturday, 20 January'. Stanley Tiquet, *It Happened Here*, p.54.

57 'Our life here is a constant strain'. Papers of George and Helena Britton, Department of Documents, Imperial War Museum

58 'He talks through his hat!'. Papers of Mrs Uttin, Department of Documents, Imperial War Museum, 88/50/1.

58 'Goebbels kept his word'. Papers of Mrs Gwladys Cox, Department of Documents, Imperial War Museum, 86/46/1.

58 'Several V-2s over during the night'. Anthony Heap, Diary, 12 March 1945, LMA/ACC 2243/19/1.

59 'We heard a child whimpering'. Quoted in Lewis Blake, *Bolts from the Blue*, p.68.

62 'Otherwise their clothing'. Papers of Reverend J.G. Markham,

Department of Documents, Imperial War Museum, 91/5/1.

62 The Smithfield Market incident, TNA/HO 186/2388, APR Incident Reports (Finsbury).

63 23 unidentified victims in Bethnal Green mentioned in George F. Vale, *Bethnal Green's Ordeal 1939-45*, p.10.

63 'We had somehow to form a body'. Frances Faviell, *A Chelsea Concerto*, pp.114-15.

64 'Emergency Mortuary and Burial Arrangements', TNA/HLG 7/762.

65 'daughter could be buried'. *South London Press*, 23 May 1945.

67 'In less than ten minutes'. Papers of Mrs E.H. Cotton, Department of Documents, Imperial War Museum, 93/3/1.

67 'Naturally the traffic'. Papers of John L. Sweetland, Department of Documents, Imperial War Museum, 97/21/1.

68 'I saw a blue flash'. *News Chronicle*, 27 April 1945.

68 The Hughes Mansions Incident Report is in TNA/HO 186/2400, ARP Incident Reports (Stepney).

69 'London is now on the air-bombing'. Anthony Heap, Diary, 17 April 1945, LMA/ACC 2243/19/1.

69 'No bombs!'. Papers of Vere Hodgson, Department of Documents, Imperial War Museum.

Details of the number and location of incidents, numbers of deaths and casualties, are taken from TNA/HO 202/10/Nos. 236-49 and TNA/AIR 20/3439 and the Metropolitan Police reports in TNA/MEPO 4/131. The statistics in the Metropolitan Police reports vary slightly from the rest, as the area covered by the Met does not correspond exactly with the area covered in London Region.

The process of clearance of debris and salvage of materials is sourced from TNA/HO 207/70.

For a detailed guide to the tasks of Civil Defence personnel see T.E. Browne, 'The Conduct of ARP Incidents. A Guide for the Civil Defence Services', Hackney Archives.

Chapter 2. The Word from the Ministry

The main secondary sources for this chapter are Ian McLaine, *Ministry of Morale* and Sian Nicholas, *The Echo of War*.

71 'If one treats'. Quoted in Ian McLaine, *Ministry of Morale*, p.251. 'Home Front Propaganda', November 1941, PRO/INF 1/251.

71 Home Security Weekly Appreciation Report, TNA/HO 202/10/No. 237, 27 December 1944-3 January 1945.

71 'In another month there will be nothing left of London'. TNA/HO 202/10/No. 243, 7 February 1945–14 February 1945.

74 'The cartoon is only one example'. Herbert Morrison, *An Autobiography by Lord Morrison of Lambeth*, pp.222–5.

77 Sandys's report on German Long Range Rocket development – 'The enemy would naturally be most anxious' – TNA/HO 186/2271.

77 'I have been looking'. Papers of Kenneth Holmes, Department of Documents, Imperial War Museum.

78 'There was intermittent air activity'. TNA/HO 207/240.

79 'No one, after considering the facts and figures'. TNA/HO 207/240.

80 'Your publication of this article'. TNA/HO 207/240/798/9/1.

80 'It seemed to the Editor-in-Charge'. Ibid.

80 'Quite apart from all question of fall of shot'. TNA/HO 207/240/798/9/1.

81 'certainly better than some of its contemporaries'. TNA/HO 207/240/798/9/1.

81 'to misconceive the intensely competitive'. Ibid.

81 Obituaries discussed in TNA/INF 1/969 and TNA/HO 207/240.

82 Morrison sent a memo to Churchill. TNA/INF 1/969.

83 fresh batch of instructions issued by Rear-Admiral Thomson on 26 April. TNA/INF 1/969.

83 *Ilford Recorder* mentioned in TNA/HO 207/240/798/9/1.

85 The Wartime Social Survey is discussed in TNA/INF 1/273.

92 'During the war years, more and more Londoners'. Mollie Panter-Downes, *London War Notes 1939–1945*, p.363.

94 Henry Moore at the Lefevre, *Spectator*, 13 April 1945.

96 *Forever Amber* 'already burst on the American market'. *Daily Mail*, 18 August 1945.

96 Anthony Heap splurged on his own copy. Diary, 5 September 1945, LMA/ACC 2243/19/1.

96 Public Morality Council on the *Forever Amber* film, LMA/A/PMC/17/1.

97 '*Brideshead* has been a success'. Evelyn Waugh, *The Diaries of Evelyn Waugh*, p.628.

97 'The theatres and cinemas'. Mollie Panter-Downes, *London War Notes 1939–1945*, p.358.

99 Home Intelligence Weekly Report, 29 December 1944, TNA/INF 1/292, No. 221.

101 'After five years of war'. Herbert Morrison, quoted in Ian McLaine, *Ministry of Morale*, p.275.

101 Resident of Chigwell in Leonard Moseley, *Backs to the Wall*, p.366.

101 'Such facilities would undoubtedly provide'. TNA/HO 186/2249.

102 'This war lasted too long'. *Croydon Advertiser*, 30 March 1945.

103 'The danger has gone'. Anon, 'Every-day War: A Diary', Kensington and Chelsea Local Studies, 940.548EVE AR/RS.

103 'The mood of the people'. Papers of Mrs P. Bell, Department of Documents, Imperial War Museum, 86/46/1.

103 'Workers continue anxious'. TNA/INF 1/292, Home Intelligence Weekly Reports, No. 221, 29 December 1944.

104 'We cannot win the war'. Quoted in Robert Hewison, *Under Siege*, p.169.

105 Wartime Social Survey on Education, TNA/RG 23/71.

105 'if Hitler invaded Hell'. Winston Churchill quoted in Ian McLaine, *Ministry of Morale*, p.201.

107 'America is not really'. TNA/INF 1/292/No. 220, 12–19 December 1944.

108 'It is always impolite to criticize'. Anon, *Over There*, p.11.

108 'America won the last war'. Ibid., p.9.

108 'Nazi propaganda'. Ibid., p.9.

108 'You are higher paid'. Ibid., p.2.

109 'People praise the Americans' fighting qualities'. TNA/INF 1/292/No. 220, 12–19 December 1944.

109 'One of the things I most look forward to'. Anthony Heap, Diary, 4 April 1945, LMA/ACC 2243/19/1.

109 'Because the British have been prepared'. Mollie Panter-Downes, *London War Notes 1939–1945*, p.398.

110 'Terribly shocked to hear'. Papers of Miss N.V. Carver, Department of Documents, Imperial War Museum, 90/16/1.

110 'I went all cold'. The Trustees of the Mass-Observation Archive, University of Sussex, FR 2229 'Death of Roosevelt', April 1945.

110 'People are saying that it is pathetic'. Anthony Weymouth, *Journal of the War Years and One Year Later*, 13 April 1945, p.387.

112 'How shall we treat the Hun?'. The Reverend J.B. Harrington Evans, Vicar of Enfield, *Enfield Herald*, 14 July 1944.

112 'It has taken the camera'. Mollie Panter-Downes, *London War Notes 1939–1945*, p.371

113 'it is no use the German people'. Papers of Vere Hodgson, Department of Documents, Imperial War Museum.

113 'After seeing the exhibition'. The Trustees of the Mass-Observation Archive, University of Sussex, FR 2248 'German Atrocities: Attitudes of Londoners', May 1945.

114 'I feel we could have prevented'. Ibid.

114 'It made me feel pretty sick'. Ibid.

114 'If, as some people think'. Mollie Panter-Downes, *London War Notes 1939–1945*, p.372.

115 'The world can and must'. Patrick Gordon Walker in *Belsen Concentration Camp: Facts and Thoughts*, 27 May 1945, BBC Written Archives.

115 'It's awful'. Anon, 'Every-day War: A Diary', Kensington and Chelsea Local Studies, 940.548EVE AR/RS.

115 'The first photographs'. Mollie Panter-Downes, *London War Notes 1939–1945*, p.372.

116 'How can we hope to re-educate'. Harold Nicolson, *Spectator*, 14 September 1945.

Chapter 3. Shelter

Richard M. Titmuss's *History of the Second World War, United Kingdom Civil Series, Problems of Social Policy* is an invaluable source on the subjects of evacuation, rest centres, resettlement of the homeless, and the increased role of social workers.

118 'After lunch, it stopped'. Papers of Gwladys Cox, Department of Documents, Imperial War Museum, 86/46/1.

119 'As soon as it was daylight'. Papers of Reverend J.G. Markham, Department of Documents, Imperial War Museum, 91/5/1.

120 'The house was badly blasted'. Papers of Mr S.M.S. Woodcock, Department of Documents, Imperial War Museum, 87/36/1.

120 'Mrs P went at luncheon'. James Lees-Milne, *Prophesying Peace*, 28 February 1944, p.30.

121 Statistics for rest centres are in LMA/LCC/WE/RC/80/1 and other details may be found in LMA/LCC/WE/RC/3.

123 'It's all right'. Frances Faviell, *A Chelsea Concerto*, p.245.

124 The *After the Raid* pamphlet may be found in TNA/INF 1/339.

124 The claims process is described in detail in 'A Short History of the War Damage Commission' available in the Department of Documents, Imperial War Museum. The total number of claims nationally for the whole war was 3,571,000.

127 'Today of all days!'. Verily Anderson, *Spam Tomorrow*, p.258.

128 Sir Ernest Gowers' report to the Minister of Home Security, TNA/HO 207/85.

129 9 million square feet of glass. Figure given in Anthony Shaw and

Jon Mills, '*We Served*': *Wartime Wandsworth and Battersea*, p.53.

130 one and a half million feet of glass in Hackney. *Hackney Gazette and North London Advertiser*, 29 October 1945.

130 132,000 men were engaged in repairs. *Daily Express*, 16 February 1945.

130 the rate of repair rose from 27,300 in January. Ibid.

130 470,900 bomb-damaged houses. *Finsbury Weekly News, Clerkenwell Chronicle and St Luke's Examiner*, 26 January 1945.

130 In Islington half of 65,900. Ibid.

130 repair men lying drunk. *South London Press*, 15 May 1945.

131 'In wartime every live rat'. *Hackney Gazette and North London Advertiser*, 3 February 1945.

131 Sir Malcolm Trustram Eve had loaned his 12-room town house. *Daily Express*, January 1945.

132 Dry rot was a common problem. *West London Press*, 8 June 1945.

133 'The Vigilantes deserve all our thanks'. *Woman*, 18 August 1945.

133 'I was desperate'. *Daily Mirror*, 4 August 1945.

134 household goods to Hackney. Hackney Archives, H/CC/2/20.

134 When a consignment of sheets. Papers of Vere Hodgson, Department of Documents, Imperial War Museum.

135 Rosie White and second-hand goods. Jess Steele, *Working Class War*, p.95.

135 'I met a lovely young wife'. Papers of Mrs Irene Byers, Department of Documents, Imperial War Museum, 88/10/1.

136 'We had a flat in London'. *News of the World*, 11 February 1945.

136 'Anyone 'ud think'. Papers of Irene Byers, Department of Documents, Imperial War Museum, 88/10/1.

137 a couple in their eighties. Papers of Reverend J.G. Markham, Department of Documents, Imperial War Museum, 91/5/1.

137 'The Christmas Day muddle'. *West London Press, Chelsea, Westminster and Pimlico News*, 5 January 1945.

138 'greatest delight is to watch the people'. *Hampstead and Highgate Express*, 13 April 1945.

138 'I am very happy here'. Ibid.

138 12,500 in the Underground. TNA/HO 207/85. Figures for the numbers sheltering in the new deep tubes are given in the same file. Figures for numbers sheltering in the tubes are also given in TNA/HO 207/386. Bunk capacity in the Underground stations is given in TNA/HO 207/226.
Hygiene in the Underground shelters is covered in TNA/HO 207/359 and welfare in TNA/HO 207/386.

138 'I stay here because I like it'. *Daily Express*, 21 April 1945.

138 'I like the early morning cup'. Ibid.

139 'It would be repugnant to public opinion'. LMA/MCC/WE/PA/2/31.

139 By July 1945 the Regional Commissioner . . . public shelters had been closed. TNA/HO 207/85.

141 German POWs . . . 'quite docile'. *Boroughs of Poplar and Stepney and East London Advertiser*, 10 August 1945. German prisoners on the building sites are also mentioned in the *News Chronicle*, 7 May 1945.

142 the salvage and removal of 331,865 tons of steel. LMA/LCC/AR/WAR/1/29. On debris clearance, see also LMA/LCC/CE/WAR/2/109.

143 Lord Rennell. *News Chronicle*, 22 February 1945.

143 Her hutment home would be built over old graves. *Hackney Gazette and North London Advertiser*, 20 July 1945 and the *Star*, 5 January 1945.

143 See 'Temporary housing in the London Region', TNA/HLG 7/1026.

143 Hornsey Housing Committee was one of several. *Hampstead and Highgate Express*, 23 February 1945.

143 The Ministry of War Transport . . . admitted to the Ministry of Health. TNA/HLG 7/1026.

144 'We are still waiting'. *Woman*, 3 February 1945.

144 'After we looked round Mary was worried'. The Trustees of the Mass-Observation Archive, University of Sussex, FR 2279 'Population and Housing in England and Wales, mid 1945', August 1945.

145 Protests against working-class flats in New End Square. *Hampstead and Highgate Express*, 2 February 1945.

145 In Wandsworth . . . 'sharp practice'. *South London Press*, 23 February 1945.

146 'I don't want to sell my freehold'. Ibid., 23 February 1945.

146 'The person whose house has been totally destroyed'. *Croydon Advertiser*, 24 August 1945.

146 'where an owner-occupier'. Ibid.

147 'beggars can't be choosers'. Ibid., 2 November 1945.

147 Shoreditch families keen to relocate to Southend. TNA/HLG 7/561.

148 Joke about a man found drowning. Anthony Weymouth, *Journal of the War Years and One Year Later*, 1 December 1943, p.267.

148 'How are people earning £3.10s'. *West London Press, Chelsea, Westminster and Pimlico News*, 5 January 1945.

148 Typically, when two flats were advertised to be let. *Daily Mirror*, 18 June 1945.

148 'Four families are living in three rooms'. Ibid.

148 'I enclose the agent's quotation'. Ibid., 11 July 1945.

149 'Londoners whose war jobs' Mollie Panter-Downes, *London War Notes 1939–1945*, p.367.

150 'They could just give me *any* of it'. The Trustees of the Mass-Observation Archive, University of Sussex, FR 2270B 'The Post-War Homes Exhibition', July 1945.

150 50,000 houses in the County of London. Figures given in Stephen Inwood, *A History of London*, p.809.

150 in 1939 there had been 1,008,000 building workers in Britain. *Spectator*, 19 January 1945.

150 'I tell him he is wrong'. *Daily Mirror*, 18 January 1945.

151 Mrs Godfrey Pyke said. *News Chronicle*, 22 February 1945.

151 the Archbishop of York said he 'could not imagine'. *News Chronicle*, 22 February 1945.

151 'indecisive footling'. *News Chronicle*, 12 April 1945.

152 'It is as though in an orchestra'. *Picture Post*, 14 July 1945.

153 'only a very grave concern'. Michael Foot, *Aneurin Bevan*, p.259.

Chapter 4. Don't Waste It

An invaluable source for this chapter is the Ministry of Food's paper 'How Britain Was Fed in War Time: Food Control 1939–45', available in the Department of Documents, Imperial War Museum.

155 'To throw your bus ticket'. Government advertisement in *Woman*, 31 March 1945.

155 frozen milk on doorstep. *South London Press*, 30 January 1945.

155 Southwark housewives besieged the Town Hall. Ibid.

155 a journey from Darlington. James Lees-Milne, *Prophesying Peace*, 24 January 1945, p.157.

156 'You had to get fuel where you could'. Lil Patrick in Rib Davies and Pam Schweitzer, *Southwark at War*, p.16.

156 'The fuel situation'. Anthony Heap, Diary, 29 January 1945, LMA/ACC 2243/19/1.

157 'We're managing, but only just'. The Trustees of the Mass-Observation Archive, University of Sussex, FR 2218 'Coal Shortage: Interviews in Chelsea', March 1945.

157 'We were frozen'. Ben Wicks, *Welcome Home*, p.175.

157 'The needs of munitions factories'. *South London Press*, 5 January 1945.

157 collapse of the electric grid system. *News Chronicle*, 3 January 1945.

159 'your fire may come out of a tap'. *Woman*, 6 January 1945.

160 'No dim-out indoors!'. *Woman*, 6 January 1945.

160 'The cold persists'. James Lees-Milne, *Prophesying Peace*, 11 January 1945, p.155.

160 'I cannot, without anthracite' Ibid., 20 January 1945, p.156.

160 'a late tea with Emerald at the Dorchester'. Ibid., 27 January 1945, p.156.

160 'And rotten bad stuff'. The Trustees of the Mass-Observation Archive, University of Sussex, FR 2218 'Coal Shortage', March 1945.

161 Mrs Doris Segal. *Star*, 4 January 1945.

161 'There was a large empty site'. Bill Goble in Shepherds Bush Local History Society, *Around the Bush – the War Years*, p.55.

161 'At the moment we are burning'. Papers of Mrs Gwladys Cox, Department of Documents, Imperial War Museum, 86/46/1.

161 'Gas and electricity are cut off'. George Beardmore, *Civilians at War*, p.187.

162 how tired, pinched and grey the people looked. Papers of Mrs E.H. Cotton (an American living in London), Department of Documents, Imperial War Museum, 93/3/1.

162 'The bus queue was another innovation'. Lola Duncan in *Home Chat*, 27 January 1945.

163 'It became a habit'. Papers of Mrs P. Bell, Department of Documents, Imperial War Museum, 86/46/1.

163 'As Dad and I were at work'. Miss Geering in Shepherds Bush Local History Society, *Around the Bush – the War Years*, p.61.

164 'We shan't know ourselves'. Anthony Weymouth, *Journal of the War Years and One Year Later*, 15 July 1941, p.40.

164 'The crude way is to tip him heavily'. *Spectator*, 28 December 1945.

165 'The outstanding problem in feeding the nation'. Frederick Marquis, the Right Honourable the Earl of Woolton, *The Memoirs of the Rt Hon the Earl of Woolton*, p.207.

167 'One day a relative gave my aunt'. Miss Geering in Shepherds Bush Local History Society, *Around the Bush – The War Years*, p.61.

168 At the Croydon and District Federation. *Croydon Advertiser*, 2 March 1945.

168 9,000 allotment holders. *Hackney Gazette and North London Advertiser*, 10 January 1945.

168 2,000-long waiting list. Ibid.

169 'It was no use relying'. Lord Woolton, *The Memoirs of the Rt Hon the Earl of Woolton*, p.248.

170 Westminster City Council . . . kitchen waste. *Islington Guardian and Hackney News*, 12 October 1945.

171 'The Upper Norwood Domestic'. *Croydon Advertiser*, 9 March 1945.

175 Westminster City Council collected 13,113 tons. *Islington Guardian and Hackney News*, 12 October 1945.

176 'I had a free day'. Anon, 'Every-day War: A Diary', Kensington and Chelsea Local Studies, 940.548EVE AR/RS.

176 'I was determined that we would not ration'. Lord Woolton, *The Memoirs of the Rt Hon the Earl of Woolton*, p.209.

178 'We made jam from hedgerow fruits'. Hornsey Historical Society, *Home Fires*, p.38.

178 'It is only possible to ration'. Lord Woolton, *The Memoirs of the Rt Hon the Earl of Woolton*, p.209.

179 'It was a "Stock Exchange" in points'. Ibid., p.212.

179 'For women it became "shopping"'. Ibid.

180 'And they were stacked'. Fred Barnes, Imperial War Museum Sound Archive, 11852/2.

181 Lord Woolton . . . application of science to nutrition. *Sunday Graphic*, 4 January 1945.

181 A Wartime Social Survey found that men complained of feeling hungry more than women, TNA/RG 23.

182 only 40 per cent of housewives. Wartime Social Survey, TNA/RG 23.

183 Marguerite Patten. Imperial War Museum Sound Archive, 16630/5/1.

183 'For a month now I have been trying'. *News of the World*, 2 September 1945.

184 'you would require the stomach'. Anthony Weymouth, *Journal of the War Years and One Year Later*, 8 January 1945, p.372.

186 Lyons Corner House menus in LMA/ACC/3527/369 and 3527/235 and 3527/371.

186 'Duly delighted to learn'. Anthony Heap, Diary, 3 January 1945, LMA/ACC 2243/19/1.

187 wry chuckles from the audience. Mollie Panter-Downes, *London War Notes 1939–1945*, p.366.

187 'The meat ration lasts'. Vere Hodgson quoted in Leonard Moseley, *Backs to the Wall*, p.334.

188 'We dine off a piece of horsemeat'. Papers of Mrs Irene Byers, Department of Documents, Imperial War Museum, 88/10/1.

188 'By rushing backwards and forwards'. Anon, 'Every-day War: A Diary' Kensington and Chelsea Local Studies, 940.548EVE AR/RS.

188 'The search for food'. Theodora Fitzgibbon, *With Love*, p.156.

188 'I never thought the day'. Papers of Mrs R.E. Uttin, Department of Documents, Imperial War Museum, 88/50/1.

189 'What do you think I have found?'. *Woman*, 27 January 1945.

189 'At the fishmonger's'. Papers of Gwladys Cox, Department of Documents, Imperial War Museum, 86/46/1.

189 'The majority of fish and chip shops'. Anthony Heap, Diary, 29 May 1945, LMA/ACC 2243/19/1.

190 'The first was asking for half-a-dozen eggs!'. Lola Duncan, *Home Chat*, 27 January 1945.

190 'Each woman would pass on'. Papers of Mrs P. Bell, Department of Documents, Imperial War Museum, 86/46/1.

191 'We can't survive without a cup of tea'. Lil Patrick in Rib Davies and Pam Schweitzer, *Southwark at War*, p.18.

191 'So now we shall be able to offer'. Papers of George and Helena Britton, Department of Documents, Imperial War Museum.

192 'Native strawberries'. Papers of Mrs E.H. Cotton, Department of Documents, Imperial War Museum, 93/3/1.

192 'Oranges today'. Papers of Vere Hodgson, Department of Documents, Imperial War Museum

194 'One thing to be careful about'. Anon, *Over There*, p.12.

194 'We always had something'. Marina Welch in Jess Steele, *Working Class War*, p.66.

194 'You was never really hungry'. Ruth Tanner, Imperial War Museum Sound Archive.

194 'It was hard not to fall into the habit'. Papers of Mrs P. Bell, Department of Documents, Imperial War Museum, 86/46/1.

194 'Mums often went short'. Papers of Mrs P. Bell, Ibid.

195 the Ritz, which 'has become fantastically fashionable'. Sir Henry Channon, *Chips*, p.221.

195 'Emerald began in true form'. James Lees-Milne, *Prophesying Peace*, 2 April 1944, p.44.

195 'We had a delicious dinner'. Ibid., 24 June 1944, p.83.

196 'Dined excellently at the White Tower'. Ibid., 5 May 1944, p.59.

197 'many impoverished or elderly people'. Theodora Fitzgibbon, *With Love*, p.117.

197 'there was no wine'. James Lees-Milne, *Prophesying Peace*, 4 April 1945, p.179.

197 'An unexpected treat'. Anthony Weymouth, *Journal of the War Years and One Year Later*, 23 December 1941, p.76.

198 'Lunch in a West-End'. Ibid., 26 December 1945, p.370.

198 'Wine, of course, has now'. Ibid., 23 September 1943, p.248.

198 'Hamish dined alone'. James Lees-Milne, *Prophesying Peace*, 20 January 1944, p.11.

199 'Ave has been to a shop'. Anthony Weymouth, *Journal of the War Years and One Year Later*, 7 December 1943, p.268.

199 'Because of having the off-licence'. Marina Welch in Jess Steele, *Working Class War*, p.66.

200 'Day after day, numbers of these young men'. Public Morality Council report, 19 March–21 April 1945, LMA/A/PMC/42.

200 'Generally we would meet'. Theodora Fitzgibbon, *With Love*, p.167.

200 'No restaurant, tea-shop or canteen'. Anthony Weymouth, *Journal of the War Years and One Year Later*, 11 March 1945, p.382.

201 'London diners eat nearly'. *Sunday Graphic*, 23 September 1945.

202 'One certainly has to pay dearly'. Anthony Heap, Diary, 22 May 1945, LMA/ACC 2243/19/1.

203 In August a boatload of bacon. *Sunday Graphic*, 12 August 1945.

204 'With extraordinary official aptitude'. *Sunday Graphic*, 15 July 1945.

204 'We must produce a great deal'. Ibid., 10 June 1945.

205 'Days when we would have roast beef'. Papers of Mrs P. Bell, Department of Documents, Imperial War Museum, 86/46/1.

205 'I read in the newspaper'. Anthony Weymouth, *Journal of the War Years and One Year Later*, p.407.

205 Smithfield meat porters were threatening. *News Chronicle*, December 1945.

205 'It is hard to realize'. Quoted in the *Australian Women's Weekly*, 20 October 1945.

206 London butcher sleeping in his shop. 'Licit or Illicit?', Philip Carr, *Spectator*, 28 December 1945.

Chapter 5. Shabby Chic

The main background source for this chapter is Colin McDowell's enormously interesting and informative *Forties Fashion and the New Look*.

207 'It was smart to be shabby'. Verily Anderson, *Spam Tomorrow*, p.140.

207 'hatless and dishevelled'. Count Edward Raczynski, *In Allied London*, p.259.

207 'We must learn as civilians'. Quoted in Colin McDowell, *Forties Fashion and the New Look*, p.82.

208 'If British civilians look dowdy'. Anon, *Over There*, p.12.

209 'Nearly all food and clothes'. Anthony Weymouth, *Journal of the War Years and One Year Later*, 10 August 1943, p.236.

210 'The surprising thing about wartime'. Raphael Samuel, *East End Underworld*, p.258.

210 'I knew a lot about the black market'. Ibid., p.259.

211 'The new ration book'. *Sunday Graphic*, February 1945.

213 'Until you have done a little shopping'. Anthony Weymouth, *Journal of the War Years and One Year Later*, 15 November 1943, p.262.

213 'Well I bought some more Savings'. Anon, 'Every-day War: A Diary', Kensington and Chelsea Local Studies, 940.548EVE AR/RS.

213 'We were not supposed to give'. Hornsey Historical Society, *Home Fires*, p.38.

214 'I have got my coupons'. Anthony Weymouth, *Journal of the War Years and One Year Later*, 15 November 1943, p.262.

215 'True economy would have been to make fewer things'. *Daily Mirror*, 15 March 1945.

216 'Fortified by VE Day'. Harold Nicolson, *Spectator*, 25 May 1945.

217 'Are you worried about elastic?'. *Woman*, 28 April 1945.

218 The Board of Trade retaliated . . . corsets. *Woman*, 3 February 1945.

219 'I was thinking this evening'. Anthony Weymouth, *Journal of the War Years and One Year Later*, 12 March 1945, p.382.

219 'Your Gossard'. Advertisement in *Woman*, 10 February 1945.

219 'At first we thought we would'. Miss Geering in Shepherds Bush Local History Society, *Around the Bush – The War Years*, p.63.

220 4,000 women queued from dawn. *Sunday Graphic*, 16 September 1945.

220 'To help out with stockings'. Mick Scott, *Home Fires: A Borough at War*, p.26.

221 'It would be illuminating'. *Sunday Graphic*, 26 August 1945.

223 'Old time social distinctions'. Anon, *Over There*, p.11.

226 'Far too many of us'. *Sunday Graphic*, 1 July 1945.

227 'This was a wonderful invention'. Theodora Fitzgibbon, *With Love*, p.168.

227 'Even if five million mass-produced hats'. *News Chronicle*, 12 April 1945.

227 'I have not worn'. Ibid.

227 'Only one in a thousand'. Ibid.

228 'I can remember a friend'. Mick Scott, *Home Fires: A Borough at War*, p.26.

228 'At this rate the theatre'. Anthony Heap, Diary, 18 May 1945, LMA/ACC 2243/19/1.

229 'The life we used to live'. Anthony Weymouth, *Journal of the War Years and One Year Later*, 25 June 1942, p.125.

229 'The frou-frou woman'. *Daily Mail*, 9 January 1945.

229 'It all started with me'. *Home Chat*, 13 January 1945.

230 'To wear clothes that have been patched'. Quoted in Colin McDowell, *Forties Fashion and the New Look*, p.112.

232 'First, I would like'. Ministry of Information, *Make Do and Mend*, p.1.

233 'Coming on top of a year'. Papers of Mrs Gwladys Cox, Department of Documents, Imperial War Museum, 86/46/1.

234 'Clothes rationing brought many problems'. Hornsey Historical Society, *Home Fires*, p.38.

234 'Here we are – you and I'. *Home Chat*, 6 January 1945.

235 'Nearly everyone's hair'. *Woman*, 3 February 1945.

236 'One of the things the English'. Anon, *Over There*, p.11.

237 'Make-up was almost unobtainable'. Theodora Fitzgibbon, *With Love*, p.122.

237 'All the quotas'. *Daily Mail*.

237 'Q: I've joined the ATS'. *Home Chat*, 27 January 1945.

239 'At the moment, Paris'. *Picture Post*, 6 January 1945.

240 *Picture Post* complained. Ibid.

240 'Paris, incidentally, talks'. *Sunday Graphic*, 26 August 1945.

241 'We must *all* have new clothes'. George VI quoted in Michael Sissons and Philip French, *The Age of Austerity*, p.25.

Chapter 6. Off the Back of a Lorry

The main background sources for this chapter are Edward Smithies's *Crime in Wartime* and Donald Thomas's *An Underworld at War*, together with the Report of the Commissioner of Police of the Metropolis for 1944 and 1945 respectively.

242 'In 1945 the war against Germany'. John Gosling, *The Ghost Squad*, p.18.

242 Report of the Commissioner of Police of the Metropolis for the Year 1945, PRO/MEPO 4/193.

244 Selection of cases taken from LMA/PS.MS/A2/115 and LMA/PS.MS A1/194.

244 'You are nothing but a contemptible young cad'. *Islington Gazette*, 21 December 1945.

245 'Against the depleted ranks'. John Gosling, *The Ghost Squad*, p.18.

246 'Lorry-loads of tea'. Ibid., p.18.

246 'No one thought they was doing'. Ruth and Fred Tanner, Imperial War Museum Sound Archive.

247 'I would rather die'. Marina Jones quoted in *News of the World*, 11 February 1945.

248 'You can't hang my soldier'. Herbert Morrison, *An Autobiography by Lord Morrison of Lambeth*, p.228.

248 'Irish Molly'. *Hackney Gazette and North London Advertiser*, 19 February 1945.

249 'are still a large number of US troops'. Public Morality Council report, 20 August–22 September 1945, LMA/A/PMC/42.

249 'The sergeant said'. *Islington Guardian and Hackney News*, January 1945.

249 'Detective Collins said the soldier'. Ibid.

250 'They [prostitutes] still patrol'. LMC/A/PMC/42/23 April 1945.

251 'At about 3 am'. *South London Press*, 2 January 1945.

251 'Police are again conducting a campaign'. LMA/A/PMC/42/22 October–18 November 1945.

251 'You killed this woman'. *Islington Gazette*, 21 December 1945.

251 When a South London woman. *Islington Guardian and Hackney News*.

252 'A nursery fire guard'. Verily Anderson, *Spam Tomorrow*, p.151.

253 'The Town Hall provided them'. Papers of Reverend J.G. Markham, Department of Documents, Imperial War Museum, 91/5/1.

253 'Detective Watson said'. *Hackney Gazette and North London Advertiser*, 8 January 1945.

254 Albert Taylor, an Essex man. *Star*, 6 January 1945.

254 'mean and un-British'. *Hackney Gazette*, 21 February 1945.

254 When Leonard Humbley. *South London Press*, 2 January 1945.

254 'These people have been bombed'. *Hackney Gazette and North London Advertiser*, 10 January 1945.

255 'Sacrifices were no longer'. *Spectator*, 28 December 1945.

255 rationing and the coupon system 'have seriously lowered standards of morality'. *Daily Mail*.

256 'One day this old boy'. Rib Davies and Pam Schweitzer, *Southwark at War*, p.17.

256 'The Ghost Squad were interested'. Raphael Samuel, *East End Underworld*, p.259.

256 'You took part in a sordid'. *South London Press*, 30 March 1945.

257 'Evidence showed that she was stopped'. *South London Press*, 19 January 1945.

257 'It was stated that Coutts'. *Boroughs of Poplar and Stepney and East London Advertiser*, February 1945.

258 'he would sooner be put against the wall'. *Hackney Gazette and North London Advertiser*, 10 August 1945.

260 'The wife . . . stopped at one of the stalls'. *Spectator*, 28 December 1945.

260 Subsequently, Arthur Gosling of Chevening Road. *Star*, 9 January 1945.

261 Lea Espir was charged. LMA/PS.MS/A2/115/22 June 1945.

261 William Donoghue. LMA/PS.MS/A2/115/6 December 1944.

261 Charles Brumwell. LMA/PS.MS/A2/115/6 February 1945.

262 'Mr Lilly, for the Wandsworth'. *South London Press*, 13 July 1945.

262 George Townshend. LMA/PS.MS/A2/115/21 June 1945.

262 Izetta Freeman complained. *Islington Guardian and Hackney News*.

263 'I remember taking my ration book'. Mrs Dolly Andretti in Jennifer Golden, *Hackney at War*, p.7.

264 'We didn't go without'. Ibid.

264 'Lilian Emily Fitzjohn'. *Hackney Gazette and North London Advertiser*, 10 January 1945.

265 'Figures at police headquarters'. *Star*, 10 January 1945.

266 'I dressed in ladies' clothes'. Ibid., 5 February 1945.

266 'There was a lot of thieving going on'. Mrs Dolly Andretti quoted in Jennifer Golden, *Hackney at War*, p.7.

267 'If it is convenient to you'. *Croydon Advertiser*, 12 January 1945.

267 'The government has governed my business'. Quoted in Donald Thomas, *An Underworld at War*, p.16.

268 'I just took it because it is so hard to get'. *Islington Guardian and Hackney News*, 12 October 1945.

268 Five other women. *South London Press*, 12 October 1945.

268 'this blackguardly minority'. *The Times*, 2 January 1945.

268 Mrs Annie Harris. *News of the World*, 13 May 1945.

269 'We were close to the docks'. Bill Gibson in Rib Davies and Pam Schweitzer, *Southwark at War*, p.16.

269 'If we went to the dock police'. *Sunday Graphic*, 20 May 1945.

269 Annie Moore. LMA/PS.MS A1/194/5 September 1945.

270 Dorothy Roberts. LMA/PS.MS A1/193/15 May 1945.

270 Winifred Brookes. LMA/PS.MS/A2/115/15 May 1945.

270 Dorothy Bristow. LMA/PS.MS A1/194/26 September 1945.

270 Marthe Feldman. LMA/PS.MS A2/115/9 April 1945.

271 Eric Simmonds. *Croydon Advertiser*, 30 March 1945.

271 Dora Murrell. Ibid.

271 In a Bow Street café. *Star*, 12 January 1945.

272 Florence Evans. LMA/PS.MS A2/116/15 January 1945.

273 Mary Kathleen Mancini. LMA/PS.MS A1/194/26 March 1945.

273 Frances Avenell. LMA/PS.MS A1/193/24 January 1945.

273 Thomas McGuire. LMA/PS.MSA/194/9 July 1945.

273 'Sometimes you would see deserters'. Mrs Dolly Andretti quoted in Jennifer Golden, *Hackney at War*, p.7.

273 Alice May Ward. LMA/PS.MS A1/194/31 March 1945.

273 Mrs Eileen Davies. *Star*, 12 January 1945 and 6 February 1945 and *Daily Mirror*, 31 January 1945.

274 'No normal woman'. *Daily Mirror*, 31 January 1945.

274 'She does not blame the nursing home'. Ibid.

274 Ronald John Gordon Candy. *Hackney Gazette*, 27 July 1945.

274 The police swoop is described in the *Daily Mirror*, 15 December 1945.

275 'They questioned every living soul'. Billy Hill, *Boss of Britain's Underworld*, p.118.

275 'For that he committed High Treason'. TNA/CRIM 1/483.

276 'Now that my dear son'. Leo Amery to Robert Barrington-Ward, Christmas 1945, *The Times* Archive.

276 'Your son's courage'. Robert Barrington-Ward to Leo Amery, December 1945, *The Times* Archive.

Chapter 7. A Brief Period of Rejoicing

'Heard that thunderstorm in the night?' The Trustees of the Mass-Observation Archive, University of Sussex, FR 2263 'Victory in Europe', June 1945.

278 'The war news is so wonderful'. Papers of Miss V. Hall, Department of Documents, Imperial War Museum.

278 'Wouldn't it be lovely?' The Trustees of the Mass-Observation Archive, University of Sussex, FR 2232 'Easter Opinions, 1945', April 1945.

278 'Now the war is ending'. William E. Hall, Diary, Hackney Archives, M4472.

279 'Well, I don't know'. The Trustees of the Mass-Observation Archive, University of Sussex, FR2232 'Easter Opinions, 1945', April 1945.

279 'The tobacconist in West End Lane'. Papers of Mrs Gwladys Cox, Department of Documents, Imperial War Museum, 86/46/1.

279 'Somehow, I fancy, none of us'. James Lees-Milne, *Prophesying Peace*, 1 May 1945, p.185.

280 'After dinner, I went along the corridor'. Sir Henry Channon, *Chips*, p.404.

280 'At about 3 am'. Quoted in Tom Pocock, *1945: The Dawn Came up like Thunder*, p.99.

281 'For five years you've brought me'. Quoted in Peter Hennessy, *Never Again*, p.57.

282 'After a heroic fight'. Quoted in Norman Longmate, *When We Won the War*, p.51.

282 'I don't know whether to start'. The Trustees of the Mass-Observation Archive, University of Sussex, FR 2263 'Victory in Europe', May 1945.

282 A woman standing at Euston. Ben Wicks, *Welcome Home*, p.7.

283 'It has been a day of expectancy'. Anon, 'Every-day War: A Diary, Kensington and Chelsea Local Studies, 940.548 EVE AR/RS.

284 'When I get to London'. Harold Nicolson, *The War Years*, p.456.

284 A description of the evening of 7 May in the West End is in the *News Chronicle*, 8 May 1945.

285 The VE Day celebrations in the West End of London are described in the Trustees of the Mass-Observation Archive, University of Sussex, FR 2263 'Victory in Europe', May 1945.

285 'The mess they're making of it!'. Ibid.

285 'People look pretty cheerful'. Ibid.

286 'The war's ending'. Ibid.

286 'Official or not'. *Stars and Stripes*, 8 May 1945.

286 'Chelsea was not mad'. Anon, 'Every-day War: A Diary', Kensington and Chelsea Local Studies, 940.548EVE AR/RS.

287 'What was that?'. Quoted in Norman Longmate, *When We Won the War*, p.60.

288 'We're from Tooting'. The Trustees of the Mass-Observation Archive, University of Sussex, FR 2263 'Victory in Europe', May 1945.

288 'It didn't surprise me'. Ibid.

288 'The desire to assist'. Mollie Panter-Downes, *London War Notes 1939–1945*, p.374.

289 'The girls in their thin, bright dresses'. *Ibid.*, p.374.

289 'Churchill for sixpence'. The Trustees of the Mass-Observation Archive, University of Sussex, FR 2263 'Victory in Europe', June 1945.

290 'Now don't go further'. Ibid.

290 'I bet Churchill's pleased'. Ibid.

291 'The way they've behaved'. Ibid.

291 'The whole of Trafalgar Square'. Harold Nicolson, *The War Years*, p.456.

292 'Yesterday at 2.41 am'. Quoted in Norman Longmate, *When We Won the War*, p.65.

293 'A wonderful day'. Noël Coward quoted in Tom Pocock, *1945: The Dawn Came up like Thunder*, p.102.

293 'The car was literally'. Norman Longmate, *When We Won the War*, p.66.

293 'At the House, Questions'. Sir Henry Channon, *Chips*, p.405.

294 'Then a slight stir'. Harold Nicolson, *The War Years*, p.457.

295 'Winston took a long time,' Ibid., p.458.

295 'This is *your* victory!' Norman Longmate, *When We Won The War*, p.72.

296 'I've never shown so much leg'. The Trustees of the Mass-Observation Archive, University of Sussex, FR 2263 'Victory in Europe', May 1945.

297 'Today we give thanks to Almighty God'. King George VI quoted in Norman Longmate, *When We Won The War*, p.74.

297 'He'll come out with the floodlighting'. The Trustees of the Mass-Observation Archive, University of Sussex, FF 2263 'Victory in Europe', May 1945.

298 'We didn't really think'. Papers of Miss F.E. Tate, Department of Documents, Imperial War Museum, 95/4/1.

298 'I remember the thrill'. Quoted in Robert Westall, *Children of the Blitz*, p.223.

299 Harold Pinter. As recounted to the author.

299 'One deadly foe'. Churchill quoted in Norman Longmate, *When We Won The War*, p.79.

300 'Why did I go to that party?'. Harold Nicolson, *The War Years*, p.458.

301 'Licensing hours were extended'. Verily Anderson, *Spam Tomorrow*, p.258.

302 Reg Neal, Imperial War Museum Sound Archive, 9573/1.

302 The mayor lit the bonfire at 10 p.m. *West London Press*, 9 May 1945.

302 George Britton. Papers of George and Helena Britton, Department of Documents, Imperial War Museum.

302 'No school today'. Stella Freeman in Shepherds Bush Local History Society, *Around the Bush – The War Years*, p.70.

302 'They ranged from modest piles'. *Croydon Advertiser*, 11 May 1945.

303 'Some men had procured'. The Trustees of the Mass-Observation Archive, University of Sussex, FR 2263 'Victory in Europe', May 1945.

304 'Well, there was a bombed area'. Elizabeth Cole in Rib Davies and Pam Schweitzer, *Southwark at War*, p.30.

304 'Some of the kids'. Papers of Mrs P. Bell, Department of Documents, Imperial War Museum, 86/46/1.

304 'For years I had prayed'. Papers of Mrs D. Pepper, Department of Documents, Imperial War Museum, 96/26/1.

305 'Our house and next door'. Rosie White in Jess Steele, *Working Class War*, p.95.

305 'My pal's dad'. Quoted in Barry Turner and Tony Rennell, *When Daddy Came Home*, p.103.

305 'That evening, after the children'. Quoted in Norman Longmate, *The Home Front*, p.229.

306 'Rose shortly before 8'. The Trustees of the Mass-Observation Archive, University of Sussex, FR 2263 'Victory in Europe', May 1945.

306 'In 1945 I was fourteen'. Arthur Welch in Jess Steele, *Working Class War*, p.89.

307 'A very pleasant Victory tea'. Quoted in Geoffrey Gillam, *Enfield at War 1939–45*.

308 'The transition from total war'. Anthony Heap, Diary, 10 May 1945, LMA/ACC 2243/19/1.

309 'I went to St Paul's'. Sir Henry Channon, *Chips*, p.406.

310 Details about the National Gallery, Sadler's Wells and the Proms from the *Spectator*, 25 May 1945, 15 June 1945, 22 June 1945.

310 At Brixton Bus Depot. *South London Press*, 8 August 1945.

311 'The whole affair has been an unseemly scramble'. *Spectator*, 24 August 1945. Queues at London's railway stations described in *Daily Mail*, 30 July 1945.

311 'All day I have been made to feel despairing'. James Lees-Milne, *Prophesying Peace*, 8 August 1945, p.220.

312 'After luncheon I go with Victor'. Harold Nicolson, *The War Years*, p.29.

313 'I am strangely unmoved'. James Lees-Milne, *Prophesying Peace*, 15 August 1945, p.221.

313 'At least the whole thing was finished'. Doris Pratt in Rib Davies and Pam Schweitzer, *Southwark at War*, p.33.

313 'We do not talk about it'. Papers of Mrs Irene Byers, Department of Documents, Imperial War Museum, 88/10/1.

313 'I was shocked'. Anthony Weymouth, *Journal of the War Years and One Year Later*, pp.400–1.

315 'Up betimes, wearing morning clothes'. Sir Henry Channon, *Chips*, p.410.

315 'The inevitable crowds'. Anthony Heap, Diary, 15 August 1945, LMA/ACC 2243/19/1.

315 'London not at its best'. Sir Alexander Cadogan quoted in Tom Pocock, *1945: The Dawn Came up like Thunder*, p.193.

316 The American sergeant who said the lack of drink was worse than Prohibition. *Daily Mail*, 17 August 1945.

316 'One longed for bands'. John Lehmann, *I Am My Brother*, p.296.

316 'the war in South-East Asia'. Tom Pocock, *1945: The Dawn Came up like Thunder*, pp.193–4.

317 'I wandered alone'. Ibid.

317 'I feel it's going to be the beginning of dreadful problems'. The Trustees of the Mass-Observation Archive, University of Sussex, FR 2228 'Special Pre-Peace News Questionnaire', April 1945.

318 'Oh, it does make you fed up'. The Trustees of the Mass-Observation Archive, University of Sussex, FR 2270A 'The General Election of 1945', July 1945.

319 'I wonder how many years of *soi-disant*'. Noël Coward quoted in Tom Pocock, *1945: The Dawn Came up like Thunder*, p.194.

319 Robb Wilton quoted in Lewis Blake, *Red Alert*, p.96.

Chapter 8. Vote for Him!

'Fancy Mr Attlee'. Papers of Miss N.V. Carver, Department of Documents, Imperial War Museum, 90/16/1.

320 'I have been stunned by the news'. Papers of Vere Hodgson, Department of Documents, Imperial War Museum.

321 'Why It Happened'. *Spectator*, 3 August 1945.

323 the Conservatives 'wanted an early cashing in'. Roy Jenkins, *Churchill*, p.790.

323 'Three days after VE Day'. Herbert Morrison, *An Autobiography of Lord Morrison of Lambeth*, p.234.

325 'I could not see why'. Papers of Gwladys Cox, Department of Documents, Imperial War Museum, 86/46/1.

328 'When these young men and women'. *Spectator*, 2 March 1945.

329 'I don't for one moment believe'. Anthony Weymouth, *Journal of the War Years and One Year Later*, pp.396–7.

329 'Churchill's all right for the war job'. The Trustees of the Mass-Observation Archive, University of Sussex, FR 2257 'Youth and the Election', June 1945.

329 'Well, it's my honest opinion'. The Trustees of the Mass-Observation Archive, University of Sussex, FR 2270A 'The General Election of June–July 1945', June 1945.

330 'Of course I shall vote'. The Trustees of the Mass-Observation Archive, University of Sussex, FR 2257 'Youth and the Election', June 1945.

330 'I found I wasn't on the register' The Trustees of the Mass-Observation Archive, University of Sussex, FR 2270A 'The General Election of June–July 1945', June 1945.

331 'Overheard two workmen'. George Beardmore, *Civilians at War*, p.197.

332 'No Socialist Government conducting'. Churchill's Gestapo speech quoted in Roy Jenkins, *Churchill*, p.792.

332 'The people were looking'. Kenneth Lindsay, *Spectator*, 3 August 1945.

333 'The PM delivered a broadside'. Sir Henry Channon, *Chips*, p.408.

334 'When I listened'. Attlee quoted in Roy Jenkins, *Churchill*, p.793.

334 'Everyone I meet is angry'. The Trustees of the Mass-Observation Archive, University of Sussex, FR 2253 'Election Questionnaire – Churchill's Gestapo Speech', May 1945.

334 'I didn't think much of it'. Ibid.

335 'Far superior to Churchill's'. Ibid.

335 'You ought to hear the women'. The Trustees of the Mass-Observation Archive, University of Sussex, FR 2270A 'The General Election of June–July 1945', June 1945.

336 'To the Editor'. Quoted in Hugh Cudlipp, *Publish and Be Damned!*, p.231.

338 Churchill's election tour in London is described in *The Times*, 5 July 1945.

338 'I watched Churchill'. Papers of John L. Sweetland, Department of Documents, Imperial War Museum, 97/21/1.

343 A *Daily Mail* reporter. *Daily Mail*, 27 July 1945.

344 'Not one word of bitterness'. Harold Nicolson, *Diaries and Letters 1945–62*, p.29.

345 As he told Captain Pim. Quoted in Peter Hennessy, *Never Again*, p.56.

345 'Evidently it does not fear'. Sir Henry Channon, *Chips*, p.410.

346 'I went to Westminster'. Ibid., p.409.

346 Colonel Clifton Brown. Michael Sissons and Philip French, *The Age of Austerity*, p.20.

346 'The new Government will have terrible tasks'. Harold Nicolson, *Diaries and Letters 1945–62*, p.29.

346 'the cold douche'. *Picture Post*, vol. 28, no. 6, 11 August 1945.

346 'a bit too business like' . . . 'Well, I shouldn't say' . . . 'Well, now, do you recall' . . . 'As for America'. The Trustees of the Mass-Observation Archive, University of Sussex, FR 2281 'The Coming Winter; Main Grumble; Ending of Lease-Lend', September 1945.

348 'We have exhausted a great part'. *Spectator*, 31 August 1945.

350 'It is certainly grim reading'. Sir Alexander Cadogan quoted in Tom Pocock, *1945: The Dawn Came up like Thunder*, p.194.

351 'Opinion in Britain'. Anthony Weymouth, *Journal of the War Years and One Year Later*, p.403.

351 Correspondence between R.H. Brand and Robert Barrington-Ward, *The Times* Archive.

Chapter 9. Little Hooligans

London children are described as 'little hooligans' in the *Hampstead and Highgate Express*, 3 August 1945.

353 'It is a fact today'. Quoted in Barry Turner and Tony Rennell, *When Daddy Came Home*, p.157.

353 'We all got the idea'. *Finsbury Weekly News, Clerkenwell Chronicle and St Luke's Examiner*, 9 February 1945 and *Hackney Gazette and North London Advertiser*, 9 March 1945.

354 'During the war years children'. Quoted in Barry Turner and Tony

Rennell, *When Daddy Came Home*, p.157 from PRO/MEPO 2/8430.

354 Juvenile crime in the capital. LMA/LCC/CH/D/13/12.

355 'trauma of being picked'. Jack Harding, Imperial War Museum Sound Archive, 88/10/1.

356 They were not used to the number of clothes. This and other aspects of evacuation are described in LMA/LCC/EO/WAR/1/1.

356 London Clothing Scheme, Ibid.

356 A number of the LCC's children's care officers were seconded to the Ministry of Health. Ibid.

357 'Arriving [after a long train journey]'. Ruth Inglis, *The Children's War*, p.32.

358 'This foster mum'. Ibid., p.33.

358 'Returning one small boy'. Papers of Mrs Irene Byers, Department of Documents, Imperial War Museum, 88/10/1.

359 'And we went underground'. Bernard Kops quoted in Ruth Inglis, *The Children's War*, p.84.

359 'with beautiful teeth'. *News Chronicle*, 7 May 1945.

360 Michael Caine quoted in Ruth Inglis, *The Children's War*, p.150.

360 'My foster-parents had masses of books'. Quoted in Ruth Inglis, ibid., p.29.

360 'On one trip to Beckenham'. Richie White in Jess Steele, *Working Class War*, p.107.

361 two boys of 13 and 11 were drowned. *Boroughs of Poplar and Stepney and East London Advertiser*, 4 May 1945.

361 The Chief Inspector of Education in London admitted. For his report and a description of the education of London children in wartime see LMA/LCC/EO/WAR/I/238.

362 'Back home after five weeks'. Papers of John L. Sweetland, Department of Documents, Imperial War Museum, 97/21/1.

363 the teacher at Stoke Newington. Papers of Miss B. Helliar, Department of Documents, Imperial War Museum, 92/49/1.

364 A woman whose father was a fire-fighter. Papers of Mrs M. Strickland, Department of Documents, Imperial War Museum, 96/18/1.

364 Joyce Barrett. Imperial War Museum Sound Archive, 9563/2.

364 Numbers of children in London at various stages of the war in the Greater London Record Office's *We Think You Ought to Go*, p.50.

364 'Lessons were somewhat disrupted'. Stella Freeman in Shepherds Bush Local History Society, *Around the Bush – the War Years*, p.69.

365 'I worry about Chris's'. Papers of Mrs Irene Byers, Department of Documents, Imperial War Museum, 88/10/1.

365 'The form master had just'. Lewis Blake, *Bolts from the Blue*, p.70.

367 'Operate London Return Plans'. Description in the *News Chronicle*, 5 May 1945.

367 *News Chronicle* report of teacher in New North Road, 4 May 1945.

368 the returns show the consequences of the bombing. LMA/EO/WAR/1/133.

368 In a paper on the return of evacuees prepared by the LCC Education Officer's department. LMA/LCC/EO/WAR/1/131 and 132.

369 System of return described in PRO/HLG 7/336.

369 A cross-section of reasons for children unable to return home. LMA/EO/WAR/1/133.

371 Daisy and Lil. *News Chronicle*, 7 May 1945.

372 Mrs S of Caversham. LMA/LCC/CH/M/7 Box 7.

372 The Minister of Health hoped to avoid bringing children back to London to an institution. Ibid.

373 If a child had been orphaned. LMA/LCC/EO/WAR/2/66.

373 'Abandoned female child'. LMA/PH/HOSP/1/46.

375 *Notes on the Return of Unaccompanied Children*. LMA/MCC/WE/PA/2/31.

376 'It was hate at first sight'. Quoted in Ruth Inglis, *The Children's War*, p.149.

376 'it wasn't the joyous homecoming'. Papers of Miss D.E. King, Department of Documents, Imperial War Museum, 97/27/1.

377 LCC's Christmas Treats Fund. LMA/LCC/EO/WAR/1/157.

Chapter 10. Reunion of Strangers

The main background sources for this chapter are Sheila Ferguson and Hilda Fitzgerald, *The History of the Second World War, United Kingdom Civil Series, Studies in the Social Services*, Penny Summerfield, *Women Workers in the Second World War*, Gail Braybon and Penny Summerfield, *Out of the Cage*, Janet M. Hook, *British Policies and Methods in Employing Women in Wartime* and the Ministry of Information papers, 'British Women at War' and 'Women in War Jobs'.

379 'Back in "Civvy Street"'. This quotation comes from 'Calling the West Indies', *Civvy Street*, by E. Laurie Stone, BBC Written Archives, Box 66610, Ram.2, 1115–200.

380 'He saw, as is natural'. Quoted in Barry Turner and Tony Rennell, *When Daddy Came Home*, p.147 from the *WVS Bulletin*, April 1945.

381 Quotes from '*Can I Help You?*' '*Civvy Street Today*' by John Morgan, BBC Written Archives.

382 Reverend Elliott. *Sunday Graphic*, 10 June 1945.

383 'Advice to Nervous Returning'. *Daily Mirror*, 18 October 1945.

384 60 million changes of address. Sheila Ferguson and Hilda Fitzgerald, *The History of the Second World War, United Kingdom Civil Series, Studies in the Social Services*, p.2.

384 families had been getting smaller. Ibid., p.4

387 Mary Beazley. Imperial War Museum Sound Archives, 16705/4.

390 Kathleen Bliss. Imperial War Museum Sound Archive, 18266/4.

391 Nancie Norman. Imperial War Museum Sound Archive, 16705/4.

391 'When you get up'. The Trustees of the Mass-Observation Archive, University of Sussex, FR 2059 'Do the Factory Girls Want to Stay Put or Go Home?', March 1944.

392 'One of the most distressing social consequences'. *Spectator*, 11 May 1945.

393 'Fifteen- to eighteen-year-old girls'. LMA/A/PMC/42.

393 'One of the most remarkable'. Sheila Ferguson and Hilda Fitzgerald, *The History of the Second World War, United Kingdom Civil Series, Studies in the Social Services*, pp.97–8.

394 'I must again refer'. Public Morality Council report, 26 December–20 January 1945, LMA/A/PMC/41.

394 Odette Lesley. Quoted in Joanna Mack and Steve Humphries, *The Making of Modern London*, p.162.

395 'To girls brought up'. Sheila Ferguson and Hilda Fitzgerald, *The History of the Second World War, United Kingdom Civil Series, Studies in the Social Services*, pp.97–8.

395 'American soldiers speak with surprise'. James Lees-Milne, *Prophesying Peace*, 14 June 1944, p.77.

395 'I ask you as a mother'. Public Morality Council, 24 January 1945, LMA/A/PMC/42.

396 'The increase of venereal disease is one of the few "black spots"'. *Woman*, 6 January 1945.

396 Rise in illegitimacy and the state's acceptance of its new responsibilities towards the unmarried mother and illegitimate child. Sheila Ferguson and Hilda Fitzgerald, *The History of the Second World War, United Kingdom Civil Series, Studies in the Social Services*, chapter 3.

398 'The first reaction of all concerned'. *Spectator*, 9 March 1945.

398 'Would-be adopters'. See Sheila Ferguson and Hilda Fitzgerald, *The History of the Second World War, United Kingdom Civil Series, Studies in the Social Services*, pp.135–6.

399 'they want nothing but British'. *Star*, 24 January 1945.

399 'fair with blue eyes'. Ibid., 7 March 1945.

399 'You must have no more'. *South London Press*, 10 July 1945.

400 Sally Solomons. *Hackney Gazette and North London Advertiser*, 25 May 1945.

400 Maurice Jakubowicz case. *News of the World*, 19 August 1945.

401 'Does absence make them'. *Spectator*, 26 January 1945.

402 'It is very easy to say'. Barbara Cartland quoted in Barry Turner and Tony Rennell, *When Daddy Came Home*, p.114.

402 'They had only a stereotyped'. Phoebe D. Bendit and Laurence J. Bendit, *Living Together Again*, p.76.

402 The *Daily Mirror* complained that lurid statements. *Daily Mirror*, 12 January 1945.

403 'The exemplary conduct and courage'. *Star*, 4 January 1945.

403 'Crowds of them haunt'. Papers of Mrs Irene Byers, Department of Documents, Imperial War Museum, 88/10/1.

403 'There was only one of the London mothers evacuated'. The Trustees of the Mass-Observation Archive, University of Sussex, FR 2205–6 'Sex, Morality and the Birth Rate', February 1945.

404 'You are urged to be like Caesar's wife'. *Home Chat*, 17 February 1945.

405 'Unless you can prove you bought it'. *Star*, 5 January 1945.

405 Alfred James Morgan. Reports from *News of the World*, 14 January 1945 and 2 September 1945.

406 Frederick James Hooker. *News of the World*, 2 September 1945.

407 Betty Weiner. Imperial War Museum Sound Archive, 9585.

408 School for Brides at Rainbow Corner. *Daily Express*, 9 April 1945.

408 'As a young war widow'. Edna Bucknill in Ben Wicks, *Welcome Home*, p.175.

409 Mr Justice Hodson. *Star*, 15 January 1945.

409 'Like a lot of girls'. Odette Lesley in Joanna Mack and Steve Humphries, *The Making of Modern London*, p.162.

410 'The vast majority of these bigamy cases'. *Daily Mirror*, 31 January 1945.

410 Ethel Barnes. *News of the World*, 6 May 1945.

411 'Monotony, Rationing, Queues'. *Daily Mail*, 27 February 1945.

411 There was an increase in prematurely grey-haired. *Daily Mirror*, 23 July 1945.

412 'Most people are agreed'. Anthony Weymouth, *Journal of the War Years and One Year Later*, p.407.

413 Evacuation of expectant mothers. LMA/LCC/PH/GEN/3/20.

414 'The Metropolitan Borough Medical Officers of Health'. LMA/LCC/PH/GEN/3/20. Expectant mothers no longer a charge on the evacuation account, LMA/LCC/CH/M/7 Box 7.

415 'Women have established their claim'. Quoted in Janet M. Hook, *British Policies and Methods in Employing Women in Wartime*, p.37.

415 'Will the Factory Girls Want to Stay Put or Go Home?' The Trustees of the Mass-Observation Archive, University of Sussex, FR 2059 March 1944.

416 'The moment you say "I will"'. *Home Chat*, 13 January 1945.

416 Mary Beazley. Imperial War Museum Sound Archive, 18266/4.

417 'Of course when we get married'. The Trustees of the Mass-Observation Archive, University of Sussex, FR 2059 'Do the Factory Girls Want to Stay Put or Go Home?' March 1944.

418 'Then I went to Rickards'. Minnie Dingwall in Anon, *All Pulling Together*.

418 'I do not think any woman'. Dorothy Sheridan, *Wartime Women*, p.220.

421 'I am strongly against equal pay'. Mass-Observation, *Speak for Yourself: A Mass-Observation Anthology*, p.184.

421 'I do feel that equal pay'. Ibid., p.185.

421 'If women were given equal'. *Hampstead and Highgate Express*, 16 February 1945.

421 'Many of us who would support the battle'. *Woman*, 10 March 1945.

422 'When my John'. *Home Chat*, 12 May 1945.

422 'Wages are very high'. Anthony Weymouth, *Journal of the War Years and One Year Later*, p.403.

423 'They will accept £1 a week'. *Sunday Graphic*, 10 June 1945.

423 'If girls would only'. Ibid., 14 October 1945.

423 'There cannot have been'. Priscilla Novy, *Housework Without Tears*, p.7.

424 'In view of the fact'. LMA/LCC/EO/WAR/2/68.

424 'The day after armistice'. Jenni Murray, *The Woman's Hour*, p.69.

425 'Oh, they'll be able to get jobs'. *Daily Mirror*, 16 February 1945.

425 Cyril Nathan and *A Four Years' Plan for Children's Nurseries*.

LMA/LCC/EO/WAR/3/33.

426 'For instance, there's the young widow'. Jenni Murray, *The Woman's Hour*, p.76.

427 'We who are urging this change'. *Spectator*, 16 March 1945.

427 'The transition to voluntary parenthood'. *The Times*, 5 June 1945.

429 Mr Percy Harper. *Croydon Advertiser*, 24 August 1945.

430 'Three young men in new suits'. J.B. Priestley, *Three Men in New Suits*, p.3.

431 'My hopes for the post-war'. The Trustees of the Mass-Observation Archive, University of Sussex, FR 2220 'British Legion Competition Essays', 14 March 1945.

432 'A man asks only'. Ibid.

432 'We disembarked, not expecting'. *Sunday Graphic*, September 1945.

433 'I have been in the Army'. *News of the World*, 26 August 1945.

434 'I woke up one day'. Ben Wicks, *Welcome Home*, p.164.

434 Mr R.C.S. of Hayes. *Daily Mail*, 20 August 1945.

434 'We lived with my parents'. Ben Wicks, *Welcome Home*, p.173.

435 'I am 27 years old'. *Picture Post*, 14 July 1945.

435 'Sir–When I started'. *Spectator*, 21 December 1945.

436 'I can remember my husband'. Kit Beasley in Ben Wicks, *Welcome Home*, p.45.

437 'I was very happy'. Dorothy Richards, Ibid., p.58.

438 'We all went down'. Joan Pender, ibid, p.78.

438 'Mum had got used'. Jess Steele, *Working Class War*, p.101.

439 'My mother and I stood'. Barry Turner and Tony Rennell, *When Daddy Came Home*, p.107.

439 'If I close my eyes'. Ibid., p.89.

440 'When my husband came home'. Louise Sedgewick in Rib Davies and Pam Schweitzer, *Southwark at War*, p.35.

440 'The atmosphere did change'. Jess Steele, *Working Class War*, p.116.

440 'When my husband went abroad'. *Home Chat*, 10 February 1945.

441 'They embraced'. Barry Turner and Tony Rennell, *When Daddy Came Home*, p.94.

441 'When my husband'. *Home Chat*, 10 March 1945.

441 'When he came back home'. Ben Wicks, *Welcome Home*, p.74.

442 'Life for me changed totally'. Barry Turner and Tony Rennell, *When Daddy Came Home*, p.90.

Epilogue: A Planner's Dream

The main sources are C.H. Holden and W.G. Holford, *The City of London*, Richard Trench, *London before the Blitz*, Sir Patrick Abercrombie, *County of London Plan, 1943*, and *Greater London Plan, 1944*, E.J. Carter and Erno Goldfinger, *The County of London Plan Explained*.

443 'The value of victory'. Lord Latham is quoted in *Islington Gazette*, 15 May 1945.

443 'Before VE Day had actually happened'. Lil Patrick in Rib Davies and Pam Schweitzer, *Southwark at War*, p.37.

448 'Families would be packed'. *North London Observer*.

A note on the currency

COPPER COINS
1/4d farthing
1/2d halfpenny ('hay-p'ny')
1d penny
3d threepence ('thruppence' or 'thrup'ny bit')

SILVER COINS
6d sixpence (or 'tanner')
1s shilling (or 'bob')
2s florin
2s 6d half-crown (or 'two and six')
5s crown

PAPER CURRENCY
10s 10-shilling note
£1 pound note
£5 5-pound note

In the old currency, there were 12 pence in a shilling and 20 shillings in a pound. One old shilling is equivalent to 5 new pence and there are 100 new pence in a pound.

To get an equivalent modern value for monetary figures given in the text, multiply by 35–40.

Bibliography

Books

All books are published in London unless otherwise specified

Abercrombie, Sir Patrick, *Greater London Plan, 1944* (1945)

Abercrombie, Sir Patrick and Forshaw, J.H., *County of London Plan, 1943* (1943)

Addison, Paul, *Now the War Is Over: A Social History of Britain* (1985)

Addison, Paul, *Churchill on the Home Front 1900–1955* (1992)

Addison, Paul, *The Road to 1945: British Politics and the Second World War* (1994)

Alanbrooke, Field Marshal Lord, *War Diaries 1939–1945*, edited by Alex Danchev and Daniel Todman (2001)

Anderson, Verily, *Spam Tomorrow* (1956)

Anon, *The Clothing Coupon Quiz* (1942)

Anon, *How Britain Was Fed in Wartime: Food Control 1939–45* (1946)

Anon, *Over There: Instructions for American Servicemen in Britain, 1942* (Oxford, 1994)

Anon, 'A Short History of the War Damage Commission' (no date)

Anon, *ARP at Home: Hints for Housewives* (no date, but probably 1939)

Anon, *Bermondsey in War 1939–45* (no date)

Anon, *Croydon and the Second World War* (no date)

Anon, 'Every-day War: A Diary', Kensington and Chelsea Local Studies, 940.548 EVE AR/RS, unpublished

Anon, *Food Facts for the Kitchen Front: A Book of Wartime Recipes and Hints with a Foreword by Lord Woolton* (no date)

Anon, *War over West Ham* (no date)

Barker, Felix and Hyde, Ralph, *London as it Might Have Been* (1992)

Barnett, Correlli, *The Audit of War: The Illusion and Reality of Britain as a Great Nation* (1986)

Bartlett, Elizabeth and Senior, Diana, *All Pulling Together: North Kensington at War 1939–45* (1990)

Bates, L.M., *The Thames on Fire* (Lavenham, 1985)

Beardmore, George, *Civilians at War: Journals 1938–1946* (1984)

Bendit, Phoebe and Bendit, Laurence J., *Living Together Again* (1946)

Bexley, London Borough of, *Home Fires: A Borough at War* (1986)

Blake, Lewis, *Bromley in the Front Line* (1980)

Blake, Lewis, *Red Alert: South East London 1939–45* (1982)

Blake, Lewis, *Bolts from the Blue: South East London and Kent under V2 Rocket Attack* (1990)

Bonham, John, *The Middle Class Vote* (1954)

Box, Kathleen, *Wartime Shortages of Consumer Goods* (Wartime Social Survey for the Board of Trade, April 1943–January 1945)

Braybon, Gail and Summerfield, Penny, *Out of the Cage: Women's Experiences in Two World Wars* (1987)

Briggs, Susan, *Keep Smiling Through* (1975)

British Information Services, *Fifty Facts about British Women at War* (New York, 1944)

Brittain, Vera, *Wartime Chronicle: Vera Brittain's Diary 1939–45*, edited by Alan Bishop and Y. Aleksandra Bennett (1989)

Brown, Irene, *One Woman's War: Recollections of a Cockney Kid* (1991)

Browne, T. E., 'The Conduct of ARP Incidents: A Guide for Civil Defence Services', Hackney Archives

Bullock, Allan, *The Life and Times of Ernest Bevin*, vol. 2 (1967)

Cadogan, Alexander, *Diaries 1938–45*, edited by David Dicks (1971)

Cadogan, Mary and Craig, Patricia, *Women and Children First* (1978)

Calder, Angus, *The People's War: Britain 1939–45* (1969)

Calder, Angus and Sheridan, Dorothy, eds., *Speak for Yourself: A Mass Observation Anthology* (1984)

Calder, Ritchie, *Carry on London* (1941)

Calder, Ritchie, *Lesson of London* (1941)

Carter, E.J. and Goldfinger, Erno, *The County of London Plan Explained* (1945)

Chamberlin, E.R., *Life in Wartime Britain* (1972)

Channon, Sir Henry, *Chips: The Diaries of Sir Henry Channon*, edited by Robert Rhodes James (1993)

Clarke, Peter, *Hope and Glory: Britain 1900–1990* (1996)

Clements, Sibyl, ed., *A Short History of the War Damage Commission 1941–62* (1962)

Collier, Basil, *The History of the Second World War, United Kingdom Civil Series, The Defence of the United Kingdom* (1957)

Colville, John, *Footprints in Time* (1976)

Cooper, Diana, Viscountess Norwich, *Trumpets from the Steep* (1960)

Bibliography

Costello, John, *Love, Sex and War* (1985)

Craig, Elizabeth, *Gardening in Wartime* (Glasgow, 1943)

Croall, Jonathan, *Don't You Know There's a War On?* (1988)

Croft, Susan, *The Stork Wartime Cookery Book* (no date)

Cudlipp, Hugh, *Publish and Be Damned!* (1953)

Dalton, Hugh, *The Fateful Years, Memoirs 1931–45 (1962)*

Davies, Rib and Schweitzer, Pam, eds., *Southwark at War: A Book of Memories* (1996)

Dean, Basil, *The Theatre at War* (1956)

Delderfield, R.F., *The Avenue Goes to War* (1958)

Faviell, Frances, *A Chelsea Concerto* (1959)

Fenner, Brockway, *Bermondsey Story: The Life of Alfred Salter* (1949)

Ferguson, Howard, *Dame Myra Hess by her Friends* (1966)

Ferguson, Rachel, *Royal Borough* (1950)

Ferguson, Sheila and Fitzgerald, Hilda, *The History of the Second World War, United Kingdom Civil Series, Studies in the Social Services*, edited by Sir Keith Hancock (1953)

Firebrace, Sir Aylmer, *Fire Service Memoirs* (Melrose, 1949)

Fitzgibbon, Theodora, *With Love* (1982)

Food, Ministry of, *The Kitchen Front: 122 Wartime Recipes Broadcast by Frederick Grisewood, Mabel Constanduros and Others* (no date)

Foot, Michael, *Aneurin Bevan* (1999)

Gardiner, Juliet, *'Over Here': The GIs in Wartime Britain* (1992)

Gardiner, Juliet, *The 1940s House* (2000)

Gilbert, Martin, *The Day the War Ended* (1995)

Gillam, Geoffrey, *Enfield at War 1939–45* (1985)

Glass, D.V., ed., *Social Mobility in Britain* (1954)

Golden, Jennifer, *Hackney at War* (1995)

Gosling, John, *The Ghost Squad* (1959)

Gough, T.W., *War-time Letters from the Tottenham Home Front 1939–45* (1994)

Graves, Charles, *Pride of the Morning* (1945)

Graves, Charles, *London Transport Carried On* (1947)

Graves, Charles, *Women in Green: The Story of the WVS in Wartime* (1948)

Green, Brian, *Dulwich Home Front 1939–45* (1995)

Greene, Graham, *The Ministry of Fear* (1943)

Haining, Peter, *The Flying Bomb War* (2002)

Hall, Professor Peter, *Abercrombie's Plan for London Fifty Years On: A Vision for the Future* (1993)

Hall, W.E., 'Civil Defence Goes Through It, Paddington 1937–47', Department of Documents, Imperial War Museum

Hampstead Borough Council, *Hampstead at War* (1946)

Hancock, Sir Keith and Gowing, Margaret, *The History of the Second World War, United Kingdom Civil Series, British War Economy* (1949)

Hardy, Clive and Arthur, Nigel, *London at War* (Huddersfield, 1989)

Hart, Valerie and Marshall, Lesley, *Wartime Camden* (1983)

Hasker, Leslie, *Fulham in the Second World War* (1984)

Heath, Ambrose, *Meat Dishes without Joints* (1940)

Heath, Ambrose, *Wartime Recipes* (1941)

Hellyer, A.G.L., *War-time Gardening for Home Needs* (no date)

Hennessy, Elizabeth, *A Domestic History of the Bank of England 1930–60* (Cambridge, 1992)

Hennessy, Peter, *Never Again: Britain 1945–51* (1992)

Henrey, Mrs Robert, *London Under Fire 1940–45* (1969)

Hewison, Robert, *Under Siege: Literary Life in London 1939–45* (1977)

Hibberd, Stuart, *This – Is London* (1950)

Hickman, Tom, *What Did You Do in the War, Auntie? The BBC at War 1939–45* (1995)

Hill, Billy, *Boss of Britain's Underworld* (1955)

Hodgson, Vere, *Few Eggs and No Oranges* (1976)

Hodson, J.L., *The Sea and the Land* (1945)

Hogan, J.P., *Hair under a Hat* (1949)

Holden, C.H. and Holford, W.G., *The City of London: A Record of Destruction and Survival* (1951)

Holden, Inez, *Night Shift* (1941)

Hook, Janet M., *British Policies and Methods in Employing Women in Wartime* (Washington, 1944)

Hopkinson, Tom, ed., *Picture Post 1938–50* (1974)

Hornsey Historical Society, *Home Fires: A North London Suburb at War* (1992)

Howgrave-Graham, *The Metropolitan Police at War* (1947)

Idle, D., *War Over West Ham* (1943)

Information, Ministry of, *Make Do and Mend* (1943)

Information, Ministry of, 'Women in War Jobs' (1943)

Information, Ministry of, 'British Women at War' (1944)

Inglis, Ruth, *The Children's War: Evacuation 1939–45* (1989)

Inwood, Stephen, *A History of London* (1998)

Jackson, Carlton, *Who Will Take Our Children?* (1995)

James, Anthony R., *Informing the People: How the Government Won Hearts and Minds to Win World War Two* (1996)

Bibliography

Jenkins, Roy, *Churchill* (2001)

Kent, William, *The Lost Treasures of London* (1947)

Kops, Bernard, *The World Is a Wedding* (1963)

Lees-Milne, James, *Prophesying Peace: Diaries 1944–45* (1977)

Lehmann, John, *I Am My Brother* (1960)

Lewis, Peter, *A People's War* (1986)

Lloyds, *Lloyds under Fire: A Tribute to the Civil Defence Services of Lloyds 1938–45* (1946)

London, Corporation of, *We Think You Ought to Go* (no date)

Long, Janet, *Brent's War: Wartime Memories of the People of Brent* (1995)

Longmate, Norman, *How We Lived Then* (1971)

Longmate, Norman, *The GIs: The Americans in Britain 1942–1945* (1975)

Longmate, Norman, *When We Won the War: The Story of Victory in Europe, 1945* (1977)

Longmate, Norman, *The Doodlebugs: The Story of the Flying Bombs* (1981)

Longmate, Norman, *The Home Front: An Anthology of Personal Experiences* (1981)

Longmate, Norman, *Hitler's Rockets: The Story of the V-2s* (1985)

Macauley, Rose, *Letters to a Sister* (1964)

Mack, Joanna and Humphries, Steve, *The Making of Modern London: London at War* (1985)

MacLaren-Ross, J., *Memoirs of the Forties* (1984)

Marwick, Arthur, *Britain in the Century of Total War* (1968)

Marwick, Arthur, *The Home Front* (1976)

Matthews, Very Reverend W.R., Dean of St Paul's, *St Paul's Cathedral in Wartime* (1946)

McCallum, R.B. and Readman, A., *The British General Election of 1945* (Oxford, 1947)

McDowell, Colin, *Forties Fashion and the New Look* (1997)

McLaine, Ian, *Ministry of Morale: Home Front Morale and the Ministry of Information in World War II* (1979)

Millin, Sarah Gertrude, *Fire out of Heaven* (1947)

Minns, Raynes, *Bombers and Mash: The Domestic Front 1939–45* (1980)

Mitchison, Naomi, *Among You Taking Notes: The Wartime Diary of Naomi Mitchison 1939–45* (1985)

Morgan, Guy, *Red Roses Every Night* (1948)

Morgan, Kenneth O., *The People's Peace: British History 1945–1989* (Oxford, 1990)

Morrison, Herbert, *How Greater London Is Governed* (1935)

Morrison, Herbert, *Prospects and Policies* (1944)

Morrison, Herbert, *An Autobiography by Lord Morrison of Lambeth* (1960)

Moseley, Leonard, *Backs to the Wall: London under Fire 1940–45* (1971)

Mosley, Diana, Lady, *A Life of Contrasts* (2002)

Murray, Jenni, *The Woman's Hour: 50 Years of Women in Britain* (1996)

Nicholas, Sian, *The Echo of War: Home Front Propaganda and the Wartime BBC, 1939–45* (Manchester, 1996)

Nicholson, Mavis, ed., *What Did You Do in the War, Mummy? Women in World War II* (1995)

Nicolson, Harold, *The War Years: Diaries and Letters 1939–45*, edited by Nigel Nicolson (New York, 1967)

Nicolson, Harold, *Diaries and Letters 1945–62*, edited by Nigel Nicolson (1971)

Novy, Priscilla, *Housework Without Tears*, foreword by Lady Beveridge (1945)

O'Brien, Terence, *The History of the Second World War, United Kingdom Civil Series, Civil Defence* (1955)

O'Leary, John, *Danger over Dagenham* (1947)

Orwell, George, *The Collected Essays, Journalism and Letters of*, edited by Ian Angus and Sonia Orwell (1968)

Panter-Downes, Mollie, *London War Notes 1939–1945* (1972)

Pearce, K.R., *Uxbridge at War, 1939–45* (1989)

Pennick, Nigel, *Bunkers under London* (Cambridge, 1988)

Pinner Association, *The Villager at War: A Diary of Home Front Pinner 1939–45* (1995)

Plastow, Norman, *Safe as Houses: Wimbledon 1939–45* (1972)

Pocock, Tom, *1945: The Dawn Came up like Thunder* (1983)

Priestley, J.B., *British Women Go to War* (1943)

Priestley, J.B., *Three Men in New Suits* (1945)

Priestley, J.B., *All England Listened: The Wartime Postscripts of J.B. Priestley* (New York, 1967)

Purdom, C.B., *How Should We Rebuild London?* (1946)

Raczynski, Count Edward, *In Allied London* (1962)

Reboul, Percy and Heathfield, John, *Barnet at War* (Stroud, 1995)

Reese, Peter, *Homecoming Heroes: An Account of the Re-assimilation of British Military Personnel into Civilian Life* (1992)

Reynolds, David, *Rich Relations: The American Occupation of Britain 1942–45* (1995)

Rhodes, Anthony, *Propaganda–the Art of Persuasion: World War II*, edited by V. Margolin (1976)

Robson, W.A., *The Government and Misgovernment of London* (1939)

Rooke, Dennis and D'Egville, Alan, *Call Me Mister! A Guide to Civilian Life for the Newly Demobilised* (1946)

Rothwell, Stanley, *Lambeth at War* (1981)

Rowbotham, Sheila, *A Century of Women: The History of Women in Britain and the United States* (1997)

Salmon, D.M., *To, For and About You: The People of Streatham* (1945)

Samuel, Raphael, *East End Underworld: Chapters in the Life of Arthur Harding* (1981)

Samways, Richard, ed., *We Think You Ought to Go: An Account of the Evacuation of Children from London during the Second World War* (1995)

Sansom, William, *Westminster at War* (Oxford, 1990)

Sayers, W.S. Berwick, *Croydon and the Second World War* (1949)

Scott, Sir Harold, *Your Obedient Servant* (1959)

Scott, Mick, *Home Fires: A Borough at War* (1986)

Shaw, Anthony and Mills, Jon, '*We Served': Wartime Wandsworth and Battersea* (1989)

Shepherds Bush Local History Society, *Around the Bush – The War Years* (1987)

Sheridan, Dorothy, ed., *Wartime Women: An Anthology of Women's Writing for Mass-Observation 1937–45* (1990)

Short, John R., *Housing in Britain: The Post-war Experience* (1982)

Sissons, Michael and French, Philip, ed., *The Age of Austerity* (1964)

Sked, Alan and Cook, Chris, *Crisis and Controversy* (1976)

Smithies, Edward, *Crime in Wartime: A Social History of Crime in World War II* (1982)

Spender, Stephen, *Citizens in War and After* (1945)

Steele, Jess, ed., *Working Class War: Tales from Two Families* (1995)

Stewart, James, *Bermondsey in War 1939–45* (1980)

Stork, *The Stork Margarine Cook Book* (no date)

Summerfield, Penny, *Women Workers in the Second World War: Production and Patriarchy in Conflict* (1984)

Taylor, A.J.P., *English History 1914–45* (Oxford, 1990)

Thomas, Donald, *An Underworld at War: Spivs, Deserters, Racketeers and Civilians in the Second World War* (2003)

Thomas, Geoffrey, *Women at Work: The Attitudes of Working Women Toward Post-war Employment* (Wartime Social Survey, 1944)

Thomas, Howard, *Britain's Brains Trust* (1944)

Thompson, George P., *Blue Pencil Admiral: The Inside Story of Press Censorship* (1947)

Times, The, When the Sirens Sounded: An Account of Air Raid Precautions in Printing House Square (1948)

Tiquet, Stanley, *It Happened Here: The Story of Civil Defence in Wanstead and Woodford 1939–45* (1947)

Titmuss, Richard M., *The History of the Second World War, United Kingdom Civil Series, Problems of Social Policy*, edited by W. K. Hancock (1950)

Trench, Richard, *London Before the Blitz* (1989)

Turner, Barry and Rennell, Tony, *When Daddy Came Home: How Family Life Changed Forever in 1945* (1995)

Vale, George F., *Bethnal Green's Ordeal 1939–45* (1945)

Waller, Jane and Vaughan-Rees, Michael, *Women in Wartime: The Role of the Women's Magazines 1939–45* (1987)

Waugh, Evelyn, *The Diaries of Evelyn Waugh*, edited by Michael Davie (1976)

Wauters, Arthur, *Eve in Overalls* (1995)

Westall, Robert, *Children of the Blitz: Memories of Wartime Childhood* (1985)

Weymouth, Anthony, *Journal of the War Years and One Year Later* (Worcester, 1948)

Wicks, Ben, *Welcome Home: True Stories of Soldiers Returning from World War II* (1991)

Williams, Gertrude, *Women and Work* (1945)

Williams-Ellis, Amabel, *Women in War Factories* (1946)

Wilson, H.A., *Death over Haggerston* (1941)

Woolton, Frederick Marquis, the Right Honourable the Earl of, *The Memoirs of the Rt. Hon. the Earl of Woolton* (1959)

Wyld, Ross, *The War over Walthamstow: The Story of Civil Defence* (1945)

Wyndham, Joan, *Love Is Blue* (1986)

Wyndham, Joan, *Love Lessons* (1986)

Yass, Marion, *This Is Your War: Home Front Propaganda in the Second World War* (1983)

Young, M. and Wilmott, P., *Family and Kinship in East London* (1957)

Ziegler, Philip, *London at War 1939–1945* (1995)

Newspapers, periodicals and magazines

Boroughs of Poplar and Stepney and East London Advertiser, Chelsea,

Bibliography

Westminster and Pimlico News, Clerkenwell Chronicle and St Luke's Examiner, Croydon Advertiser, Enfield Gazette, Enfield Herald, Finsbury Weekly News, Hackney Gazette and North London Advertiser, Hampstead and Highgate Express, Islington Gazette, Islington Guardian and Hackney News, Kensington Gazette, Kensington News and West London Times, North London Observer, North London Press, Paddington News, Paddington Press, South London Press, Wembley News, West London and Chelsea Gazette, West London Press, Westminster Chronicle

Daily Express, Daily Herald, Daily Mail, Daily Mirror, Evening News, Evening Standard, News Chronicle, News of the World, Star, Stars and Stripes, Sunday Express, Sunday Graphic, The Times

Economist, Illustrated London News, Listener, Picture Post, Radio Times, Signal, Spectator, Tribune

Australian Women's Weekly, Britannia and Eve, Home Chat, Lady, Vogue, Woman, Woman and Home, Woman's Journal

Papers of the following in the Department of Documents, Imperial War Museum

Mrs P. Bell, Kathleen Bliss, Mr and Mrs George Britton, Mrs H. Broadway, Mrs Irene Byers, Miss N. V. Carver, D.J. Clough, Mrs M. Cossins, Mrs E.H. Cotton, Mrs Gwladys Cox, Mrs R.C. Desch, Dr H. Enoch, Mrs D. Farrall, Mrs E.M. Green, H.F. Grey, Miss V. Hall, Miss B. Helliar, Miss Vere Hodgson, Mrs B.M. Holbrook, Kenneth A. Holmes, G. Inward, D.W. Johns, A. V. Monk, C.A. Newbery, Miss J.M. Oakman, Miss N. O'Connor, Mrs O. Pepper, Mrs V. Shoulder, Ms V.J. Staunton, Mrs M.E. Stevenson, Mrs U.M. Streatfield, John L. Sweetland, Miss F.E. Tate, Miss G. Thomas, Mrs R.E. Uttin, Mrs E. Varah, Miss P. Warner, R.A. Weir, R. Wells, Mr S.M.S. Woodcock

Interviews with the following from the Imperial War Museum Sound Archive

Fred Barnes, Joyce Barrett, Mary Beazley, Jack Harding, Ivy Heard, Betty Hill, Mr J. Murray, Reg Neal, Nancie Norman, Marguerite Patten, Ruth and Fred Tanner, M. Waschauer, Betty Weiner

Index

Index

Picture Acknowledgements

The author and publisher would like to thank the following for permission to reproduce illustrations:

Plates: Page 10 (above) © Bettmann/CORBIS. Page 14 (above left) © Hulton-Deutsch Collection/CORBIS. Pages 6–7 Bancroft Library. Pages 5 (below), 11 (above), 13 (below), 21 and 23 (below) Hulton Archive. Page 1 Imperial War Museum D6412. Page 2 (above) Imperial War Museum HU634. Page 3 (above) Imperial War Museum D5945. Page 5 (above) Imperial War Museum HU81422. Page 9 Imperial War Museum D12032. Page 11 (below) Imperial War Museum ZZZ8951C. Page 12 (below) Imperial War Museum ZZZ19226H. Page 14 (above right) Imperial War Museum HU36203. Page 14 (below) Imperial War Museum D8956. Page 15 Imperial War Museum HU63758. Page 17 (above) Imperial War Museum H41849. Page 18 (above) Imperial War Museum EA65802. Page 18 (below) Imperial War Museum PL65767. Page 19 Imperial War Museum AP65763. Page 20 (above) Imperial War Museum EA75894 NIXF. Page 23 (above) Imperial War Museum HU81423. Pages 2 (below), 3 (below), 4 (above), 4 (below), 8, 12 (above), 16, 17 (below), 22 and 24 popperfoto.com. Pages 10 (below) and 20 (below) Southwark Local Studies Library.
Integrated: Pages 158, 174, 349 and 222 © Crown Copyright. Pages 341 and 287 © Mirrorpix. Page 87 Imperial War Museum MH15564. Page 231 Imperial War Museum LDP297. Page 388 Imperial War Museum MH4735. Page 238 with thanks to the manufacturer of Odo Ro No. Pages 165 and 184 © We'll Eat Again, the Imperial War Museum.

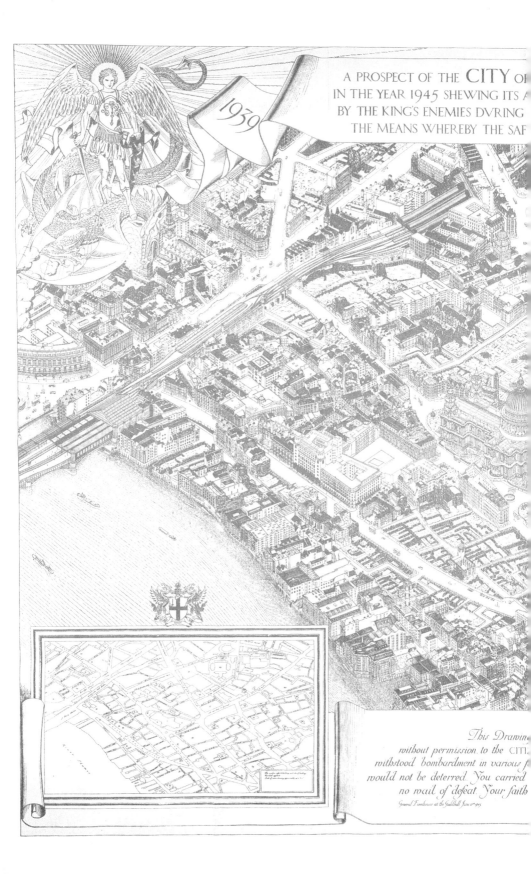

A PROSPECT OF THE **CITY** OF
IN THE YEAR 1945 SHEWING ITS A
BY THE KING'S ENEMIES DVRING
THE MEANS WHEREBY THE SAF

1939

This Drawin
without permission to the CITY
withstood bombardment in various f
would not be deterred. You carried
no mail of defeat. Your faith

General Eisenhower at the Guildhall June 12th 1945